Reading and Writing in Medieval England

Reading and Writing in Medieval England
Essays in Honor of Mary C. Erler

Edited by

Martin Chase
Maryanne Kowaleski

THE BOYDELL PRESS

First published 2019
The Boydell Press, Woodbridge

ISBN 978 1 78327 355 3

The Boydell Press is an imprint of Boydell & Brewer Ltd
PO Box 9, Woodbridge, Suffolk IP12 3DF, UK
and of Boydell & Brewer Inc.
668 Mt Hope Avenue, Rochester, NY 14620–2731, USA
website: www.boydellandbrewer.com

A CIP catalogue record for this book is available
from the British Library

The publisher has no responsibility for the continued existence or accuracy
of URLs for external or third-party internet websites referred to in this book,
and does not guarantee that any content on such websites is, or will remain,
accurate or appropriate

This publication is printed on acid-free paper

Contents

Illustrations

Plates

Figures

The editors, contributors, and publishers are grateful to all the institutions and persons listed for permission to reproduce the materials in which they hold copyright. Every effort has been made to trace the copyright holders; apologies are offered for any omission, and the publishers will be pleased to add any necessary acknowledgement in subsequent editions.

Contributors

Allison Adair Alberts is an academic dean and member of the English faculty at Sacred Heart, Greenwich. Her dissertation, which studied female suffering in medieval and early modern literature, was completed under the guidance of Mary Erler at Fordham University. Her most recent publication, "Spiritual Suffering and Physical Protection in Childbirth in the *South English Legendary* Lives of Saint Margaret" (*Journal of Medieval and Early Modern Studies* 46 [2016]: 289–314), examines the way saints were invoked during childbirth in the later Middle Ages. Her current project focuses on sanctity and motherhood in medieval and early modern England.

Caroline M. Barron is Professor Emerita of the History of London at Royal Holloway, University of London. Her publications include *London in the Later Middle Ages: Government and People* (Oxford, 2004) and *Medieval London: Collected Papers*, edited by Martha Carlin and Joel T. Rosenthal (Kalamazoo, 2018). She has worked with Mary Erler on the great altar table at Syon Abbey and on the fifty or so medieval manuscripts containing London Chronicles.

Heather Blatt is Associate Professor of English Literature at Florida International University. She is celebrating the recent publication of first book, *Participatory Reading in Late-Medieval England* (Manchester, 2018). She was a student of Mary Erler's at Fordham University, where she received her Ph.D. in 2011.

Martin Chase is Professor of English and Medieval Studies at Fordham University. He has published on a variety of subjects relating to medieval English and Old Norse/Icelandic devotional literature. He is the author of *Einarr Skúlason's Geisli* (Toronto, 2005) and *Eddic, Skaldic, and Beyond: Poetic Variety in Medieval Iceland and Norway* (New York, 2014).

Joyce Coleman is the Rudolph C. Bambas Professor of Medieval English Literature and Culture in the English Department at the University of Oklahoma. Her research focuses on late medieval literary reception, performance, and patronage. Her publications include *Public Reading and the Reading Public in Late Medieval England and France* (Cambridge, UK, 1996), a co-edited interdisciplinary anthology titled *The Social Life of Illumination: Manuscripts, Images, and Communities in the Late Middle Ages* (Turnhout, 2013), and many articles in anthologies and journals.

Maryanne Kowaleski is Joseph Fitzpatrick S.J. Distinguished Professor of History and Medieval Studies at Fordham University. She has authored books and articles on medieval English towns, trade, women, demography, and maritime history. Her publications include two essay collections co-edited with Mary Erler: *Women and Power in the Middle Ages* (Athens, GA, 1988) and *Gendering the Master Narrative: Revisiting Women and Power in the Middle Ages* (Ithaca, NY, 2003). Her current projects focus on the maritime industries of medieval London, the origin of scolding indictments, and borough courts in medieval England.

Sheila Lindenbaum is Associate Professor Emeritus at Indiana University, where she was director of the Medieval Institute; she now lives in London. She has published articles on the city's late medieval ceremonies and tournaments and on dramatic activity at Westminster Abbey. She has also written on various aspects of London's literate practice, including Hoccleve's poetry and the kinds of literacy represented in Richard Whittington's "deathbed" picture. The essay in this volume is part of a book-length project on "Intellectual London," which investigates the many university graduates who worked in the city and the impact of their learning on ordinary citizens.

Joel T. Rosenthal is SUNY Distinguished Professor Emeritus after a long career in the History Department of Stony Brook University. He has published on medieval English social history – widows, children, old age, marriage, family letters – on ecclesiastical benefaction, and on the personnel of the episcopate. He is a founding co-editor of *Medieval Prosopography* and has served on national committees of the AAUP. He currently co-edits *Studies in Medieval and Renaissance History*.

Michael Sargent is Professor of English at Queens College and the Graduate Center of the City University of New York. He earned his doctorate from the Centre for Medieval Studies of the University of Toronto, and worked for four years as a Lehrbeauftragter in the Institut für Anglistik of the Universität Salzburg and as a research assistant to James Hogg in the project of editing the fifteenth-century *cartae* of the General Chapter of the Carthusian Order. He has been a member of the faculty of City University since 1985. He has produced a full critical edition of Nicholas Love's *Mirror of the Blessed Life of Jesus Christ* (Exeter, UK, 2004), a recently published edition of Book II of Walter Hilton's *Scale of Perfection* (Oxford, 2017), and is presently at work completing an edition of *Scale* I.

Kathryn A. Smith is Professor of Art History at New York University. She is the author of books, articles, and reviews on early Christian and later medieval art, especially the illuminated manuscripts of Gothic England. She is founding series editor of *Studies in the Visual Cultures of the Middle Ages* (Brepols) and co-edits the journal *Studies in Iconography.* Current projects include studies of late medieval English alabaster sculpture, word and image in an illuminated Anglo-Norman French Bible, and the chapter on English Gothic illumination for the forthcoming second edition of *A Companion to Medieval Art*, edited by Conrad Rudolph.

Abbreviations

BL   British Library

BnF   Bibliothèque nationale de France

Cgm   Codex Germanicus Monacensis

ÍF   *Íslensk fornkvæði / Islandske Folkeviser*, ed. Jón Helgason. 8 vols. Copenhagen, 1962–81.

Íf   Íslenzk fornrit

ÍGSVÞ   *Íslenzkar gátur, skemtanir, vikivakar og þulur*, ed. Jón Árnason and Ólafur Davíðsson . 4 vols. Copenhagen, 1887–1904.

ÍM   *Íslenzk Miðaldakvæði / Islandske Digte fra Senmiddelalderen*, ed. Jón Helgason. 2 vols. Copenhagen, 1936–1938.

KD   *Kvæði og Dansleikir*, ed. Jón Samsonarson. 2 vols. Íslensk Þjóðfræði. Reykjavík, 1964.

LMA   London Metropolitan Archives

MED   *Middle English Dictionary*

OED   *Oxford English Dictionary*

OPL   Oxford-Paris-London Moralized Bible

PML   The Morgan Library & Museum (formerly Pierpont Morgan Library)

STC   *A Short-Title Catalogue of Books Printed in England, Scotland, & Ireland and of English Books Printed Abroad, 1475–1640*, ed. Alfred W. Pollard, et al. 2nd ed. 3 vols. London, 1976–1991.

T&C   *Troilus and Criseyde*

TAMO   John Foxe, *The Unabridged Acts and Monuments Online*

TNA   The National Archives

WLC   Wollaton Library Collection, University of Nottingham

Wing   *Short-Title Catalogue of Books Printed in England, Scotland, Ireland, Wales, and British America and of English Books Printed in Other Countries, 1641–1700*, ed. Donald Goddard Wing and Alfred W. Pollard. 3 vols. New York, 1945–1951.

Introduction:
Bibliography in the Service of Biography

MARTIN CHASE AND MARYANNE KOWALESKI

Mary Erler's scholarship has been at the forefront of what has been called a "remarkable efflorescence" or "second wave" in studies of the history of the book and the material text that began in the last decade of the twentieth century.[1] Her vision has expanded the scope of questions that can be asked – and answered – and has helped to break down traditional boundaries between periods, genres, media, social classes, religious states, and genders. Her approach is focused and distinctive enough to constitute a method in itself, but it also engages a variety of other methods to analyze and assess the larger picture. Her interdisciplinary work has interacted with and contributed to book studies, literary studies (new philology, new historicism, feminism), social history, ecclesiastical history, and good old-fashioned intellectual history, among others. Erler's work realigns earlier ideas about periodization: much of it is situated in the unsettled times of late fifteenth- and early sixteenth-century England, and so deals with early printed books as well as late manuscript codices. Her writings consider a broad range of groups, including Catholics (lay and religious), Lollards and Anglicans, men and women, aristocrats and bourgeoisie.

The material object, be it printed volume, manuscript, or legal document, is invariably the starting point of her enquiry, but the primary object of interest is always the human subject who produced, read, shared, inherited, bequeathed, or treasured it. The term Erler associates with her work – "bibliographical study" – may strike some as old-fashioned or even pedestrian, but in Erler's hands "bibliographical study" is cutting-edged, nuanced, and deeply revealing. "Bibliography" is tellingly the first word of her ground-breaking study, *Women, Reading, and Piety in Late Medieval England* (2002):

> Bibliography has sometimes been moved by what might seem an especially pure form of the historical impulse: the wish to use physical objects, books, to reveal something about non-physical realities: about intellectual lives, about

1   Heidi Brayman, Jesse M. Lander, Zachary Lesser, "Introduction," in *The Book in History, the Book as History: New Intersections of the Material Text. Essays in Honor of David Scott Kastan*, ed. Heidi Brayman, Jesse M. Lander, and Zachary Lesser (New Haven, 2016), 10.

1

manners or habits in the past. Viewed in this way, books have continued to signal seductively their potential as guides and markers to another age's sensibility. In fact current fascination with book provenance has perhaps derived from the insight of the *histoire du livre* school that research into book ownership could offer a novel way in to social history, one which might make visible even the elusive matters of personal preference and personal taste, always particularly difficult to recover.[2]

She takes up the idea again in the introduction to her second acclaimed study, *Reading and Writing during the Dissolution* (2013):

The starting point of this book has been bibliographical. All of the chapters but one began as bibliographical problems, but I have regularly thought of bibliography as a way of exploring lives – and so in what follows, bibliography finds itself in the service of biography. Both these disciplines, in turn, make their contribution to the social and religious history of a period narrowly outlined but satisfying to examine because of the rich material it displays.[3]

All of the essays in this volume engage with Erler's characteristic use of bibliography in the service of biography by investigating how the physical object of the book can enlighten our understanding of medieval readers and writers. They focus on a variety of themes that her own work has highlighted: the culture of medieval reading practices, especially those of women (Coleman, Barron, Sargent, Blatt, and Alberts), across social classes (Lindenbaum, Rosenthal, Chase), and in terms of the transition between the pre- and post-Reformation periods (Blatt, Chase, Alberts); the fluidity of genre boundaries (Coleman, Smith, Chase); and changes in devotional reading and writing in this liminal period (Lindenbaum, Smith, Sargent, Blatt, Chase, Alberts). Our contributors range from friends and colleagues with whom Erler has collaborated over the years to younger scholars who, inspired by her work, are now expanding how we see books and people.

Joyce Coleman's nuanced essay shows how Chaucer himself used bibliography in the service of biography. In his description of the aristocratic Criseyde reading with female companions in a "paved parlor," Chaucer shows us a women's reading circle like those that have been so central to Erler's work. Coleman argues that Chaucer's depiction of this scene may have been influenced by his

2 Mary C. Erler, *Women, Reading, and Piety in Late Medieval England* (Cambridge, UK 2006), 1.
3 Mary C. Erler, *Reading and Writing during the Dissolution: Monks, Friars, and Nuns 1530–1558* (Cambridge, UK, 2013), 2.

youthful service in the court of Elizabeth de Burgh, countess of Ulster and daughter-in-law of Edward III. Coleman also draws particular attention to the material object of the book and reading practices – the tension that arises as the reading group (and book itself) compete with Pandarus for Criseyde's attention, the importance to Criseyde of a key passage written in rubricated script, and the ease with which the women jump through the book to a favorite passage about the attack on the city of Thebes. Chaucer refers to the book the women are reading as a romance, but this may not mean that it is women's fiction – it may be called a romance because it is written in French. It is clear that the women regard it as serious history – an interpretation of the past that can help them understand the present. Coleman demonstrates how Chaucer's subtle intertextuality gives us biographical insight into his characters by showing us what they read, why they read, and how they read, but she also ponders the relationship between overtones of sex and violence in *Troilus and Crisyede*, in the *Roman de Thèbes*, and in Chaucer's own life.

Caroline Barron also pursues bibliography in the service of biography by using – as Erler often has done – documented bequests of books to provide insights into the worlds of testators. By examining carefully what books Beatrice Melreth, the widow of a wealthy mercer of London, owned and to whom she bequeathed them, Barron draws conclusions about her relationships with her family (two husbands, children, siblings, and in-laws) as well as her devotional life. Beatrice chose to leave all six of her books, mostly vernacular works of personal piety, to one of her three sisters, Agnes, suggesting a shared literary culture that was both secular and familial. She could probably read three languages, since half of her books were in French, including a Book of Hours that she received from Agnes; another text was in Latin and English, and the two others probably in English. Beatrice's most unusual book was a French copy of the apocryphal *Gospel of Nicodemus*, which no other Englishwoman is known to have owned. Even more significantly, she did not possess any of the popular texts of affective piety that often surface in the wills of fifteenth-century medieval Englishwomen studied by Erler and other scholars. Barron points out that Beatrice's spirituality appears to have been firmly grounded in her lay state with no aspirations to a mixed or vowed life, which makes her "ordinary" life, as reflected by her books, exceptional.

Also looking at what Londoners were reading in the fifteenth century, Sheila Lindenbaum focuses on the interaction between the literate bourgeoisie and university-educated intellectuals, most of them clergy. Like Mary Erler, she examines a series of encounters between different social groups over texts, particularly the *Eclogue* of Theodulus (a schoolboy grammar based on a Christianized selection of poetic debates from Virgil) and Wyclif's *Trialogus* (a

3

summa of his religious doctrine that appropriates the *Eclogue*'s structure and characters). Lindenbaum queries Sylvia Thrupp's long-standing assertion that London citizens lacked intellectual curiosity. While Thrupp rightly saw an absence of critical thinking among Londoners, Lindenbaum argues that she did not realize that their "aversion to questioning and debate was a dangerous anti-intellectualism produced in the course of religious and political controversy, and not just a function of their preoccupation with commerce."[4] Yet Lindenbaum also recognizes how the classicizing civic rituals initiated by the merchant elite helped to distinguish them socially from artisans, and usefully speculates how and why Londoners appear to have co-opted a "softer" form of logic centered around political discussions and writings.

Joel Rosenthal draws on another type of document: testimonies to establish proof of age for heirs that were tenants-in-chief of the crown. Witnesses testified to their memory of the heir's birth by associating it with specific events that they regarded as significant and memorable, such as monastic professions, ordinations, and pilgrimages. The recorded testimonies attest to the existence of documents no longer available at the time of witness, i.e., the witness's recollection *that* an event was recorded is deemed credible based on another event associated with its recording. Witnesses also recall particular books – liturgical books, martyrologies, Bibles – in which dates were recorded, and they often have a memory of having held, or seen, the book in question, or a recollection of just where in a church the book was kept. This links to interest in the book as physical object – one remembers a baptism because one associates it with the material object in which it was recorded. The memory of the book itself becomes as authoritative as the memory of the event.

A well-known lavishly illuminated manuscript book, the Queen Mary Psalter, is the focus of Kathryn Smith's study, which centers on how the Psalter's Old Testament preface reshaped the story of the ancient Israelites into something resembling chivalric romance. In noting the permeability of genre boundaries between Scripture and romance, Smith thus follows Mary Erler, as she does also in assessing how the physical object of the Queen Mary Psalter speaks to the enigma of its commission and intended owner. Smith argues that the artists consciously employed pictorial models from romance manuscripts to satisfy the patron's wishes, and responded to other contemporary attitudes on Jews and the roles of art in worship, as well as to the particular political environment in early fourteenth-century London. Even though the identity of the artists, owner, and viewers of the Psalter remain uncertain, Smith demonstrates that its Old

---

4   Lindenbaum, "How Intellectual Were Fifteenth-Century Londoners?" 79.

Testament preface "brilliantly synthesizes the diverse intervisual, multilingual strands of early fourteenth-century England's rich artistic and readerly cultures."[5] Michael Sargent's extensive work on book production, transmission, and ownership has often intersected with Mary Erler's, and he here offers another particular point of contact with Erler's work: Walter Hilton's *Scale of Perfection*. The Carthusians were great readers and promoters of Hilton's works, and this enthusiasm was shared by the Brigittine nuns of Syon Abbey, whose reading habits Erler has done so much to elucidate. Sargent examines how the nuns read such texts as the *Scale*, and he invokes Mark Amsler's theory of "affective literacies" to investigate the ways in which interaction with the book itself as a physical object invokes "a completely embodied reading." Contact with the material form of a devotional text – with its rubricated headings (like those Criseyde noted in her French romance)[6] and its mix of English and Latin – linked the reader, physically as well as cognitively, to the monastic *opus* of the Divine Office, producing an experience "neither clerical nor lay . . . neither Latin nor vernacular . . . neither theological nor devotional . . . [but rather] deeply, materially, both."[7] Sargent concludes that the experience of the nuns is an example of the construction of a religious women's literacy analogous to but distinct from clerical literacy and lay literacy.

Heather Blatt also takes Syon Abbey as the starting point for her research, and like most of the authors in this collection, she is especially concerned with materiality. But the physical objects she investigates are not the texts themselves, rather what she calls "book furniture" and bookmarkers – objects that facilitated the reading of books and that can reveal something about the practices of their readers. Blatt shares Erler's interest in the reading practices of women, and she finds the double monastery of Syon a perfect site for determining how practices were gendered. While, as most of the essays in this volume demonstrate, boundaries were more fluid than we might expect, Blatt nevertheless discerns general trends where practices differed. The reading of the monks at Syon tended to be "professional" and liturgical: they used theological books for study and liturgical books for ritual. These books tended to be large, and often required book-stands, desks, and other related "furniture." The reading of the nuns, on the other hand, tended to be devotional and recreational. The books they

---

5 Smith, "Crafting the Old Testament in the Queen Mary Psalter," 129.
6 See Coleman, "'Within a Paved Parlour,'" 11. Sargent notes that David of Augsburg's *Formula novicorum*, cited in the Syon text *Disce mori*, refers to the tale of Troilus as an example of the tendency of corrupted lovers to poison one another with flattery (Sargent, "Affective Reading," 145).
7 Sargent, "Affective Reading," 136.

used were smaller and could be held in their hands, leading to a more intimate involvement with at least the object, and perhaps consequently with the text, as well. The nuns carried their small books from room to room, while the larger books of the monks had to be read in a library, scriptorium, or church. Blatt's study of "register bookmarkers," clusters of ribbons attached to the spine of a volume, also suggests different reading practices. The monks used bookmarkers to navigate the complicated use of liturgical books for Mass and Divine Office, while the nuns used them for "nonlinear" devotional reading. Blatt's research on bookmarkers confirms from another point of view the nonlinear reading practices discussed by Joyce Coleman and Michael Sargent elsewhere in this volume.

Martin Chase's contribution deals with an "English Poem" (*Enska Vísan*) produced in Iceland at the end of the Middle Ages that has strong affinities with the Middle English *Sir Orfeo*. The transmission of the text of this poem shows that scribal networks and reading communities in Iceland were remarkably similar to the English equivalents studied by Mary Erler. The poem itself is an example of the fluid genre boundaries discussed elsewhere in this volume by Joyce Coleman, Kathryn Smith, and Michael Sargent. It has characteristics of devotional poetry and of romance, and although a product of post-Reformation Iceland, it reflects an earlier style associated with Catholic religious poetry. Some of the scribes and commissioners of the manuscript copies were clerics, others were lay, and the poem occurs in some collections in which all the other poems are devotional, and others in which all the other poems are secular. Wills reveal that several early manuscript owners were women. Chase shows how active reading communities on the farms and in the towns of northern Iceland bequeathed, exchanged, and copied one another's books. These communities remained active well into the nineteenth century, and their correspondence reveals a social nexus of provincial Icelanders and antiquarian scholars in Denmark and England – not unlike the London networks described by Sheila Lindenbaum.

Allison Alberts uses Foxe's *Book of Martyrs* as a resource for investigating the reading practices of early modern married women and mothers. Both the female subjects and the female readers of the *Book* provide insights into how literacy affected the ideas and lives of sixteenth-century women, particularly how marriage and motherhood were in themselves viewed as a Christian ideal and a form of witness. By examining the examples of particular women readers – bibliography in the service of biography – Alberts shows how women read the *Book of Martyrs*. Lady Margaret Hoby's diary describes nightly reading of the *Book of Martyrs* before bed. Grace Mildmay's autobiography, recommending the *Book* to her daughters and granddaughters, recounts her reading of the book beginning in her childhood and continuing throughout her long life. The lives Alberts reconstructs present women actively engaged in domestic administration and child-rearing who, seeing their suffering reflected in the lives of Foxe's maternal martyrs, find meaning and hope.

"Show me your library, and I'll tell you who you are," goes the saying. The essays in this collection reflect Mary Erler's passion for exploring lives – especially the lives of late medieval and early modern women and men – through the books they owned and read. If we can know little of their deeds and achievements, we can learn much about *who* they were. We can know what they read, why they read, how they read, and with whom they read. What is perhaps most affirming is to know simply *that* they read, and how reading affected and changed their lives. Their gifts and bequests of books, sometimes through generations, show how highly the books themselves were valued – owning a treasured text could be as important as reading it. Books were important for community life and relationships. Reading and book exchange sometimes cemented friendships and social groups and sometimes facilitated understanding between otherwise mutually exclusive social groups. During the times of turbulent religious and civic changes in the transition from the late Middle Ages to the early modern period, books and reading provided both an anchor in tradition and a guide to the way forward. Mary Erler, with an equal passion for texts, books, and lives, has given us new approaches and new insights. We present this book to her with our happy acknowledgment and with profound thanks.

"Withinne a Paved Parlour":
Criseyde and Domestic Reading in a City under Siege

JOYCE COLEMAN

When Boccaccio's Pandaro makes his first visit to Criseida as go-between for Troiolo, the text says only that "he made his way to where Criseida abode. And she, seeing him coming to her, stood up and greeted him from afar, and Pandarus her. And, taking her by the hand, he led her with him into an apartment" (sen gì ver dove Criseida stava; / la qual, veggendo lui a sé venire, / levata in pie, di lungi il salutava, / e Pandar lei, cui per la man pigliata / in una loggia seco l'ha menata).[1] There the two of them talk and joke, until Pandaro gradually reveals that Troiolo is in love with her. After much discussion, Criseida agrees to accept Troiolo's love.

When Chaucer's Pandarus makes his first visit to Criseyde as go-between for Troilus, he asks some of "hire folk" where she is, and is directed to her "paved parlour," where she and two of her ladies are sitting, listening to a maiden read aloud to them. Pandarus and Criseyde do an elaborate little dance around the book, both verbally and spatially, until they fall into a conversation that starts with Criseyde asking for news of the siege and then is guided by Pandarus into mutual praise of Troilus' successes in defending Troy. Next Criseyde wants to consult Pandarus concerning her estates; her people draw away as the two sit down together, and Pandarus turns the conversation back to his friend. After much discussion, Criseyde agrees merely to be nice to Troilus – to "maken him good chere."[2]

---

1   Boccaccio, *Il Filostrato*, parte 2, stanza 8, lines 4–8. The English is from R. K. Gordon, ed. and trans., *Il Filostrato*, in *The Story of Troilus* (Toronto, 1978), 23–127, at 43; the Italian is from *Il Filostrato*, in Boccaccio, *Tutte le opere*, vol. 2, ed. Vittore Branca (Milan, 1964), 37. I feel very privileged to have been invited to participate in this festschrift, in honor of a friend and scholar whom I have known and respected deeply for many years. I offer my essay in gratitude and admiration for all that Mary has done for me and for all of us. I am also grateful for feedback and insight from Caroline Barron and Martha Carlin, as well as for the help of Jason Lubinski.
2   *Troilus and Criseyde* 2:78–595; quotes from 2:79, 82, 471. All references to Chaucer's works are from *The Riverside Chaucer*, 3rd edn., ed. Larry D. Benson (Oxford, 1987).

Given her social standing, Boccaccio's Criseida would have had a household of attendants and servants around her, just like her English counterpart, but it was Chaucer's choice to make these "folk" visible, as a mini-throng through whom Pandarus must navigate in order to get Criseyde alone. Chaucer also invented the reading in the paved parlor, and in doing so, not only complicated Pandarus' task of proxy seduction but also inaugurated a complex exploration of the nature of reading, of women, and of women reading.

The famous parlor scene, and particularly the interaction between uncle and niece, have attracted varied scholarly explications over time. Earlier assessments tended to find it charming: the scene "portrays domestic happiness as vividly as it is portrayed anywhere in English literature";[3] Pandarus "maintains an affectionate flirtation."[4] As feminist readings developed, the view grew more ominous: Criseyde is aware "that her uncle is manipulating her, but . . . she simply cannot dissolve the realities and constraints of her position and her past."[5] Finally, scholars began to discover overt invocations of seduction, incest, and rape: "Pandarus' courting has disquietingly sexual overtones . . . [his touches] are uncomfortably cozy and intimate."[6] While many scholars have explored the dyad of uncle and niece in this scene, and the implicit triangle of uncle, niece, and Troilus, I would argue that we might really be dealing, at least initially, with a quaternion of uncle, niece, book, and Troilus. In order to explicate these complexities, I will start by going over the familiar parlor-reading, charting its textual/sexual permutations. I will then explore five "layers" that, I suggest, underlie Chaucer's shaping of the scene, and will close with speculations on a potentially disturbing relationship between the morally ambiguous pursuit of Criseyde and the creation of poetry.

From the moment he walks into the room, Pandarus is aware of the book and its communal readership as rivals for Criseyde's attention. Both are embedded in his greeting:

> Quod Pandarus, "Madame, God yow see,
> With youre book and all the compaignie!"

(T&C 2:85–86)

3   H. M. Smyser, "The Domestic Background of Troilus and Criseyde," Speculum 31 (1956): 297–315, at 314–15.
4   Richard Firth Green, Poets and Princepleasers: Literature and the English Court in the Late Middle Ages (Toronto, 1980), 209.
5   David Aers, "Criseyde: Woman in Medieval Society," Chaucer Review 13 (1979): 177–200, at 183.
6   Gretchen Mieszkowski, Medieval Go-Betweens and Chaucer's Pandarus (New York, 2006), 143.

10

Criseyde rises to welcome Pandarus, then sits with him on a bench. He apologizes for interrupting "youre book ye preysen thus" (2:95) – although she has said nothing to him about the book. "What seith it?" he asks. "Is it of love? O, som good ye me leere!" (96–97). Pandarus' question and request seem to imply a fear that the book is *not* about love, that it may be directing the minds of its auditors in some more serious direction. His statement pushes back against that possibility by setting up a flirtatious tone – to which Criseyde responds with her famously ambiguous but apparently humorous statement: "Uncle, . . . your maistresse" – his mastery or his mistress – "is nat here" (98). Criseyde then explains, getting into the story as she goes:

> This romaunce is of Thebes that we rede;
> And we han herd how that kyng Layus deyde
> Thorugh Edippus his sone, and al that dede;
> And here we stynten at thise lettres rede –
> How the bisshop, as the book kan telle,
> Amphiorax, fil thorugh the ground to helle.
>
> (*T&C* 2:100–5)

The materiality of the book, and its pull on Criseyde, are strongly felt in these words. One has to imagine that she has left the bench where she was sitting next to Pandarus and gone over to the table where the book was lying, so that she could point at the rubricated words introducing the episode of Amphiorax's disappearance. We should also note the first-person plural pronouns that Criseyde employs: "we rede"; "we han herd"; "we stynten." The shared public reading has melded its audience into a community of listeners. Pandarus now must try to separate his niece both from that community and from their book.

His first move is to characterize the book, and the reading of it, as boring:

> Al this knowe I myselve,
> And al th'assege of Thebes and the care;
> For herof ben ther maked bookes twelve.
>
> (*T&C* 2:106–8)

One imagines a yawn at "Al this know I myselve" and heavy stresses (abetted by the words' position at line-end) on "the *care*" and "bookes *twelve*." Pandarus, moreover, has apparently pursued Criseyde over to the table, for his next words strongly imply that he is touching her. At "Do wey youre barbe, and shew youre face bare" (110), he may be imagined pulling down the cloth that widows wore to conceal their chin and neck. "Do wey youre book," he continues – is he closing

11

it? – "rys up, and lat us daunce, / And lat us don to May som observaunce" (111–12). Criseyde has evidently sat down at the table in her absorption with the book and its rubric, and now Pandarus could be pulling her up and drawing her into some dance figure. These small but intimate and slightly invasive touchings, of chin and arm, would possibly be meant to evoke in the widowed Criseyde some physical arousal.[7]

In any case, Criseyde presumably pulls away from Pandarus at this point, protesting too-muchly:

> "I! God forbede!" quod she. "Be ye mad?
> Is that a widewes lif, so God yow save?
> By God, ye maken me ryght soore adrad!
> Ye ben so wylde, it semeth as ye rave."
>
> (*T&C* 2:113–16)

Having been invited not just to dance but to engage in Mayday celebrations – associated in medieval as in ancient times with sexual license[8] – Criseyde retreats, whether flirtatiously or in true distress, to imaginations of even chaster reading matter and location. "It satte me wel bet ay in a cave," she says,

> "To bidde and rede on holy seyntes lyves;
> Lat maydens gon to daunce, and yonge wyves."
>
> (2:117–19)

Layer 1. Intertextuality: Chaucer / Statius / *Roman de Thèbes* / Ovid

There are passages in Chaucer's work that are intensely layered, combining astute psychology with intertextual citation, historical observation, gender *realpolitik*, and authorial self-referentiality. Such passages seem to accrue particularly around women characters, and the scene of Criseyde's reading in the paved parlor is one of them.

I count at least five layers here. To unpeel them, we can begin with intertextuality. The reading group's femaleness, and Criseyde's use of the word "romaunce"

---

7   These ideas about the movements implicit in the text emerged during a 2005 project in which I and a graduate class filmed the parlor scene, with Profs. Elisabeth Dutton and Dan Ransom portraying Criseyde and Pandarus. The short film can be viewed at mednar.org or on YouTube.

8   E. K. Chambers, *The Mediaeval Stage* (1903; repr. Mineola, NY, 1966), 160–81.

(*T&C* 2:100) to describe their text, might incline a modern reader to assume that this is a group of courtly ladies entertaining themselves with, as one scholar has put it, "softheaded romantic fiction."[9] But the story of Thebes passed for history in Chaucer's time. Criseyde's Theban story could also be called a "romaunce" because it was apparently in French. Statius' *Thebaid* was the classical source for the siege of Thebes, but since Criseyde's text includes the story of Oedipus and calls Amphiorax a "bisshop" (105) – elements not present in Statius – Criseyde and her ladies should probably be imagined as reading the twelfth-century *Roman de Thèbes* or one of its prose redactions.[10] (Criseyde's Amphiorax is Amphiaraus in the *Thebaid* and Amphariäs in the *Roman de Thèbes*; for consistency's sake I am going to call him Amphiaraus from now on.)

Criseyde's reference to how "kyng Layus deyde / Thorugh Edippus his sone" (*T&C* 2:101–2) also tells us something interesting about her reading session, or sessions. Scholars have speculated about the insights Criseyde could have achieved if only Pandarus had not interrupted her reading. She would have encountered the family history of her future lover Diomede, for example, or even, if her manuscript happened to include the *Roman de Troie*, read her own fate.[11] However, if Criseyde and her ladies had already, in that one session, read continuously from Oedipus' patricide to just before Amphiaraus' fall, they would have been more than ready to break off at Pandarus' appearance – since Laius is dead by line 244, while Amphiaraus' fall starts at line 5053.[12] Within the verisimilitude of Chaucer's story, we would have to suppose either that the group had been reading its way, over many days, through the entire *Roman de Thèbes*; or

9   John V. Fleming, *Classical Imitation and Interpretation in Chaucer's "Troilus"* (Lincoln, NE, 1990), 96.

10   Boyd Ashby Wise, *The Influence of Statius upon Chaucer* (1911; repr. New York, 1967), 8–9.

11   E.g., Alain Renoir, "Thebes, Troy, Criseyde, and Pandarus: An Instance of Chaucerian Irony," *Studia neophilologica* 32 (1960): 14–17; Catherine Sanok, "Criseyde, Cassandre, and the *Thebaid*: Women and the Theban Subtext of Chaucer's *Troilus and Criseyde*," *Studies in the Age of Chaucer* 20 (1998): 41–71, at 49–54; Carole E. Newlands, *Statius, Poet between Rome and Naples* (London, 2012), 134. The *Roman de Troie* follows the *Roman de Thèbes* in Geneva, Bodmer Foundation 18; BnF, MS fr. 60, and BnF MS fr. 375; Aimé Petit, "Introduction," in *Le roman de Thèbes*, ed. and trans. Petit, Champion Classiques: Moyen Âge (Paris, 2008), 7–63, at 8.

12   The full *Roman* survives in five manuscripts, which present variant texts. We cannot, of course, be sure what manuscript, surviving or not, and containing which variants, Chaucer knew. I follow here Aimé Petit's edition, based on BnF MS fr. 784 (*Le roman de Thèbes*, Champion Classiques: Moyen Âge [Paris, 2008]). All quotes from the *Roman* are from this edition.

13

that in this one session they had begun with Oedipus, then jumped to one or more favorite passages later in the story, and were about to start on the Amphiaraus section when Pandarus turned up. Arguably, Chaucer achieved several goals by arranging for the women to read this way, or for Criseyde to mention these two widely separated passages: it serves to establish that they are reading the *Roman de Thèbes'* version of the story; it sets up Pandarus' annoyingly superior invocation of the Latin *Thebaid* (which, unlike the *Roman*, has "bookes twelve" [2:108]); and it casts a certain irony, or pathos, over the entire procedure.

This irony lies in the context of their reading. When we realize what "this romaunce of Thebes" is about, we understand that the text has a stark relevance to the world outside the cozy, paved parlor. "In a city under siege," as Carolyn Dinshaw has noted, "Criseyde reads a romance about a city under siege."[13] Chaucer suggests how resonant this parallel is for the group by having Criseyde point to and read the rubric describing how "Amphiorax . . . fil thorugh the ground to helle" (*T&C* 2:105). Thus carefully framed, the story is this: a Greek army has been besieging a city, and is now attacking it. Suddenly, the ground opens before the chariot of one of the war-leaders and swallows it and him up whole. From this isolated moment of text, the audience of Trojan women, whose besieged city is constantly being attacked by a Greek army, could derive a reassuring hope, or daydream – that the gods might yet intervene on their behalf and render similar havoc on their enemies.

Catherine Sanok suggests a possible difficulty in this reading, in her assumption that Criseyde's group would not know the story related in the Amphiaraus passage, since they had stopped at the rubric that introduces it.[14] I think this is too literal an approach, however. Chaucer clearly meant his readers to associate the reading event with that incident, since he signaled it so precisely. (It is not likely that he was signaling the text just *before* Amphiaraus' fall, because it consists of Amphiaraus charging along in his chariot, killing Thebans.) Moreover, based on medieval reading practices, this is much more likely to be a rereading of a familiar text than a first perusal of it. The number of books in even a noble household would never have been very great, and favorite material would be read repeatedly over time. Medieval references to pleasant evenings spent reading sections of romances or chronicles in groups imply that the listeners were familiar with the texts and had chosen favorite

---

13 Carolyn Dinshaw, *Chaucer's Sexual Poetics* (Madison, WI, 1989), 52; see also Sarah Stanbury, "The Voyeur and the Private Life in *Troilus and Criseyde*," *Studies in the Age of Chaucer* 13 (1991): 141–58, at 142.
14 Sanok, "Criseyde, Cassandre, and the *Thebaid*," 50.

portions for re-experiencing.[15] Edward III's esquires — one of whom was, at a certain point, Geoffrey Chaucer — kept "honest company" in evenings in "lordez chambrez within courte," in piping, harping, singing, and "talkyng of cronycles of kinges and of other polycyez [books on government]."[16] Presumably, with such a mix of entertainments, the reading sessions were short and selective. Similarly, *A Talkyng of þe Loue of God* — a series of prayers produced in the mid- to late-fourteenth century — suggests that readers "bi ginnen and leten in what paas. so men seoþ. þat may for þe tyme ȝiven mest lykynge" (begin and leave off at whatever place people may find gives most pleasure at that time).[17]

Another difficulty might seem to be that, in the case of Thebes, both the attackers and the defenders were Greek; as the reference to Oedipus would remind us, the antagonists were his two sons, Polynices and Eteocles. After their father's abdication, the brothers had agreed to take turns ruling Thebes, but Eteocles refused to step down when his turn was over. Polynices, in alliance with his Argive in-laws (including Amphiaraus), thus began the famous siege. Yet the fact that Criseyde and her ladies were reading the *Roman de Thèbes* means that they had help in forgetting that the city's defenders were just as Greek as the attackers. The French text obscures this "reality" by speaking consistently of "les Griex" (the Greeks) attacking "cil de la vile" (those of the city) or "ceus de Thebes" (those of Thebes) (lines 4562, 4553, 5030).[18]

Assuming that Criseyde and her ladies had been interrupted while rereading an already familiar text, the anxiety-allaying quality of the story would only have carried on for them, following Amphiaraus' fall. The *Roman de Thèbes* describes in great detail how the event plunged "les Grecs" into despair:

> They were greatly sorrowful, sad, and thoughtful,
> convinced they would never escape alive.
> Each man considered he was doomed
> because they had lost Amphiaraus.
> For him they mourned, for themselves they doubted,

---

15 Joyce Coleman, *Public Reading and the Reading Public in Late Medieval England and France* (Cambridge, UK, 1996), 130–31; Andrew Taylor, "Fragmentation, Corruption, and Minstrel Narration: The Question of the Middle English Romances," *Yearbook of English Studies* 22 (1992): 38–62.

16 A. R. Myers, ed., *The Household of Edward IV: The Black Book and the Ordinance of 1478* (Manchester, 1959), 129.

17 M. Salvina Westra, ed., *A Talkyng of þe Loue of God* (The Hague, 1950), 2. Translations are mine unless otherwise stated.

18 Chaucer himself, in *Anelida and Arcite*, describes the war as a conflict between "Thebes and Grece" (line 53).

to return home they desired.
[Mout sont dolent, tristre et pensif,
ja n'en cuident eschaper vif.
Chascun se tient a confondu
d'Ampharïas qu'il ont perdu.
De lui font deul, d'eus sont dotex,
du retorner sunt couvoitex.]

(lines 5143–48)

The Thebans, by contrast, rejoice, deriding their attackers and declaring:

your master has jumped into a big hole.
By him God has given you a sign
that you are not worthy of our land.
[vostre mestre a grant saut sailli.
Par lui vos demoutre Dex signe
de nostre terre n'estes digne.]

(lines 5166–68)

In a council the next day, the Greeks agree. The Duke of Vincennes laments:

There's nobody so crazy that he doesn't clearly see
that God does not approve our path.
How can you think to succeed,
if God does not will this enterprise?
[N'i a si fox qui bien ne voie
que Diex ne veut pas nostre voie.
Comme en cuidiez vos a chief trere,
se Diex ne veut icest afaire?]

(lines 5223–27)

It is not hard to imagine how comforting such passages would be to women living in daily danger of their city falling to Greek invaders. For them, the desirable stopping-point in the text would presumably have been line 5237, when the tide of opinion begins to turn. The army decides to elect a new bishop, who can lead them in penance and sacrifice. Their prayers induce God to close the hole into which Amphiaraus had fallen (at line 5389), and the Greeks resume their attacks on Thebes.

Putting the women's reading into context reveals Criseyde's paved parlor for the flimsy protection it is. Any audience aware of the story of Troy would think

16

forward to the fates of Andromache, Cassandra, Hecuba, and Polyxena.[19] In a daring moment, Chaucer allows the ugliness of war and the savage treatment of women on the losing side to shimmer through the courtly veil of his narrative. The moment is the more remarkable in that it is set against another, preceding intertextuality, one that mixes aubade with Ovidian rape and metamorphosis. On the day of his visit to Criseyde, Pandarus is awakened to his "pimp's errand" by the song of "the swalowe Proigne" (Procne), lamenting "How Tereus gan forth hire suster take."[20] Yet the reading group's choice of text wards off such invocations of male violence: even though Thebes does inevitably fall, in the *Roman de Thèbes* neither Antigone nor her sister Ismene dies, and they, and the other women of Thebes, are neither enslaved nor raped.[21]

It is easy to imagine that Criseyde and her ladies would want to hear, over and over again, the story of a Greek general destroyed by the gods as he was attacking a besieged city – even if their enjoyment required some strategic misreading and selective remembering. Hopefully, scholars are now beyond blaming Chaucer's female readers – the Wife of Bath is the other notorious offender[22] – for skewing male-authored texts to make their own lives more bearable. Criseyde and her women misread in order to render their exposed position as women in a besieged city less intolerable. Under these circumstances, there is a certain heroic quality

19 Cf. Winthrop Wetherbee, *Chaucer and the Poets: An Essay on "Troilus and Criseyde"* (Ithaca, NY, 1984), 116. Chaucer's audience would have derived their knowledge of Trojan history primarily from Virgil's *Aeneid* (c. 25 BCE), Dictys Cretensis' *Ephemeridos belli Trojani* (fourth century CE), Dares Phrygius' *De excidio Trojae historia* (fifth or sixth century), Benoît de Ste-Maure's *Roman de Troie* (c. 1160), and/or Guido de Columnis' *Historia destructionis Troiae* (1287). Dares provides a relatively happy outcome for Hecuba, Cassandra, and Andromache, who are all taken by Helenus (respectively their son, brother, and brother-in-law) to the Chersonese. In every other source, Cassandra is dragged from the temple of Minerva (but not raped) and later given to Agamemnon. Andromache is also dragged from the temple in Benoît, and then in all but Dares given to Neoptolemus/Pyrrhus. Virgil has Aeneas meet Andromache later in Chaonia, now married to Helenus but still traumatized by the past. In every text, Polyxena is sacrificed to Achilles, and in Dictys and Benoît, her mother Hecuba goes mad, curses the Greeks, and is stoned to death. Guido's account follows Benoît's in every case.

20 Fleming, *Classical Imitation*, 188; *T&C* 2:64–70, quotes from lines 64, 69.

21 In the *Roman de Thèbes*, Antigone's sister Ismene becomes a nun after her lover, Atys, dies in battle (lines 6161–98). In most manuscripts of the romance, Antigone herself is not mentioned again after a short remark on her anxiety about her lover, Parthenopeus (lines 8667–72). In BnF MS fr. 375, however, she dies of love nine days after Parthenopaeus' death; Rosemarie Jones, *The Theme of Love in the Romans d'Antiquité* (London, 1972), 24.

22 For a thorough denunciation of the Wife as reader, see D. W. Robertson, Jr., *A Preface to Chaucer: Studies in Medieval Perspectives* (Princeton, 1962), 317–31.

to the carefully framed focus on Amphiaraus' fall. There is narrative irony, as well, for readers who know that Criseyde would ultimately escape the rapes of Troy – only to become a byword for female faithlessness.

Layer 2. Physical Site: The Paved Parlor

In his opening assault on Criseyde's chastity, as this close reading has sought to demonstrate, Pandarus' biggest challenge seems to be to get his niece to close her book. Even though her book turns out to be history, not saints' lives or some other Christian text that Chaucer might have imported with equal anachronism into ancient Troy, the scene of women sharing a public reading in a close, domestic environment recalls the sort of devotional female reading circles that Mary Erler and others have discussed.

To explore Criseyde's circle, we can begin with its physical site, which Chaucer designates as carefully as he does the textual site at which the group reading halts. The paved parlor, like the reading that takes place within it, is Chaucer's addition to his source. In Boccaccio, the architectural layout is vague, but different. Pandaro goes "dove Criseida stava" (where Criseida lived). She sees him coming and greets him; he takes her hand and leads her "in una loggia," where their conversation takes place.[23] Although R. K. Gordon, as quoted above, translated *loggia* as "apartment," the word probably designated a far less private space: a room open on one side, with pillars, possibly on the upper floor of an internal courtyard.[24] Chaucer's Troy is a lot more like the less balmy London (also known, of course, as New Troy).

Scholars agree that the houses inhabited or visited by the characters of *Troilus and Criseyde* play an important part in the narrative, and that their layouts match closely those of medieval English houses.[25] In 1956 H. M. Smyser helpfully explained for literary critics the standard form of a late fourteenth-century aristocratic English residence. Based on a house-type that had evolved since the twelfth century, the core of this building was a rectangular hall, either at ground level or raised over an undercroft. At one end were "offices" – a pantry and buttery, and beyond them, the kitchen – separated from the main part of the hall by a screen and passageway. The rest of the space served in turn as meeting and business venue, dining room, and dormitory. "Chamber blocks" or "solar blocks" were sometimes added, as an extension of the hall or attached at a right angle to the hall's upper end. These

23 Boccaccio, *Filostrato*, parte 2, stanza 34, lines 1–8; quotes from lines 4 and 8.
24 I am grateful to my colleague Jason Houston for his help in visualizing Boccaccio's *loggia*.
25 Smyser, "Domestic Background," 297; Barry Windeatt, *Oxford Guides to Chaucer. "Troilus and Criseyde"* (Oxford, 1992), 192–95.

would be one or two stories, with one or two rooms per story, providing private rooms for the masters and/or mistresses of the house.[26]

Not much mentioned in the architectural histories – even the literary ones – is the one room we are most interested in, the parlor. Yet it turns out that parlors have a particularly interesting history, especially in the context of Chaucer's Criseyde. The medieval Latin word *parlatorium*, the Anglo-Norman *parlur*, and the Middle French *parloir* were in use in England from the twelfth century, but the *Oxford English Dictionary*'s earliest citation of "parlour" as an English word dates to c. 1225. At that point it means "a room or place for talking; *spec.* an apartment in a monastery or (esp. in later use) a convent, in which residents may converse with people from outside the establishment or amongst themselves." It is not until around 1378 that we get the first citation of the word in a secular context, as "a smaller room separate from the main hall, reserved for private conversation or conference . . . [i]n a manor house, or large public building."[27]

The actual room, as a secular space, occurs earlier than the word's first citation in English, but associated only with the heights of society. A document from 1291 shows that Corfe Castle, for example, included a queen's chamber and parlor.[28] It took until about the second quarter of the fourteenth century, however, for the royal innovation to percolate down to the aristocracy and gentry, and until the third quarter of the century to reach the merchant class.[29] The room's novelty in that period can be felt in the text cited by the *OED* as the word's first appearance in English. This is William Langland's famous complaint:

> Elenge is the halle, ech day in the wike,
> Ther the lord ne the lady liketh noght to sitte.
> Now hath ech riche a rule – to eten by hymselve
> In a pryvee parlour . . .
>
> (*Piers Plowman* B-Text, X:96–99)[30]

26 Smyser, "Domestic Background," 297–99, diagram on 298; John Blair, "Hall and Chamber: English Domestic Planning 1000–1250," in *Manorial Domestic Buildings in England and Northern France*, ed. Gwyn Meirion-Jones and Michael Jones (London, 1993), 1–21.

27 *OED*, s.v. "parlour": Etymology; Sense A.I.1 (cf. *MED*, s.v. "parlour" Sense 2); Sense A.I.2.a (cf. *MED*, Sense 1).

28 TNA PRO E. 101/460/27; cited at www.british-history.ac.uk/rchme/dorset/vol2/pp52–100.

29 John Schofield, *Medieval London Houses* (New Haven, 1994), 66; Caroline M. Barron, *London in the Later Middle Ages: Government and People 1200–1500* (Oxford, 2004), 24, 252.

30 William Langland, *The Vision of Piers Plowman*, ed. A. V. C. Schmidt (London, 1978). The *OED* dates the Langland passage to 1400, based on the date of the manuscript

[Ailing is the hall, each day in the week,
Where neither lord nor lady likes to sit.
Now each rich one has a rule – to eat by himself
In a private parlor]

Since Chaucer wrote *Troilus and Criseyde* around 1385, only a few years after Langland's complaint about the room's new-fangledness, Criseyde's parlor would presumably have struck contemporary audiences as a recent domestic innovation. It would carry strong overtones of the conventual parlor, especially as it was occupied – until invaded by Pandarus – by a chaste group of female readers.

From the time of the queen's parlor at Corfe, the room also had a particular association with women. Geoff Rector has characterized the chamber as the site of literary cultivation among Anglo-Norman magnates in the twelfth and thirteenth centuries.[31] But gender complicates the situation. Baudri de Bourgueil may have enveloped his encomium to Adèle de Blois in an elaborate description of her *thalamos* (chamber),[32] but like most medieval "chambers," Adèle's was also a bedchamber. And while men could entertain mixed groups in bedchambers, it would be less appropriate for women to welcome men to theirs: compare the ease with which Pandarus, Helen, Deiphebus, and Criseyde move in and out of Troilus' bedchamber at Deiphebus' house, with the conniving and creeping around involved in getting Troilus into a bedchamber containing Criseyde.[33]

Like its conventual antecedent, the secular parlor provided elite women with a respectable place of encounter with male visitors, as well as a retreat for themselves. In the terms of architectural "access analysis," which works on the assumption that "the permeability of each room in a complex has a social meaning,"[34] parlors would be halfway permeable. One would have to get into the hall first, to get to the parlor, but the parlor would be more accessible than the

quoted (Oxford, Bodleian Library, MS Laud Misc. 581), but notes that the text itself dates to c. 1378.
31 Geoff Rector, "Literary Leisure and the Architectural Spaces of Early Anglo-Norman Literature," in *Locating the Middle Ages: The Spaces and Places of Medieval Culture*, ed. Julian Weiss and Sarah Salih (London, 2013), 161–74; Geoff Rector, "*En sa chambre sovent le lit*: Literary Leisure and the Chamber Sociabilities of Early Anglo-French Literature (c. 1100–1150)," *Medium Ævum* 81 (2012): 88–125.
32 Ibid. 101–3.
33 Respectively, *T&C* 2:1666–1703; 3:59–211; and 3:631–973. Pandarus actually calls the room he brings Criseyde to a "closet" (3:663), but it feels more like a bedchamber, in that it contains a curtained bed and a fireplace.
34 Amanda Richardson, "Gender and Space in English Royal Palaces c. 1160–c. 1547: A Study in Access Analysis and Imagery," *Medieval Archaeology* 47 (2003): 131–65, at 131.

(bed)chamber upstairs.[35] The fact that Chaucer replaced Pandaro's "pathless" approach to Criseida with Pandarus' passage through the hall of Criseyde's house and encounter with "hir folk," en route to her parlor, suggests that the author was well attuned to and wanted his audience to register these fine socio-spatial calibrations.

The other suggestive physical datum about Criseyde's reading is, of course, that her parlor was paved. As late as 1524, in a letter to Cardinal Wolsey's physician, John Francis, Erasmus complained that the floors of English houses

> are generally spread with clay and then with rushes from some marsh, which are renewed from time to time but so as to leave a basic layer, sometimes for twenty years, under which fester spittle, vomit, dogs' urine and men's too, dregs of beer and cast-off bits of fish, and other unspeakable kinds of filth. As the weather changes, this exhales a sort of miasma which in my opinion is far from conducive to bodily health.[36]
> [Tum sola fere sunt argilla, tum scirpis palustribus, qui subinde sic renovantur, ut fundamentum maneat aliquoties annos viginti, sub se fovens sputa, vomitus, mictum canum et hominum, projectam cervisiam, et piscium reliquias, alias que sordes non nominandas. Hinc mutato coelo vapor quidam exhalatur, mea sententia minime salubris humano corpori.][37]

Presumably Criseyde's floor would have been exempt from some of the ingredients listed by Erasmus. But by writing explicitly of a *paved* parlor, Chaucer was communicating to his contemporary audience that the reading scene took place in an atmosphere of unusual cleanliness and unsmelliness.

"Paved" at this time could designate a floor of stone slabs or the fancier option of plain or decorated ceramic tiles,[38] tiling being usually associated with religious houses and with royal palaces or aristocratic residences such as,

---

35   Parlors became progressively more private over the later fifteenth and into the sixteenth century, as the great chamber developed as an alternate space to receive and entertain guests. See John Schofield, "Social Perceptions of Space in Medieval and Tudor London Houses," in *Meaningful Architecture: Social Interpretations of Buildings*, ed. Martin Locock (Aldershot, Hampshire, 1994), 188–206, at 202–3.

36   Letter no. 1532 in *The Correspondence of Erasmus: Letters 1356 to 1534, 1523 to 1524*, trans. R. A. B. Mynors and Alexander Dalzell, annotated by James M. Estes, Collected Works of Erasmus 10 (Toronto, 1992), 470–72, at 471.

37   Quoted in Frederick J. Furnivall, Jr., "Forewords," in *Early English Meals and Manners*, ed. Furnivall, Early English Text Society o.s. 32 (London, 1868), i–lxviii, at lxvi.

38   The *OED* defines "to pave," from c. 1325, as "to lay paving, a pavement, or (later also) any hard surfacing material on (a road, floor, etc.); (also) to tile (a floor)" (Sense 1.a).

perhaps, Criseyde's. The expense and *cachet* of such flooring is suggested by the records: in 1439, for example, Cardinal Henry Beaufort (Chaucer's nephew by marriage) spent £6 to buy 2,000 paving tiles for his parlor at Bishop's Waltham in Hampshire – the equivalent of about £3,000 today.[39]

We may thus imagine Pandarus and Criseyde playing out their drama on a pavement of tiles carrying connotations not only of cleanliness but also of value, prestige, and beauty. The importance of this room, and its connotations, to Chaucer's opening portrait of Criseyde can be gauged by a surprising fact: not only is her parlor not entered or even mentioned again in the rest of *Troilus and Criseyde*, but Book 2's reference to Criseyde's "paved parlour" is the only time the word or the thing itself appears anywhere in Chaucer's writings.

Layer 3. Women's Reading Communities

Criseyde's paved parlor, with its overtones of conventual meeting-rooms and of a state of physical purity symbolically appropriate to the inhabitants of convents, seems a fitting site for an all-female reading group. Since the women were pagan Trojans, it would have stretched credibility too far, and lost the intertextual undertones of anxiety, if Chaucer had actually given them a book of saints' lives to read. That he has Criseyde refer to saints' lives as suitable reading for widows, however, suggests that he wanted his audience to make the connection.

One thinks inevitably, in this context, of BL MS Add. 70513, the Campsey Ash Priory collection of saints' lives, with its famous inscription: "ce livre [est] deviseie a la priorie de Kampsie de lire a mengier" (fol. 265; this book [is] given to the priory of Campsey to read at mealtime). The work of scholars such as Jocelyn Wogan-Browne and Virginia Blanton has shown how Campsey Ash and other houses were centers of female book ownership and communal readership.[40] In this the institutions were following long-standing monastic tradition, going back as far as the Augustinian Rule – which Campsey Ash, as a house of Austin nuns,

39 C. M. Woolgar, *The Great Household in Late Medieval England* (New Haven, 1999), 70. Price conversion from the U.K. National Archive's Currency Converter, which equates £6 in 1440 with £2,816 in 2005 (the last date offered for calculation) (http://www. nationalarchives.gov.uk/currency-converter/). On tiled floors in medieval London, see Schofield, *Medieval London Houses*, 112–13; Alun Graves, *Tiles and Tilework of Europe* (London, 2002), 20–21.
40 Jocelyn Wogan-Browne, "Powers of Record, Powers of Example: Hagiography and Women's History," in *Gendering the Master Narrative: Women and Power in the Middle Ages*, ed. Mary C. Erler and Maryanne Kowaleski (Ithaca, NY, 2003), 71–93; Virginia Blanton, *Signs of Devotion: The Cult of St. Aethelthryth in Medieval England, 695–1615* (University Park, PA, 2007), 195–201.

would have followed. The rule prescribed: "When you come to the table and until you rise, listen to what is being read aloud to you according to custom, making no noise or disturbance; [for] it should be not only your jaws that are chewing food but your ears that are thirsting for God's word" (Cum acceditis ad mensam, donec inde surgatis, quod vobis secundum consuetudinem legitur, sine tumultu et contentionibus audite; nec solae vobis fauces sumant cibum, sed et aures esuriant Dei verbum).[41] Mary Carruthers quotes an undated but later medieval rule for women that describes not only how the audience should behave but also how they should feel: "With absorbed, intent mind, she should actively, emotionally enter into the reading. She sighs anxiously when, in prophecy or historical narrative, the word of God shows enmity to the wicked. She is filled with great joy when the favor of the Lord is shown to the good" (Tunc uniuscujusque mens sobria intenta sit dulcedini verbi Dei, suspiret anxia, cum propheticus aut historicus sermo Dei saevitiam monstrat in pravos. Gaudio repleatur immenso, cum benignita Dei annuntiatur in bonos).[42] One thinks of Criseyde's joy at the destruction of the invading Greek, Amphiaraus.

Devotional works produced for men and women in secular life continued to valorize shared reading. Jocelyn Wogan-Browne quotes a compilation of Anglo-Norman penitential texts (Cambridge, Trinity College, MS R.1.47), created in the third quarter of the thirteenth century, that addresses itself to "sweet dear brothers and sisters in God, men and women of religious life, and to all those, male and female, who will read this writing or will hear it read by others" (duz chers freres e suers en deu, hommes e femmes de religion, e a tuz icels e celes [ke] cest escrit lirront ou de autre lire le orrunt).[43] Again one gets the feeling of public reading building a community whose interaction augments and deepens the benefits of reading the text. The perception carries through right across the time of *Troilus and Criseyde*'s composition into the fifteenth century and a text such as *The Nightingale*, composed in 1446. An anonymous Christian allegorization dedicated to Anne, Duchess of Buckingham, the poem envisions a court and reading practice rather like the one we glimpse in Chaucer's Troy. The duchess will

---

41 Translation from Adolar Zumkeller, *Augustine's Ideal of the Religious Life*, trans. Edmund Colledge (New York, 1986), 287–95, at 290; Latin from www.thelatinlibrary. com/augustine/reg.shtml.

42 Translation from Mary J. Carruthers, *The Book of Memory: A Study of Memory in Medieval Culture*, 2nd edn. (Cambridge, UK, 2008), 208; Latin from *Patrilogia latina* 30. 435C-D.

43 Jocelyn Wogan-Browne, "'Cest livre liseez . . . chescun jour': Women and Reading c. 1230–c. 1430," in *Language and Culture in Medieval Britain: The French of England c. 1100–c. 1500*, ed. Wogan-Browne et al. (York, 2009), 239–53, at 253; Wogan-Browne's translation.

call vn-to hyr high presence
Suche of hyre peple, that are in lustynesse
Fresschly encoragyt, as galantus [lovers] in prime-tens [springtime],
Desyrous for to here the amerouse sentensce
Of the nyghtyngale, and in there mynde enbrace,
Who favoure moste schall fynd in loues grace,

Commandyng theym to here wyth tendernesse
Of this your nightyngale the gostly [spiritual] sense.[44]

Here Anne is offered a strategy, as text-chooser and chief listener, of using the reading event not just to unite but to shape the young members of her *familia*, redirecting their distracting erotic impulses into a more spiritual, and also more disciplined consortium. Criseyde's reading session employs a similar strategy to a different end, with a book chosen for its ability to amuse its audience while subvocally, as it were, assuaging anxieties about sexual violence.

In its pagan and secular context, the Trojan parlor reading taps into medieval secular models of reading as well. History was a topic that attracted both female and male audiences, although there are many more accounts of male readers – possibly corresponding to the relative paucity of female authors. The limited evidence suggests that the medieval French *estoire* or Middle English *istorie*, both of which mixed the modern senses of "history" and "story," tended to tip in different directions for each gender. In accounts of all-male groups reading historical material in colleges, inns of court, and noble or royal households, the "history" side seems to predominate.[45] The sort of history being read by Criseyde and by other medieval women inclines more toward the "story" side. We might call this genre "romanticized history," meaning that what was or was thought to be actual history – for example, the exploits of Alexander the Great or Charlemagne, or the fall of Thebes – incorporated active female protagonists, some of whom at least would have love relationships (re)oriented around the rules of *fin' amor*. This form of *estoire* possibly co-originates with the romance itself, as the earliest examples trace back to the period and patronage of Eleanor of Aquitaine. The *Roman de Thèbes*, whose references to Poitiers and London link the work to Eleanor, is in fact the first known romance. Aimé Petit notes the scholarly hypothesis that Eleanor and her husband Henry II underwrote a

---

44 "The Nightingale," in *Lydgate's Minor Poems: The Two Nightingale Poems (A.D. 1446)*, ed. Otto Glauning, Early English Text Society e.s. 90 (London, 1900), 2–15, at 2, lines 9–16.
45 Joyce Coleman, "Talking of Chronicles: The Public Reading of History in Late Medieval England and France," *Cahiers de littérature orale* 36 (1994): 91–111.

series of romanticized histories – consisting of the *Roman de Thèbes*, *de Troie* (by Benoît de Ste-Maure), and *d'Eneas*, with Wace's *Brut* and Benoît's *Roman de Rou* – intended to align the history of the Plantagenets with a high classical pedigree. Several manuscripts survive that compile two or more of these texts together.[46]

While both monarchs might have been involved, however, Eleanor's influence is clear in the augmented role given to female actors. For example, in the *Roman de Thèbes*, Jocasta is an astute politician called upon to handle important negotiations. Rosemarie Jones notes that Jocasta's "mission to the camp of Polynices is a festive occasion, quite unlike the account in the *Thebaid* where we see a trembling old woman failing in her attempt to bring peace and scurrying ignominiously back to the city."[47] The Argive widows not only seek Theseus' help to bury their husbands but actually enable the Athenians' victory by tearing down the ramparts of Thebes. And Criseyde owes her very (literary) existence to Eleanor's (possible) sponsorship of the *Roman de Troie*, in which Benoît invented a love affair between Troilus and Calchus' daughter Briseis (later renamed Criseida by Boccaccio). Of course, the argument for Eleanor's patronage is largely circumstantial, and in any case we have no record of her, or Henry, reading these works.

Though the *Troilus and Criseyde* scene is probably the most detailed and important account of female reading of romanticized history that we have, other traces do survive. In his *Mirur* (Mirror) of c. 1250, for example, Robert de Gretham notes that his patroness, Dame Aline la Zouch,

> loves very much to hear and read
> Songs of deeds and of *estoire*
> And commits many of them to memory.
> [mult amez oir e lire.
> Chancon de geste e destoire
> E mult i metez la memoire.]
>
> (*Mirur*, lines 4–6)[48]

It would probably be fair to translate *estoire* here as "romanticized history," especially as it is contrasted with the more deed-oriented *chansons de geste*. And the statement that Aline loved "oir et lire" (to hear and read) these texts suggests that at least sometimes she shared the reading with at least a prelector, and most probably (given medieval social structures) with some of her household as well.

46 Petit, "Introduction," 24–26; see also Newlands, *Statius*, 131.
47 Jones, *Theme of Love*, 20.
48 Transcribed from Nottingham, WLC/LM/4, f. 57 (mssweb.nottingham.ac.uk/ document-viewer/medieval-women/theme7/document1/09-1111m-7-1_1.asp).

Across genres, a persistent feature of reading groups is the creation and, one could say, in some cases the management of community. Moving out of early monastic contexts into secular life, vernacularity allowed the practice to retain its spiritual impact while expanding into new social situations. For laywomen, it may have provided an especially welcome opportunity both to meet away from the various pressures of male company and to insert themselves into literate culture, on their own terms.

One would suppose that Chaucer, with his many modes of courtly service, would have been familiar with the idea of aristocratic women reading together in small groups. But there is a generally overlooked period of his courtly service that may have particularly influenced his account of the reading in Criseyde's paved parlor.

Layer 4. Elizabeth de Burgh and her Connections

Chaucer's first courtly post was as a page in the household of Elizabeth de Burgh, countess of Ulster and wife of Edward III's second surviving son, Lionel of Antwerp. Thanks to two binding fragments that preserve expense records of Elizabeth's household from June 1356 to April 1359 (BL MS Add. 18632, fols. 2b–2, 101b–101), we know that "Galfridus Chaucer" was issued various items of clothing in 1357, and apparently continued in Elizabeth's service until sometime in 1359.

Elizabeth is a largely unknown figure in Chaucer's life; I assemble here what is, as far as I know, the first attempt since 1885 at an overview of her short life.[49] The Elizabeth de Burgh whom Chaucer knew was the heir of her considerably more famous grandmother of the same name and rank (Fig. 1.1). Elizabeth senior was co-heir of the vast estates of her father, Gilbert de Clare, earl of Gloucester and Hertford, and became countess of Ulster through her first marriage.[50] Her son, William de Burgh, earl of Ulster, married Maud or Matilda of Lancaster, daughter of Henry, earl of Lancaster, and sister of Henry de Grosmont, first

49 Cf. Emily S. Holt, "Elizabeth, Duchess of Clarence," *Journal of the Architectural, Archaeological, and Historic Society, for the County, City, and Neighbourhood of Chester* 3 (1885): 391–408. Holt was a historical novelist and biographer, who dug deeply into administrative documents to reconstruct Elizabeth's life (without the aid of the account fragments, which had not then been published). Nonetheless, at various points her interpretations now seem questionable.

50 On Elizabeth de Burgh senior's life and activities, see Frances A. Underhill, "Elizabeth de Burgh: Connoisseur and Patron," in *The Cultural Patronage of Medieval Women*, ed. June Hall McCash (Athens, GA, 1996), 266–87; Underhill, *For her Good Estate: The Life of Elizabeth de Burgh*, New Middle Ages (Basingstoke, Hampshire, 1999).

26

Geneaology of Elizabeth de Clare / de Burgh; Maud / Matilda of Lancaster; and Elizabeth de Burgh

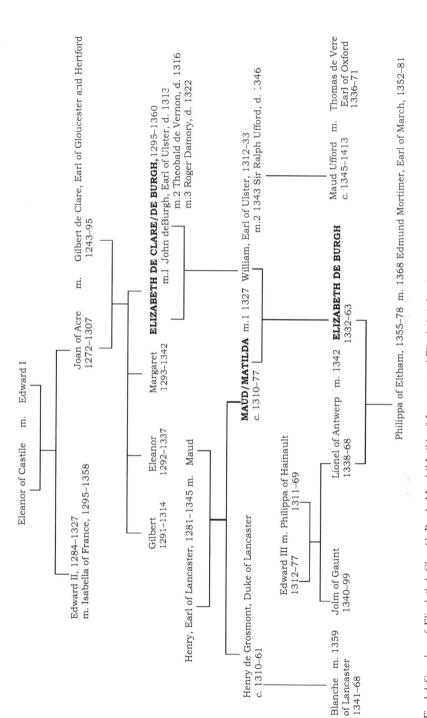

Fig. 1.1 *Genealogy of Elizabeth de Clare/de Burgh, Maud/Matilda of Lancaster, and Elizabeth de Burgh.*

duke of Lancaster. Their daughter, Elizabeth junior, was born in Ireland on July 6, 1332, in Carrickfergus Castle.[51] Less than a year later, on June 6, 1333, the twenty-one-year-old William was murdered near Carrickfergus by his own men, and Maud fled with her baby daughter to England.

Although Elizabeth now became a ward of the crown, Edward III allowed Maud to keep the child with her until, allegedly to please his Irish subjects, he betrothed Elizabeth to Lionel in May 1341.[52] No doubt her status as heiress to the Clare and de Burgh lands also figured into Edward's decision. The prospective bride joined her groom-to-be in the royal household. Edward did not wait long before securing Lionel's claim on Elizabeth's inheritance; their marriage took place on Assumption Day, August 15, 1342, in the Tower of London. Elizabeth, bedecked in pearls and wearing a gold coronet and ruby ring given to her by the king, was ten years old; Lionel, three.[53] Meanwhile, in 1343 Edward married Maud off to Sir Ralph Ufford, brother of the earl of Suffolk. The king then appointed Ralph justiciar of Ireland and sent the couple to Dublin to oversee Lionel's prospective claims. After two strenuous and frustrating years, Ralph died, in April 1346. Maud, back in England with another infant daughter, took the veil.[54] Elizabeth and Lionel's first and only child, Philippa of Eltham, was born on August 16, 1355.[55]

Since 1353, when she came of age, Elizabeth had been receiving an Exchequer annuity of £100 for the maintenance of her own *familia*, "separate from her husband's, consisting of *domicelle*, a clerk or clerks, probably an esquire or esquires, yeomen (*valetti*) of the chamber, a page or pages, and a chaplain."[56] The first record of Chaucer's presence in this household dates from April 4, 1357, when he was outfitted for Easter; he is recorded again on May 20 and December 20 of the same year. Late in 1359, when Lionel came of age, his

51   Edmund Curtis, *A History of Ireland*, 6th edn. (New York, 2004), 91–92.

52   Underhill, *For her Good Estate*, 94; *Foedera, conventiones, litterae, et cujuscunque generis acta publica inter reges Angliae . . .*, vol. 2, pt. 2, ed. Thomas Rymer and Robert Sanderson (London, 1821), 1159.

53   W. M. Ormrod, "The Royal Nursery: A Household for the Younger Children of Edward III," *English Historical Review* 120 (2005): 398–415, at 411 n. 74, citing a marginal note in TNA PRO E 36/204, fol. 26v; Holt 1885: 395, citing the Exchequer issue rolls for Michaelmas, 16 Edward III.

54   Robin Frame, "Matilda [Maud] of Lancaster, countess of Ulster (d. 1377)," *Oxford Dictionary of National Biography* (Oxford, 2004–); Frame, "Ufford, Sir Ralph (d. 1346), justiciar of Ireland," *Oxford Dictionary of National Biography* (Oxford, 2004–).

55   Underhill, *For her Good Estate*, 184 n. 41.

56   *Calendar of the Patent Rolls: Edward III*, vol. 9: *1350–1354*, 495; Martin M. Crow and Clair C. Olson, eds., *Chaucer Life-Records* (Austin, TX, 1966), 17.

and Elizabeth's households probably merged, with Chaucer moving into Lionel's service;[57] certainly, Chaucer was in France with Lionel by September 1359.[58] On November 4, 1360, Elizabeth de Burgh senior died, and Elizabeth junior and Lionel (now back in England) inherited the Clare lands (as well as de Burgh lands that Elizabeth senior had held for life). On July 1 of the following year, Edward III appointed Lionel royal lieutenant of Ireland, and on September 15, 1361, Lionel and Elizabeth arrived in Dublin.[59] Chaucer seems to have stayed behind.[60] On December 10, 1363, Elizabeth died in Dublin, cause unknown.

Early in 1364 her body was transported to England, at the Crown's expense, and buried in the family mausoleum at Clare Priory, Suffolk.[61] Her daughter had apparently been with her in Ireland, as arrangements were made in March 1364 to send the child, then eight, back to England.[62] Lionel himself left in April for a nine-month break in England, perhaps partly out of a need to reconnect with his family after his wife's death.[63] He presumably participated in the memorial celebration in December 1364, a year after Elizabeth's death, for which expenses are recorded in the accounts of the royal Wardrobe. Furred mourning robes were provided for Queen Philippa and for her namesake and godchild, Lionel and Elizabeth's daughter Philippa.[64] While still in England Lionel arranged to set up a chantry in St. Patrick's church, Dublin, to pray "for the soul of Elizabeth that was the duke's wife," as well as other family members.[65]

Scholarship has usually passed lightly over Chaucer's period of service in Elizabeth's household, to move on to his more muscular, male associations in the service of Lionel and then of Edward III. In fact, Elizabeth is often simply subsumed into her husband. One medievalist has recently written, for example, that Chaucer "had grown up in St. Martin in the Vintry but left there in adolescence for the courtly life he lived with the Duke of Clarence, and then in

57 Crow and Olson, *Chaucer Life-Records*, 13–15, 18.
58 Derek Pearsall, *The Life of Geoffrey Chaucer: A Critical Biography* (Oxford, 1992), 41.
59 W. M. Ormrod, "Lionel [Lionel of Antwerp], duke of Clarence (1338–1368), prince," *Oxford Dictionary of National Biography* (Oxford, 2004–).
60 Crow and Olson, *Chaucer Life-Records*, 21.
61 Ormrod, "Lionel, duke of Clarence."
62 *Foedera*, vol. 3.2, 725.
63 Philomena Mary Connolly, "Lionel of Clarence and Ireland, 1361–1366" (PhD diss., University of Dublin, 1977), 322–23. Her itinerary for Lionel records his absence from Ireland from April 23, 1364, to February 7, 1365.
64 Holt, "Elizabeth, Duchess of Clarence," 408.
65 *Calendar of the Patent Rolls: Edward III*, vol. 12: *1361–1364*, 522.

the king's rather itinerant household" – erasing Elizabeth while identifying her husband by the title he gained through her Clare inheritance.[66]

Yet it is surely significant that at the impressionable age of seventeen, or younger,[67] the wine-merchant's son's first immersion in an aristocratic milieu came in the court of a woman, and – in the context of his future composition, *Troilus and Criseyde* – of a young woman known to have had a small group of female attendants. One of these (adding to the intensity of the experience, perhaps) was probably the boy's future wife, Philippa de Roet. Elizabeth's accounts include four expenditures for a "Philippa Pan" – the "Pan" being written with an elevated punctus after the *n*. This was probably Philippa de Roet, who married Chaucer around 1366. The "Pan" would derive from the forename of her father, Sir Paon de Roet, a courtier who came to England in the train of Queen Philippa of Hainault, Elizabeth's mother-in-law.[68] Three other *domicellae* are attested via records of annuities granted them for service to Elizabeth: in May 1357, Maud de Pudyngton, who had apparently moved from Queen Philippa's household to Elizabeth's; in June 1359, Alice Dautre; and in February 1365, Margaret Dyneley.[69]

It is hard to think that the adolescent Chaucer would not have been awed and fascinated by the young countess and the round of courtly entertainments he probably accompanied her to: Easter in Reading (1357), St. George's Day at Windsor Castle (1357 and 1358), Pentecost in Woodstock (1357), Christmas at Hatfield in Yorkshire (1357; John of Gaunt was one of the visitors), Epiphany at Bristol (1358). Other events he may have attended in some capacity include the entry of the captive King Jean II of France into London, on May 24, 1357; a visit to the lions in the Tower of London, in November 1358; Isabella of France's funeral on November 27, 1358, in London; the betrothal of Elizabeth and Lionel's daughter to Edmund Mortimer, earl of March, in late 1358 or early 1359; and John of Gaunt's wedding to Blanche of Lancaster at Reading and the subsequent tournament at Smithfield in London, in which Lionel participated, in May 1359.[70] Among the less elaborate of these courtly events – not involving any expenditure, so not appearing in the accounts – might well have been group

66   Paul Strohm, *Chaucer's Tale: 1386 and the Road to Canterbury* (New York, 2014), 67.
67   Chaucer's birthdate is usually given as around 1340, but some scholars argue for 1343 (see Pearsall, *Life*, 9–11).
68   Pearsall, *Life*, 35. The expenditures for Philippa are dated July 24, 1356; May 20 and December 20, 1357; and April 21, 1358; Crow and Olson, *Chaucer Life-Records*, 13–15.
69   *Calendar of the Patent Rolls: Edward III*, vol. 10: *1354–1358*, 531; *Calendar of the Patent Rolls: Edward III*, vol. 11: *1358–1361*, 245; *Calendar of the Patent Rolls: Edward III*, vol. 13: *1364–1367*, 100.
70   Crow and Olson, *Chaucer Life-Records*, 18; Ormrod, "Lionel, Duke of Clarence."

readings such as the one Chaucer later ascribed to the young female aristocrat Criseyde.

While no direct evidence survives of Elizabeth's character, some actions of her husband are suggestive. When the couple arrived in Dublin in 1361, Lionel acted to protect his wife from what she felt was a hazardous posting (the danger arising chiefly from the Irish-born English, leery of interference from "headquarters"): "Bearing in mind the treacherous murder of her father by the colonists, their threats against her mother after that event, and their malignity when she [Maud] returned with her second husband, the Viceroy, D'Ufford, Lionel issued a proclamation, forbidding any man born in Ireland to approach his camp."[71] His actions directly following his wife's death, described above, seem to suggest genuine grief. In 1364, the year after Elizabeth's death, Lionel acted for her mother in establishing an abbey of Minoresses at Bruisyard (Suffolk), which Maud later joined.[72] In October 1368, when Lionel fell mortally ill just a few months after his marriage to Violante Visconti in Milan, he ordered that his body be returned to England and buried at Clare Priory, next to Elizabeth.[73] Such acts of consideration and devotion may indicate that Lionel had genuinely loved

71 J. T. Gilbert, *History of the Viceroys of Ireland; with Notices of the Castle of Dublin and Chief Occupants in Former Times* (Dublin, 1865), 218. The *Annales Hibernie* report the order – Lionel "clamavit in exercitu suo quod nullus nativus de Hibernia appropinquaret exercitui suo" (*Annales Hibernie*, in *Chartularies of St. Mary's Abbey, Dublin*, vol. 2, ed. John T. Gilbert [London, 1884], 303–98, at 395) – but I have been unable to confirm Gilbert's account of Lionel's motive from more recent published sources. However, most of these conform to a male-oriented historiography that tends to exclude female agency or influence. There may be more information in unpublished documents of Lionel's lieutenancy held in the National Archives and other sites (for a list of these, see Connolly, "Lionel of Clarence," 343–44). In any case, recent historians have not suggested any other motive for Lionel's decree. Given that her father had been murdered by the Anglo-Irish and that her mother twice had to flee the country (and cited her fear of the place in numerous petitions to the king [e.g., *Calendar of the Patent Rolls: Edward III*, vol. 4: *1338–1340*, 21; *Calendar of the Patent Rolls: Edward III*, vol. 5: *1340–1343*, 189–90; *Calendar of the Patent Rolls: Edward III*, vol. 6: *1343–1345*, 246]), it seems entirely feasible that Elizabeth distrusted the Irish and that Lionel issued his decree on her behalf. On the other hand, Connolly could find no evidence for such an order in the surviving administrative records, causing her to doubt its existence (Connolly, "Lionel of Clarence," 153).
72 "House of Minoresses: Abbey of Bruisyard," in *A History of the County of Suffolk*, vol. 2, ed. William Page, Victoria County History (London, 1975), 131–32, at 131; David Allen, "A Newly Discovered Survival from the Muniments of Maud of Lancaster's Chantry College at Bruisyard," *Proceedings of the Suffolk Institute for Archaeology & History* 40, pt. 2 (2006): 151–74, at 153–54.
73 Ormrod, "Lionel, duke of Clarence."

his first wife, and thus that she was a woman who could attract the admiration of others as well, including her young page.

Elizabeth was only in her mid-twenties when Chaucer was part of her *familia*. However, the countess's female relations put her in a context of literacy, patronage, and, indeed, of Campsey Ash. Her grandmother had been celebrated for her patronage of intellectual life, expressed particularly in her refoundation of Clare Hall (now Clare College), Cambridge, in 1346.[74] She celebrated the birth of her granddaughter by sending Maud an illuminated book worth the spectacular sum of £36 (equivalent to over £16,000 today);[75] one can imagine the girl often perusing what must have been a very beautiful manuscript. In her biography of Elizabeth senior, Frances Underhill notes that Elizabeth junior frequently visited her grandmother. Underhill considered it "very possible that he [Chaucer] accompanied her on these visits."[76] Female reading groups might well have been a feature of life with the elder Elizabeth. It is also worth noting that if Chaucer did indeed have access to Jean II's copy of Guillaume de Machaut's works while the king was staying at John of Gaunt's Savoy Palace, as some have hypothesized,[77] it would have been while Chaucer was in Elizabeth's household and therefore, most likely, through his connection with her.

The younger Elizabeth had important connections through her mother, as well. In 1347, Maud became a canoness in Campsey Ash Priory, where she had buried her second husband in 1346. The priory, which had enjoyed Ufford patronage since 1319, welcomed Maud as an important, resident patron. She brought with her a rich dower and founded a chantry of a warden and four chaplains to pray for her relations;[78] in 1358, she used her influence with the king to exempt the sisters from taxation.[79] Ordinances prescribed in 1356 by Maud for her chantry's priests echo the Augustinian Rule in declaring: "we will and ordain that at all

---

74 Underhill, "Elizabeth de Burgh," 273–77.
75 Ibid., 274–75. The price calculation is from http://www.nationalarchives.gov.uk/currency-converter/, based on 2005 rates.
76 Underhill, *For her Good Estate*, 184 n. 45.
77 James I. Wimsatt and William W. Kibler, "Introduction" to Guillaume de Machaut, *Le jugement du roy de Behaigne* and *Remede de Fortune*, ed. Wimsatt and Kibler, The Chaucer Library (Athens, GA, 1988), 3–57, at 53. Jean II was in residence at the Savoy from May 24, 1358 to April 4, 1359; H. d'Orléans, "Notes et documents relatifs à Jean, roi de France, et à sa captivité en Angleterre," in *Miscellanies of the Philobiblon Society* 2 (London, 1855–56), 1–190, at 27–44.
78 "Houses of Austin Nuns: Priory of Campsey," in *A History of the County of Suffolk*, vol. 2, ed. William Page, Victoria County History (London, 1975), 112–15. For the chantry's complicated history, see Allen, "A Newly Discovered Survival."
79 *Calendar of the Patent Rolls: Edward III*, vol. 11: *1358–1361*, 138.

ordinary meals and collations, at the beginning and at the end they are to have a reading from Holy Scripture, or from any other book which shall be able better to stimulate the hearers to devotion" (volumus et ordinamus quod in omne refeccione et collacione ordinaria, in principio ac fine, lectionem habeant de sacra scriptura vel de aliquo alio libro quo melius ad deuocionem audientes poterunt excitari).[80] Obviously, Maud herself was a good candidate to participate in the sort of conventual prelections of saints' lives or other material associated with Campsey Ash and BL Add. 70513. It is a nice symmetry that the widowed mother of Chaucer's first patron had access to Campsey Ash's famous collection of saints' lives, while Criseyde, in Troy, connects the reading of saints' lives with widowhood.

Composed of a thirteenth-century core with early fourteenth-century additions, BL Add. 70513 compiles thirteen lives, in French, which collectively "provide a plethora of role models for women . . . [and] a very full guide to the concerns of elite women in or associated with religious lives."[81] The book would surely have made exciting and enjoyable listening for the canonesses – and their guests. It was common for nuns to receive visits and even return them;[82] and in fact, Elizabeth's accounts show that she left her baby daughter with her mother at Campsey on two occasions. In April 1358 Elizabeth seems to have been there herself, since "Bette panetarie" (Betty the pantry-mistress) is recorded as having received 20 shillings "[de] dono domine apud Campsey" (by the lady's gift at Campsey).[83] This information reinforces the likelihood that Maud had her own small household within the priory – a trend specific to female houses in the fourteenth and fifteenth centuries,[84] and one likely to facilitate shared familial readings. As Mary Erler notes, there was a "reciprocal relation between cloister and world . . . Nunneries in fact might be thought of as foci for female interaction, as other institutions were for male meeting. Since they were not members of choir schools, of university colleges, of law courts, of military bands, both religious and laywomen found in female houses a singular opportunity for proximity."[85]

---

80 Edited and translated in Allen, "A Newly Discovered Survival," 169.
81 Wogan-Browne, "Powers of Record," 78.
82 Jo Ann Kay McNamara, *Sisters in Arms: Catholic Nuns through Two Millennia* (Cambridge, MA, 1996), 279.
83 "Fragments of an Account Bound up with a Manuscript of the British Museum; – Additional Ms. 18,632," in *Life-Records of Chaucer* III: *Chaucer as Page in the Household of the Countess of Ulster, Wife of Lionel, 3rd Son of King Edward III, A.D. 1356–9*, ed. Edward A. Bond, Chaucer Society, second series 21 (London, 1886), 105–13, at 111–12.
84 Roberta Gilchrist, *Gender and Material Culture: The Archaeology of Religious Women* (London, 1994), 123, 127.
85 Mary C. Erler, *Women, Reading, and Piety in Late Medieval England* (Cambridge, UK, 2002), 11–12. For further comment on the interrelationship of lay and religious women's

There is no guarantee that a young woman such as Elizabeth de Burgh, going the round of family festivities with her prince-husband, devoted herself solely to devotional texts. If Elizabeth read books with her ladies, they may have been romances, what I have called historicized romances, or a variety of other material, on a spectrum from secular to sacred. The countess and her court may also have played audience to or even inspired some of the "Ditees and . . . songes glade" in honor of Venus that Chaucer's friend, John Gower, later described him as having written "in the floures of his youthe."[86]

A tentative but intriguing clue that Elizabeth de Burgh was an important person in Chaucer's personal history, or his wife's, is the name of a girl sometimes assumed to have been their daughter: an Elizabeth Chausier who was nominated to be received as a nun in the priory of St. Helen's Bishopsgate on July 27, 1377. The priory was only a third of a mile from Chaucer's then-lodgings in Aldgate. The likelihood that this Elizabeth was indeed a family member is further increased by the fact that the patent letter admitting her to St. Helen's was issued on the same day and recorded directly after one admitting Margaret Swynford to Barking Abbey. This benefit bestowed on Katherine Swynford's daughter, in an order issued by Richard II eleven days after his coronation,[87] suggests the influence of John of Gaunt, the king's uncle and Katherine's lover. It is thus likely that the Elizabeth Chausier who received a similar benefit on the same day was being similarly patronized, as Katherine's niece.

In later life, Chaucer had at least vicarious access to the habits of elite female readers, through his wife's and sister-in-law's service in the courts of Queen Philippa and of John of Gaunt's first and second duchesses. Nonetheless, it seems justifiable to emphasize his earliest, most "embedded," and surely indelible exposure to such scenes in his first courtly post, in the household of a young countess with notable intellectual antecedents. Though it is doubtful that Elizabeth de Burgh resembled Criseyde in character, surely some of her aristocratic demeanor, perhaps her beauty, and perhaps also her reading practices may be reflected in Chaucer's Trojan heroine.

---

reading, see Felicity Riddy, "'Women Talking about the Things of God': A Late Medieval Sub-Culture," in *Women and Literature in Britain, 1150–1500*, ed. Carol M. Meale (Cambridge, UK, 1993), 104–27.

86 John Gower, *Confessio Amantis*, book 8, lines *2946, *2943, in *The English Works of John Gower*, 2 vols., ed. G. C. Macaulay, Early English Text Society e.s. 81–82 (London, 1900–1).

87 Crow and Olson, *Chaucer Life Records*, 545 n. 3; *Calendar of the Patent Rolls: Richard II*, vol. 1: *1377–1381*, 20.

Layer 5. Pandarus as Sexual/Textual Predator

Ricocheting across the four layers we have discussed above – intertextuality, the paved parlor, women's reading communities, and Elizabeth de Burgh – are the double issues of sex and violence, with violence doubled as alternately martial and sexual. The intertextuality plays the Trojan women readers' fantasy of rescue from siege against the Middle English readers' knowledge of the rapes and murders due to befall the Trojan women. The parlor and the reading community it harbors represent a female attempt to assert bodily and psychological integrity, repelling violence by managing it through their choice of text. Yet the need to seek such spaces, companions, and texts implies the dangers that lie outside the circle. Elizabeth de Burgh seems to represent a strong female figure who perhaps echoes in Criseyde's assertions of autonomy ("I am myn owene womman, wel at ese", *T&C* 2:750) – a countess in charge of her own *familia*, her young page among them. Yet Elizabeth's life was bounded by violence: her father murdered when she was a baby, and an early death finding her in an insurgent Ireland, where she had feared to return.

The last layer of the paved-parlor scene returns us to Pandarus, who acts as the vector bringing all these issues and layers into play – i.e., who launches the plot. That the reader of *Troilus and Criseyde* sees the reading in the paved parlor through the eyes of the man who enters to interrupt it emphasizes the sense of an enclosed female space. Pandarus, as a man stepping into that space, with intent to engage Criseyde in an affair with his patron, carries many echoes of penetration – from a sperm entering a womb to an archangel entering a *hortus conclusus* to an enemy soldier invading a city or house. Pandarus' determined attack on the book that preoccupies his niece succeeds in drawing her away from it and from her ladies, and then turns into a deliberate reshaping of the reading experience he had just interrupted. Instead of safety among her women, and book-fed fantasies of the gods intervening to repel the Greeks, Pandarus offers a different solution to her anxiety: an affair with a valiant defender of Troy.

To move her in this direction, Pandarus devalues the book and by implication the reading circle, offering instead physical touch and dance and Mayday celebration. In the chat that follows, he carefully redirects her focus. Just after she has informed him that widows should sit in caves and read holy saints' lives, he tells her that he has good news. She asks eagerly: "is than th'assege aweye? / I am of Grekes so fered that I deye" (*T&C* 2:124–25). The audience of *Troilus and Criseyde* knows that the alleged good news is that Troilus is in love with her, not that the war is over. But playing off of the fears revealed in Criseyde's choice of reading, Pandarus delays that information, beginning with praise of Hector that quickly diverges into praise of Troilus' many virtues: "alle trouthe and alle

35

gentilesse, / Wisdom, honour, fredom, and worthinesse" (160–61). It is Criseyde herself who jumps from moral to martial worthiness: "men tellen that he doth / In armes day by day so worthily" (185–86), she exclaims. Pandarus is quick to echo her praise, calling Troilus "sheld and lif for us" (201). In the corresponding scene in Boccaccio's *Filostrato*, Pandaro ignores the war, focusing instead on the pleasures of having a noble lover. Pandarus' emphasis on Criseyde's anxiety and Troilus' valor is, therefore, Chaucer's addition.

Pandarus moves in closer to his goal, declaring that a fair "aventure" has befallen Criseyde (*T&C* 2:224), and again that she is "fortunat" and may have "goodly aventure" (280–81). Finally, he announces outright: "Good aventure, O beele nece, have ye / Ful lightly founden, and ye konne it take" (288–89). There seems to be a clear, though cracked, echo of the Annunciation: the salutation "O beele nece" recalling the "Ave Maria," and the evocation of "good adventure . . . Ful lightly founden" recalling the "benedicta tu in mulieribus." The wording and overtones throw us back to the paved parlor, re-presenting Criseyde and her ladies, but especially Criseyde, in the role of chaste reader interrupted in her reading as Pandarus, an anti-Gabriel, enters to announce that, fortunate among women, she has won the love of a great prince. Pulled both by fear and desire, when Criseyde next convenes her ladies, it is to wander in a pleasure garden and hear her niece Antigone sing of love.

So Rudely Forced

Underlying all these layers, queasily, is some other possible thing – a conclusion I have resisted but that has kept surfacing as I have been writing this essay. It is a commonplace of criticism that in his stage-managing of Troilus and Criseyde, Pandarus seems to function as an alter-ego to the story's narrator and to the real-world author Geoffrey Chaucer. He not only engineers the romance, he uses authorial language in deciding how to do so. In the parlor scene, Pandarus is "a skilled, self-conscious rhetorician who approaches the task of seducing his niece Criseyde on behalf of his friend Troilus as a problem of rhetorical invention," using literary terms of art such as "endite," "entencioun," "conclusioun," and "matere" (*T&C* 2:257–59, 261, 267).[88] As he first starts thinking about how to entrap his niece, Pandarus draws on architectural metaphors derived from Geoffrey of Vinsauf's discussion of literary composition (1:1065–69); later, the narrator draws on the same source in explaining that the consummation scene is all set: "This tymbur is al redy up to frame" (3:530). Next, having literally tossed one protagonist into bed with the other, Pandarus famously sits by the fire "to

---

88 Martin Camargo, "Chaucer and the Oxford Renaissance of Anglo-Latin Rhetoric," *Studies in the Age of Chaucer* 34 (2012): 173–207, at 200.

looke upon an old romaunce" (3:980), suggesting a *mise en abyme* by which he is reading the story of the romance he has just "written," behind him.

But if the pander Pandarus is channeling Chaucer and authorship here, what does that say about Chaucer, and about authorship as Chaucer saw it? The question is especially pressing, given the many auctorial echoes of rape or attempted rape with which Chaucer surrounds key scenes. As scholars have pointed out, the day that starts with Pandarus hearing Procne lamenting her sister's rape ends with Criseyde listening to a nightingale sing "a lay / Of love" (*T&C* 2:921–22).[89] The recap is devoid of mythological references, as though the non-latinate Criseyde experiences the nightingale directly and innocently, while for her latinate uncle, the swallow-sister of the raped Philomela-turned-nightingale is experienced through a filter of myth and corruption. Just before entering the room in Pandarus' house where Criseyde is lying in bed, Troilus prays for success. He invokes, among other classical stories, Jove's abduction of Europa, Apollo's pursuit of Daphne, and Mercury's ambiguous attempt to get access to Herse (3:722–23, 726–77, 729–30).[90] Another rape, that of Proserpina, is evoked in Troilus' speech lamenting Criseyde's failure to return from the Greek camp (5:319–20).[91]

The dilemma grows more intense still when one considers the association that the heavily emphasized Philomela myth[92] draws between rape and poetry. Philomela, violated by Tereus, becomes the passionate nightingale, whose suffering is appropriated and transgendered so that the bird becomes the type of the male poet; note that Criseyde's nightingale sings "in *his* briddes wise" (*T&C* 2:921; my emphasis). In the Daphne myth, as well, Daphne fleeing Apollo becomes the laurel tree, whose leaves go to crown poets. In this male-centric view, the god, and his human followers, attain to lyric inspiration through the suffering caused by (what is presented as) a tragic romantic loss of the beloved. Surrounded by such myths, Chaucer's alter-ego Pandarus sexually pursues a prized female – as a proxy for his patron, but nonetheless generating personal overtones of

89 E.g., Robert Sturges, "Ascalaphus and Philomela: Myth and Meaning in Chaucer's *Troilus and Criseyde*," *American Notes & Queries* 4 (1991): 63–67; and Louise O. Fradenburg, "'Our owen wo to drynke': Loss, Gender and Chivalry in *Troilus and Criseyde*," in *Chaucer's Troilus and Criseyde: Subgit to alle poesye: Essays in Criticism*, ed. R. A. Shoaf (Binghamton, NY, 1992), 88–106, at 98–100.

90 See Elizabeth Robertson, "Public Bodies and Psychic Domains: Rape and Female Subjectivity in Geoffrey Chaucer's *Troilus and Criseyde*," in *Representing Rape in Medieval and Early Modern Literature*, ed. Robertson and Christine M. Rose (New York, 2001), 281–310, at 301.

91 Sturges, "Ascalaphus and Philomela," 64–65.

92 The nightingale also appears in the consummation scene; *T&C* 3:1233–39.

voyeurism, sadism, inappropriate intimacy, and even incest.[93] All of this is in the interests of producing the most ambitious piece of poetry in Chaucer's career, or in the history of English literature to that date – the work that is sent off, at its end, to "kis the steppes where as thow seest pace / Virgile, Ovide, Omer, Lucan, and Stace" (*T&C* 5:1791–92).

So, did Chaucer learn from the classics that, bluntly, the invidious pursuit or rape of women, and the suffering that results, is the crucible from which emerges great poetry? Did he take the mythic pattern and rework it in the form of a human woman pursued by human men, in the interests of augmenting his own ambition to apotheosize from "maker" to "poet"? All I can say is: maybe, yes and no. Yes, in that the plot of *Troilus and Criseyde* clearly (to modern eyes) has Pandarus (and Troilus) exploiting Criseyde's fears and vulnerabilities in order to get her into bed. No, in that once past the consummation scene – with its multiple forms of deceit and aggression – Criseyde seems to participate willingly in and to enjoy the affair.

And no, in that while his characters are pagans, Chaucer was not. To him, Tereus and Philomela, Apollo and Daphne were myths, subject in the Middle Ages to moralization and allegoresis. The *raptus* committed by the gods, and the sufferings of their nymph-victims, could be read metaphorically, as the poet's arduous pursuit of inspiration – or, to adopt another classical trope, of his muse. Chaucer may "sample" the mythic pattern, but his Criseyde loses neither her human form nor her tongue. She stubbornly remains her own, complex self, and in a way outlasts all the romantic males of Troy. Granted, she has taken up with Diomede, and her name will be "rolled . . . on many a tonge" (*T&C* 5:1061) as a result. But, like the women of Thebes – and unlike Andromache, Cassandra, Hecuba, Polyxena, and most of the other women of Troy – she escapes enslavement, rape, and murder. Here is a kankedort[94] for the Chaucerians: which fate is preferable?

93   Cf. Robertson, "Public Bodies."
94   Cf. *T&C* 2:1752.

Beatrice Melreth:
A London Gentlewoman and her Books

CAROLINE M. BARRON

When she drew up her will in 1448 Beatrice Melreth bequeathed to her sister, Agnes Burgh, a small collection of devotional books and rolls, some written in French, some in English, and others in Latin.[1] Beatrice also left a Psalter-Hours (a primer and psalter bound together in one volume) to her son-in-law Henry Bardolf, and a "black primer" to one of her executors. Her small collection of devotional books was distinctive and suggests that Beatrice was a pious woman who valued her spiritual texts and was able to read several languages.[2] She is, in fact, exactly the kind of medieval woman that Mary Erler's painstaking scholarship has done so much to draw out of the shadows. Beatrice listed the contents of her small collection with considerable care and it is clear that the rolls and books were important to her. She did not leave these to a clerk or priest or member of a religious house, but to her sister, Agnes Burgh. Beatrice had two other sisters whom she named and to whom she made bequests of girdles and clothing, but it was Agnes who was to receive this special collection of pious texts. This distinctive collection of books prompts further investigation. Who was Beatrice Melreth and what is it possible to find out about the world, or worlds, in which she lived? Beatrice was the – probably eldest – daughter of John and Joan Waleys, who held the manor of Glynde in Sussex: a reasonably prosperous

1   London, Lambeth Palace, Register of Archbishop Stafford, fols. 165–66. Large parts of the will are printed in translation in Hilary Jenkinson and G. Herbert Fowler, eds., "Some Bedfordshire Wills at Lambeth and Lincoln," *The Publications of the Bedfordshire Historical Record Society* 14 (1931): 79–131, at 123–25. The translation is not entirely accurate, and in this essay I reference the original Register copy of the will. I am very grateful to Dr. Jenny Stratford, who read an earlier version of this essay and made a number of very helpful suggestions for its improvement.

2   Beatrice Melreth's collection of books has already been noticed: see Carol M. Meale, "'. . . alle the bokes that I haue of latyn, englisch, and frensch': Laywomen and their Books in Late Medieval England," in *Women and Literature in Britain, 1150–1500*, ed. Meale (Cambridge, UK, 1993), 128–58, at 132; Anne F. Sutton, "The Acquisition and Disposal of Books for Worship and Pleasure by Mercers of London in the Later Middle Ages," in *Manuscripts and Printed Books in Europe*, ed. Emma Cayley and Susan Powell (Liverpool, 2013), 95–114, at 111.

manor which yielded £80 *per annum* at the end of the fourteenth century. The family resources were augmented by income from other local manors, and amounted to some £120 *per annum* in all. As Professor Nigel Saul has observed "A figure of this order represented a not insubstantial income for a knightly family. Many would have had to subsist on a good deal less."[3] John Waleys in 1409 had inherited the estates from his father, with whom, however, he had had a protracted dispute over the distribution of the Waleys manors between various male heirs. But John need not, perhaps, have been so troubled about his lands because his wife Joan, whom he had married in 1398, was the only child of Sir Robert Turk, and so his heiress. Robert was born into a London family of fishmongers and, following his marriage to Joan's mother, Beatrice Kendale, he had acquired extensive lands, particularly in Hertfordshire, where he established his seat in Hitchin. He retained extensive London contacts and London properties which yielded some £95 *per annum*, and all these properties came to Joan on the death of her father on December 28, 1400.[4] So John and Joan Waleys were comfortably established and, considering the source of much of their prosperity, it was entirely appropriate that they named their first daughter Beatrice after her maternal grandmother.

The London contacts were also significant: Robert Turk's friends Bartholomew Seman, a prosperous goldbeater, and Richard Jepe, the rector of All Saints, Honey Lane, both came down to Glynde to witness the delivery of seisin of some manors to John and Joan on their marriage.[5] It seems likely that Beatrice

3   Nigel Saul, *Scenes from Provincial Life: Knightly Families in Sussex, 1280–1400* (Oxford, 1986), 14–27, esp. p. 21.
4   For a biography of Sir Robert Turk, see J. S. Roskell, Linda Clark, and Carole Rawcliffe, eds., *The History of the House of Commons 1386–1421*, 4 vols. (Stroud, Gloucestershire, 1993), 4:673–75. The date of his death is established by the provision of a perpetual obit to be celebrated on that day in Hitchin church (R. R. Sharpe, ed., *Calendar of Wills Enrolled in the Court of Husting, London*, 2 vols. [London, 1889–90], 2:460).
5   Saul, *Scenes from Provincial Life*, 180. For another instance of Seman and Jepe in 1406 acting for Robert Turk, see A. H. Thomas, ed., *Calendar of Select Plea and Memoranda of the City of London 1381–1412* (Cambridge, UK, 1932), 282. There is no surviving will for Robert Turk, but it seems likely that Bartholomew Seman and Richard Jepe acted as his executors. Richard Jepe was the rector of All Saints, Honey Lane, from 1398 until his death in 1429. In his will, drawn up on March 2, 1428, Jepe left 10 marks to pay for a chaplain to celebrate in All Hallows for his soul and that of Sir Robert Turk and his wife Beatrice. He held a tenement jointly with Bartholomew Seman and this was to go to the Nuns of Cheshunt, Hertfordshire, to pray for the souls of Robert and Beatrice Turk. Bartholomew Seman was one of Jepe's executors (London Metropolitan Archives [LMA], Commissary Register 9171/3, fol. 220). In 1429, when Seman was thinking about drafting his own will, he left London properties to Michaelhouse, Cambridge, to

and her brother and sisters will have spent some time in London where their parents and relatives had considerable property. We do not know how Beatrice spent her childhood, nor where she was educated and learned the French and – perhaps – Latin that fuelled her later piety. There are no family wills surviving and so it is impossible to know if the Waleys household was a bookish one. Beatrice had three sisters, two of them called Joan and the youngest Agnes. They had a brother John, but he died before being able to claim his inheritance, so the Waleys and Turk lands in Sussex, Hertfordshire, and London were divided among the four sisters, although this was challenged on behalf of their cousin, William Waleys III, termed "the idiot," who was, in the end, deemed incapable of inheriting.[6]

How Beatrice and her sisters (or their parents) chose their husbands remains unknown, but by 1415 Beatrice was the wife of Reginald Cockayne, the eldest son and heir of John Cockayne, a prosperous and successful Justice of the Common Pleas. Just as Beatrice had been named after her maternal grandmother, so Reginald had been named after his maternal grandfather, his mother Ida's father, Reginald, Lord Grey of Ruthin. John Cockayne had risen to the Bench by virtue of his service to the House of Lancaster and he used the profits of his office (which were considerable) to buy the Bedfordshire manor of Bury Hatley (now Cockayne Hatley) in 1417.[7] He and his wife Ida had ten children, five sons and five daughters, and it was the eldest son, Reginald, who married Beatrice Waleys. Beatrice would have known her parents-in-law, because they both lived until the mid-1420s, and it is likely that she lived with them, and her husband, at Bury Hatley.

Like the Waleys family, the Cockaynes had strong links with London. John Cockayne had been the Recorder of London from 1394 to 1398, and as a royal justice he had to spend time at Westminster. On February 6, 1401 he and his wife purchased a life interest in a large mansion within the close of St. Bartholomew's Hospital from Alice and William Cressewyk, who had been one of the London

---

fund two poor scholars who were to be known as "Turkeschildren." They were to pray for the souls of Sir Robert Turk and his wives, Alice and Beatrice. In case of default, the properties were to go to Clare Hall on the same conditions, *Husting Wills*, 2:459–60.

6 Saul, *Scenes from Provincial Life*, 89–90. In the end the manor of Glynde passed to Joan Waleys and her husband Nicholas Morley, and it remained in their family for several generations.

7 S. J. Payling, "Cokayne, John (d. 1429), justice," *Oxford Dictionary of National Biography* (Oxford, 2004–); Maureen Jurkowski, "John Fynderne of Findern, Derbyshire: An Exchequer Official of the Early Fifteenth Century, his Circle and Lollard Connections" (PhD diss., University of Keele, 1998), 104–11.

undersheriffs, and was also a member of the Mercers' company.[8] In addition to the mansion, John and Ida were to receive a weekly allowance of bread and ale from the Hospital.[9] Later John acted for the hospital as a witness or arbiter in the years 1424 to 1426, and in his will, dated February 10, 1428, he left bequests to Robert Fossard, the Hospital chaplain; to John Wakeryng, the energetic master of the Hospital; 3s. 4d. to every brother, chaplain, and sister there; and 6d. to every poor bedridden person in the Hospital.[10] His executors were to lodge in the mansion house (where Cockayne kept several chests bound with iron bands as well as a bed with hangings) for a year to oversee the execution of his will, and it was then to pass to the master, brothers, and sisters of the Hospital forever in return for their annual observance of his obit.[11]

As might be expected, John Cockayne had a considerable library, most of which he left not to his eldest son, Reginald, who inherited the manor of Bury Hatley and the lion's share of his father's chattels, but to his fourth son, Thomas.[12] Thomas was a lawyer like his father and already had in his possession all his father's books of civil and canon law. Now his father passed on to him a book called "magn' summarum" (perhaps the *Summa Theologica* of Thomas Aquinas), a psalter called "Hampell Sauter" (a psalter glossed by the hermit Richard Rolle of Hampole), a book of the works of Isidore of Seville, and a book which begins "parce mihi domine".[13] But heading the list of books bequeathed to his son were "a great psalter" and "a book of miracles of Blessed Mary," both of which he specified were in London, which suggests that the other books were at Bury Hatley. It is very likely that the "great psalter" is a manuscript now in the Bibliothèque nationale de France (MS lat. 765). This finely illuminated psalter, dating from the third quarter of the fourteenth century, is known as the Fitzwarin Psalter from the arms on fol. 23. Two obits are added on fols. 1

8   Caroline M. Barron, *London in the Later Middle Ages* (Oxford, 2004), 357; Cressewyk drew up his will in October 1406 (*Husting Wills*, 2:370).

9   LMA, Husting Roll 129/92; Jurkowski, "John Fynderne," 330.

10   Nellie J. M. Kerling ed., *Cartulary of St Bartholomew's Hospital: A Calendar* (London, 1973), nos. 148, 149, 246, 890, 1660.

11   London, The National Archives (TNA), PROB 11/3, fol. 40. The will is translated in *Bedfordshire Wills proved in the Prerogative Court of Canterbury, 1383–1548*, ed. Margaret McGregor, Bedfordshire Historical Record Society 58 (Bedford, 1979), 8–11.

12   Of the ten children of John and Ida, four sons (Reginald, Henry, John, and Thomas) and two daughters (Elizabeth and Margaret) were alive at the time of their father's death.

13   Jurkowski, "John Fynderne," 330. The words "parce mihi domine" come from Job chapter 7 and would have been very familiar since they were used in the Office of the Dead. It is not clear which particular book is indicated here.

and 22.[14] The first records the death of "Ide Cokayn quondam uxoris Johannis Cokayn justiciarii domini regis que obiit anno domini MCCCCXXVI," and the second that of "Johannis Cokayn nuper justiciarii domini regis qui obiit anno domini MCCCCXXIX".[15] It may be that John Cockayne purchased the psalter in London, or perhaps received it in lieu of a legal fee. In his will John Cockayne refers to other books that he had been given: a book of statutes given to him by Thomas Overton, the rector of the London church of St. Magnus, and also a psalter given to him by a woman named Alice Vynter.[16] Since it was to his son Thomas that Sir John bequeathed his "great psalter" it seems likely that it was Thomas who recorded his parents' obits in the volume. The year before his father died, Thomas had become an apprentice at law at the Middle Temple, and ten years later, on October 27, 1438, he was elected Recorder of the city of London as his father had been. But he died within two years, leaving a will in which there is no mention of his father's "great psalter".[17] How it reached the Bibliotèque nationale remains a mystery.

Sir John Cockayne's books were largely theological and legal, many in Latin, and they were rather different from the books of personal piety which the judge's daughter-in-law, Beatrice, owned and bequeathed in her will. But if they lived together at Bury Hatley for a decade or so, it is likely that Sir John and Beatrice were at least aware of each other's books. And they would both have known the books and furnishings in the chapel in the manor house. John Cockayne left the chapel furnishings to his heir, Reginald, but stipulated that they were to remain in the chapel for the service of God. He specified a missal and breviary, the red and green vestments, and the silver cruets, all of which twenty years later in her will, Beatrice (as the heir of her husband) also listed and left to her son John.[18]

14   For a full description of this manuscript, see Francis Wormald, "The Fitzwarin Psalter and its Allies," *Journal of the Warburg and Courtauld Institutes* 6 (1943): 71–79; Lucy Freeman Sandler, *Gothic Manuscripts 1285–1385*, 2 vols., A Survey of Manuscripts Illuminated in the British Isles 5 (London and Oxford, 1986), 2:133–35.
15   Ida died June 1, 1426 and her husband on June 22, 1429.
16   Cockayne will, 8–9. Thomas Overton drew up his will on December 2, 1405 and died the following year, TNA, PROB 11/2A/97. He left several books in his will but does not refer to John Cockayne. It has not been possible to locate Alice Vynter.
17   See John H. Baker, *The Men of Court 1440–1550: A Prosopography of the Inns of Court and Chancery and the Courts of Law*, 2 vols., Selden Supplementary Series 18 (London, 2010), 491; TNA, PROB 11/3, fol. 218v.; Barron, *London in Later Middle Ages*, 174 n. 6 and p. 356.
18   Cockayne will, 8; Beatrice will, fol. 165.

Beatrice and Reginald Cockayne were married for about twenty years and they had at least two sons, John and Thomas, and two daughters, Edith and Marion.[19] Reginald died in 1433 and within a year Beatrice herself had married again to a wealthy and successful London widower, the mercer and alderman William Melreth.[20] They may have met through Cockayne's membership of the Mercers' Company or, perhaps, because the village of Meldreth in Cambridgeshire, where William Melreth probably grew up, is only ten miles as the crow flies from Bury Hatley in the neighbouring county of Bedfordshire.[21] However they met, William and Beatrice lived together in London in a house at the northern end of Milk Street in the parish of St. Lawrence Jewry, an area much frequented by wealthy mercers and near to the Guildhall. It seems likely that Beatrice would now have spent most of her time in London, leaving the manor house at Bury Hatley to her son John.[22] William Melreth was at the height of his career: he was a ship owner much engaged in overseas trade and was three times an MP for the city. While married to Beatrice he twice served as warden of the Mercers' Company and took part in parliamentary elections, although he did not himself serve again as an MP after 1432.[23] At the time of his marriage to Beatrice his lands in London and elsewhere were valued at £80 *per annum*. He was one of only ten London merchants whose lands were worth this much annually.[24] His estate would have been considerably enlarged when Beatrice and her sisters in 1436 established their claim to the Waleys lands in Sussex, bringing the manors of Hawkesden and Baynden to the Melreths.[25] William already had two daughters, both of whom were married to mercers: Emma to Thomas Tykhill and Margaret to

19   By the time Beatrice drew up her will in 1448, Edith was married to John Wilton and Marion to Henry Bardolf. Beatrice does not mention the wives of her two surviving sons, and Thomas was not, in fact, yet of age. His mother placed him in the custody of William Pickering, a mercer who had been an executor of William Melreth's will.
20   William Page, ed., *Victoria History of the County of Bedfordshire*, 3 vols. (London, 1904–12), 2:216. For a biography of William Melreth, see Matthew Davies, "William Melreth," in *The House of Commons 1422–1461*, ed. Linda Clark (London, forthcoming). I am grateful to the History of Parliament Trust for allowing me to see this article in draft. See also Anne F. Sutton, *Wives and Widows of Medieval London* (Donington, Lincolnshire, 2016), 132 n. 60.
21   Lisa Jefferson, ed., *The Medieval Account Books of the Mercers of London: An Edition and Translation*, 2 vols. (Farnham, Surrey, 2009), 1:274, 283.
22   A. E. Cockayne, *Cockayne Memoranda: Collections towards a Historical Record of the Family of Cockayne* (Congleton, 1873), 148 and pedigree inserted in back pocket of the volume.
23   He had served as an MP in 1427, 1429 and 1432 (Davies, "William Melreth").
24   Sylvia L. Thrupp, *The Merchant Class of Medieval London, 1300–1500* (Ann Arbor, MI, 1962), 378–85.
25   Richard F. Dell, ed., *The Glynde Place Archives* (Lewes, Sussex, 1964), xiii.

Bartholomew Stratton, who had been Melreth's apprentice.[26] Whether they were already wives when their father married Beatrice is not known, but they may have lived for a time with their stepmother in London. The fact that Beatrice later remembered both of her stepdaughters in her will with bequests of cloth suggests a certain closeness.

What sort of man was Beatrice's new husband? William Melreth's mercantile activities and his rise up the ladder of civic office are not out of the ordinary, but it may be surprising that he was not elected an alderman until five years after he had served as sheriff, and although he was then an alderman for fifteen years he was never elected mayor. The surviving records suggest that he focused his attention on his company, the Mercers. His will suggests, perhaps, that he was a self-made man and that his primary concern was for himself.[27] Unlike many of his contemporaries, the extensive provisions that he made for commemorative prayer after his death were only for his own soul and the souls of his benefactors (unspecified). He does not mention his parents, nor his wives, nor his children nor, indeed, the faithful departed who are so often included in such commemorations. He directed that he was to be buried in "tumba honesta" (costing the considerable sum of 40 marks) by his seat in the parish church of St. Lawrence Jewry. He did not ask for burial with either of his wives and, indeed, he did not even name his first wife, whose identity remains unknown. Such charitable bequests as he made, he furnished with conditional clauses specifying exactly the terms on which the bequests were to be made by his executors, as in the case of his bequests to his two daughters. There were no bequests to the poor, nor to the sick in hospitals: the objects of his charity were the marriage of poor girls "of good reputation," the making and repair of roads, and the delivery of debtors from prison provided that their creditors gave security that they would not pursue them further. Only five people received individual bequests: Thomas Key of Meldreth, his two servants Robert Westneye and William Key, and his two apprentices, Robert Moyn and William Whitwey, who were, however, instructed to help his executors to recover the debts owing to their master.[28] William's main concern, in his two wills, was to

26 Jefferson, *The Medieval Account Books of the Mercers*, 1:415, 417.

27 Two wills dated January 13 and 14, 1445, TNA, PROB 11/3, fols. 257–58. The second will, relating to the lands to support the Lady Mass in St. Lawrence Jewry and the bequests to his two daughters, is also enrolled in the Husting Court, LMA, Husting Roll, 174/8; *Husting Wills*, 2:506–7.

28 Robert Moyn was apprenticed to Melreth in 1442–43 and issued from his apprenticeship in 1447–48 (Jefferson, *The Medieval Account Books of the Mercers*, 1:566, 2:636). According to the account books, it was Robert Whitwey who was Melreth's apprentice, and William Whitwey was the apprentice of William Pickering, one of Melreth's executors (ibid., 587, 800).

provide for a clerk, "skilled in singing and well instructed and informed," to sing a daily mass in honor of the Virgin in the church of St. Lawrence Jewry, and to pray for the soul of William Melreth.[29] He also left a silver-gilt chalice and paten to be used at the altar of St. John in the parish church on condition that the vicar, every Sunday, would from the pulpit "especially recommend my soul to the parishioners and other Christians." By comparison with wills of other wealthy aldermen, it is a very egocentric, very detached, will.

Beatrice, as civic custom required, was left half Melreth's goods as dower. She was not, however, appointed as one of his executors (although this was usual among London merchants at this period), which suggests, perhaps, that she had little involvement with his business affairs. But there is one clause that may throw a shaft of light on the relationship between William and his wife. He left "meum librum missale" to the church of St. Lawrence to be used at the high altar and at the altar of St. John the Evangelist. But this bequest was only to come into effect after the death of Beatrice. This may suggest that they had together used this volume in their private chapel and that William wanted Beatrice to continue to have access to this missal there until her own death. Such a bequest indicates perhaps a shared concern for spiritual matters or, at the least, that William acknowledged Beatrice's interest in having such a missal in her own home.

Remarkably this missal survives in the British Library (MS Arundel 109), and it has been perceptively discussed by Sheila Lindenbaum.[30] This is a large missal of the Use of Sarum, probably made in London during Melreth's lifetime. There are 265 folios, eleven with illuminated initials and elaborate borders.[31] On folio 262v an image of the Trinity has been added, with God the Father holding the crucified Saviour and the dove of the Holy Spirit hovering over the head of Christ. Kneeling at the foot of the Trinity is the figure of William Melreth wearing his aldermanic furred gown and holding a scroll with the text "utinam

29　In 1548 the six tenements in Milk Street given by Melreth to support a "Singing man at the Lady Altar, and obit", yielded £7 6s. 8d., although the "singing man" received £11, so the parish must have made up his salary from other funds. See C. J. Kitching, ed., *London and Middlesex Chantry Certificate 1548*, London Record Society 16 (London, 1980), 27.

30　Sheila Lindenbaum, "Literate Londoners and Liturgical Change: Sarum Books in City Parishes after 1414," in *London and the Kingdom: Essays in Honour of Caroline M. Barron*, ed. Matthew Davies and Andrew Prescott, Harlaxton Medieval Studies 6 (Donington, Lincolnshire, 2008), 384–99, esp. 390–94.

31　There are surviving illuminations for saints Andrew, John the Baptist, Peter and Paul, Anne, Michael, and the Virgin, but a number of the illuminations are missing. See Kathleen Scott, *Later Gothic Manuscripts 1390–1490*, Survey of Manuscripts Illuminated in the British Isles 6, 2 vols. (London, 1996), 2:380–81.

dirigantur viae meae ad custodiendas justiticationes tuas" (O that my ways may be directed to keep thy statutes, Psalm 118:5) wafting heavenwards above his head. To the right are two shields, one bearing the arms (presumably) of Melreth and the other his merchant's mark of an intertwined W and M.[32] These shields, which sit awkwardly in the image, may have been added later. In the hanging behind the figure of the Trinity, and beneath the image, are the words "Blessyd be the Trinite" and a laborious Latin poem of fourteen lines reciting in rhyming hexameters Melreth's bequest of the missal to the high altar, and to the altar of St. John, and his endowment of a priest to sing the Lady Mass in the church. The verse concludes by providing, in a convoluted formula, the date of Melreth's death: January 16, 1445 (two days after sealing his will).

It may be that this image and verse were inserted into the missal by the vicar of the church, Robert Rooke, who was one of Melreth's executors, and who may well have discussed with him the various bequests that he made to the church. Rooke himself was a graduate of Balliol College, Oxford, which had presented him to the living of St. Lawrence Jewry in 1438, where he remained until his death in 1458. He had been a fellow of Balliol and was clearly a learned man with a considerable library of theological works, which he ultimately bequeathed to the College.[33] It seems likely that he encouraged Melreth's benefactions toward the parish church, and he may have been responsible for the depiction of the Holy Trinity and the kneeling Melreth to be found in the Arundel missal. Perhaps, as Sheila Lindenbaum has suggested, Rooke was anxious to draw a distinction between the very basic Latinity of the text attributed to Melreth, a mere layman, and the more sophisticated Latin learning of the educated cleric exemplified in the verses.[34] Rooke's verses were, however, characteristic of the "complimentary versifying" that was practised by educated clerics in London at the time.[35] It

32   The arms appear to be per fess argent and sable in chief five ermine spots in base three mullets of four points or. It has not been possible to trace Melreth's arms recorded elsewhere, for instance in the various sixteenth-century London armorials, where his coat of arms is left blank. I am very grateful to Matthew Payne for help in describing and tracing the Melreth arms.

33   A. B. Emden, *A Biographical Register of the University of Oxford to A.D. 1500*, 3 vols. (Oxford, 1959), 3:1589. In his will, dated November 9, 1453, Rooke bequeathed at least fifteen carefully listed books to Balliol, in addition to those he had already given to the College, see TNA, PROB 11/4, fols. 108v–109. Rooke had a further dozen or so liturgical books which he distributed to friends.

34   Lindenbaum, "Literate Londoners," 393–94.

35   See V. H. Galbraith, "John Sewarde and his Circle: Some London Scholars of the Early Fifteenth Century," *Medieval and Renaissance Studies* 1 (1941–3): 85–104; James G. Clark, *A Monastic Renaissance at St Albans: Thomas Walsingham and his Circle*, Oxford Historical

may well be that William Melreth did not participate to any great extent in the Latin learning and word play of the educated London clergy, but he presumably liked Robert Rooke well enough to embellish his church, and he trusted him sufficiently to make him an executor of both his wills. It is possible that Beatrice did not share her husband's attachment to Rooke. It may be significant that, just as William had omitted her from his anniversary prayers and obit, so Beatrice is not placed kneeling with her husband at the foot of the Trinity image. It looks as if the artist almost expected a second balancing donor figure on the right side of the miniature, and the two shields were added to fill the awkward space. When she came to draw up her own will three years after her husband, Beatrice did not choose Rooke as one of her executors.

Beatrice's own will, drawn up at Bury Hatley, could hardly be more different from that of her second husband.[36] She asked to be buried with one of her husbands: either with Melreth if she died in London or with Cockayne if she died in Bedfordshire. If she was buried in Bury Hatley with Reginald she wanted both their arms to be made in brass and placed on the tomb, and she left bequests for making a window in the bell tower of the church there, and 10 pounds for a ten-year annual obit. She set out in detail the arrangements for her funeral: twelve men to carry torches, 100s. to be distributed to the poor, and 3s. 4d. to every priest present at her obsequies. She appointed Master Thomas Tunley, a Cambridge graduate, at a salary of 10 marks *per annum*, to celebrate daily for two years for her soul, and for the souls of Reginald and William, for her parents and benefactors, and all the faithful departed.[37]

Having made provision for her soul and the souls of others to whom she was bound, Beatrice turned to the disposal of her estate. By 1448 she appears to have had four surviving children: two sons, John and Thomas, and two daughters, Edith and Marion. She left everything in the manor house at Bury Hatley (including the furnishings of the chapel, which she listed) together with the crops in the fields and the produce and cattle in the barns to her eldest surviving son,

Monographs (Oxford, 2004), 218–26. I am very grateful to Professor Clark for helping to provide the context for the laudatory poem in Melreth's missal.

36 See n. 1 above. The will of her first husband, Reginald Cockayne, has not survived.

37 Beatrice further stipulated that Tunley was to visit the church where she was buried on the day of her obit to pray especially for her and for those she had specified. She also laid down that if Tunley received a benefice within the two years, then another Cambridge scholar was to be found to take his place. In fact, Tunley appears not to have gained a benefice until 1457, when he became vicar of Hackney, Middlesex. He moved later to Rochford, Essex, and to St. Margaret Lothbury in London, before ending his life at Phillack in Cornwall, where he was buried in 1471. See A. B. Emden, *A Biographical Register of the University of Cambridge to 1500* (Cambridge, UK, 1963), 596–97.

John. Clearly Beatrice anticipated some opposition from John and stipulated that if he made trouble for her executors, then he was to receive none of the goods that she had bequeathed to him. Thomas, the younger son, was probably still a minor. To him Beatrice left the 100 marks which she was owed by William Pickering the ex-apprentice, mercer and one of the executors of William Melreth's will. Presumably Pickering had not paid over to Beatrice all that she was owed as dower under Melreth's will drawn up three years earlier.[38] Beatrice further left to Thomas all the furnishings in her London house in Milk Street.[39] Robert Osbarn, a member of the notable family of London civil servants, was given responsibility for looking after this money and providing young Thomas with 10 marks every year. Robert, described as "dearly beloved," was also made the supervisor of Beatrice's will and so, presumably, was deemed particularly trustworthy.[40] Beatrice's two daughters, Edith and Marion, were made residual legatees of Beatrice's goods should her two sons die, but otherwise they were not richly endowed. Edith and her husband, John Wilton, received "a cloth and towel of the better quality." Marion was given her "best gown of scarlet trimmed with grey." It looks as if Marion may have married the widower Henry Bardolf soon after Beatrice drew up her will, because she has added a clause at the end giving a "cloth and towel of the best" to "Henry Bardolf and Marion his wife, my daughter."[41] Beatrice's two stepdaughters, Emma Tykhill and Margaret Stratton, also received cloth and towels of the "second best quality," to distinguish them, perhaps, from Beatrice's own daughters.

38 Pickering completed his apprenticeship with Melreth in 1442–43 and was admitted to the livery ten years later (Jefferson, *The Medieval Account Books of the Mercers*, 1:562, 2:725, 761); Melreth in 1445 had left 20 marks to the common box of the Mercers, but Pickering did not hand over the final installment of this bequest (which is recorded in the Mercers' accounts as £20) until 1458–59 (ibid., 715, 723, 739, 781, 847).

39 It is not clear what became of Thomas: he may be the Thomas Cockeyn who in 1455–59 paid rent to the Mercers' Company for a property in Coleman Street ward (Jefferson, *The Medieval Account Books of the Mercers*, 2:867).

40 Robert was the nephew of Richard Osbarn, who had been the City Chamber Clerk, or Controller, from 1400 to 1437. Both men, like many members of the Osbarn family, were closely associated with the Mercers' Company. See R. A. Wood, "The Life and Network of the Chamber Clerk, Richard Osbarn 1400–1438: A Man of Many Accomplishments," *Transactions of the London and Middlesex Archaeological Society*, forthcoming.

41 Earlier in the will, Beatrice left a bed of red worsted and a primer and psalter in one volume to Henry Bardolf; his son Edward was to have 40s. for his schooling, and his daughter Elizabeth was to have a bed. An Edmund Bardolf, senior, was made an executor of Beatrice's will. The Bardolfs may have been a local family.

A distinctive feature of Beatrice's will is the attention which she pays to her sisters: Joan married to Robert Lee, another Joan married to Nicholas Morley, and Agnes married to John Burgh. The four sisters as co-heirs of the Glynde estates had recently acted together to resist the claims of William Waleys III. Although they had won their case in 1436, the judgment was challenged and the sisters (and their husbands) had to continue to maintain their rights against Waleys and his supporters.[42] This need for communal action may have kept the sisters in close touch. To Joan, who was married to Nicholas Morley, Beatrice left her "best girdle of red silk harnessed with silver and gilt," and to the other Joan, married to Robert Lee, her "best girdle of russet silk harnessed with silver, and a scarlet gown lined with tarteryn." It would appear that Joan Lee, together with her daughter Marion, may have been living in Beatrice's household, since they were to share the cloth in Beatrice's chests with two of her household servants.[43]

But it was to her sister Agnes, married to John Burgh, that Beatrice left her small collection of devotional works. She described them carefully: a book "merce and gramarce" written with gold letters; a roll containing the passion of our Lord Jesus Christ, the Epistle of Nicodemus written in French; a book (unspecified) in English and Latin; a primer (or Book of Hours) "de gallic" which Agnes had earlier given to her; and a roll of the Fifteen Joys of the Virgin.[44] The book "merce and gramarce" is probably to be identified with the book now more commonly known as *Le livre de seyntz medicines* or *The Book of Holy Medicines*, written by Henry of Grosmont, Duke of Lancaster (d. 1361). This work of pious instruction seems, in the fifteenth century, to have been known not by the title in the colophon to the text, but rather from the opening lines of the main text: "Beau sire Dieux, de trois choses vous sui jeo principalment tenuz a dire: Sire, mercye & graunte mercye."[45] Thomas of Otterbourne (c. 1420), writing about Henry of Grosmont, said that he ran the whole course of his life "sub istis duobus verbis *Mercy* et *graunt Mercy*."[46] And John Capgrave (1393–1464) explained that Henry of Lancaster

42 *The Glynde Place Archives*, xii–xv.

43 The word used for the cloths or covers is "flameola."

44 Lambeth Palace Library, Register of Archbishop Stafford, fol. 166. I am very grateful to Julia Boffey, Jenny Stratford, Sue Powell, and Tess Tavormina for their help in describing the books owned by Beatrice.

45 For a translation and discussion of the text, see Catherine Batt, trans., *Henry of Grosmont, First Duke of Lancaster, "Le Livre de Seyntz Medicines / The Book of Holy Medicines,"* Medieval and Renaissance Texts and Studies 419, The French of England Translation Series 8 (Tempe, AZ, 2014).

46 Thomas Hearnius [Thomas Hearne], ed., *Duo Rerum Anglicarum Scriptores Veteres, viz. Thomas Otterbourne et Johannes Whethamstede, Ab origine gentis Britannicae usque ad Edvardum IV*, 2 vols. (Oxford, 1732), 1:116.

had written a "librum devotum . . . cuius titulus est *Mercy, Gramercy*."[47] It is not surprising that Beatrice gave this text – perhaps the most impressive volume in her collection, since it was illuminated with gold letters – the title by which it was commonly known in the fifteenth century.[48] Although the *Livre* was written by a noble soldier reflecting on chivalric practices and courtly life, and might be considered very much a masculine work, there are long passages devoted to the Virgin and to her feminine and motherly qualities: indeed, the author identifies to a remarkable extent with the intimate and physical pleasures of motherhood.[49] It is thus quite fitting to find the book among Beatrice's collection. The author writes with remarkable directness about the spiritual conflicts and temptations of courtly life and the necessary remedies provided by prayer, contrition, and confession.[50]

Beatrice's second text was a little roll (*rotulus*) with the Passion of Jesus Christ. This was probably one of the small parchment rolls, known as *Arma Christi* rolls, which contain a poem in English of some 150 lines, sometimes known as the Vernicle from its opening words.[51] In the poem some twenty objects associated with Christ's passion inspire short verses which meditate upon the sufferings of Christ and direct the reader toward personal reflection. Twenty medieval copies of this work are known and ten are rolls, like Beatrice's, with symbols and instruments of the passion painted in the margins. These rolls are often completed with an indulgence.[52] Ann Eljenholm Nichols has argued that the poem was intended not to encourage the reader to meditate on the suffering of

---

47 Francis C. Hingeston, ed., *Johannes Capgrave Liber de Illustribus Henrici*, Rerum Britannicarum Medii Ævi Scriptores 7 (London, 1858), 163–64; see Batt, *Henry of Grosmont, Le Livre*, 68 n. 5

48 Only two manuscripts of this work are known to exist, and one of them (Clitheroe, Lancashire, Stonyhurst College, MS 24) is illuminated with gold letters. This manuscript was given to Humphrey, Duke of Gloucester (d. 1447) by "baron de Carew," probably Sir Thomas Carew (d. 1431). It is possible that this copy of the *Livre* was given to a member of the Cockayne family, and hence to Beatrice. See E. J. F. Arnould, "Henry of Lancaster and his *Livre des Seintes Medicines*," *Bulletin of the John Rylands Library* 21 (1937), 1–37.

49 See M. Teresa Tavormina, trans., "Henry of Lancaster: *The Book of Holy Medicines (Le Livre de Seyntz Medicines)*," in *Cultures of Piety: Medieval English Devotional Literature in Translation*, ed. Anne Clark Bartlett and Thomas H. Bestul (Ithaca, NY, 1999), 19–40.

50 Batt, *Henry of Grosmont, "Le Livre,"* 34, 63, 255–72.

51 Lisa H. Cooper and Andrea Denny-Brown, eds., *The Arma Christi in Medieval and Early Modern Material Culture. With a Critical Edition of 'O Vernicle'* (Farnham, Surrey, 2014).

52 Ann Eljenholm Nichols, "The Footprints of Christ as Arma Christi: The Evidence of Morgan B.54", in ibid., 113–41, esp. 135–37.

Christ, but rather was written to aid in the examination of conscience and so to be used as a preparation for confession.[53] The next item in Beatrice's collection was a French version of the Gospel of Nicodemus, the learned Jew who appears in St. John's Gospel assisting Joseph of Arimathaea in burying Christ. The apocryphal work, which describes in considerable detail the trial, death, and resurrection of Christ, was later attributed to him and known as the Gospel of Nicodemus.[54] It was widely popular, was translated into several vernaculars, and formed the basis for a number of the English mystery plays.[55] Beatrice appears to have owned a French version of this work, which may have been written in either prose or verse.[56]

The Book of Hours (*primer de gallic*) had been given to Beatrice by her sister Agnes, to whom she now bequeathed it. Books of Hours were the most popular devotional texts of the laity (especially women) in the later Middle Ages. These were sometimes sumptuous volumes, beautifully illustrated, and might contain a calendar, gospel lessons, the Hours of the Virgin, the Hours of the Cross and of the Holy Spirit, prayers to the Virgin, the Penitential Psalms, the Office of the Dead, and further individual suffrages or prayers seeking the intercession of saints to whom the owner might have a special devotion.[57] These primers focused particularly on the cult of the Virgin and were compiled to assist lay people in their private devotions at home, or to be read while the clergy celebrated mass in church. Books of Hours were usually written in Latin, but some contained vernacular elements such as the calendar, the rubrics, and some prayers. Since Beatrice describes her primer as *de gallic* this may suggest that the vernacular elements were, in this case, in French. Or the primer may have been imported

---

53 Ann Eljenholm Nichols, "'O Vernicle': Illustrations of an Arma Christi Poem," in Marlene Villalobos Hennessy, ed., *Tributes to Kathleen L. Scott: English Medieval Manuscripts: Readers, Makers and Illuminators* (Turnhout, 2009), 139–69, esp. 143.

54 See M. R. James, *The Apocryphal New Testament* (Oxford, 1924), 94–146.

55 Rosemary Woolf, *The English Mystery Plays* (London, 1972), esp. 269–76.

56 Gaston Paris and Alphonse Bos, eds., *Trois versions rimées de l'Evangile de Nicodème, par Chrétien, André de Coutances et un Anonyme*, Société des Anciens Textes Français (Paris, 1885); Ruth J. Dean and Maureen B. M. Boulton, *Anglo-Norman Literature: A Guide to Texts and Manuscripts*, Anglo-Norman Text Society, Occasional Publications Series 3 (London, 1999), 273–75.

57 See Roger S. Wieck, *Time Sanctified: The Book of Hours in Medieval Art and Life* (New York, 1988), esp. 27–38; Mary Erler, "Devotional Literature," in *The Cambridge History of the Book in Britain*, vol. 3: *1400–1557*, ed. Lotte Hellinga and J. B. Trapp (Cambridge, UK, 1999), 495–525, esp. 495–99; Charity Scott-Stokes, *Women's Books of Hours in Medieval England*, Library of Medieval Women (Cambridge, UK, 2006), 1–24.

from France like many Books of Hours in England in the fifteenth century.[58] The volume might well have been illuminated, though Beatrice does not describe it as such (unlike the *Merce et Gramarce*), but this may be because she did not need to identify it since she explained that it was the book that had been given to her by Agnes.

The final item mentioned in Beatrice's will is a roll of the Fifteen Joys of the Virgin. This meditation links the events of the Virgin's life to fifteen virtues. It is to be found in Latin, French, and Anglo-Norman versions, both in prose and verse, in the fourteenth century. In the fifteenth century John Lydgate produced an English version in verse for Isabella, countess of Warwick (d. 1439).[59] This has been described as a "rosary poem, with an Ave to be said after the remembrance of each joy."[60] Although the Fifteen Joys is often included in Books of Hours it can also be found alone, as appears to be the case here.[61]

How unusual was Beatrice in having her own collection of devotional books? And were such books commonly found in private households? As a number of writers have demonstrated, women were often the owners of books and the agents for their transmission between generations. But there are, perhaps, some aspects of Beatrice's collection that are distinctive. Among her six texts, three were written in French, one in English and Latin, and the remaining two rolls probably contained English poems. This would suggest that Beatrice was able to read comfortably in French and English and could cope, to some degree, with Latin. In her study of religious literature owned by women in England in the period 1350 to 1500, Anne Dutton found that women's use of this literature was "almost exclusively in the vernacular."[62] But Beatrice's attention to French vernacular texts is distinctive, since the use of French religious treatises by women was declining in the fifteenth century.[63] A Book of Hours would be the standard

---

58 See Roger S. Wieck, *Painted Prayers: The Book of Hours in Medieval and Renaissance Art* (New York, 1998), 10; Scott-Stokes, *Women's Books of Hours*, 21–22.

59 Ibid., 32, 96–100; Mary C. Erler, *Women, Reading, and Piety in Late Medieval England* (Cambridge, UK, 2002), 58.

60 Derek Pearsall, *John Lydgate*, Poets of the Later Middle Ages (Charlottesville, VA, 1970), 71, 274. See Henry Noble MacCracken, ed., *The Minor Poems of John Lydgate*, Early English Text Society e.s. 107, 2 vols. (London, 1911), 1:260–67.

61 Dean and Boulton, *Anglo-Norman Literature*, 413.

62 Anne M. Dutton, "Passing the Book: Testamentary Transmission of Religious Literature to and by Women in England 1350–1500," in *Women, the Book and the Godly*, ed. Lesley Smith and Jane H. M. Taylor, Selected Proceedings of the St. Hilda's Conference, 1993 (Cambridge, UK, 1995), 41–54, at 50. See also Dutton, "Women's Use of Religious Literature in Late Medieval England (PhD diss., University of York, 1995), 142–46.

63 Dutton, "Passing the Book," 51.

book in the possession of a female member of the gentry or merchant class at this date, and the rolls containing the *Arma Christi* poem and the verses on the Fifteen Joys of the Virgin are also what might be expected.[64] Perhaps the most exceptional items are Henry of Grosmont's *Livre de seyntz medicines* and the French version of the Gospel of Nicodemus, both of which were substantial works. Only one other woman is known to have owned a copy of the *Livre*: Maria, Lady Roos, who bequeathed "libro gallico de Duce Lancastriae" in 1394 to her kinswoman Isabella Percy.[65] No other woman has so far been identified who owned a copy of the Gospel of Nicodemus. In her study of women's wills in late medieval England, Anne Dutton most frequently encountered Walter Hilton's *Scale of Perfection*, *The Chastising of God's Children*, the *Pore Caitif*, the *Mirror of the Blessed Life of Jesus Christ*, and lives of the saints.[66] Beatrice Melreth does not seem to have associated with these works of affective piety.

What was also, perhaps, distinctive about Beatrice was that she was not a vowess, nor did she have any particular links to female religious houses. She does not appear to have relatives, whether male or female, who were members of religious communities, and in her will she makes no bequests to monasteries or nunneries. In this respect, Beatrice differs considerably from the Norwich woman Margaret Purdans and her associates, examined by Mary Erler. There is no evidence in Beatrice's will, or in her list of books, of the affective and intense piety of some of these fifteenth-century women.[67] Felicity Riddy has pointed out that nuns and pious gentlewomen in this period had a shared literary culture; in contrast, Beatrice Melreth seems to have shared her literary culture not with nuns but, exclusively, with her sister Agnes.[68]

Agnes Waleys, perhaps the youngest daughter of John and Joan Waleys, appears to have married a London "armiger," John Burgh, who was presumably still alive when Beatrice drew up her will in 1448, since she refers to her sister as Agnes Burgh. But by November 1452, when Agnes drew up her own will, she had remarried, to another "armiger," John Padyngton, and they were living in

64 Two noblewomen owned rolls of the Passion of Jesus Christ, and there were several other copies of "The passion of Our Lord" recorded in women's wills of the period. See Dutton, "Women's Use of Religious Literature," Appendices 2 and 3.
65 Felicity Riddy, "'Women Talking about the Things of God': A Late Medieval Sub-Culture," in *Women and Literature in Britain 1150–1500*, ed. Carol M. Meale, Cambridge Studies in Medieval Literature 17 (Cambridge, UK, 1993), 104–27, esp. 108, 120.
66 Dutton, "Women's Use of Religious Literature." Dutton's sample was based on wills (largely printed) from the period 1350 to 1500, probate inventories, and manuscripts known to have been owned by women.
67 Erler, *Women, Reading, and Piety*, ch. 3.
68 Riddy, "'Women Talking about the Things of God,'" 110–11.

the parish of St. Andrew Cornhill (Undershaft) in London. Unfortunately, Agnes says nothing in her own will about the books which she had been bequeathed by her sister. But the will, in fact, deals exclusively with lands and property, most of which she left to her new husband for life, and thence to her only surviving child, Johanna.[69] John Padyngton himself died very soon after his wife and in his will made conscientious attempts to fulfil the wishes of his wife and to leave to her daughter, Johanna Burgh, all the lands she had specified as well as a generous collection of plate and clothing.[70] But there is no mention of books.

It seems likely that Beatrice was buried with Reginald in the church at Bury Hatley but, if so, nothing now remains of their tomb, although there are brass fragments from the earlier tomb for Reginald's parents, Judge John Cockayne and his wife Ida.[71] Beatrice's will has, however, provided an insight into the lifestyle and religious practices of an educated woman whose life appears to have been lived entirely in the secular world. She moved between manors in Sussex and Bedfordshire and town life in London, was twice married, brought up four children, kept in touch with her three sisters, fought legal cases to defend her inheritance, supported scholars from Cambridge, and collected together a small library of books which would help her to reflect on her life, confess her sins, and find reassurance in the example of the Blessed Virgin and in the death of her Saviour. It is easier to find extraordinary people in the past: Beatrice's very ordinariness makes her exceptional.

---

69 LMA, Commissary Register 9171/4, fol. 273v. Agnes had acted as the executor of her husband John Burgh, and appointed as her own executors her new husband, John Padyngton, and her brother-in-law, Nicholas Morley, who had married her sister Joan. For Morley, described as "unscrupulous and tenacious," see *The Glynde Place Archives*, xv–xvi.

70 Lambeth Palace Library, Register of Archbishop Kempe, fols. 273v–275. By this date Johanna was described in Padyngton's will as Johanna Grey: she had married Ralph Grey of Brent Pelham, Hertfordshire.

71 William Lack, H. Martin Stuchfield, and Philip Whittemore, eds., *The Monumental Brasses of Bedfordshire* (London, 1992), 50–53; Cockayne, *Cockayne Memoranda*, records that the tomb of Chief Baron Cockayne was removed from the nave in the mid-nineteenth-century by the then rector, the Revd. and Hon. Henry Cockayne Cust, "while improving the church," 23.

How Intellectual Were Fifteenth-Century Londoners?
Grammar versus Logic in the Citizens' Encounters with Learned Men

SHEILA LINDENBAUM

One of the most striking themes to emerge from Sylvia Thrupp's magisterial study, *The Merchant Class of Medieval London*, is the Londoners' lack of "intellectual curiosity or initiative." Wherever she looks in the merchants' culture, despite the impressive evidence of literacy and book ownership that emerges, Thrupp can find only a faint "intellectual stirring," one that "fed primarily upon religious interests" in a disappointingly "meditative and reflective" way. To a social historian of the 1940s like Thrupp, that is scarcely intellectual activity at all – nothing like the "fully developed religious or political ideas" she admires in the vibrant debates of the Calvinist reformers. Thrupp is clearly frustrated by the Londoners' failure to question "dominant assumptions" about the social order or to "probe" the political issues they faced as governors of the city. "When business affairs were laid aside, they could listen with interest to preaching; otherwise they preferred convivial relaxation to intellectual discussion."[1]

What are we to make of these views today, given our present understanding of the Londoners' religious and political culture? Has our view of the Londoners' intellectuality changed because we know they had their own passionate reformers, orthodox and Lollard, or because we understand the forms of censorship that produced "intellectual inhibition" in the public sphere? For many scholars, Thrupp's formulations have continued to be highly influential: for example, Malcolm Richardson remarks on the "intellectual limits" and lack of "intellectual curiosity" in the citizens' letter writing and commonplace books. But others have used her terminology to make the opposite point. Anne Sutton finds the London mercers to be "intellectually curious" and "intellectually ambitious" owners of historical and literary texts, who occasionally ventured into Lollardy and alchemy. Mary Erler, the dedicatee of this volume, has emphasized the intellectual potential of the books London women shared with their learned

1   Sylvia Thrupp, *The Merchant Class of Medieval London, 1300–1500* (Ann Arbor, MI, 1948), 161, 247, 181, 315, 99, 163.

spiritual advisors, which though mainly devotional, could sometimes demand sophisticated interpretive strategies and critical thinking.[2]

Taking my cue from Erler's pairings of London women and their learned advisors, I propose to revisit the question of the Londoners' intellectuality by looking at a series of encounters between citizens and the *bona fide* intellectuals in their midst – the university graduates who brought academic learning to the metropolis and disseminated it there.[3] I hope to get a more specific purchase on the various senses in which Londoners can be regarded as intellectual, or not, by seeing how they respond to the instructional overtures of highly educated men. I will be thinking of intellectual work in this period as deriving from university learning and academic skills, as recent scholarship has tended to do, but I will also refer to Thrupp's more general sense of what counts as intellectual activity. As will be seen, her emphasis on questioning and discussion is surprisingly resonant with the speculative and disputational aspects of medieval university study.

The three encounters I will discuss are diverse: they involve intellectuals of very different stripes, engaging with artisans as well as merchants, in each case employing the Latin *Eclogue* of Theodulus or its scholarly offshoot, Wyclif's *Trialogus*, for their own special purposes. Taken all together, however, they show the importance of the university arts curriculum as the ground on which university scholars and urban laity could meet, and the significance of grammar and logic, the most fundamental skills of the arts curriculum, as rival claimants for the citizens' attention. As I hope to show, the intellectual history of London citizens in the mid-fifteenth century can usefully be told in terms of the antagonism between these two disciplines, particularly as it was fueled by the forces of religious controversy.

---

2   Mishtooni Bose refers to the "intellectual inhibition" of this period, though her main focus is on "intellectual fresh starts" and positive creativity ("Intellectual Life in Fifteenth-Century England," *New Medieval Literatures* 12 [2010]: 333–60, at 336–37). See also Malcolm Richardson, *Middle-Class Writing in Late Medieval London* (London, 2011), 155, 173; Anne F. Sutton, *The Mercery of London: Trade, Goods and People, 1130–1578* (Aldershot, Hampshire, 2005), 164–69; Mary C. Erler, "The Library of a London Vowess, Margery de Nerford," in *Women, Reading and Piety in Late Medieval England* (Cambridge, UK, 2002), 48–67.

3   A penetrating analysis of the issues to be considered when applying the modern term "intellectuals" to medieval scholars can be found in Rita Copeland, *Pedagogy, Intellectuals, and Dissent* (Cambridge, UK, 2001), 1–50.

John Seward and his Students at Cornhill

As will be seen in all three of these encounters, Londoners were well accustomed to the presence of learned men. Not only did graduates of Oxford and Cambridge inhabit the city's own institutions of higher learning, the scola of the fraternal orders, where the equivalent of the arts course at Oxford and Cambridge was taught, but they could also be found in every parish: they were heads of religious houses and rectors of the city churches, secretaries and chaplains of the great, and administrators in the offices of the church and crown. There were also men with university training in grammar and dictaminal practice in the city's schools. In the mid-fifteenth century, the period I am focusing on here, there was a busy two-way traffic between the universities and the city; notably, when scholars in both places cooperated to raise funds from the citizens for the new anti-heretical colleges and Oxford's divinity school.[4] Through such contacts, academic developments at the universities were soon communicated to the city's academic population, and the ground prepared for the citizens' interaction with learned men.

One of the most important of these developments, at least for the civic elite, was the early fifteenth-century revival of classical learning at Oxford. This movement was characterized by a dramatic shift of emphasis from logic to grammar and rhetoric within the liberal arts, and a fresh interest in the ancient authors and twelfth-century classicizing poets who exemplified the newly favored disciplines. Although it had little effect on the official university curriculum, this new enthusiasm for the classics can be detected in learned sermons, the Ciceronian oratory of the day, and the production of new grammatical and rhetorical texts for those engaged in higher learning.[5] In London, we can see it in the teaching

4   A. B. Emden documents hundreds of ecclesiastical benefices and government offices held by Oxford graduates in London in *A Biographical Register of the University of Oxford to A.D. 1500*, 3 vols. (Oxford, 1957–59). Here, as in his *Biographical Register of the University of Cambridge to 1500* (Cambridge, UK, 1963), Emden benefits from the lists of the city's graduate rectors in George Hennessy, *Novum Repertorium Ecclesiasticum Parochiale Londinense* (London, 1898). Oxford's fundraising in London is extensively documented in *Epistolae Academicae Oxon: (Registrum F)*, ed. and trans. Henry Anstey, Part I (Oxford, 1898); see particularly the form letter to be sent to the many city rectors who served as executors of wealthy citizens (277–78).

5   James G. Clark offers an eloquent account of the classical revival in *A Monastic Renaissance at St Albans* (Oxford, 2004), 210–17. See also *Monastic Renaissance* (226–34) for Ciceronian rhetoric and classicizing sermons in the work of the Oxford Benedictine Hugh Legat, and for the new taste for classical literary works outside of the official Oxford curriculum (212). For the "significant revival of interest in rhetoric and the literary arts, including both the classical poetry of antiquity and the classicizing Latin poetry of the twelfth century," see also Martin Camargo, "The Late Fourteenth-Century

of John Seward, who brought it from Oxford to his school in Cornhill where it was transmitted in modified form to the sons of the elite. In encounters between grammar masters like Seward and their students, this strong intellectual current became the basis of a classically inspired civic ritual, where it served to mark the superiority of the city's merchants over its shopkeepers and artisans.

Although Seward's Oxford career is obscure, it is highly likely that he came to London as a Master of Grammar, a respected attainment for scholars who wanted to become heads of grammar schools.[6] While residing in London, from about 1404 to his death in 1435/6, he continued to communicate with famous grammarians and devotees of classical literature at the university. Among the many learned dedicatees of his poetry was the university chancellor, Richard Courtenay, an aristocratic supporter of the arts revival, who may have been the first to solicit books from the Lancastrian dukes when they were needed for the "liberal arts and three philosophies," as the arts curriculum was called. Seward was never ordained as a priest, but lived in Cornhill with a wife and daughter, taking part in parish life, acquiring a little property, and developing rewarding friendships with prosperous citizens and their families as well as fellow schoolmasters nearby. Like his London contemporary Thomas Hoccleve, he employed his professional skills in moonlighting jobs: he was commissioned by his friend John Whitby, the rector of St. Peter Cornhill, to compile a cartulary of properties belonging to the church and its chantries, including an index composed according to academic practice, but in English for use in the parish. Seward was also hired to write business letters in Latin on behalf of the London skinner Richard Swan, the father of one of his students, Thomas Swan. These letters were to Richard's brother, William, a papal notary, mainly on behalf of wealthy Londoners seeking legal representation at the papal court, and they show that Seward had useful if unremarkable dictaminal skills.[7]

Renaissance of Anglo-Latin Rhetoric," *Philosophy and Rhetoric* 45 (2012): 107–33, at 109; and his "Chaucer and the Oxford Renaissance of Anglo-Latin Rhetoric," *Studies in the Age of Chaucer* 34 (2012): 173–207 (see 180 for the renewed interest in ancient Ciceronian treatises).

6 "The M. Gram. degree gave considerable status to its holder both in terms of advantages at Oxford over the *alii quam magistri* who held no master's degree, and outside Oxford as a proof of competence, but it was not of course ranked with the other masters' degrees." David Thomson, "The Oxford Grammar Masters Revisited," *Mediaeval Studies* 45 (1983): 293–310, at 301.

7 Rents paid to a John Seward in 1411 are recorded in The National Archives (TNA) E40/2175. The cartulary, formerly Guildhall MS 4158, is now in the London Metropolitan Archives, P69/PET1/D/001/MS04158. For Seward's career and associates, with transcriptions of letters written to William Swan, see V. A. Galbraith,

In his day job, however, Seward was an extraordinarily accomplished scholar whose students could benefit from the high standards of Latin grammar exemplified in his pedagogical treatises on metrics (an important aspect of grammatical study) and his impressive first-hand knowledge of classical authors. These are skills that would come significantly into play when he introduced his students to the classics through the *Eclogue* of Theodulus, a centuries-old literary text that was the main vehicle for this purpose in London schoolrooms, as elsewhere.[8] Theodulus' poem is a Christianized take on the poetic contests in Virgil's eclogues: a pagan goatherd (Pseustis, a Liar) and a beautiful shepherdess of David's line (Alithea, Truth) alternately compose quatrains based on stories from their respective cultural repertories: for example, the goatherd's verses on the great flood from which Jupiter saves Deucalion are countered by the maiden's on Noah's flood. After the shepherdess is revealed to be a Christian, a third figure, Mother Wisdom (Phronesis), finally proclaims her the winner, but only after the goatherd has introduced a large host of Ovidian and Virgilian personages and their myths for the grammar students' edification.[9]

In teaching this text to Thomas Swan and his other students, Seward would have used glossed versions of the *Eclogue*, together with his own knowledge, to explain difficult words and constructions, label the parts of speech, work out the meter (his specialty), identify characters, and give fuller versions of the mythological and biblical stories referred to in the poem. For the first line of the prologue (*Ethiopum terras iam feruida torruit estas*), for instance, one commentary he may have used gives the derivations and meanings of all the key words, indicates conjugations and declensions (*feruidus-a-um*), lists related words (such as all four seasons when glossing *estas*), and notes that *iam* is an adverb of time. For "*axis solis*" in the next line, it is noted that this is an example of synecdoche, the "*axis*" actually referring to "*ipse sol*," and information is given about the movement of

"John Seward and his Circle," *Mediaeval and Renaissance Studies* 1 (1941): 85–104. For the letters to Swan, see also E. F. Jacob, "To and From the Court of Rome in the Early Fifteenth Century," *Essays in Later Medieval History* (Manchester, 1968), 58–78. Seward refers to Richard Swan's son as his student ("meum discipulum") in a letter to William Swan probably written in 1419 (Galbraith, 101).

8   An unglossed copy of the *Eclogue* from fifteenth-century London, in a non-professional hand, survives in BL MS Add. 37075. It is gathered into a book with excerpts from Priscian and other grammatical authorities, composition exercises, and hymns. There was also a copy of the *Eclogue* among the schoolbooks given to St. Paul's school in 1358 along with a number of classical literary texts (Thomson, 306).

9   See Patrick Cook's introduction to this poem, with an English translation, in "The *Ecloga Theoduli*," in *Medieval Literature for Children*, ed. Daniel T. Kline (New York, 2003) 188–203.

the spheres. For mythological characters and events, the commentary often refers to Ovid and Virgil. The long gloss on Saturn situates that figure in Ovid's Golden Age (an opportunity to list all four ages of the world), prior to commenting on his grim visage and astronomical significance as the malevolent planet, his identification with the King of Crete who devoured his children, his castration by Jupiter and the grotesque birth of Venus, and other details of the Greco-Roman creation myth.[10] The schoolmaster is encouraged to treat each word as an opportunity to add to the student's knowledge of the Latin language, Greco-Roman mythology, and the biblical narratives referred to in the poem.

In comparison to the catechetical instruction also purveyed in grammar schools in the shape of predetermined questions and answers to be learned by rote – What are the four cardinal virtues? How do you recognize the comparative degree of an adjective? – this was interesting, even stimulating work. It may well have included role playing: the text invites the young male student to impersonate the girl versifier as well as the boy, and it miraculously endows Alithea, with whose feminine weakness a young schoolboy might identify, with the skill to win the contest.[11] There was also a compelling vocational impetus to the students' work, since they were pursuing a course of study that defined them as future leaders. Because it was the foundational discipline of the liberal arts, grammar was frequently associated with the entire curriculum of the "arts and three philosophies," the branch of university study considered most useful to great rulers, and the source of the many encyclopedic texts and works of moral philosophy that scholars translated for princely patrons.[12] This link between the arts and successful rulership was a well-worn theme when applied to royalty: when imploring the duke of Bedford to support the arts curriculum, Oxford predictably argues that such learning "is the noblest of noble things, it is at once the glory and defense of kings, the source and strength of good government; it

10 I quote from the commentary of Odo Picardus printed in London in 1515 by Wynkyn de Worde (Early English Books Online, STC 23943, images 1–3, 5–6). Odo's gloss, which incorporates material from earlier commentaries, was written in 1406–7 for children of the French court, and it was well known in England prior to its entry into print. It contains a layer of interpretation according to the four senses of the Bible along with the matter discussed here.

11 For therapeutic role playing of this kind, see Marjorie Curry Woods, "Weeping for Dido," in Latin Grammar and Rhetoric: From Classical Theory to Medieval Practice, ed. Carol Dana Lanham (New York, 2002), 284–94.

12 Charles Briggs, "Teaching Philosophy at School and Court: Vulgarization and Translation," in The Vulgar Tongue: Medieval and Postmedieval Vernacularity, ed. Fiona Somerset and Nicholas Watson (University Park, PA, 2003), 99–111. Briggs's article concerns moral philosophy, one of the three studied as the culmination of the arts curriculum (the others being natural philosophy and metaphysics).

composes strife, encourages justice and renders subjects obedient . . . ."[13] But these ideas were more than a commonplace for the sons of London's most prosperous citizens, in that their association with the "noble" liberal arts materially assisted their aspirations to become important members of the city's ruling elite or local governors among the gentry.[14] The spectacular pageant of the seven liberal arts and Lady Sapientia performed on Cornhill in 1432 was intended to describe the aristocratic education of its primary audience, the eleven-year-old Henry VI; but it also spoke to the city's grammar students, including those in Seward's nearby school.[15]

Yet despite the attractions of the *Eclogue*, Seward's students would not have used it to venture beyond the grammatical study and elementary rhetoric that was their province. Although the poem dramatizes a contest, their study emphasized the accumulation of knowledge rather than discussion or debate, and there was little encouragement to engage in literary interpretation beyond elucidating the literal sense of the text and moralizing the characters. The more advanced reaches of grammar were reserved to Seward himself, working at the full extent of his powers, pursuing technical difficulties and theoretical issues with his academic peers, and reading at the superior level of poetic invention and allegorical meaning which became the ground of his own writings. He would, for instance, have understood that Theodulus' maiden uses a sophisticated Christian hermeneutics in her account of the flood and other Old Testament narratives, whereas the goatherd is trapped on the literal level. In his own major work, the *Somnium Seward*, he moves beyond the practices of the schoolroom to a higher level of study, seeking out the superior example of ancient authors under the patronage of an allegorical Lady who stands for the liberal arts in their ideal, uncorrupted form (Fig. 3.1).[16] His

---

13 Translated from the florid Latin by the editor, Henry Anstey, in *Epistolae Academicae Oxon: (Registrum F)*, Part I, 81; and see also 53–54, 106–7, 107–8.

14 In a valuable piece of research, Hannes Kleineke identifies the career paths of students at St. Paul's school in 1434, noting that they were likely to become London merchants, landed gentry active in local government, or men-at-law. See "The Schoolboy's Tale: a Fifteenth-Century Voice from St. Paul's School," in *London and the Kingdom: Essays in Honour of Caroline M. Barron*, ed. Matthew Davies and Andrew Prescott, Harlaxton Medieval Studies 6 (Donington, Lincolnshire, 2008), 146–59, at 154–55. Seward's student Thomas Swan, the son of a moderately prosperous skinner, took a different but equally prestigious path, becoming the long-standing rector of St. Mary at Hill in London, after leaving Oxford as a Bachelor of Civil Law.

15 *Henry VI's Triumphal Entry into London*, in *John Lydgate, Mummings and Entertainments*, ed. Claire Sponsler (Kalamazoo, 2010), line 238.

16 *Somnium Johannis Seguard*, Edinburgh University Library, MS 136, fol. 44v. I am much indebted here to Clark's interpretation of the *Somnium* (*Monastic Renaissance*, 225). On

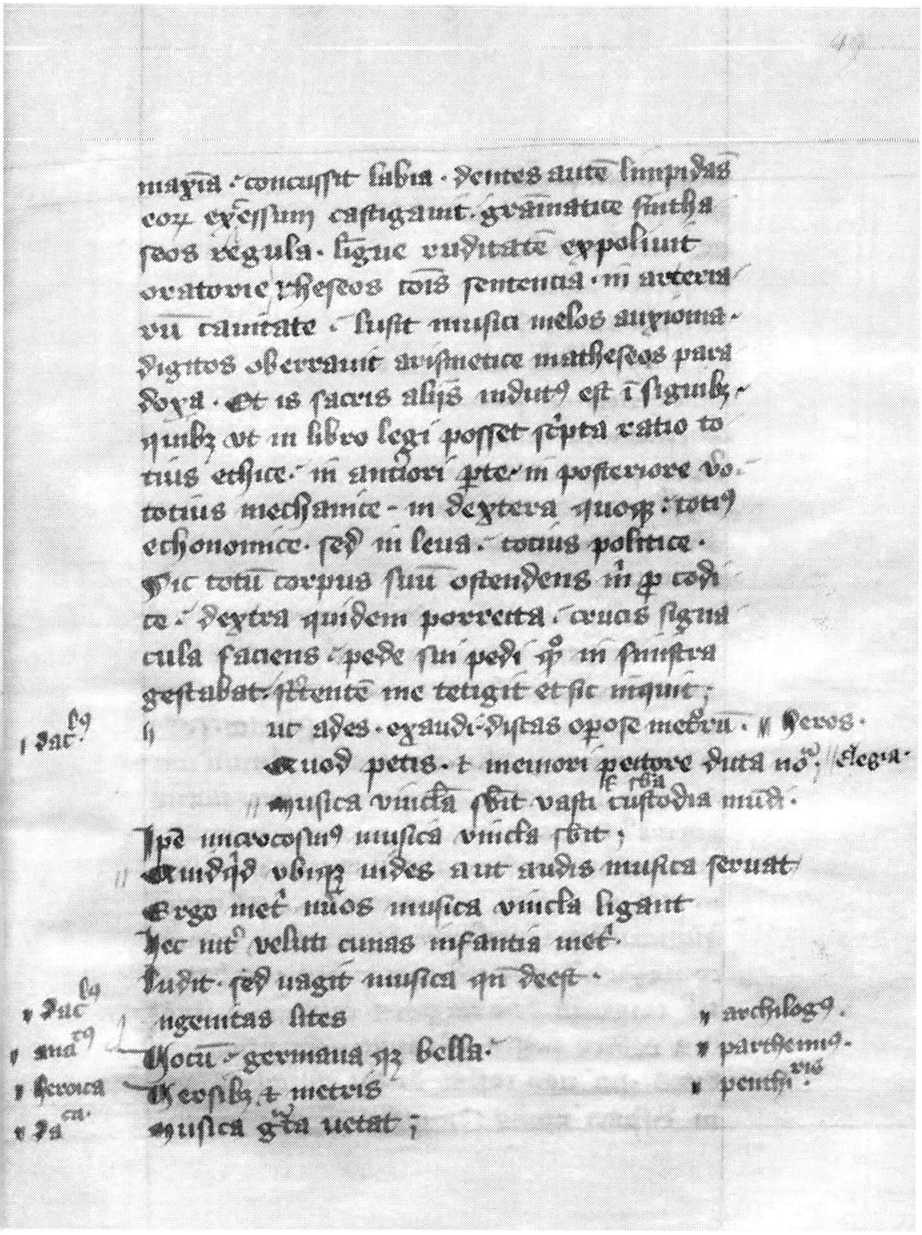

Fig. 3.1 Somnium Johannis Seguard, *Edinburgh University Library MS 136, fol. 44v.*

metrical scholarship is excessively pedantic, to be sure, but it is also adventurous in the way it treats grammar as a theoretical discipline whose rules could be investigated, debated, and established as well as slavishly followed – and it was conducted with passionate enthusiasm. One is reminded of the fervor with which Poggio Bracciolini searched German monasteries for ancient manuscripts of the classical authors – not as far a stretch as it might seem, since in 1419, when Seward was in mid-career in Cornhill, Poggio was living at Winchester Palace across the river as secretary to bishop Henry Beaufort.[17]

In their own future careers, however, the merchants' sons who studied with Seward applied their learning in a more pragmatic way, consistent with the elementary nature of their studies and the narrow political objectives to which their literary activities were directed. While they honored the liberal arts, they preferred to delegate poetic invention and scholarly inquiry to specialists, restricting themselves to the more passive role of sponsoring vernacular offshoots of the classical revival and providing a discerning audience for such initiatives.

We see this with great clarity in one of their best-known literary ventures, the mumming the Mercers company commissioned from John Lydgate to honor their mayor, the rich and well-connected William Estfield, a younger son of the gentry who had been apprenticed in London. Lydgate's mumming seems to have been inspired by commentaries on Theodulus' *Eclogue* that describe the author traveling the ancient world in search of learning, and it is remarkably evocative of the older poem. In the mumming, Jupiter descends from his celestial mansion, passing through various regions of the world mentioned in classical mythology and the Old Testament. His first stop is Jerusalem, but he then pauses at Parnassus with its classical "rethorycyens" and poets, and their modern descendants Boccaccio and Petrarch, before alighting in Europa. One of his messengers has taken a similar journey by water from Egypt via the Red Sea and the shores of the River Jordan ("where Jacob passed"), through exotic locales inhabited by Circe and Neptune (but identifiable as sources of the mercers' wares), before reaching "Brutes Albyon" and finally London, where he is in charge of admitting "certein estates" to the mayor's feast. Here we have the same dual appropriation of classical learning and biblical lore, the same brief references to a range of stories, the same appeal to accumulated literary knowledge, as in the students'

---

the demarcation between the two levels of study, Marjorie Curry Woods argues that approaches to standard rhetorical texts in the schoolroom and university classroom were "mutually exclusive" ("A Medieval Rhetoric Goes to School – and to the University," *Rhetorica* 9 [1991]: 55–65, at 55).

17 G. L. Harriss, "Beaufort, Henry [called the Cardinal of England] 1375?–1447," *Oxford Dictionary of National Biography* (Oxford, 2004–).

reading of Theodulus, in a work requiring of the viewer the same level of literary expertise. In the copy of the mumming made by the London anthologist John Shirley, there are even glosses similar to the ones schoolmasters employed when teaching the *Eclogue*: "Poetes feynen that the gret god Jupiter came doune from heven forravisshe a kynges doughter cleped Europa. after whame alle the cuntreys of Europ berethe the name."[18]

As at school, the elite citizen needs no profound understanding of this material. A comfortable, general familiarity is enough to distinguish him from the ordinary artisan and tradesman and confirm the superior status that gains "certein estates" entrance to the mayor's feast.[19] Just being recognized as a patron of the liberal arts may have been enough to identify a merchant with the gentry, and to judge by the growing call for places at London's grammar schools, these and other strategies used to integrate classical learning into the merchants' own cultural practices were a political success.[20] How "intellectual" this makes the merchants is a separate question, however, one that can be addressed by recalling Sylvia Thrupp's association of intellectual activity with "curiosity or

---

18 *Mumming for the Mercers of London*, in *John Lydgate, Mummings and Entertainments*, ed. Sponsler, line 238. See also a recent edition of the mumming for contemporary performance with extensive "explication" of the theatrical aspects by Meg Twycross and Elisabeth Dutton, in *The Medieval Merchant*, ed. Caroline M. Barron and Anne F. Sutton (Donington, Lincolnshire, 2014), 310–49. This work is usually dated to Estfield's first mayoralty in 1430. I am grateful to Hannes Kleineke and the History of Parliament project for allowing me to see Matthew Davies's biography of William Estfield, soon to be published on www.historyofparliamentonline.org.

19 Much as I do here, Maura Nolan views this mumming as the "attempt of a socially elite but non-noble group to identify itself as consumers of aristocratic cultural capital" in the form of classical learning and European poetic culture, but she thinks that London's civic elite would find the references "intimidatingly learned," rather than comfortably familiar, and she does not relate them to what was taught in grammar schools (*John Lydgate and the Making of Public Culture* [Cambridge, UK, 2005], 99–106, at 100). Claire Sponsler likewise emphasizes the unfamiliarity of the classical material even to a "well educated and intellectually curious" civic elite, stressing the process by which "foreign culture is made native" for their benefit (*The Queen's Dumbshows: John Lydgate and the Making of Early Theater* [Philadelphia, 2014], 44–51, at 50, 44).

20 On the Londoners' need for more grammar schools, see Nicholas Orme, *English Schools in the Middle Ages* (London, 1973), 210–13, 308–9; Caroline M. Barron, "The Expansion of Education in Fifteenth-Century London," in *The Cloister and the World*, ed. John Blair and Brian Golding (Oxford, 1996), 219–45; and Anne F. Sutton, "The Hospital of St. Thomas of Acre of London: The Search for Patronage, Liturgical Improvement, and a School, under Master John Neel 1420–63," in *The Late Medieval English College and Its Context*, ed. Clive Burgess and Martin Heale (York, 2008), 199–229.

initiative." The merchants' classically inspired pageantry and mummings are certainly important intellectual "initiatives" in that they give academic learning, in the form of grammar, a home at the center of city government, and they also give the poet an acknowledged role in the public sphere. But these initiatives engage only modest linguistic and interpretive skills on the merchants' part, and they encourage the accumulation of knowledge rather than speculation and "curiosity." The invention is all the poet's, and since the objective is to present the merchants' superiority as an unquestioned attribute of their group, even the poet will refrain from the critical inquiry and investigation of new territory that accompanied the classical revival in its more ardent, academic form.

Ralph Mungyn and William Estfield

In addition to promoting the elite citizen's social aspirations, the classical learning purveyed in London's grammar schools implied a politically safe religious orthodoxy. It is impossible to imagine John Seward violating archbishop Arundel's prohibition against schoolmasters teaching "materia theologica," expounding scripture, or permitting their pupils to dispute on such matters in the manner of university students. His teaching was restricted to *primitiva scientia*, as the skills needed to read and write Latin were called, and it was accompanied by the pious exercises appropriate to laymen.[21] In Ralph Mungyn, however, we have a London intellectual who could be Seward's dark twin, also trained at Oxford, living in London at the same time, but potentially as challenging to the religious authorities and their lay adherents as Seward was supportive of them. An unbeneficed Wycliffite priest, he brought to the city an academic habit of logical argument that was antagonistic to the classical learning and elitist political agenda of the city's grammar schools. A dramatic encounter with the prominent mercer William Estfield, which led to Mungyn's trial for heresy, illustrates this antagonism and helps explain the resistance to intellectual questioning that characterized London's political and religious cultures.

Mungyn had been a logic student of Peter Payne, the notorious Wycliffite who in 1413 escaped from Oxford to become a leader of the Hussites and a

---

21 William Lyndwood, *Provinciale seu constitutiones Angliae* (Oxford, 1679), 248. As noted above, BL MS Add. 37075 contains pious hymns for the use of schoolboys. See Jo Ann Hoeppner Moran, *The Growth of English Schooling, 1340–1548* (Princeton, 1985), 38–39, for evidence that some grammar schools may have anticipated university study by teaching logic (dialectic) to their students and holding disputations. The evidence is scanty and problematic, however; some of it seems to refer to recreational debates about the rules of grammar or to disputations in the "schools" of cathedral chapters and the friars' studia

formidable controversialist on the international stage.[22] Mungyn thus brought with him to London some knowledge of Wyclif's theology along with the professional expertise in academic argument he acquired by studying with Payne. He would also have carried with him a disapproval of classical learning as taught by grammar-school masters like Seward, with their mystical reverence for the liberal arts. For Wycliffites, it was necessary to study grammar, and especially logic, only because they were useful tools of biblical study. It was "heathenish" to believe, as Seward did, that the liberal arts could ennoble their practitioners by restoring the knowledge man naturally possessed before the Fall. Grammar was not an avenue to classical learning and the wisdom it could impart, but a skill needed to elucidate the literal sense of scripture. Even the highly valued art of logic, to which Wyclif himself had contributed an important textbook, was studied not to regain prelapsarian knowledge but because the ability to examine a proposition and argue its validity was essential to the search for scriptural truth.[23]

While the kind of learning Mungyn sought to impart to Londoners is fairly clear from his study with Payne, it can be inferred more precisely from Wyclif's *Trialogus*, a text we know he possessed (Fig. 3.2). *Trialogus* is a summa of religious doctrine that was intended to bridge the gap between Wycliffite scholars with university training and the lay public. It follows the topical outline of Peter Lombard's *Sentences*, the core text of university theological study, with the doctrine altered to reflect Wyclif's views, and the *quaestio* form of the university summa modified to meet the needs of those engaged in pastoral instruction. It seems to have been intended for Wycliffite priests who had not quite progressed to theological study, but had enough training in the arts to understand the logical principles being employed in the text, in the hope that they could convey something of these principles along with the work's doctrinal content as they went about teaching and preaching to the laity. As such, the work was ideally suited to Mungyn's level of learning and his London mission.[24]

22 At his trial, Mungyn admitted that he had studied logic but not "doctrina" (theology) with Payne: *The Register of Henry Chichele, Archbishop of Canterbury*, ed. E. F. Jacob, 4 vols. (Oxford, 1937–47), 3:195–205, at 198. For a detailed account of the London heresy trials of 1428, including Mungyn's, see Charles Kightly, "The Early Lollards. A Survey of Popular Lollard Activity in England 1382–1428" (DPhil thesis, University of York, 1975), 535–48.

23 Wyclif's opposition to the notion that the liberal arts were redemptive is pursued in a stimulating article by Kantik Ghosh ("Logic and Lollardy," *Medium Ævum* 76 [2007]: 251–67). For "heathenish" learning, see *Johannis Wyclif, Tractatus De Logica*, ed. Michael Henry Dziewicki, vol. 1 (London, 1893), 1.

24 *Wyclif: Trialogus*, trans. Stephen E. Lahey (Cambridge, UK, 2013), *Introduction*, 13–15 (audience). At his trial, Mungyn admitted having once owned a copy of this prohibited

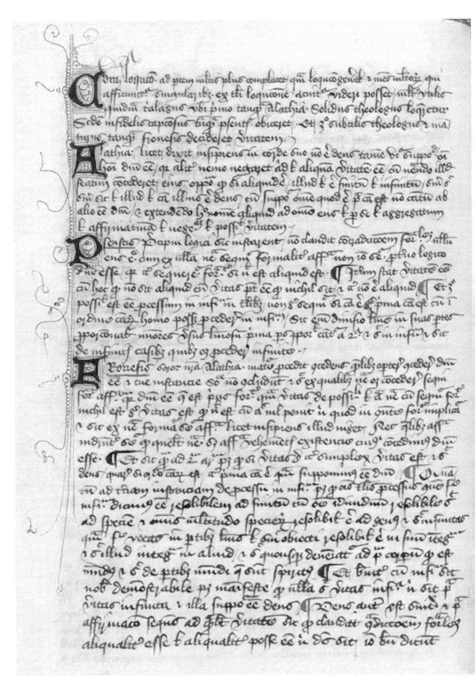

Fig. 3.2 A fifteenth-century copy of John Wyclif's Trialogus *of English provenance. Florence, Biblioteca Medicea Laurenziana MS Plut. 19.33, fol. 57v. Reproduced by permission of MiBACT : any further reproduction by any means is prohibited.*

Mungyn would also have found an ideal teaching scenario modeled in *Trialogus*. Here Wyclif makes a point of replacing the classically oriented learning of grammar schools with the logical argument characteristic of university study. Appropriating Theodulus' *Eclogue* for this purpose, he unburdens the three characters in the singing contest of their ancient narratives and recasts them as participants in a quasi-academic debate: the pagan goatherd becomes a fallacious "pagan" friar ("infidelis captiosus"), the maiden Alithea a "sound philosopher" ("solidus philosophus"), and Phronesis a theologian "subtillis . . . et maturus," a figure for Wyclif himself, who evaluates and corrects the others.[25] The three figures are then redeployed to dispute the many points of doctrine taken up in the course of the work – from the nature of God and the world, to the moral virtues, the sacraments, the Last Things, and the heavenly "experiences of the blessed" – with digressions on the evils of clerical endowment added to Peter Lombard's subject matter.

This is obviously a more demanding mode of instruction than Seward's teaching of *primitiva scientia*. Reading Theodulus' *Eclogue* in a grammar school, as we have seen, meant absorbing the wealth of information contained in the text's mini-narratives and glosses so that it that could be recalled when needed as evidence of the elite student's privileged status. In contrast, the emphasis in *Trialogus* is on questioning – and how to go about it. At times, there is almost as much discussion of how to test propositions as there is argument itself. This is especially true of the initial questions about God and the universe: in her opening speech alone, Alithea refers to three of the principles (contradiction, affirmation/negation, and the theory of propositions) that Wyclif treats in his logic textbook.[26] There are no explicit directives for how to adapt this sophisticated discourse to a lay audience, but in the less formal sections of the work, when Alithea prompts Phronesis to expound on the sacraments and the vices with their corresponding virtues, his responses begin to sound more like works of instruction for the adult laity, and we sometimes hear the voice of the preacher as well.[27]

book, but claimed he sold it some years earlier (*Register of Henry Chichele*, 3:198). I am very grateful to Stephen Lahey for his generous help with the manuscripts and intended audience of Trialogus.

25 *Trialogus*, 38.

26 For later tracts which also teach argumentative skills along with Wycliffite doctrine, but less systematically and in English, see Fiona Somerset, "Wycliffite Prose," in *A Companion to Middle English Prose*, ed. A. S. G. Edwards (Cambridge, UK, 2004), 195–214, at 202–6.

27 While the intent of these sections of *Trialogus* may be to provide a model for teaching, Copeland stresses the difficulty of adapting academic modes of instruction to the lay classroom: "we cannot look to university instruction for a practical model of lay adult education among the Lollards" (*Pedagogy, Intellectuals, and Dissent*, 18). She argues instead

There can be little doubt that Ralph Mungyn's attempts to evangelize the London laity resonated strongly with this work. At his trial, not only was he said to have introduced the same controversial matter found in *Trialogus* into his sermons, preaching frequently against the worldly possessions of the friars and religious orders, but he was also conspicuously "subtilis" in his preaching style: he employed the skills of a trained logician to the extent that he was difficult to understand (a typical complaint about preachers who applied logic to matters of the faith).[28] Moreover, the heretical statements on clerical disendowment that he allegedly made in informal conversation with William Estfield and others, which I will discuss below, suggest that he was trying to pursue specific arguments found in Wyclif's works, including *Trialogus*.

What support he had from Londoners in these efforts is unclear. We know that he was a priest at St. Stephen Walbrook for a time, but about seven or eight years before his trial, bishop Richard Clifford removed him from the cure of souls when he preached an offensive sermon. After that, he managed to continue preaching locally, and to judge from his acquaintance with other Lollards in the London area, it seems that he may have quietly worked as a Lollard teacher. Although not actually in hiding, he may have lived much like Wyclif's elusive disciple John Purvey, who was discovered in obscure London quarters, with a few books, after the Oldcastle revolt.[29] Whatever opportunities Mungyn discovered for preaching or teaching in the 1410s and 1420s, he evidently did his part to keep what Kantik Ghosh calls the characteristic Lollard habit of "intellectual criticism and questioning" alive in some form, in some corners of the city, working for over fifteen years among the obscure Londoners, lay and clerical, who presumably gave him the means to survive.[30]

---

for a Lollard pedagogy based on a radical redefinition of the literal sense and a collapsing of the hierarchical relationship between teacher and student, neither of which seems to be Wyclif's brief in *Trialogus*.

28   At the preliminary *inquisitio*, John Loverton, "capellanus" at Shadworth's parish church of St. Michael Bassishaw, testified "quod est ita subtilis in sermonibus suis quod eum non clare intelliget, sed maxime loquitur contra religiosos et fratres" (*Register of Henry Chichele*, 3:203).

29   Mungyn appears as an unbeneficed priest of St. Stephen Walbrook in a clerical tax return of 1419–20, but he was deprived of that post by August 1421 (BL MS Add. 35096: Original tax return, Diocese of London, benefices and chaplains 1419–20). *Register of Henry Chichele*, 3:199. Maureen Jurkowski, "New Light on John Purvey," *English Historical Review* 110 (1995): 1180–90.

30   Kantik Ghosh, "Bishop Reginald Pecock and the Idea of Lollardy," in *Text and Controversy from Wyclif to Bale: Essays in Honour of Anne Hudson*, ed. Helen Barr and Ann M Hutchinson (Turnhout, 2005), 131–62, at 162.

But it was an uphill battle, given the civic authorities' belief that his mode of address was dangerous to the laity. On this matter, and especially when acting against heretics in their midst, they agreed entirely with the prosecutorial speaker in Hoccleve's famous chastisement of John Oldcastle. Intellectual questioning by the laity is nothing more than "sly coloured argumentes." Logic is the language of heresy and insurrection, grossly repellent in the populace and equally "unsemeli" when used by a layman of gentle status like Oldcastle himself. Instead of debating religious doctrine, Oldcastle should have been reading exemplary tales of Trojan heroes and Old Testament kings, the same classical and biblical figures we have seen Londoners studying in their grammar schools.[31]

The extraordinary encounter with William Estfield that brought Mungyn's London career to a halt is further evidence of this view on the part of the civic elite. The meeting took place one day in February 1428, when Mungyn improbably sat down to dinner with prominent citizens in the house of a former mayor, John Shadworth, having been invited there by Shadworth's chaplain. We do not know if the elderly Shadworth, who was in failing health, was aware that a persistent Lollard would be dining with him that day, along with his own friend, William Estfield, other mercers, and members of the local clergy.[32] But whatever his role in the affair, this was a gathering that could come to no good, for not only was Estfield a candidate for mayor at a time when London mayors were almost by definition keen detectors of heretics, he was also a close friend of William Alnwick, bishop of Norwich, England's most avid Lollard hunter. He was, moreover, an adherent of cardinal Henry Beaufort, the king's kinsman and chief financier, who, according to the very latest news of the day, was soon to lead an English army against Mungyn's teacher, Peter Payne, and the Hussites in Bohemia.[33]

---

31 *Hoccleve's Works I. The Minor Poems*, ed. Frederick J. Furnivall, Early English Text Society e.s. 61 (London, 1892), 8–24.

32 Shadworth's role in the affair remains murky. He may have been sheltering his Lollard chaplain, or he could have been the one to detect Mungyn and the chaplain, as was required by church law of those who noted signs of heresy. His eventful career is summarized by Carole Rawcliffe in J. S. Roskell et al., *The History of Parliament: The House of Commons 1386–1421* (Stroud, Gloucestershire, 1993).

33 For Estfield's contacts with the great, see Rosemary Hayes, "William Estfeld, Mercer (died 1446) and William Alnwick, Bishop (died 1449): Evidence for a Friendship?," *The Ricardian* 13 (2003): 219–59, and Davies' biography cited above. For the aborted crusade, see G. A. Holmes, "Cardinal Beaufort and the Crusade against the Hussites," *English Historical Review* 88 (1973): 721–50.

In the presence of such a guest, the remarks Mungyn was said to have made in reference to Beaufort's crusade were conversation stoppers of the first order: it was against the commandment "thou shalt not kill" to fight the Hussites, and (no doubt in reference to the Hussites' plundering of Bohemian monasteries) it was permitted for the needy to take from the rich because "all goods should be in common" ("omnia bona essent communia"). In response to a question about indulgences, presumably those being offered to Beaufort's supporters, Mungyn allegedly replied that the pope had no more power to issue indulgences than did Mungyn himself.[34]

As reported almost without variation by Estfield and five other witnesses at Mungyn's trial, these remarks are obviously simplifications of the complex views that Mungyn was trying to convey, couched in terms most likely suggested to the witnesses by overly zealous prosecutors. Indeed, that all goods should be in common is one of the beliefs attributed to heretics by the prosecutorial speaker in Hoccleve's Oldcastle poem, similarly without regard to the elaborate arguments developed for and against clerical disendowment by Wyclif and his opponents in decades of extensive scholarly debate. The clergymen among Shadworth's guests would presumably have known something of these arguments, but the narrow frame of reference implied by the citizens' reductive testimony suggests how difficult it was for a university-educated priest like Mungyn to convey positions developed within the academy to uninitiated laymen. This is not to say that Shadworth's guests were indifferent to what the crusade might mean for their city in practical terms – their dinner conversation obviously went far beyond the "convivial relaxation" that Thrupp thought was the order of the day on these occasions. But Estfield and his fellow mercers were not equipped by their educations in grammar to contend with the ideological context of Mungyn's remarks, or with the tradition of academic argument which was so foreign to their milieu. This was not Prague, where Mungyn's mentor, Peter Payne, could find merchants sympathetic to his cause, and where the citizens could hear public debates on the theological arguments for reform, pro and con.[35] This was London, where the instinctive response of a city governor to such views was to report them to the bishop, as Estfield or one of his fellow diners eventually did in Mungyn's case.

34 *Register of Henry Chichele*, 3:204.
35 Michael Van Dussen comments that, in Prague, Wycliffite doctrine was "spilling ou of the halls of the Carolinum and into the streets" (*From England to Bohemia* [Cambridge UK, 2012], 65). F. Šmahel states that a disputation in 1429 that lasted several days "wa attended by large numbers of the public" ("Payne, Peter [Peter Engliss], Wycliffite and Hussite heretic," *Oxford Dictionary of National Biography* [Oxford, 2004–]).

Looking at William Estfield's role in this story, it is tempting to write him off as one of Sylvia Thrupp's unintellectual Londoners, a merchant simply not interested in probing the theological and political issues that Mungyn raised at Shadworth's table. But he was not unintellectual in every respect; after all, this is the same Estfield whose company would soon be commissioning a classically inspired mumming in his honor. And as regards his testimony at Mungyn's trial, we might say that he was not so much unintellectual as knowingly *anti-intellectual*, in the spirit of those proceedings. Indeed, the distaste for intellectual questioning that often accompanied orthodox religious views, not least among churchmen known for their Christian classicism, was particularly evident on that occasion. This was the trial of a university graduate, convened in the chapter house of St. Paul's, during Convocation, before an imposing gathering of eminent theologians and other high churchmen ("in multitudine copiosa"), with the foremost doctor of canon law in England appearing as prosecutor, but there was no hint of the quasi-disputational exchange of ideas that took place at the trial of Richard Wyche back in 1402–4, when the defendant was asked to respond to questions about the Eucharist, using the tools, if not the full procedures, of academic argument. Instead, the prosecutor, William Lyndwood, presented Mungyn with a list of fourteen brief charges which could be answered with a simple admission or denial. A few of the charges pertained to the incriminating statements reported by Shadworth's guests, but most referred to the superficial signs of Lollardy that Lyndwood was currently in the process of encoding in his commentary on Arundel's Constitutions: for example, had Mungyn consorted with other Lollard suspects or circulated certain forbidden books.[36] It is to Mungyn's credit that he insisted on qualifying his answers and steadfastly refused to abjure the stated crimes.[37]

The immediate purpose of the list, other than the failed attempt to extract a confession from the defendant in an efficient manner, was to construct an official summary of Mungyn's heretical opinions to proclaim at St. Paul's, as evidence that England could become another Bohemia if Londoners did not support Beaufort's crusade. The more far-reaching goal was to construct a body of vigilant citizens who could readily detect heresy to the authorities on

36 *Register of Henry Chichele*, 3:198–200 (trial). Lyndwood, *Provinciale*, 302–3 (signs of heresy). From this evidence, I would argue that inquisition was not always "an intellectually creative activity for English churchmen," as proposed in *The Culture of Inquisition in Medieval England*, ed. Mary C. Flannery and Katie L. Walter (Cambridge, UK, 2013), 4.

37 It is not clear why Mungyn's repeated refusals to abjure on any point did not lead to his execution (Kightly, 545). His punishment was life imprisonment unless the archbishop chose to mitigate his sentence (*Register of Henry Chichele*, 3:205), and he is not heard from after his trial.

the basis of such a list, without having to engage in any way with the heretics' arguments. At Mungyn's trial, this determined campaign to banish academic argument from the public arena captured all in its train: the prosecuting clergy who shelved their learning for the occasion, the civic elite who took a stand against intellectual questioning on their turf, and the general public who were indoctrinated by the publicized list. Of course, the campaign did not cleanse London completely of intellectual argument. The discipline of logic continued to be practiced by scholars at the cathedral school and the scola of the friars, as part of the arts curriculum they offered or in theological disputations among the clergy. But outside of these academic venues, the animus against logical questioning proved to be long-lasting and pervasive in London's civic culture, eventually reaching into the milieu of the lesser citizens as well as the civic elite.

Reginald Pecock and the Mercers' Servants

In the years immediately following Mungyn's trial, there was taking shape in London a more considered response to the problem of heresy than we observed in that affair. This was the system of doctrinal instruction devised by Reginald Pecock, a project he conceived in the 1430s under the banner of orthodox reform and vigorously pursued until his own trial for heresy in 1458. Pecock had come to London as master of Whittington College, a house of priests overseen by the Mercers' company, and he continued to reside in the city even after he became bishop of St. Asaph and then of Chichester. He was therefore well integrated with the citizenry and thought of them as his primary audience, addressing those of high and low station, orthodox and Lollard, at various points in his extensive writings.[38] What concerns us here, however, is his eventual falling out with the citizens, and, about five years before his trial, a bitter encounter with the Mercers' servants in which the disciplines of grammar and logic played a part. The servants' rejection of Pecock's logic-based teaching shows how entrenched in London society the distaste for logical argument had become, and how the citizens looked instead to the persuasive rhetoric that was joined to the study of grammar.

Although Pecock's project was identified with logical argument, the instructional books he produced for Londoners refer to grammar as well. While his system is unique, in that it substitutes his own categories of knowledge for the Ten Commandments and other essentials of the faith, it is organized with the familiar cursus of medieval education in mind, in which logic succeeds

38 For Pecock's involvement with the Mercers in executing Richard Whittington's bequests, see Wendy Scase, "Pecock, Reginald (b. c. 1392, d. in or after 1459), bishop of Chichester and religious author," *Oxford Dictionary of National Biography* (Oxford, 2004–).

grammar on the way to philosophy and then theological study. In keeping with this scheme, Pecock's most important instructional work, the *Reule of Crysten Religioun*, begins with a Boethian dream vision much like John Seward's mystical vision of Lady Liberal Arts. A "multitude of persoonys ful comely and faire" appear to the author, signifying the "truthis of universal philosophy" – Pecock's term for the theological doctrines in Peter Lombard's *Sentences*. This dramatic appearance in the *Reule* signifies that the student has gone beyond the simple statements of doctrine in Pecock's *Donet*, the book he named after the elementary Latin grammar of Donatus, to a higher level of instruction where academic argument comes into play. At this point, the student must reject the frivolous aspects of classical learning ("strange stories, fablis of poets, new inventions") that plague the sermons of Pecock's fellow clergy, and take up the art of syllogistic logic, the best means of testing religious truths. It is important to Pecock's project, however, that the fair "truths" in his vision seem to belong to the world of "the liberal arts and three philosophies," rather than to speculative theology, as these disciplines are a more comfortable ground on which the theologian and lay reader can meet.[39]

Here one begins to see the many points of contact between Pecock's *Reule* and Wyclif's *Trialogus*, the text owned by Ralph Mungyn and one that Pecock knew very well.[40] Doctrinally, the two works belong at opposite ends of the religious spectrum, but as pedagogical projects they are remarkably akin. They are both convenient *summae* on the model of Lombard's *Sentences*. Both recognize the university arts curriculum as the most fruitful meeting point for adult learners and the learned clergy, and both focus on the moral and philosophical aspects of theology rather than the highest reaches of theological speculation. Both feature a strong magisterial figure engaged in quasi-academic debate with less qualified interlocutors. Pecock quotes his opponents rather than representing them in a Pseustis-like speaker, but the dutiful Son in the *Reule* often prompts his master, the Father, with apt questions and possible objections to his teaching, just as Alithea prompts Phronesis in Wyclif's work. Finally, both offer actual instruction in logic along with religious doctrine. It could be argued that Pecock fulfills the instructional potential of *Trialogus*, a book in Latin for priests, by writing a *summa* of the same kind in English for

---

39 *The Reule of Crysten Religioun*, ed. William Cabell Greet, Early English Text Society o.s. 171 (Oxford, 1927), 34–35.

40 Pecock responds at length to the arguments for clerical disendowment made in *Trialogus*. See *The Repressor of Overmuch Blaming of the Clergy*, ed. Churchill Babington (London, 1860), 1:275–2:415 (Part Three). For an example of Pecock's logic instruction, see *The Repressor*, 9.

laymen. Unlike Wyclif, however, Pecock believes that the academic learning in his works dignifies his readers and enables them to achieve salvation. A redemptive view of the arts and philosophy is at the root of his project, along with his dependence on logic.

Until the end of his career, Pecock hoped that his monumental project, conceived within the safe framework of the liberal arts, but promising to enhance the lay reader's understanding by means of logical reasoning, would prove so effective against heresy that it would be adopted by the English Church. But his writings record a growing chorus of opposition. By the time he was himself made heretical in 1458, his work had been condemned not only by high churchmen and fellow theologians, the powerful city rectors, irate courtiers, and the king himself, but also by the mayor and the civic elite, the most respected segment of his primary audience, who had been much praised in his writings for their superior intellectual capacities. Jeremy Catto attributes the unanimous hostility of these groups to the loss of Pecock's important supporters at court, together with fears that his opinions might exacerbate the social turbulence that was so threatening in the 1450s; certainly these factors account for the opposition of the city governors, for whom stability was always the prime object. Their belief that Pecock was a destabilizing presence was surely reinforced by the scandal that ensued after he defended non-preaching bishops in 1447.[41]

But this does not explain why his project was also "scornyd and reprouyd" by the Mercers' servants, a group of lesser Londoners, when one of Pecock's books "came into her handis and was of hem rad."[42] These "servants" were mercers who after their apprenticeship lacked funds to become members of the livery, the company's superior branch. They worked for liveried mercers or had shops in which women manufactured goods such as shirts and ribbons, as opposed to engaging in the large-scale overseas trade that made liveried mercers like William Estfield rich. They and their fellow artisans were a volatile, often disaffected group within the London population. At just the time they were reading Pecock's book, the servants were fighting the senior mercers' efforts to squeeze them out of the company. A few years later, they would rise to attack Italian merchants whom they suspected of cutting into their trade.[43] Clearly the servants' objection

41 Jeremy Catto, "The King's Government and the Fall of Pecock, 1457–58," in *Rulers and Ruled in Late Medieval England*, ed. Rowena E. Archer and Simon Walker (London, 1995), 201–22.

42 *The Folewer to the Donet*, ed. Elsie Vaughan Hitchcock, Early English Text Society o.s. 164 (Oxford, 1924), 176–77.

43 Anne Sutton, "The Shopfloor of the London Mercery Trade, c. 1200–1500: The marginalisation of the artisan, the itinerant mercer and the shopholder," *Nottingham Medieval Studies* 45 (2001): 12–50. Sutton, *The Mercery of London*, 230–31 (Italian merchants).

to Pecock was not motivated by fear of disorder, as they themselves were part of that problem.

Rather, the servants were objecting to the logical tenor of Pecock's works. As the Son in Pecock's *Folewer to the Donet* reports, the servants had found something obviously wrong ("yuel") in the book they read, something that earned their scorn and disapproval and caused Pecock to accuse them of "detraccion" and "diffamose, maliciose, synful clateryng" (gossip). We discover elsewhere in the *Folewer* that the "evil" opinion to which they objected was Pecock's insistence that his own books, with their logical proofs of religious doctrine, were more efficacious than popular sermons. This was an assertion that had been attacked in the city's pulpits by its highly respected rectors for some time. Indeed, Pecock complains that these preachers have poisoned the minds of his prospective readers, lying and defaming him with "vnsemeli" attacks against his use of logic; for they "wolden lauȝe and calle 'sophym,' whanne it was alleggid that a trouth was prouyd by sillogisme."[44] Evidently, the sentiment against logical argument was still so persistent in London that the servants ignored the grammatical aspect of Pecock's curriculum, the simple Donets written for their benefit, and joined the preachers and the elite in opposing the entire project.

Given the uncertain circumstances of their lives, it is not difficult to see how the Mercers' servants might have preferred the comforting and unassailable essentials of the faith to the idiosyncratic, argumentative instruction in Pecock's books. In taking this stand, however, they were cutting themselves off from one of the chief models of intellectual questioning available in their milieu, the other being the Lollard classroom, of which we have little evidence from London at this time. And having rejected logic, they could not fall back on the resources of grammar as the city's elite could do. As Anne Sutton has pointed out, these lesser freeman were literate, but had "only basic reading, writing and arithmetic and the Latin picked up from a primer and the liturgy"; it was the liveried members of the company who were likely to have "Latin grammar." Pecock himself calls attention to this deficiency by haughtily responding to their attack in Latin: "Cum recte viuas, ne cures verba malorum" (If you live righteously, you need not mind the words of the wicked). This moral is from Cato's *Distichs*, an elementary

44 *The Folewer*, 176–78, 10–11. Pecock made a formal accusation of libel against the city rectors in these same terms, claiming that they slandered him "asserendo illas [conclusiones] esse sophisticas et continentes intra se terminos incompetentes et indebitos" ("by asserting that his conclusions were sophistical and were arrived at using improper and unacceptable logical terms"), to the great confusion of many in the city of London. This document is printed at the end of *The Repressor*, ed. Babington, 615. R. M. Ball identifies Pecock's detractors as the city rectors in "The Opponents of Bishop Pecock," *Journal of Ecclesiastical History* 48 (1997): 230–62.

Latin schoolbook often found in the company of Theodulus' *Eclogue*, a book for the elite in a language the servants did not understand. Nor did the servants have ready access to Cato in the vernacular where he was often quoted; according to Sutton's research, the books they owned were mainly primers and devotional aids. The cost of books was an issue for artisan readers, as Pecock himself was well aware, having written a short, cheap version of the *Donet* for this audience called *The Poore Mennis Myrrour*.[45]

Having rejected logic, and without access to grammar, the Mercers' servants and their fellow artisans would seem to be a truly unintellectual group of London citizens, *if* we did not know of their enthusiasm for sermons. Thrupp briefly suggests sermons as a possible source of intellectual nourishment for Londoners, and indeed the standard of preaching in the city's parishes was conspicuously high at this time, thanks to the influx of learned clergy in the 1430s and after. Although almost none of their repertory has survived, we know that the city's learned preachers collected vast resources of scriptural commentary and patristic lore for use in their London sermons. While they were averse to theological questioning and speculation, their preaching reflected an equally serious intellectual enterprise grounded in the study of the Church Fathers, and, in doing so, it incidentally offered the artisans an indirect way to experience grammar. Because the preachers favored the literal sense of the biblical text, their scholarship had important affinities with elementary grammatical study, and the ideas of eloquence they derived from the Church Fathers, though restrained and directed to the acquisition of Christian wisdom, had much in common with the Ciceronian rhetoric that was introduced in grammar schools.[46] A surviving sermon on the Annunciation by one of Pecock's London contemporaries illustrates both of these tendencies, first going over the biblical text line by line, with unusually close attention to the meanings of words and proper names, and then developing the five virtues of the Virgin and

---

45 *The Folewer*, 176 (Cato). Anne Sutton, "The Acquisition and Disposal of Books for Worship and Pleasure by Mercers of London in the Later Middle Ages," in *Manuscripts and Printed Books in Europe 1350–1550*, ed. Emma Cayley and Susan Powell (Liverpool, 2013), 95–114, at 95.

46 I discuss the London rectors' ministry, books, and sermons in "London after Arundel: Learned Rectors and the Strategies of Orthodox Reform," in *After Arundel: Religious Writing in Fifteenth-Century England*, ed. Vincent Gillespie and Kantik Ghosh (Turnhout, 2011), 187–208. For Ciceronian rhetoric at the grammar school level, see Marjorie Curry Woods, "The Classroom as Courtroom," *Ciceroniana* n.s. 13 (2009), 203–15.

their opposite vices as they apply to secular lords, using Ciceronian techniques of praise and blame.[47]

On the whole, however, the Mercers' servants confirm the wide applicability of Thrupp's conclusions regarding the merchants' lack of intellectual curiosity. Particularly important for all groups of citizens is her recognition that their impressive degree of literacy did not necessarily imply critical thinking. This is an observation to keep in mind when we consider the various forms of legal proceeding, documentary practice, and practical information gathering that have been taken rather loosely to exemplify medieval intellectual activity. What Thrupp did *not* see was that the Londoners' aversion to questioning and debate was a dangerous anti-intellectualism produced in the course of religious and political controversy, and not just a function of their preoccupation with commerce. She therefore did not recognize what a potent weapon this attitude could be when unleashed against Ralph Mungyn and Reginald Pecock, for instance, or how it could be used to reduce the city's artisans to conformity. As for positive evidence of intellectual activity, Thrupp also failed to take account of the classicizing "initiatives" launched by the merchants in their campaign to distinguish themselves from the artisans, probably because these pageants and entertainments did not produce the lively ideological debates she hoped to find.

What needs to be investigated more fully in regard to such debates is the potential of grammar-school rhetoric for taking on the burden of logical argument in London's public sphere. As it appears, the Londoners' distaste for intellectual argument was focused on academic logic and did not extend to the less formal, persuasive reasoning that belonged to the discipline of rhetoric and historically was the method of choice when discussing public policy. As codified in Cicero's *De inventione* and introduced to advanced students in grammar schools, this "softer" form of logic had long been available to Londoners in legal and parliamentary proceedings, literary works by the great London poets, and books of advice to rulers, but it took on special importance when the Lancastrian-Yorkist conflict produced a wave of political discussion in the city. In the collection of political documents and treatises compiled for the great draper Thomas Cook junior, around 1480, there is a telling example: a chapter from Sir John Fortescue's *Governance of England* that addresses the same issue of property ownership raised by the logician Ralph Mungyn, but does so under the rules of rhetorical argument. Like Mungyn, Fortescue refers to Bohemia, where a cruelly impoverished populace looted the rich and "made all their goodes to be commen," but for him Bohemia does not call to mind

---

47 "The Annunciation of the Blessed Virgin Mary (John Dygon)," in *Preaching in the Age of Chaucer: Selected Sermons in Translation*, ed. Siegfried Wenzel (Washington, DC, 2012), 165–81.

the recondite proofs used to argue against clerical property in academic tracts like *Trialogus*: it is rather one of many likely consequences, similar cases, and disadvantageous results a rhetorician could bring to bear against the bad policy of keeping the commons poor.[48] It would seem that in the readers of such arguments about policy we have something close to the intellectually engaged Londoners Thrupp desired. If so, that would be a triumph for grammar, but not a total defeat for logic.

48   For these and other "attributes of actions" in Cicero, see M. C. Leff, "The Topics of Argumentative Invention in Latin Rhetorical Theory from Cicero to Boethius," *Rhetorica* 1 (1983): 23–44. For the kinds of argument proper to rhetoric and their origin in formal logic, see Hanns Hohmann, "Logic and Rhetoric in Legal Argumentation: Some Medieval Perspectives," *Argumentation* 12 (1998): 39–55. For Cook's copy of Fortescue, see *The Politics of Fifteenth-Century England: John Vale's Book*, ed. Margaret Lucille Kekewich et al. (Stroud, Gloucestershire, 1995), 240–42, at 241.

Social Memory, Literacy, and Piety in Fifteenth-Century Proofs of Age

JOEL T. ROSENTHAL

This essay draws on Proof of Age hearings that were conducted by a local jury of twelve men as part of royal Inquisitions Post Mortem to establish that an heiress or an heir had reached the age of majority and could now claim her or his estate.[1] The oral testimony of the jurors consists largely of memories that indicate how and why the critical day of the heir's birth or baptism – many years earlier – sticks in their minds. These all-male juries offer a large number of very terse (or compressed) testimonies – hundreds and hundreds of "memories" providing us with an array of mnemonic tales, mostly in the form of one-line recollections. What light do these memories shed on the jurors' world, mixing recollections of the mundane with the picturesque, the highly personal with the disinterested or what was learned at second or third hand? I argue here that even if many of the memories offered are formulaic, in some instances perhaps the mere recitation of a standardized, boiler-plate recollection, they are nevertheless of great interest because of what memories and what kinds of memories – whether genuine or not – have been selected. As Brian Stock reminds us, "the single great storehouse of meaning is memory," and there was a vast array of memories and false memories

---

1   The first volume of the Inquisitions Post Mortem appeared in 1904, covering the reign of Henry III, and since the series reached the reign of Edward III in 1909, the volumes have included the Proofs of Age. See also Christine Carpenter, "General Introduction to the New Series," in Kate Parkin, ed., *Calendar of Inquisitions Post Mortem*, vol. XXII, 1–42, at 34–6, dealing with the proofs of age; and S. S. Walker, "Proofs of Age of Feudal Heirs in Medieval England," *Mediaeval Studies* 35 (1973): 306–23. Unfortunately, Proofs of Age receive almost no attention in Michael Hicks, ed., *The Fifteenth-Century Inquisitions Post Mortem: A Companion* (Woodbridge, Suffolk, 2012). Though it appeared too late to be incorporated into this paper, William Deller's "Proofs of Age 1246 to 1430: Their Nature, Veracity, and Use as Sources," in *The Later Medieval Inquisitions Post Mortem: Mapping the Medieval Countryside and Rural Society*, ed. M. A. Hicks (Woodbridge, Suffolk, 2016), 136–60, is an excellent overview of these sources.

Special thanks to Maryanne Kowaleski, who asked me to contribute to this volume, and to Caroline M. Barron for some specific references and a generous interest in my findings.

81

from which to pick and choose.[2] Here we are dealing with "social memory" – memory articulated in public before one's peers, by men participating in a formal act of inquiry.

This essay focuses on several specific categories of testimony, of memory, that have been selected from the wide assemblage of jurors' testimonies because they complement two themes characteristic of Mary Erler's scholarship. One is that of literacy, written records, and books. The other is more diverse: memories that reflect the laity's interest in, knowledge of, and involvement in matters of the church; that is, with the church as the guardian of a belief system and as an institution overseeing and touching upon much of daily life. Memories of this latter sort rest on the proposition that the lives of the laity were closely interwoven with the rituals, structure, and personnel of the church and, furthermore, that the laity were aware of and knowledgeable about such issues.[3] In the discussion that follows, the memories have been plucked from the nine volumes of *Inquisitions post Mortem* that run from 1399 to 1447.[4]

2   Brian Stock, *The Implications of Literacy: Written Language and Models of Interpretation in the Eleventh and Twelfth Centuries* (Princeton, 1983), 13.

3   Of Mary Erler's many publications, those closest to the themes developed below are *Women, Reading, and Piety in Late Medieval England* (Cambridge, UK, 2002); "The Laity," in *A Companion to the Early Printed Book in Britain, 1476–1558*, ed. Vincent Gillespie and Susan Powell (Cambridge, UK, 2014), 134–49; "Religious Women after the Dissolution: Continuing Community," in *London and the Kingdom: Essays in Honour of Caroline M. Barron*, ed. Matthew Davies and Andrew Prescott, Harlaxton Medieval Studies 6 (Donington, Lincolnshire, 2008), 135–45; "Widows in Retirement: Locale, Patronage, Spirituality, Reading at the Gaunts, Bristol," *Religion and Literature* 37 (2005): 51–75; "Devotional Literature," in *The Cambridge History of the Book in Britain*, vol. 3: *1400–1557*, ed. Lotte Hellinga and J. B. Trapp (Cambridge, UK, 1999), 495–525; "Three Fifteenth-Century Vowesses," in *Medieval London Widows*, ed. Caroline M. Barron and Anne F. Sutton (London, 1994), 163–84.

4   J. L. Kirby, ed., *Calendar of Inquisitions Post Morten and other Analogous Documents*, vol XVIII: *1–6 Henry IV: 1399–1405* (London, 1987); J. L. Kirby, ed., *Calendar of Inquisition Post Mortem*, vol. XIX: *7–14 Henry IV: 1405–1413* (London, 1992); J. L. Kirby, ed., *Calendar of Inquisitions Post Mortem*, vol. XX: *1–5 Henry V: 1413–1418* (London, 1995); J. L. Kirby and Janet H. Stevenson, eds., *Calendar of Inquisitions Post Mortem*, vol. XXI: *6–9 Henry V: 1418–1422* (Woodbridge, Suffolk, 2002); Kate Parkin, ed., *Calendar of Inquisitions Post Mortem*, vol. XXII: *1–5 Henry VI: 1422–27* (Woodbridge, Suffolk, 2003); Claire Noble ed., *Calendar of Inquisitions Post Mortem*, vol. XXIII: *6–10 Henry VI: 1427–32* (Woodbridge Suffolk, 2004); M. L. Holford, S. A. Mileson, C. V. Noble, and Kate Parkin, eds., *Calendar of Inquisitions Post Mortem*, vol. XXIV *11–15 Henry VI: 1432–1437* (Woodbridge, Suffolk 2010); Claire Noble, ed., *Calendar of Inquisitions Post Mortem*, vol. XXV: *16–20 Henry VI 1437–1442* (Woodbridge, Suffolk, 2009); M. L. Holford, ed., *Calendar of Inquisitions Post*

The purpose behind the aggregation of the twelve jurors' memories at the Proof of Age hearing was to piece together a body of testimony to support the claim that the heiress or heir to an estate was now of age and therefore able to take in hand what had been held by a guardian during the years of minority. The basic question put to each juror by the escheator, the king's local official and representative, was "how do you know that she or he is now of age," or "how do you remember that the date of birth or baptism was the requisite number of years ago" – the critical age being twenty-one for a male heir, sixteen for an unmarried heiress, and fourteen for the heiress if married.[5] Accordingly, the aggregation of jurors' memories was pegged to their recollection of events that had occurred on or near the day of birth or baptism. Those memorable events might be focused on the infant – the baptism or some such – or sometimes on *other* memorable events that had more or less coincided with the heir's first appearance. Though in some cases the twelve memories revolved around a common theme, such as all the jurors having been in the church and having seen the baptism, usually there is some spread of content and timing. As well as memories of a personal nature, such as the burial of a parent or a spouse, we have memories of other ecclesiastical affairs and of various secular matters. The events recalled may have affected or occurred to the juror himself, or they could be something he knew about and now chose to offer as his contribution to the collective process.

There is controversy and/or skepticism about the reliability of many of the memories so offered.[6] Some of the statements offered do seem, in all likelihood, to be drawn from a standard repertoire, or even pre-fabricated, and occasionally

---

Mortem, vol. XXVI: *21–25 Henry VI: 1442–1447* (Woodbridge, Suffolk, 2009). References to the entries are given, in parentheses, as (18/325).

5   E. R. Stevenson, "The Escheator," in *The English Government at Work, 1327–1336*, vol. II: *Fiscal Administration*, ed. William A. Morris and Joseph R. Strayer (Cambridge, MA, 1947), 109–67. In a quantitative check Proofs of Age were but a small part of the serious matter of the transmission of real property. In vol. XXVIII of the *Inquisitions Post Mortem* (and the volume was chosen at random) there are fifty Proofs of Age among over 1,100 entries, most of them being Inquisitions Post Mortem designed to take an inventory of the deceased's estate and his or her next heir (though there are also a fair number of documents that assigned a widow her dower).

6   Matthew Holford, "'Testimony (to some extent fictitious)': Proofs of Age in the First Half of the Fifteenth Century," *Historical Research* 81 (2008): 1–25; though skeptical of their veracity, Holford provides a thorough survey of the discussion of the value or reliability of the Proofs as a source; also, John Bedell, "Memory and Proof of Age in England, 1272–1327," *Past & Present* 162 (1999): 1–27. For an assessment that considers the Proofs generally reliable (without denying the problems they pose), see Joel T. Rosenthal, *Telling Tales: Sources and Narration in Late Medieval England* (University Park, PA, 2003), 1–62. Much of the discussion of the value and veracity of the Proofs is to be found in reviews of

show up in virtually the same wording at hearings well separated by time and distance. "Memories" of this sort may have been handed out to jurors by the escheator, whom we might think of as passing around the fifteenth-century version of the three-by-five notecard. The frequent repetition of certain kinds of memories and phrases certainly does argue for a routinized approach with ready-made recollections. However, whatever their "reality," the memories offered always did the job. In the discussion below we shall consider such routinized memories only briefly. Most jurors in this "theater of baptism" recall such things as having been sent to fetch the midwife or the wet nurse, assisting in the baptism itself, summoning godparents, meeting those going to or returning from church (with or without the baby), fetching wine or water for the ceremony or the celebration, and so forth.[7] The heirs to the estates themselves are but names off stage: they never play an active part in the proceedings that were so much in their interest.

Two categories of what may be standardized recollections reveal something of the nature of the pre-fabricated memories. Whether they reflect "real" events of twenty-one years ago, or whether they were offered so frequently simply because virtually any memory was sufficient, does not seem to matter. One popular and oft-used form of these stock recollections has to do with the memory of a broken shin, usually – though not always – the shin of the juror himself. If the broken-bone tales rest on reality then it would seem that a good many of the men of fifteenth-century England were walking around with a serious limp. Such memories were frequently cited, and appear in most volumes of the *Inquisitions*. In volume XIX (1405–13) we have separate memories of eight broken shins, four broken arms, and one broken finger (in addition to some fatal accidents). There is the occasional extra touch: the man had been "badly crushed," or had fallen from a horse and broken a shin, "whence he has suffered much pain," or even, "whence he has *often* suffered pain." We also find slight variations: it might have been the right shin or the left arm, while one juror recalled a finger had been broken when he "played at bucket play." And if a fall from a horse was the main culprit in volume XIX, in other volumes we have comparable tales of shins broken through wrestling, playing football, being in the wrong place at the wrong

volumes of the *Inquisitions*; Bedell, Holford, and Rosenthal all go through this material though they differ in their conclusions.
7   Taken from vol. 26: 587 for fetching the midwife, 149 for fetching the wet nurse, 142 for assisting at the baptism, 464 for summoning the godparents, 144 and 146 (among others) for fetching wine or water for the ceremony. We can add the juror who was merely in church and saw the baptism – he being but one of many who offered such a memory (142) – and the juror who met the godparents on their way to church (354).

time at a bear-baiting, slipping on the ice, leaping a ditch, being hit by an arrow, or falling off a ladder.[8]

Memories of great windstorms also appear repeatedly. These storms seem to have been as memorable as falls from a horse, and almost as frequent. We might doubt that such memories were actually based on meteorological reality, since they rather give the impression that the villages and hamlets of the kingdom lay in the path of hurricanes, tornadoes, and cyclones. We can mine vol. XXIII of the *Inquisitions* (1427–32) for tales of this sort. One juror remembered that "such a wind blew up on the day that he and others feared the collapse of their weakened houses." Even in the middle of Norwich such a storm could happen: "in the city . . . many houses collapsed." One juror's grange was "demolished by a storm," while another recollected that "his apple tree was brought to the ground." Yet another remembered that his building "beside the churchyard of the church" had been blown down. Even today memories of weather tend to be dramatic, and not always credible, and it seems little has changed. Nonetheless, the circumstantial dressing was invariably good enough for the escheator.[9]

Occasionally a juror offered a memory of some unusual secular event, whether it had affected him personally or was something he just happened to know about and could now remember. Such tales, in contrast to the broken shins and high winds, sound more convincing, the sort of events that would stick in the memory. We have the juror who remembered the key date because it was when he began his journey to Berwick "to fight the king's enemies, the Scots" (24/396). Men in the west told tales of rebellion along the Welsh border: a juror had seen Henry, prince of Wales, "first born of Henry IV ride with a great army" as he moved toward Monmouth (23/140). One could well remember that "on the same day the Bretons entered Ilfracombe and there took two men and set out to sea with them" (26/143). Equally memorable was the time when "Owyn Glendordy

---

8   Chosen at random from the nine volumes, the eight broken shins recalled in vol. 19 are: 186, 603, 777, 782, 786, 898, 996 (juror saw the abbot of Malmesbury fall and break his right shin), and 339 (daughter Joan broke her shin). In addition we find at 666 a juror who had fallen while returning home from the baptism and had broken his arm; and at 778, one who fell into a ditch and has "often suffered pain." At 191, a simple fall from a horse is recalled; at 997, just a fall. Some comparable memories were rather grim: at 781 we learn that a chaplain "broke his neck . . . and they [two jurors in unison] attended before the coroner to view the body."

9   As found in vol. 23 (and typical of all the volumes of *IPMs*): 141 (and numerous other cases) for the wind that blew so hard it was feared houses would collapse; 593 for "many houses collapsed" in Norwich; 421 for the grange being demolished; 718 for the apple tree having been blown down; and 716 for the building beside the churchyard being blown down.

came with his large army to the gates of Cardiff" (20/184). It was an unruly world, and we have a man who had been taken by Welsh rebels in 1408, when they "plundered all his belongings" (23/417). Still another man – touching two of our themes – "was injured in the head and shin at the Battle of Shrewsbury" (22/529). Though the Proofs mostly reflect the world of village and countryside, one vivid London memory was offered: "in that year in London in the month of May two fine ridings, of the fishmongers and goldsmiths, all parading and celebrating on horseback as was never before seen" (20/842). And to move from the national to the local, there was a memory of when the town bailiff "placed Alice Blast on the tumbril . . . for many defaults and transgressions perpetrated by her to the harm of the whole vill" (22/673). A man who says he remembers the date because it was when his daughter died of plague seems credible (24/562), though whether this was a secular memory event touching medical history, or one best seen as a personal and family tale, is an open question.

Social memory, as noted above, is memory offered in oral form and set within a social context, which means in the presence of one's fellows – contemporaries, neighbors, kinsmen, companions in work and play. Each juror's statement, whether vivid or formulaic, his own or pre-fabricated, highly personalized or nodding toward some generality of the human condition or an external event, had to be credible within the context of the day's proceedings. And though the hearing invariably moved toward a foregone conclusion, it was a legal as well as a socio-economic affair, its findings to be recorded and then preserved in the king's records. Every "memory" had to stand as a useable social memory, regardless of whether the event being recalled had actually happened, or had happened at the time of the birth or baptism, or was a mere legal fiction that sufficed for the purpose. Furthermore, each juror's testimony was his specific and personal contribution to the aggregation of the twelve memories. In most instances we have twelve separate memories from twelve jurors, though very often there are individualized repetitions of the same event and even joint memories with three or four or even six men of the twelve affirming as one. And whether we have twelve separate memories or some lesser number, all the statements were ultimately bound together into a collective and oralized affirmation regarding age of the heir. Our jurors point us down the path that leads from orality, memory, and perhaps local lore, toward the relatively fixed world of the written record.[10]

Social or collective memory and the transition from oral testimony to the written record enshrined and perhaps highlighted what, for us, can seem little more than existential assertions about age and recollection. Though they were

---

10   M. T. Clanchy, *From Memory to Written Record: England 1066–1307*, 3rd edn. (Chichester 2013) – a groundbreaking work that remains the basic text.

self-referential or self-contained, memories of this sort were good enough for the business of the day, as when a juror recounted that he "had a daughter . . . of the same age [as the heir] . . . and [the priest] baptized her in that church on the same day" (18/315). It might be even more assertive: "In the week . . . William, my own son, was born who is now 16 years of age and more" (23/597), with no need to articulate the rest of the syllogism. There were occasional hints at more detail, not forthcoming or at least not recorded and presumably not needed: "the other jurors, separately examined, agree and say that they know for the following reasons, all referring to events that happened 21 years ago" (22/189). Most tantalizing of all is the bland statement, "the jurors had other notable evidence if it were necessary to produce it" (19/901). But to set against the charges of standardized testimonies (probably a valid critique in numerous cases) and self-referential memories, we must keep in mind when assessing and assembling these recollections that the jurors did have to satisfy common sense; that is, they had to ensure that their testimonies did not undermine the memories or credibility of their peers, who were presumably standing or sitting right beside them. What any given juror said had to be reasonable in the context of his age, his social standing, and his role in the social web of village, community, or neighborhood.[11] A juror in Kent, known to have never crossed the Thames, was unlikely to reminisce about having been wounded fighting the Scots, nor would a man who had always been a local fixture be likely to talk about the date of his return from Jerusalem. Social memory was a guiding or controlling force. It may not always give us the lived reality we might wish for but, whatever the mnemonic being offered, it had to carry some semblance of conviction in the face of the other eleven jurors, as well as seeming believable to the king's officer who would convey the day's findings back to headquarters.[12]

Let us now turn to those memories that touch on the literacy theme and that thereby, either explicitly or implicitly, acknowledge the power, the mystery, and

11 Carpenter, "General Introduction," 18–19, on the social status of the jurors; they were middling-level men, for the most part, and presumably locals since they had been there *then* and were still on hand to testify the requisite number of years later. Each juror gave his age; the questions raised by these self-stated ages are discussed in J. T. Rosenthal, *Old Age in Medieval England* (Philadelphia, 1996), 33–43. See James Fentress and Chris Wickham, *Social Memory*, New Perspectives on the Past (Oxford, 1992), 91, on why different social groups remember differently.

12 The estate's guardians rarely objected to either the hearing or its conclusions, 23/314: the two custodians "attended but could give no reason why the lands and tenements should not be freed to the heir." For a dispute that touched on both the heirs' ages and claims to the estates, see Christine Carpenter, ed., *The Armburgh Papers* (Woodbridge, Suffolk, 1998).

the relative permanence of the written record. There is an air of solemnity to these one-liners that marks them as particularly noteworthy, coming as they do alongside hundreds of laconic statements about baptism, marriage, and death. We will look at two categories of memory that rest on the recollection of something having been set down in writing. There are those memories that attest to the creation of a written record of the heiress's or heir's birth or baptism – a memory directly tied to the critical ceremony that defined the day when the counting began and that was recorded in a service book. The other category of recollections that defers to the power of the written word covers the many memories of secular transactions recalled because they had been finalized by a document – a charter, deed, indenture, or a written and sealed contract of some sort – at or around the critical time.

Some of these testimonies are of particular interest, resting as they do on recollections of *the* key date because that date and the events that made it memorable had been written down in some fashion.[13] Most often the tale is along the lines of a juror's memory of the priest putting down the date of the baptism, though we also have memories that attribute some action by or agency to the juror himself, a layman's dip into the swirling waters of literacy and service books. Our juror might have held the book for the priest during the service. In the memories covered by this theme of books and writing we get an idea of the reverence, among these middling-level men, for that which was set down on the page. Though there are variations on the theme, as we have said, the basic scenario was much along the lines of "John de Dalton, chaplain of Alexander, wrote the name and date of Thomas' birth in a missal in the church and this writing proves his age" (18/530). A common variation was "Thomas the father asked the then rector to write the day and year of the birth in a martyrology, and so it is now recorded and they [the four jurors who offer this as a common memory] know the date" (18/996). Another common recollection was of someone who had participated in the ceremony or perhaps had simply been a close witness: he had "heard mass . . . and held the book for the priest at the baptism" (18/1178). At times a juror might ascribe a more active role to himself, for instance having been the sacristan of the parish church during the ceremony (24/562). One man said he had been "in church reading the third morning lesson and heard William [the heir] crying at the font" (18/674) – perhaps a testament to lay literacy as well as

13   In 1439 Pope Eugenius IV told the Armenian church that "Among all the sacraments holy baptism holds the first place because it is the gateway to the spiritual life; by it we are made members of Christ and belong to His body, the Church" (Council of Florence, Decree for the Armenians, in *The Christian Faith in the Doctrinal Documents of the Catholic Church*, ed. J. Neuner and J. Dupuis, rev. edn. (New York, 1981), 390 (§1412).

to memory. Things seen and things heard are mentioned: he "heard the rector to order the clerk . . . to enroll William's name and the time of his birth in the book of benefactors [*mortilagium*] . . . as a perpetual memorial of the birth" (22/530). A significant level of involvement is evident for the juror who "wore a surplice and held the book from which the rector read during the baptism" (26/466).[14]

Given how many jurors in our survey cited the memory of something being written – and these recollections generally seem genuine – any additional scrap of detail is more than welcome. While the social status of these jurors makes it unlikely that they owned their own Books of Hours (that "best seller of the Middle Ages"), they certainly knew to distinguish the different service books. Along with the martyrology referred to above we have a juror who "was then the parish clerk and held the Bible in his hands while Christine was baptized" (22/235). The date could be verified: it was possible in one instance to "know his age by inspection of a book of martyrs . . . in which the birth was noted" (18/309). A comparable memory takes us to the psalter: "the date of the marriage was entered in a psalter . . . and by inspection of that he knows the date" of the baptism, a phrasing that seems to indicate the juror's own literacy (19/188). There is a little more detail in one memory: "He recorded John's birth in the table of contents of his psalter," probably referring to the first recto page within the covers (21/876). At one hearing we have both a Bible-based memory and a recollection of the juror himself having played a role. He "saw the parson write the day of . . . birth in the church Bible and then read the writing there," while a fellow juror said that he himself had written "his son's age in his book called 'Prymer,'" thereby seeming to suggest both his own literacy and a role in the ceremony (22/530). Odd touches of memory give an extra degree of credibility, not that the testimonies were ever questioned; for example, "He saw the parson write John's age in a book kept in the south part of the chancel" (21/874). In a common memory offered by four jurors speaking as one, they saw the parson write the date in a missal, though they had actually come to the church "to make offerings before a picture of the Virgin Mary" and just happened to catch the baptism (19/777). It is more common for a memory to invoke the priest's literacy than the juror's, for example in the recollection that "He saw the parson write the day of Philip's birth in the church Bible and then read the writing there" (22/530). But there probably was a note of pride in recounting a participatory role, as in the case of the juror who

---

14　Another recollection, though it contains no actual mention of writing, yet outlines a complicated business: the juror sold a horse "on condition that it proved the best of John's horses," and he received the handsome sum of £10. But the horse injured itself and he returned 40s. as compensation (22/530).

remembered being asked by the godfather "to write the time of birth in books of three men and others" (19/777).

In a world of written Latinity, a reference to the vernacular catches the eye: "The date was written in English in a book and read out whilst they were there," a common memory offered by two jurors, though they "separately say" that it took place (20/131). For another memory resting on a parental request, we have "the father asked the parson to write in a missal in English" (20/272). The memory that really crowns this topic is one that attests, once more and quite explicitly, to the permanence and special nature of the written record: the "proctors of the church delivered a missal to the rector in the presence of the parishioners, [it] to remain in the church for use in perpetuity" (23/716). In one unusual recollection the juror "saw the monk write Joan's age in a missal" (25/298); the monk was in the church because he had accompanied his abbot, who was one of the godparents.[15]

Other memories that refer to the use of writing as a mnemonic take us out of the church and point, instead, to a variety of secular transactions. Few of these are particularly striking or out of the ordinary, were we looking at them in the setting of the local economy or manorial studies; we encounter references to leases, indentures, charters, deeds, receipts, rent rolls, apprenticeships, court rolls, and the like. What is of interest here, however, is that the memory of the date of secular business was offered to verify what was both a legal and an ecclesiastical issue. Here too, as with the date written into the missal, it was the act of writing that fixed the memory of the transaction and set the date in stone. Given the importance of these various secular affairs in the lives of the jurors who now recounted them, such memories may have been at least as vivid and important – to the juror – as those memories of a birth date of someone else's child as set down in a service book. In most of these secular recollections, at least as reported some years later, the jurors had been active parties rather than mere witnesses or bystanders.

The purchase of land or of a tenement could be formalized by a written accord: "that day seised of a messuage . . . by a charter, written at Stonor by the rector," as one juror briefly recounted (20/265). A prolonged complaint concerning an accusation of trespass was settled with "a general acquittance" on the critical day (20/265). Whatever lay behind the bald testimony of a juror in Northampton, his tale of a kinsman "who gave him his inn called 'Clyntons Inne' in Towcester by

---

15 One instance of writing concerns a will rather than a service book, and the act of writing was not done in the church. Instead, the chaplain came to the juror's house to write his wife's will: "She made him her executor and so he [the juror] knows by the date of the will" (19/780).

charter and put him into possession" would be an affair to remember and a date that was not hard to recall (21/871). One man recollected that he had come to the church to finalize the renting of 6 acres at 6s. 8d. per annum from the baby's grandfather, and after that business had been transacted the baptism had taken place; "he sealed the deed . . . and knows by the date of the deed" (19/664). We note here the parish church as the venue for the conclusion of secular business, as well as for the sacrament that welcomed the grandchild into Christ's flock.[16] It probably suited the grandfather, presumably a man of more substance than the juror, to take care of both matters at once. One juror told of having been the "receiver of rents of the manor . . . and by his receipt for the payment of the rent [he] has evidence of the age [of the heir]" (18/1178). Another knew the requisite number of years "by the date of the charter" that sealed a purchase of some land (19/158).

A transaction marked with a seal sounds quite formal, all the more likely to have been offered (and accepted) as a memory. In one record we discover business had been conducted with the prior of Haverholm and the juror still has "an indenture sealed with the common seal of that house" (23/139).[17] Another juror recalled a less happy event that marked the day: "he was arrested by servants of the vill's bailiffs by virtue of the king's writ to respond . . . in a plea of trespass at Westminster on the following quindene of Easter" (22/830). The purchase of a horse on what sounds like an installment plan also had to be covered by paper: the juror had bought a horse "called 'morel Gray' . . . for 10 marks English money, payable the following Easter . . . They made a deed of obligation . . . and they still have it in their custody" (24/560). And we might ask if a concord of peace and amity between two feuding parties might be considered as secular business? One Walter Rede and the abbot of Torre settled their quarrel in the church and "the releases were written by a monk of the abbey on the same day" (25/298).[18]

---

16 The juror said that "on the day of her birth he met many men and women coming from church who told him that Joan was baptized and a Christian" (24/268).

17 Though a monastic house would be expected to have a seal, recent scholarship has extended their use down the social scale. See P. D. Harvey and A. F. McGuiness, *Guide to British Medieval Seals* (Buffalo, NY, 1996); and Elizabeth A. New, *Seals and Sealing Practices*, Archives and the User 11 (London, 2010). For a survey of urban sealing, though focusing on an earlier period, see John A. McEwan, *Seals in Medieval London 1050–1300: A Catalogue*, London Record Society, e.s. 1 (London, 2016).

18 There are numerous references to an act of writing that finalized a secular transaction, including references to an indenture of apprenticeship (19/188), and the ceremony of homage for a tenement settled with "a letter of homage" (23/139).

Let us turn now from references to reading and writing that serve to fix the critical date in mind and memory, and consider those memories/testimonies that open the window on lay knowledge of and interest in matters ecclesiastical. These straddle the boundary between the spiritual and the secular: they focus on the date of a baptism, a sacramental proceeding, and yet they are also (and simultaneously) sited in and recorded because of their role in a secular-cum-legal proceeding, the Proof of Age inquiry. Given the importance of the church in secular and lay life, it is hardly a surprise that many memories go back to church matters that left an impression upon the ordinary men who make up our juries. We know, from those memories of birthdates inscribed into service books at a father's request and then held up for all to see, that the jurors had been spectators and semi-participants in many aspects of public life, both in and out of church and in matters both spiritual and secular.

Two types of memory of particular interest are those relating to what we can think of as personnel movements within the church and those relating to pilgrimage. The first focuses on the church as a vast reservoir of human resources, drawing upon its reserve army of labor and pointing us in the direction of such mundane issues as careers and mobility as well as toward vocation and commitment. One common memory is of a priest (or another clerk, however labeled) performing his first mass just around the day of the infant's baptism. That the priest so named and so remembered in the testimony often (or usually) was the son of the juror himself makes it a rather poignant recollection. And just as there seem to have been legions of men who went about with a limp, thanks to all those broken shins, so any alleged shortage of clerics might have been alleviated had the ranks of all those new priests paraded before us been adjusted upward on a national basis. While ordination and first mass were probably credible as *real* events of which a father might reasonably boast, that the promotion or ordination had occurred so as to coincide with (or shortly before or after) the day of baptism does seem, at the very least, fortuitous. And yet, who could deny a father's pride in harking back to this solemn ceremony, taking place the requisite number of years ago. At a lesser level, or perhaps as the first step on this ladder, we have the father who remembered the date because it was then that he "placed Richard his son in the schools at Cambridge . . . there to study grammar" (25/351).[19]

As with other lines of recollection there was a standard formulation for this particular category of remembrance, a basic and terse summation of a great event. It was much along the lines of the testimony of a juror who "had a son

---

19 The outcome could be tragic, as for the juror who sent his son "to Salisbury that day to be confirmed by the Bishop. He died there" (23/143).

ordained in that year who said his first mass in that church about the following 30 November" (18/1180). An occasional variation might be: "John his son took holy orders long before that day, and celebrated his first mass" on the day of the baptism (22/360). And even among priests, having been ordained by the bishop of London was evidently worth mentioning; the sacrament was performed by the "then bishop of London," one man recalls, looking back some twenty-one years (22/189). There was also the juror's son "promoted to priest's orders at York as appears by his letters shown to them" (18/857). It did not always have to be a son. There are a few references to a juror's brother who "that day celebrated his first mass after he was ordained" (22/363), or even to an uncle (23/143). On one occasion, it had been the ordination of and first mass by an unspecified kinsman, though kinship terminology usually gives us a more precise pointer (25/336). Other ranks and forms of clerical office were also offered in the testimonies, or at least they were so distinguished. Edmund Peese recounted that "Walter Halybred, clerk, was inducted and instituted as vicar . . . and baptized Edmund Peese his son in the font" (24/128). Or it might simply be that the juror "was in the church on that day when Robert de Coton, chaplain, celebrated his first mass" (21/671), or perhaps it was a "clerk" doing the same (21/875). Nicholas Greneham "was chosen parson of the church of Seaton before the birth of John," giving this statement a populist touch with the word "chosen" (26/588). Alternatively, the memory might be about the advancement of a canon: we find recollections that a "first born son was elected canon to the Benedictine monastery of Dorchester" (25/127), and of one John Seteryngton, unrelated to the juror but remembered as "professed as a canon in the abbey of Old Malton" (25/611). One memory captured one of those common exchanges of a living: the rector, a prebendary of York, "resigned for an exchange and Thomas Garton was inducted and instituted" (19/341).

These were all personnel moves or promotions within the ranks of the secular clergy. But the jurors also had some knowledge of life and lives within the regular ranks. On the day of the baptism at issue one juror recalled that "his son was professed as a monk" (22/363), or "his son made his profession as a monk at Fountains Abbey on the 1 January before the birth" (23/309), or he "professed as a monk on the day Elizabeth was born" (23/722). Another mentions a move to the "abbey of St. John in Colchester" (23/310). The day on which one juror's brother-in-law, a canon of the Carthusian priory of Witham, "was made prior" clearly remained a memorable one in family lore (21/876) – unusually, the precise date is recalled, May 26, 1400, perhaps a further sign of family pride in the event (which was recounted on July 1, 1421).

While a newly ordained priest might not be sure of which living he would receive, a newly sworn mendicant had presumably been free to choose his house:

one juror's son "was professed as a Franciscan friar in the friars' convent at Exeter on the same day as Christine was baptized" (22/228). In similar fashion, the son of a juror at Sudbury had chosen "the habit of the friars minor in Babwell" (19/785). Some of the testimonies indicate that our middling-level men kept an eye on the affairs of their betters. At a hearing at Cheriton in Kent we can see a local and lay awareness of and interest in neighborhood issues: the date of birth was remembered in one instance because "Agnes Bongesett, prioress of St. James's hospital, Canterbury, died that year [that is, the year of the baby's birth]. Lady Clemency prioress from the death of Agnes has been so since the death of Agnes, for 21 years" (20/846).[20] Another juror recalled that "John his son was elected abbot of Pipewell" – an event that would certainly help fix this time in the memory (23/422). Similar is the recollection that "On that day John Leek was elected as prior of Markby priory" – a Proof of Age from 1436 and referring to an election held some twenty-one years before (24/721). In a hearing at Dorchester a juror "swears that Thomas, abbot of Dorchester, was elected on the Monday after Philip's birth" [June 21].[21] Since the Proof of Age was taken in 1437, we are looking back to June 1417 (25/127). One juror, perhaps a man of somewhat higher status, recalled that he had ridden with his brother to see his wife's brother, Thomas Blysworth, "one of the canons [at Chalcombe Abbey] made abbot on 12 February 1400" (21/871).

Another ecclesiastically focused activity that seemed to stay in the memory was pilgrimage, or rather the memory of pilgrimage, either personally undertaken or

20   This is the hospital of St. James at Thanington by Canterbury. It was established in the eleventh century for (twenty-five) leprous women, but it eventually became a hospital with twenty-three sisters and a prioress, before the Black Death, and still had "brethren, sisters, and chaplains" in 1415 (David Knowles and R. Neville Hadcock, *Medieval Religious Houses, England and Wales* [London, 1971], 397).

21   Because of gaps in the record and the uncertainty of names it is not possible to verify these claims against the lists of men as given in David M. Smith, *The Heads of Religious Houses, England and Wales*, vol. III: *1377–1540* (Cambridge, UK, 2008). At Markby, a house of Augustinian canons, John Leek was prior from 1395 until he resigned in 1438. He was also known as John Fenthorpe de Leek and as John Fenton (Smith, 46–77); at Dorchester, Robert Codesdone had been abbot in 1393–94, John Wynchestre was referred to as the late abbot in 1341, and John Clifton seems to have been abbot between 1438 and his death in 1445 (Smith, 423); at Witham, John de Evercriche was cited in 1386, Nicholas de la Felde in 1402 (no source given), and William FitzWilliam from 1408 until he was relieved of office in 1421 (Smith, 364–65); for Pipewell, Roger had been abbot from 1383 until 1401, succeeded by John de Coventre in 1405 and mentioned as late as 1418, then Stephen de Rysshton (who was dead by 1436), and John Green, who presided from 1436 into the 1450s (Smith, 319–20). As these details show, finding matches between the reference book and the jurors' memories is not an easy task.

the recollected journey of another – kinsman or friend – whose departure and/ or return was well known. We have about two dozen memories of this sort, and we find that journeys to St. Thomas at Canterbury, to Jerusalem, and to Rome (sometimes referred to as the Roman curia) were of about equal popularity, each drawing some six or seven pilgrims or memories. A few others had gone to Santiago de Compostella in Spain, while others had chosen to stay closer to home – York, Bridlington, and "St. Margaret's."[22] Here too there was a basic memory, a bald statement: "on the Tuesday after that day [he] set out for the court of Rome" (18/1178). A journey to Jerusalem might be labeled in several ways: one juror recalled when he "began his pilgrimage to the Holy Land" (32/722). But not everyone, as we have noted, felt the call to go so far from home. One man said he had bought a horse "to ride on pilgrimage to St. Thomas of Canterbury" (25/298), and others of his countrymen were content to visit York (25/563). The pilgrim who set off for Canterbury was going from Exeter so it was a fair journey, if a lesser undertaking than a trek to Spain; the man who sought York was another with a lower horizon. Mostly the pilgrims, whether the jurors or someone about whom they spoke, had a successful journey, though one such undertaking ended on a sad note: "on the morrow of the baptism John his brother set out for the Holy Land and died on the journey" (19/999). Exotic travel clearly left memories that were out of proportion with the time the adventure occupied – for those who returned safely – and memorable dates and memorable journeys remained a reasonable pairing for recollection and testimony.

Against the hundreds of laconic recollections of the basic realities of life and death that make up the majority of our imposing list of memories in the volumes of the *Inquisitions*, there are a few that go their own way (though usually not very far). Some of these merely focus on the parish church, that most familiar physical presence of the faith and the center of the community. A juror might recall something about the construction of or repairs to the building, as when four men had acted together to contract with a carpenter "for repairing a chantry, called 'Chelrey Chantry,'" and while negotiating on this they witnessed the baptism (20/268).[23] One juror told of seeing a window installed in the church,

22 Jonathan Sumption, *Pilgrimage: An Image of Medieval Religion* (Totowa, NJ, 1975), esp. ch. 11 (pp. 168–210), "The Journey." For a fourteenth-century Proof of Age testimony that involves a pilgrimage, see Diana Webb, *Pilgrims and Pilgrimage in the Medieval West*, International Library of Historical Studies 12 (London, 1999), 175. It is of interest to note that there is no reference to pilgrimage to Walsingham in Norfolk among the jurors' recollections.

23 The baby's maternal grandfather had been a Chelrey and, presumably, the founder of the chantry. This means it was still being adequately endowed one or two generations later.

"in which the date is written" (19/188), taking us back in an unusual way to our "things written." The communal aspects of life can also be attested to: "he and other neighbours bought the gret bell of the church, called 'sweet maria of Shorehoge'" (26/148); or there is the tale of the juror who had been in church "to receive 20 marks from parishioners in payment for building a new roof for the church and also received 13*s.* 4*d.* for himself" (20/269). But it was not all wine and roses: "the parochial church . . . was burgled that day and stripped by thieves of chalice, Bible, and altar cloth" (22/362). It could get worse: "on 23 April 1385 the church of Weaverthorpe . . . was polluted by bloodshed . . . and was reconsecrated [in 1407] by the suffragan of [the] archbishop of York on the day of the birth" (19/342). A similar task fell to the suffragan of Winchester, cleansing a church after "the effusion of blood and pollution" (19/1002), while another memory turned to the cleansing of the graveyard after "pollution by the effusions of blood" (20/184). Compared to these crises, the consecration of the altar of St. John the Baptist "on the same day" was not all that dramatic, though no doubt it had been an event of note in the village (26/148).

A few memories stand out for the level of detail they offer, as with the juror who said the date of the baptism was memorable because it was on that day that Nicholas Boister killed John Curteys, Dominican friar, "in self-defense near the churchyard" (22/366). Though the testimonies are generally devoid of such material, there is one breath of scandal, the day of the baptism having just preceded that day on which "Margaret Morys . . . was then pregnant by Thomas Holm, chaplain, and for shame took her goods on the following morning [of the baptism] and left the town" (19/783). A more decorous memory came from the juror who had been sent to see if the parish church had been decorated in preparation for the baptism; he was able to report that he had found "the altar hung with ten gold clothes and the font suitably decorated with ten white silken cloths" (23/596). But the heavy hand of social control was also to be reckoned with, and we have one case of a juror who recalled that he had declined an invitation to be the godfather because "such a spiritual relationship could in future, be an impediment to marriage" (23/309).[24] One memory opened a window on social hierarchy and current views about the link between sexual activity, pregnancy, and lactation: the juror's wife agreed to be the nurse for three

---

24 See James A. Brundage, *Law, Sex, and Christian Society in Medieval Europe* (Chicago 1987), on impediments, with attention to the later Middle Ages in ch. 10. For an idea of how often the rules about marriage were ignored or broken, leading to petitions to the papal curia, see Peter D. Clarke and Patrick N. R. Zutshi, eds., *Supplications from England and Wales in the Registers of the Apostolic Penitentiary, 1410–1503*, 3 vols., The Canterbury and York Society 103–5 (London, 2012–15).

years and our poor juror left town "because John de Holand forbade him to have marital relations with Isabel [his wife] during that time" (21/149).

Two memories went back to what the jurors asserted had been miracle cures. One man told of how and when "a miracle took place . . . [when] one of Richard's boys . . . was exhausted by fever to the point of death but he was saved by St. William [of York] on that day," as he related in a proceeding at Ripley, Yorkshire (23/309).[25] But St. William of York was not allowed to monopolize this rich field of popular belief; another man told of St. Osmund coming to the rescue. The juror in this case had broken his leg (he "fell from his cart") but was lucky enough to have "friends [who] carried him to Salisbury and placed him before the tomb of St. Osmund in the chapel of St. Mary in the cathedral church . . . he was then miraculously healed" (22/828). Given the high incidence of broken shins and arms, such medical aid would have been very welcome, though it seems to have been in short supply.

To us, though not necessarily to the men of the day, two memories that talk of Lollards and Lollardy stand out. One recollection was laconic: the comment that "a heretic was burned at Smithfield" was given as testimony at a hearing in 1432, and takes us back to 1411 (23/718). But the other tale of the Lollards is one of the longest and most arresting of all the jurors' memories. At a hearing held at Brentwood (Essex) on October 29, 1435, a juror told of events of some twenty-two years before. John Kempe, now sixty-three and more, says that:

> On the day and year abovesaid, at Horndon on the Hill many Lollards gathered with insurgents against the church's power and privileges and, like disturbers, destroyed the king's peace, proposing that the young be not baptised, to the prejudice, destruction and scorn of the entire church. Thomas Malgrave . . . said that Richard [the heir] would be killed unbaptized, ordered many armed men, of whom he was one, for defence and to destroy the force and their diabolic intention. They fought the Lollards on the same evening . . . and two-hundred of them were thrown to the ground and killed. Richard was born and baptized on the same day and this battle happened twenty-two years ago. (24/566)[26]

25 The testimony tells us that the translation of St. William is celebrated on June 8 in the province of York, that also being the date of the heir's birth and of the miracle which "took place after prayers and divine service in honour of St. William."

26 This rather dramatic event receives a one-line reference in E. F. Jacob, *The Fifteenth Century, 1399–1485* (Oxford, 1961), 132.

So our tapestry nears completion, displaying some brightly colored strands to set against the dun ones of so much reminiscence and testimony. In a sweep of this sort it is likely that it will be the odd memories, the one-offs, and some of those that are highly personalized that are most likely to hold our attention. In running through those hundreds of memories that all went back to the basic assertion of being at or near the baptism, or of giving a daughter in marriage, or of burying a parent or a spouse on the critical day, we are likely looking with interest at the odd tale of a suicide,[27] or of a thief being put to the gallows, or of a would-be godmother who arrived too late, let alone at an account of a Lollard uprising or of an expedition into Scotland. But we must keep in mind that it is the ordinary, the day-in and day-out, that provides the firm foundation on which social history – with its colorful ration of anecdote and eccentricity – rests. We pay heed to this when we choose to privilege memories that resonate with our own interests – those touching on occasions of reading and writing and relating to the workings of and interactions with the church.

These efforts to pursue lines of inquiry that reflect themes covered by Mary Erler in a long and productive career is, however, incomplete, since Erler's invaluable work on women of piety and of books – an important subset of lay piety and literacy – has hardly made an appearance. Though many of our "boys' club" memories actually revolve around or focus on women and women's activities (such as giving birth and/or being churched or serving as nurse or midwife), the agency of these women only comes through to us, in the Proofs of Age, by way of some male juror's recollection; it always was *his* memory, *his* account of having been in the right place at the right time, of remembering *her* role. A proper examination of the role of the women who stood beside our hundreds of jurors must await a further inquiry.[28] But in regard to literacy and to the special aura of books and what is written therein, our jurors have much

---

27 Alexander Murray, *Suicide in the Middle Ages*, vol. 1: *The Violent against Themselves* (Oxford, 1998). Murray's statistics (pp. 405–8) indicate that hanging was the usual or preferred method. Obviously, suicide left a lasting memory, as a number of jurors cited such an event: "on that day at Wilcote, John Wargon hanged himself from a tie-beam [*laqueo se suspendebet*] and he [the juror] came to Wilcote to see John hanging. Returning he met a woman . . . carrying Thomas to Wilcote church for baptism" (22/528).

28 See also Fiona Harris-Stoertz, "Remembering Birth in Thirteenth- and Fourteenth-Century England," in *Reconsidering Gender: Time and Memory in Medieval Culture*, ed. Elizabeth Cox, Liz Herbert McAvoy, and Roberta Magnan, Gender in the Middle Ages (Cambridge, UK, 2015), 45–59; B. Gregory Bailey et al., "Coming of Age and the Family in Medieval England," *Journal of Family History* 33 (2008): 41–60. A fuller account of life as reconstructed on the basis of the memories in the Proofs is presented in my *Social Memory in Late Medieval England: Village Life and Proofs of Age* (Cham, Switzerland, 2018).

to offer. They also open windows onto the laity's perception of the church and its personnel, and onto the broad intersection of the secular and the spiritual. Our jurors were rarely eloquent, rarely prolix (given the nature of the source as recorded) but, in their numbers, they steer us to the sort of transactions, events, and memories from which so much of everyday life is constructed and on which it rests.[29] While this tale of fifteenth-century men and their memories has led us, once more, into that strange country of the past, we can conjecture that it may not have been all that different – that we too might have been called upon to tell our own tales, had we been pushed forward, offering some mnemonic about an event that had befallen us some fourteen or sixteen or twenty-one years ago.

29 Carpenter, "General Introduction," 33: "The anecdotes offered . . . to establish their memory of the child's birth or baptism are wonderful vignettes of the minutiae of ordinary lives, quite often of the lives of people about whom we would normally know nothing on this scale." This theme was picked up many years ago by Walter Rye, *Records and Record Searching*, 2nd edn. (London, 1897), quoting "the late W. D. Cooper" in vol. 12 of the *Sussex Archaeological Collections*, as in his paper on Sussex families, pp. 102–3, touching briefly on many of the themes covered above.

Crafting the Old Testament
in the Queen Mary Psalter

KATHRYN A. SMITH

For elite audiences in the late Middle Ages, the act of reading was often as much about contemplating pictures as it was about consuming texts. Imagery and texts in richly illustrated, intricately designed one-off volumes may structure, reinforce, gloss, explicate, vivify, inflect, and even challenge or contradict one another, enriching and complicating the messages they were intended to convey, and, by extension, the reader-viewer's experience of them. Careful selection and editing could shade illustrated texts and captioned pictures toward the timeless or the topical. Indeed, as scholarship on the medieval illustrated book has richly demonstrated, examination of the relationship between word and image in any single example may reveal "a space of intellectual struggle, historical investigation, and artistic/critical practice," as W. J. T. Mitchell put it, and thus may suggest the conditions of an artifact's crafting as well as its reception.[1]

1   W. J. T. Mitchell, "Word and Image," in *Critical Terms for Art History*, ed. Robert S. Nelson and Richard Schiff, 2nd edn. (Chicago and London, 2003), 60.
     I first encountered Mary Erler at the conference Women and the Book, held at St. Hilda's College, Oxford, in summer 1993. It is a pleasure to contribute this essay in honor of a scholar whose work on medieval books and their readers I have long admired, not least for her recognition of the importance of images to medieval reading practices. My great thanks go to Delbert Russell, Distinguished Professor of French Emeritus, University of Waterloo, who prepared most of the transcriptions and translations of the Anglo-Norman French texts in the Queen Mary Psalter Old Testament preface, published here in the context of our collaborative work on that preface. Missing text is enclosed in square brackets; abbreviations have been expanded in italics, the acute accent is added to final tonic -e, and initial letters of proper nouns capitalized. Earlier versions of this research were presented at English Fourteenth-Century Illuminated Manuscripts in the British Library: A Conference, sponsored by The British Library and AMARC (December 1, 2014); Reading and Writing in City, Court, and Cloister: A Conference in Honor of Mary C. Erler, the thirty-fifth Annual Conference of the Center for Medieval Studies, Fordham University (March 7, 2015); the New York Comics and Picture-Story Symposium, Parsons/The New School (September 29, 2015); and the seminar of the Consejo Superior de Investigaciones Cientificas–Spanish National Research Council, CCHS-Instituto de Historia, Madrid

These ideas have resonance with respect to the Queen Mary Psalter (BL MS Royal 2 B. VII), among the most impressive English manuscripts of the fourteenth century.[2] The Psalter is exceptional not only for its sheer bulk and pictorial abundance – 319 folios displaying over 800 images – but also for its harmonious design, lavish production, and rich presentation of Christian salvation history. The manuscript opens with an Old Testament preface covering Creation through the story of Solomon, after which follow four full-page miniatures detailing the lineage and kin of Jesus in the male and female lines and the prophetic and apostolic foundations of the faith. A Sarum calendar embellished with narrative imagery of the monthly labors and zodiac signs precedes the Latin psalter, canticles, and litany, texts that are framed and articulated by eighty-seven full- or half-page miniatures depicting the Life of Christ and Christological, Marian, eschatological, and devotional themes as well as twenty-three historiated initials at the main text divisions. The lower margins of every folio of these texts display drawings – 464 in total – comprising several thematic series, including bestiary themes, Marian miracles, hagiographic narratives, combatant grotesques, and

(November 5, 2015). For their kind invitations to speak and astute comments, advice, and questions, I am grateful to the following colleagues and friends: Lucy Freeman Sandler, Kathleen Doyle, Susan L'Engle, Marc Michael Epstein, Alixe Bovey, Michael A. Michael, Julian Luxford, Nigel Morgan, T. A. Heslop, Michael Kauffmann, Stella Panayotova, Christopher Barrett, Paul Binski, Maryanne Kowaleski, Martin Chase, Thelma Fenster, Jocelyn Wogan-Browne, Nina Rowe, Nicole Rice, Martha Carlin, Joel Rosenthal, Ben Katchor, J. J. Sedelmaier, Therese Martin, and Esperanza Alfonso. I am particularly indebted to Kathleen Doyle of The British Library for granting me access to the psalter, and to Christina Duffy of The British Library for undertaking the multispectral imaging that enriched my understanding of the artist's working methods. Jonathan Alexander, Anne Rudloff Stanton, and Maryanne Kowaleski read earlier versions of this essay, and their comments improved it significantly. All links cited in the notes were active as of November 15, 2017.
2   Major bibliography for the Psalter includes George Warner, *Queen Mary's Psalter* (London, 1912); Lucy Freeman Sandler, *Gothic Manuscripts, 1285–1385*, A Survey of Manuscripts Illuminated in the British Isles 5, gen. ed. J. J. G. Alexander, 2 vols. (London, 1986), 2:64–66, no. 56; Kathryn A. Smith, "History, Typology and Homily: The Joseph Cycle in the Queen Mary Psalter," *Gesta* 32 (1993): 147–59; Anne Rudloff Stanton, *The Queen Mary Psalter: A Study of Affect and Audience* (Philadelphia, 2001), with her earlier important studies; and the catalog entry by Deirdre Jackson in *Royal Manuscripts: The Genius of Illumination*, ed. Scot McKendrick, John Lowden, and Kathleen Doyle, with Joanna Frońska and Deirdre Jackson (London, 2011), 272–75, no. 85. For additional bibliography and the fully digitized manuscript, see The British Library's Digital Catalogue of Illuminated Manuscripts, continually updated, at http://www.bl.uk/catalogues/illuminatedmanuscripts (search for "Queen Mary Psalter").

101

vignettes of courtly and urban entertainment, material that extends the Psalter's program into the realm of contemporary aristocratic ideals and experience.

This lavishness and pictorial plenitude are all the more impressive because, as is generally agreed, all of the imagery in BL Royal 2 B. VII was executed by "a single artist of exceptional talent," the illuminator known as the Queen Mary "Master."[3] From the evidence of the manuscripts executed by this illuminator and others working in the Queen Mary style, it appears that some of the artists of the Queen Mary group were itinerant, while others were local to London. Moreover, the volumes to which they contributed, diverse in respect to destination as well as genre, include religious, devotional, liturgical, legal, and historical manuscripts executed for institutional, monastic, ecclesiastical, and lay patrons or clients in Kent, East Anglia, Bangor (Wales), and Paris as well as London and Westminster.[4]

As enigmatic as the origins and training of the Queen Mary Master are the identities of the manuscript's original intended owner and the circumstances of the commission. Traditionally dated to c. 1310–1320 on the basis of style, the Psalter has always been assumed to have been made for a recipient of the highest rank, a member of the English royal circle, with the most frequently suggested candidates being Edward II (r. 1307–27), his queen, Isabella of France (1295–1358), and their son Edward III (b. 1312; r. 1327–77).[5] Yet the Psalter resists definitive contextualization, as it contains no early fourteenth-century owner or

3   Jackson, in *Royal Manuscripts*, 272.
4   For the localization, patronage, and ownership of Queen Mary group manuscripts, and for the London book trade, see Sandler, *Gothic Manuscripts*, 1:30–31, and 2:13–14, 64–83, nos. 1 and 56–76; Lynda Dennison, "An Illuminator of the Queen Mary Psalter Group: The Ancient 6 Master," *The Antiquaries Journal* 66, part 2 (1986): 287–314; M. A. Michael, "Oxford, Cambridge and London: Towards a Theory for 'Grouping' Gothic Manuscripts," *The Burlington Magazine* 130, no. 1019 (1988): 107–15, at 112–13; and Lynda Dennison, "'Liber Horn', 'Liber Custumarum' and Other Manuscripts of the Queen Mary Psalter Workshops," in *Medieval Art, Architecture and Archaeology in London*, ed. Lindy Grant, The British Archaeological Association, Conference Transactions for the Year 1984 (Leeds, 1990), 118–34; C. Paul Christianson, *A Directory of London Stationers and Book Artisans, 1300–1550* (New York, 1990); Ralph Hanna, *London Literature, 1300–1380* (Cambridge, UK, 2005), 68–82; and M. A. Michael, "Urban Production of Manuscript Books and the Role of the University Towns," in *The Cambridge History of the Book in Britain*, ed. Nigel J. Morgan and Rodney M. Thomson (Cambridge, UK, 2008), 185–86, with additional bibliography.
5   Warner, *Queen Mary's Psalter*, 7, suggested that the Psalter was made for either Edward I or Edward II. Stanton (*Queen Mary Psalter*, 216–44) surveys possible candidates and summarizes the major hypotheses as well as putting forward her own.

donor portraits, coats of arms, inscriptions, or calendar entries that might aid in identifying the intended recipient.

The scope, visual homogeneity, and synthetic narrative conception of the Queen Mary Psalter make the search for sources and analysis of its illustrations a daunting task. These comments are perhaps nowhere more pertinent than with respect to the Old Testament preface, whose sixty-six folios display 223 drawings, delicately tinted in mauve, peach, green, and brown washes, usually arranged two per page and enclosed in vivid red frames. These pictures are accompanied by captions in Anglo-Norman French, or "insular French," England's principal vernacular of learning, culture, law, record, and lay devotion and religious instruction from the Norman Conquest through the early fifteenth century.[6] The captions are written in one, two, or even three columns, a variability of layout that evinces an intricate relationship between pictures and text. Moreover, alone among surviving psalter prefatory cycles, the one in BL Royal 2 B. VII also includes *un*illustrated summaries in Anglo-Norman French, some several pages long, preceding or interspersed among the picture series associated with several Old Testament figures. These summaries cover much of the same material as do the captioned pictures and are, like the captions themselves, written in an unusual mixture of prose and "verse in prose format," although they often differ from the captions in the amount and nature of the detail that they present.[7] Unlike the quiring of the Psalter proper, that of the Old Testament preface is irregular, and Anne Rudloff Stanton plausibly suggested that the apparently unique prefatory text was created expressly for this project, and that the text and gatherings of the preface were composed simultaneously or nearly so, a scenario that would

6   For the roles and significance of French in England see *Language and Culture in Medieval Britain: The French of England c. 1100–1500*, ed. Jocelyn Wogan-Browne, with Carolyn Collette, Maryanne Kowaleski, Linne Mooney, Ad Putter, and David Trotter (York, 2009), especially Wogan-Browne's "General Introduction: What's in a Name: The 'French' of England,'" 1–13.

7   Unillustrated summaries are included for all or part of the stories of Joseph (fol. 14r), Moses (fols. 20v–22r), Jael (conflated with Deborah) and Sisera and Gideon/Jerobaal (fols. 31v–32v), Gideon/Jerobaal and Abimelech (fols. 35r–35v), Jephthah (fol. 39v), Samson (fols. 41v–42r), and Ruth (fol. 46v). Warner, *Queen Mary's Psalter*, transcribed and translated the Anglo-Norman French captions but not the unillustrated summaries; Stanton, *Queen Mary Psalter*, 245–55, transcribed all of the unillustrated summaries. For analysis of the preface see Warner, *Queen Mary's Psalter*, 8–22; Anne Rudloff Stanton, "Notes on the Codicology of the Queen Mary Psalter," *Scriptorium* 48 (1995): 250–62; Stanton, *Queen Mary Psalter*, 26–31, here quoting 29; and Ruth J. Dean with Maureen B. M. Boulton, *Anglo-Norman Literature: A Guide to Texts and Manuscripts*, Anglo-Norman Text Society, Occasional Publications Series, 3 (London, 1999), no. 465.

have entailed an exceptionally close level of cooperation and collaboration among text-compiler, scribe, and artist.[8] The use of tinted drawing for the Old Testament preface and full painting and gilding for the miniatures and initials embellishing the psalter, canticles, and litany registers the Christian view of the primacy of the New Testament, the scriptural, the liturgical, and the Latinate over the Old Testament and vernacular paraphrase.

This essay is concerned with multiple dimensions of the production and reception of the Queen Mary Psalter's fascinating illustrated preface. It advances new suggestions concerning sources and models that the book artisans consulted in crafting, or recrafting, Old Testament history. It examines some of the ideas, images, and objects that appear to have informed the artisans' treatment of their subjects, as well as offering glimpses into the illuminator's working methods. Yet a larger aim of this essay is to sketch the contours of what Jacques Le Goff memorably dubbed the *imaginaires*, or "imaginaries," of the artisans and their client(s) – that is, to explore the visual, intellectual, and cultural environments and experience of the manuscript's early fourteenth-century makers and putative intended audience.[9] On account of its lavishness, the Queen Mary Psalter may seem a volume better suited to admiration than actual use. Moreover, the preface, with its simplified storyline and frequent omission, conflation, or misidentification of characters, may seem to the modern reader-viewer to possess the quality of "scripture-lite." Yet the version of Old Testament history presented on its pages is both astutely edited, and, in key scenes, highly particularized in its details. How this carefully crafted account of biblical history recasts the story and image of the ancient Israelites in relation to elite medieval readerly tastes, widely held attitudes toward contemporary Jews, Christian attitudes toward the roles of art in connection with worship, and the turbulent political ambient and vibrant artistic context of early fourteenth-century London and Westminster, are the principal concerns of this essay.

8   Stanton, "Notes on the Codicology;" idem, *Queen Mary Psalter*, 14–17.

9   Jacques Le Goff, *L'Imaginaire médiéval* (Paris, 1985); translated as *The Medieval Imagination* by Arthur Goldhammer (Chicago, 1988), and more congenially as "imaginary" in Michael Camille, *Mirror in Parchment: The Luttrell Psalter and the Making of Medieval England* (Chicago and London, 1998), 307. My use of the term "imaginaire" is also indebted to Lucy Freeman Sandler, "Bared: The Writing Bear in the British Library Bohun Psalter," originally published in *Tributes to Jonathan J. G. Alexander: The Making and Meaning of Illuminated Medieval & Renaissance Manuscripts, Art & Architecture*, ed. Susan L'Engle and Gerald B. Guest (London, 2006), 269–82; reprinted in Lucy Freeman Sandler, *Illuminators and Patrons in Fourteenth-Century England: The Psalter & Hours of Humphrey de Bohun and the Manuscripts of the Bohun Family* (London and Toronto, 2014), 217–27, at 225 n. 3.

The Queen Mary Master's crafting of the very first picture in the Old Testament preface conveys a sense of the artist's command of his visual sources and powers of synthesis, as well as the capacity of images to enrich the book-bound experience of medieval readers (Fig. 5.1). The apparent subject of the picture is stated matter-of-factly in its caption: "How Lucifer fell from heaven and became the Devil, and a great multitude of angels were with him."[10] The drawing is both more expansive in scope and subtler in its details. Employing the rings familiar from English Creation imagery produced from the Anglo-Saxon period forward, the artist portrayed the Deity accomplishing several acts associated with the First Day of Creation, including the Creation of Light and the Division of Light from Darkness (Gen. 1:3–5).[11] Not told in Genesis but established by Augustine in his *De Civitate Dei*, following earlier Jewish and Christian writers, is the idea that God also created the angels on the First Day when he said, "Be there light." The kneeling angels flanking the Creator within the upper ring and the seraphim hovering just outside it may refer to this divine act and to the angels' participation in the light of God's wisdom.[12]

For other elements of this picture, the artist appears to have turned to a Continental model that was close at hand: the full-page Creation miniature in the Oxford-Paris-London (hereafter OPL) Moralized Bible, one of the four early thirteenth-century versions of this monumental work, all produced in Paris under French royal sponsorship, a manuscript known to have been brought to London sometime in the thirteenth century (Fig. 5.2).[13] John Lowden convincingly showed that the three prefatory pictures in the English Holkham Bible Picture Book (c. 1327–1340), including its first dramatic Creation image, were produced in light of the frontispiece and colophon images in the OPL Moralized Bible.[14] The artist

10   "Coment lucifer chayit de ciel e devient diable, e *grant* multitudo des angeles ovesq*ue* li" (BL Royal 2 B. VII, fol. 1v).
11   Herbert R. Broderick III, "The Influence of Anglo-Saxon Genesis Iconography on Later English Medieval Manuscript Art," in Paul E. Szarmach and Joel T. Rosenthal, eds., *The Preservation and Transmission of Anglo-Saxon Culture* (Kalamazoo, MI, 1997), 211–42; C. M. Kauffmann, *Biblical Imagery in Medieval England 700–1550* (London and Turnhout, 2003), 33–72 and 215–28.
12   Frederick Van Fleteren, "Angels," in *Augustine through the Ages: An Encyclopedia* (Grand Rapids, MI, 1999), 21. Isa. 6:1–2 describes two seraphim on either side of God's throne.
13   Now divided among Oxford, Bodleian Library, MS Bodley 270b; BnF MS lat. 11560; and BL MSS Harley 1526–1527; see John Lowden, *The Making of the Bibles moralisées*, 2 vols. (University Park, PA, 2000), 1:185–87.
14   BL MS Add. 47682, fol. 2r; John Lowden, "The Holkham Bible Picture Book and he *Bible Moralisée*," in *The Medieval Book: Glosses from Friends & Colleagues for Christopher*

of the Holkham Bible Picture Book followed his Parisian model in portraying God not as an architect using a pair of dividers to *measure* the cosmos, as in many earlier depictions of this theme, but rather as an artist using a compass to *draw* it, an image richly resonant with the compass-drawn roundels that organize the pages of the Parisian manuscripts, and with the activities of the artists who produced the illustrations.[15]

The Queen Mary Master, too, showed God wielding a compass to draw the rings of his Creation, which are arranged in a rough diamond-shape that echoes the lobed frame enclosing the Deity in the French miniature (Figs. 5.1 and 5.2). While the upper and lower rings in the picture are compass-struck, the artist drew the lateral rings partly free-hand, positioning the stylus of the compass so that it rests on the inner arc of the side ring near the Deity's right leg, as if the Creator has just finished drawing that very circle. In a further, bravura display of draftsmanship, one possibly intended to call attention to his role in endowing the Creator with pictorial form, the artist disposed the Deity so that the hole made by the point of the compass doubles as the Lord's navel. Moreover, in order to convey the ideas of God's omnipotence and his responsibility for the whole of Creation, the artist positioned the Deity so that he touches each ring: seated at the intersection of the lateral rings, God rests one foot on the upper ring and the other on the lower.

The artist's attention to seemingly small yet meaningful details extends to the portrayal of the Fall of Lucifer and the Rebel Angels, an event also traditionally associated with the First Day of Creation. In the lowest ring, three rebel angels plunge headlong from the clouds directly above three snub-nosed, hairy devils, a deft visualization of the moment of the angels' transformation from beings of

de Hamel, ed. James H. Marrow et al. (T'goy-Houten, 2010), 75–83. Elizabeth Marer-Banasik, "The Creator with the Cosmos and a Compass: The Frontispieces of the Thirteenth-Century Moralizing Bibles," *Rutgers Art Review* 15 (1995): 7–32, noted the iconographic connections among the Creation pictures in the Moralized Bibles, the Queen Mary Psalter, and the Holkham Bible Picture Book, but she did not distinguish between the architect's dividers that God holds in some examples from the Anglo-Saxon, Romanesque, and Gothic periods, and the artist's compass that God wields in the Moralized Bibles, BL Royal 2 B. VII, BL Add. 47682, and other manuscripts. For the Holkham Bible Picture Book, see also M. R. James, "An English Bible Picture Book of the Fourteenth Century," *The Walpole Society* 11 (1922–23): 1–27; W. O. Hassall *The Holkham Bible Picture Book* (London, 1954); F. P. Pickering, *The Anglo-Norman Text of the Holkham Bible Picture Book*, Anglo-Norman Texts 23 (Oxford, 1971); Sandler, *Gothic Manuscripts* 2:105–7, no. 97; and Michelle P. Brown, *The Holkham Bible Picture Book: A Facsimile* (London, 2007).

15 Lowden, "Holkham Bible Picture Book," 79.

light into creatures of darkness. The larger, center devil, equipped with a beast's head at his groin signifying his exceptional depravity, is Lucifer himself. Like the delicately rendered seraphim at the top of the picture, the monstrous Lucifer wears a narrow stole knotted at his chest, a reference to his putative membership before his Fall of the order of seraphim, the highest order of the Celestial Hierarchy. Yet as worn by Lucifer, the stole has acquired a sinister function. The ends of this garment are wrapped around the wrists of the two devils crouching at his knees, binding these creatures to their master and making them the Devil's minions.

Among the most widely acknowledged features of the Old Testament preface is its liberal infusion of extra-biblical material, including apocryphal episodes and legendary motifs collected in great Latin compilations such as Petrus Comestor's *Historia Scholastica* (c. 1173), as well as fanciful alterations and embellishments of plot paralleled in Continental and insular vernacular biblical paraphrases and metrical biblical romances, developments amply witnessed in the visual arts from the years around 1200.[16] In the introduction to his partial facsimile of the Queen Mary Psalter, George Warner made a formidable start at identifying textual analogs of some of the extra-biblical motifs in the preface.[17] Writing eighty years later, Nigel Morgan characterized the preface as exemplifying an approach to the visualization of biblical narrative at once indebted to and distinct from earlier English Gothic Old Testament cycles in which the very character of biblical storytelling itself is transformed, so that the events, values, and social and interpersonal relationships in biblical stories are reframed and presented as biblical or chivalric romance, a favorite reading matter of the later medieval laity.[18]

An apparent drive to transform scripture into chivalric romance appears to inform numerous scenes in the Old Testament preface. Yet I submit that their romance flavor derives not solely from their makers' or beholders' familiarity

16 For the French biblical paraphrases see Jean Bonnard, *Les Traductions de la Bible en vers français au Moyen Age* (Paris, 1884); and Samuel Berger, *La Bible française au Moyen Age: Étude sur les plus anciennes versions de la Bible en langue d'Oïl* (Paris, 1884; repr. Geneva, 1967). More recent overviews of different aspects of this topic containing essential bibliography include Nigel Morgan, "Old Testament Illustration in Thirteenth-Century England," in *The Bible in the Middle Ages: Its Influence on Literature and Art*, ed. Bernard S. Levy, Medieval & Renaissance Texts & Studies 89 (Binghamton, NY, 1992), 149–98; James H. Morey, "Peter Comestor, Biblical Paraphrase, and the Medieval Popular Bible," *Speculum* 68 (1993): 6–35; Kauffmann, *Biblical Imagery*; and Brian Murdoch, *The Medieval Popular Bible: Expansions of Genesis in the Middle Ages* (Cambridge, UK, 2003).

17 Warner, *Queen Mary's Psalter*, 9–20.

18 Morgan, "Old Testament Illustration," 172.

with the *literature* of romance, but rather also from the artist's consultation of *pictorial* models derived from the burgeoning, increasingly sophisticated tradition of illuminated romance manuscripts. In the portrayal of David's first, fateful glimpse of Bathsheba, the wife of Uriah the Hittite (Fig. 5.3, bottom), for example, text-compiler and artist dispensed with key scriptural elements of this episode, including Bathsheba's bath and the messenger whom David sent to bring her to him, details typically favored by Gothic patrons and book artisans, including the makers of the French Old Testament Picture Book in the Morgan Library (c. 1240–50).[19] In a cluster of Parisian versions of this theme – including the Beatus pages of the St. Louis Psalter and its "sister" manuscript, the Psalter and Hours "of Isabelle of France" (both c. 1255/60–70), as well as a profusely illuminated picture Bible and saints' lives illuminated in the early fourteenth century by the Fauvel Master and an associate – a rapt David spies from his castle window a partially (or entirely) naked Bathsheba at her bath, attended by a female servant or servants.[20]

19 Stanton, *Queen Mary Psalter*, 120, 126; New York, Morgan Library & Museum, MS M. 638, fol. 41v; for the manuscript, see William Noel and Daniel Weiss, eds., *The Book of Kings: Art, War, and the Morgan Library's Medieval Picture Bible* (London and Baltimore, 2002); and numerous essays in Colum Hourihane, ed., *Between the Picture and the Word: Manuscript Studies from the Index of Christian Art* (Princeton, 2005). All of the folios are viewable through CORSAIR at http://ica.themorgan.org/manuscript/158530, and in the online exhibition The Crusader Bible, at http://www.themorgan.org/collection/Crusader-Bible; for this folio see http://www.themorgan.org/collection/crusader-bible/82.
20 For the St. Louis Psalter Beatus page (BnF MS lat. 10525, fol. 85v) see Harvey Stahl, *Picturing Kingship: History and Painting in the Psalter of Saint Louis* (University Park, PA, 2008), 184–201; and for the manuscript see Alison Stones, *Gothic Manuscripts 1260–1320, A Survey of Manuscripts Illuminated in France*, ed. François Avril et al., 2 parts (Turnhout and London, 2013), Part I, vol. 2:20–23, no. I-11, with additional bibliography; the psalter is fully digitized at http://gallica.bnf.fr (search for "St Louis Psalter" then select "Manuscrits" in the 'Type de document' panel on the left).
        For the Psalter-Hours "of Isabelle of France" (Cambridge, UK, Fitzwilliam Museum MS 300, fol. 13v), see Paul Binski and Stella Panayotova, eds., *The Cambridge Illuminations: Ten Centuries of Book Production in the Medieval West* (London and Turnhout, 2005), 178–80, no. 72; and Stones, *Gothic Manuscripts 1260–1320*, Part I, vol. 2:25–27, I-13. For the picture Bible and saints' lives (New York, New York Public Library, MS Spencer 22, fol 71r), see François Bucher, *The Pamplona Bibles*, 2 vols. (New Haven, 1970); the catalog entry by Lucy Freeman Sandler in Jonathan J. G. Alexander, James H. Marrow, and Lucy Freeman Sandler, *The Splendor of the Word: Medieval and Renaissance Illuminated Manuscript at the New York Public Library* (London/Turnhout and New York, 2005), 97–100, no. 20; the catalog entry by Elizabeth Morrison in Morrison and Anne D. Hedeman, *Imagining*

In the Queen Mary Psalter preface, no messengers or servants mediate the protagonists' encounter. David atop his "chastel" propositions Bathsheba directly, and Bathsheba, an elegantly dressed *châtelaine*, replies in consent from the crenellated parapet of her own abode.[21] Indeed, Bathsheba resembles nothing so much as the ladies communing with knightly suitors from battlemented towers in illustrated Arthurian romances such as the well-known *Lancelot propre*, richly illuminated c. 1310–15 in Picardy by the artist known as the Master of Sainte Benoîte and his associates (Fig. 5.4, left).[22]

Similarly, the vignette in the Psalter preface of the Egyptian handmaid Hagar in the wilderness holding the swaddled Ishmael resembles closely the depiction in the Morgan *Lancelot propre* of the Lady of the Lake holding the infant Lancelot (Fig. 5.5, bottom, and Fig. 5.6). Here, too, the captioned picture offers a radical simplification and reworking of biblical narrative in the service of enhancing its romance flavor. In Genesis, Hagar experiences two wilderness sojourns. In the first (Gen. 16:6–13), the pregnant handmaid flees into the wood in order to escape the harsh treatment of her former mistress, Sarah. There, "by a fountain of water in the wilderness . . . in the way to Sur in the desert" (Gen. 16:7) she is comforted by an angel who instructs her to return home, where, months later, she gives birth to Abraham's son Ishmael. Hagar's second, far longer wilderness sojourn occurs years later, when, at Sarah's urging, Abraham turns out of the house both Hagar and the youth Ishmael. The sorrowing Hagar abandons Ishmael to die by a tree in the wilderness of Beersheba, but God saves the starving pair by guiding Hagar to a spring (Gen. 21:9–20).

Both of these episodes were known to English audiences. They are elaborated in several biblical paraphrases, including the Middle English poems *Genesis and Exodus* (mid-thirteenth century) and *Cursor Mundi* (c. 1300), the latter an epic account of Christian salvation history from Creation to Doomsday.[23] Moreover,

the Past in France: History in Manuscript Painting, 1250–1500 (Los Angeles, 2010), 137–40, no. 14; and Julia A. Finch, *"Bibles en images*: Visual Narrative and Translation in New York Public Library Spencer MS 22 and Related Manuscripts" (PhD diss., University of Pittsburgh, 2011).

21 "Coment David mountaunt soun chastel vist Bersabee la femme Urye e la priast de fornicacion e ele consenti" (BL Royal 2 B. VII, fol. 56v, bottom). As Stanton (*Queen Mary Psalter*, 120, 126) put it, Bathsheba in this picture is in no way "represented as the passive recipient of [David's] gaze."

22 Morgan Library & Museum MS M. 805–806; Morrison and Hedeman, *Imagining the Past*, 121–23, no. 10; Stones, *Gothic Manuscripts 1260–1320*, Part I, vol. 2:438–49, no. III-93.

23 For the Middle English *Genesis and Exodus*, see *The Story of Genesis and Exodus, an Early English Song, about A.D. 1250*, ed. Richard Morris, Early English Text Society o.s. 7

although lengthy Hagar cycles are uncommon in thirteenth- and early fourteenth-century art, Hagar's two distinct wilderness sojourns are set out in scrupulous detail in the *bas-de-page* of the English Isabella Psalter, made c. 1303–1308 for Isabella of France in connection with her betrothal to Edward II, a manuscript whose visual program offers numerous parallels with that of BL Royal 2 B. VII, as Stanton showed.[24]

Text and image in the Queen Mary Psalter preface conflate these two scriptural episodes (Fig. 5.5, bottom). Hagar flees only once into the wilderness, where, in contradiction to scripture, she gives birth to Ishmael. She then abandons her infant by a tree because she cannot nurse him, but returns and recovers him at the command of the angel, who advises her that she will find a fountain there that will sustain them.[25] With the aid of his French model(s), the Queen Mary Master transformed Hagar into a veritable "Lady of the Fountain" (Fig. 5.5,

(London, 1865; rev. edn. 1873; repr. 1996); and *The Middle English Genesis and Exodus*, ed. Olof Arngart (Lund, 1968). For the earlier, Northern version of *Cursor Mundi*, see *Cursor Mundi*, ed. Richard Morris, Early English Text Society o.s. 57, 59, 62, 66, 68, 99, 101 (London, 1874–93; repr. 1961–66); and for broader discussion, see John J. Thompson, "The *Cursor Mundi*, the 'Inglis tong', and 'Romance,'" in *Readings in Medieval English Romance*, ed. Carol M. Meale (Cambridge, UK, 1994), 99–120.

24 Munich, Bayerische Staatsbibliothek, Cod. Gall. 16, fols. 26v and 28v; major bibliography includes D. D. Egbert, "A Sister to the Tickhill Psalter: The Psalter of Queen Isabella of England," *Bulletin of the New York Public Library* 39 (1935): 759–88; idem, *The Tickhill Psalter and Related Manuscripts* (New York, 1940); Sandler, *Gothic Manuscripts* 2:33–34, no. 27; Anne Rudloff Stanton, "The Psalter of Isabelle of France, Queen of England: Isabelle as the Audience," *Word and Image* 18 (2002): 1–27; idem, "Turning the Pages: Marginal Narratives and Devotional Practice in Gothic Prayerbooks," in *Push Me, Pull You: Imaginative and Emotional Interaction in Medieval and Renaissance Art*, ed. Sarah Blick and Laura D. Gelfand, 2 vols. (Leiden and Boston, 2011) 1:75–121; and Munich, Bayerische Staatsbibliothek, *Illuminierte Prachtpsalterien der Bayerischen Staatsbibliothek vom 11. bis zum 16. Jahrhundert* (Luzern, 2011), 16–17 and no. 7. The manuscript is fully digitized; see https://www.digitale-sammlungen.de (search for "Cod. Gall. 16").

For depictions of Hagar's story in French and English Gothic art, and for additional relationships between the programs of the Isabella and Queen Mary psalters, see Stanton, *Queen Mary Psalter*, 90–126.

25 "Coment la drener femme Abram qe estoit sa chambrere s'en est alee par despiit denz un boys si est delivceré de un fitz e ne le pout susteyner. e le met desuit un arbre en boys, pur ceo q'ele ne voleit mye qe l'enfaunt morut de mesaise qe ele le viit e s'en ala. Si acountre le angel Deu, qe la fiit returner, e q'ele trovereyt une founteyne de quei hii serroint sustenous" (How the most recent wife of Abram, who was the maidservant, went into the woods out of spite and gave birth to a son, whom she could not nurse, and she put him under a tree in the woods because she did not wish the infant to die of hunger while she could see him, and she left. And she met the angel of the Lord who made her

bottom, and Fig. 5.6). Moreover, the artist's ingeniously constructed composition ensures that the viewer first beholds Hagar's abandonment of her son and then her reunion with him, with the vignette of Hagar holding the swaddled Ishmael doubling as a representation of both narrative moments.

It might be argued that these two examples register merely a consonance of ethos between the illustration of chivalric romance and the illustration of biblical narrative *presented as* romance, a consonance enhanced by the Queen Mary Master's elegant, courtly style. Nonetheless, another picture in the Old Testament preface, a dramatic episode from the story of David, is more clearly suggestive of the artist's direct knowledge of or access to illustrated romance manuscripts or models. Saul's younger daughter Michal, David's first wife, learns of her father's intention to have David killed, and she devises a plan to ensure her husband's escape. She helps David to climb out through a window and tricks her father's soldiers into thinking that David is still at home, sick in bed, by placing in their bed a *teraphim*, a life-size statue of a household god, with a goatskin on it to imitate hair (1 Sam. 19:11–16). While Saul's unsuspecting soldiers keep the house under surveillance, Michal clasps David in a final embrace as he steps through the arched window (Fig. 5.7, top).

Gothic treatments of this story, including the one in the Morgan Old Testament Picture Book, tend to follow scripture in showing Michal hastily covering the *teraphim* so that only its goatskin hair is visible above the bedcovers while David makes his escape (Fig. 5.8). In a suite of *bas-de-page* illustrations in the English Tickhill Psalter (c. 1303–1314), Michal gives David a boost through the window and then stalls Saul's servants with the *teraphim*-decoy.[26] When the soldiers return and fling back the bedclothes, they discover the *teraphim* – described in the Latin inscriptions on the banderoles as a "statue" (statuam) and a "simulacrum" (simulachrum) (text derived from the Vulgate) – and, intriguingly, portrayed by the artist as a statue of a bishop of a type familiar from the façades and walls of Gothic churches (Figs. 5.9–5.11).[27]

return, and told her she would find a fountain that would nourish them) (BL Royal 2 B. VII, fol. 10r, bottom).

26 New York Public Library MS Spencer 26, for which see Egbert, *Tickhill Psalter*; Sandler, *Gothic Manuscripts* 2:32–33, no. 26; and Sandler's catalog entry in *Splendor of the Word*, 201–7, no. 41.

27 For the varied, shifting meanings of the terms "simulacrum" and "statua" in the Middle Ages, see Michael Camille, *The Gothic Idol: Ideology and Image-Making in Medieval Art* (Cambridge, UK, 1989), 43–44, 283, and 287; Beate Fricke, *Fallen Idols, Risen Saints: Sainte Foy of Conques and the Revival of Monumental Sculpture in Medieval Art*, trans. Andrew Griebeler, Studies in the Visual Cultures of the Middle Ages 7 (Turnhout, 2015), 52, 54, 56, 151, 159; and Assaf Pinkus, *Sculpting Simulacra in Medieval Germany, 1250–1380*

Although the caption for the picture in BL Royal 2 B. VII mentions the "ymage" covered by a goatskin,[28] the artist eliminated that plot element from the drawing and focused, instead, on the couple's passionate farewell, which strongly echoes in both form and conception the striking image of Lancelot and Guinevere's first kiss in the Morgan *Lancelot propre* (compare Fig. 5.7, top, and Fig. 5.12, left). As Alison Stones has shown, the Master of Sainte Benoîte's portrayal of this theme had an enduring impact on the Continental tradition of Arthurian manuscript illumination.[29] There is rich evidence for contact and collaboration among French and English scribes and illuminators generally, and within the Queen Mary group of manuscripts itself.[30] Thus, it seems eminently possible that the Queen Mary Master, a visual omnivore with an expansive pictorial repertoire, could have known this influential depiction of the first kiss of the most famous lovers of romance – a chivalrous knight and his royal *amie* – and repurposed it to depict the parting embrace of the chivalric biblical hero and his royal Israelite bride. In a recent discussion of the "interpenetration of sacred and profane texts and images" in French Gothic manuscript illumination, Anne D. Hedeman suggested that medieval designers and artists deployed particular motifs from one

(Aldershot, Hampshire, 2014), esp. "Introduction: Medieval *Symulachra*," 1–27, with additional bibliography.

The discovery of the *teraphim* is portrayed in some illuminated German world chronicle manuscripts, including Munich, Bayerische Staatsbibliothek, MS Cgm 5, fol. 135v, made c. 1370. In this manuscript, the illuminator portrayed the *teraphim* as a lumpish, humanoid, but otherwise featureless object and did not include the goat-skin hair. For the image, see http://daten.digitale-sammlungen.de/bsb00079954/image_276.

28 "Coment Saul maunda gentz des armes pur tuer D*a*vid en nuitant [MS: mytaunt]. E Michol sa femme q*e* fust la file Saul [MS: D*a*vid] lessa David passer p*ar* une fenestre, e mist en son lit une ymage e la teste coveri de pels de chevere" (How Saul dispatched soldiers to kill David in the night, and Michal his wife, who was the daughter of [Saul], let David escape by a window, and put in his bed an image and covered its head with goatskin) (BL Royal MS 2 B. VII, fol. 52r, top).

29 Alison Stones, "Illustrating Lancelot and Guinevere," in *Lancelot: A Case Book*, ed. Lori J. Walters (New York and London, 1996), 125–57; see also Michael Camille, "Gothic Signs and Surplus: The Kiss on the Cathedral," *Yale French Studies*, Special Issue: *Contexts: Styles and Values in Medieval Art and Literature* (1991): 162–64.

30 For collaborations between early fourteenth-century English and French book artisans, see Sandler, *Gothic Manuscripts*, 1:19. For BnF MS lat. 17155, a volume of some of the works of Aristotle executed in Paris by French scribes and containing illumination in the Queen Mary style by an English artist and penwork decoration by a French and an English artisan, see Sandler, *Gothic Manuscripts*, 2:78–79, no. 70; and François Avril and Patricia Danz Stirnemann, *Manuscrits enluminés d'origine insulaire VIIe–XXe siècle* (Paris 1987), 141–42, no. 177.

genre "to make an intentional *intervisual* reference" to another literary genre.[31] "Did artists ever deliberately create a secular image with a sacred resonance or a sacred image that has a secular resonance," as Hedeman further put it, in a conscious effort to "shape a reader's response?"[32] I believe that the Queen Mary Master's recourse to pictorial romance models was not only self-conscious, but was also intended for the eyes of a reader-viewer or -viewers who likely understood and appreciated, and perhaps even requested, these genre-crossing references.

The life of Moses in the Old Testament preface is both substantially edited and replete with "legendary accretions."[33] Equally intriguing, its program evinces its makers' ostensible theological sophistication, and, sometimes even in the same captioned picture, their conversance with what might be called contemporary "urban legend." The drawing of Moses appearing to the Israelites after his second sojourn on Mount Sinai shows the patriarch displaying the renewed Tables of the Law to a clutch of eager if apprehensive Israelites (Fig. 5.13, bottom). Moses holds the round-topped tablets in a veiled left hand, while with his right hand he wraps a portion of the veil around his head, obscuring one of the two horns with which he was often portrayed in northern Gothic art but leaving visible the second.[34] Moses wore the veil to hide his glorified, shining, "horned" (*cornuta*) countenance, as the Vulgate puts it, so that he could speak to the Israelites without frightening them (Exod. 34:29–35). As interpreted by Paul (2 Cor. 3:7–18), the veil, which "covered the faded . . . splendor of the old covenant," was removed by Jesus.[35] Yet although Moses' veil figures prominently in Christian exegesis, depictions of the prophet with the veil are not plentiful, and even rarer are portrayals of Moses with the veil, the Tables of the Law, *and* the horns: one must look back to the depiction of this episode in the Illustrated Old English Hexateuch, begun at Canterbury c. 1025–50 – the earliest surviving artifact in which Moses is portrayed with two horns – for an earlier image of the patriarch with all three attributes.[36] Moreover, as in some depictions of Moses in the Old

31 Anne D. Hedeman, "Gothic Manuscript Illustration: The Case of France," in *A Companion to Medieval Art: Romanesque and Gothic in Northern Europe*, ed. Conrad Rudolph (Malden, MA, and Oxford, 2006), 427.

32 Ibid.

33 Warner, *Queen Mary's Psalter*, 18.

34 Ruth Mellinkoff, *The Horned Moses in Medieval Art and Thought* (Berkeley and Los Angeles, 1970); idem, "More about the Horned Moses," *Journal of Jewish Art* 12/13 (1986/87): 184–98.

35 Adam S. Cohen, *The Uta Codex: Art, Philosophy, and Reform in Eleventh-Century Germany* (University Park, PA, 2000), 127.

36 BL MS Cotton Claudius B. IV, fol. 105; for the manuscript and the image see Benjamin C. Withers, *The Illustrated Old English Hexateuch, Cotton Claudius B. IV: The Frontier*

English Hexateuch, in this picture in the Psalter the patriarch's one visible horn appears to emerge or grow from a circular band or diadem, a detail only faintly visible in the Queen Mary Master's drawing.[37] The Queen Mary Master's picture may register that strand of interpretation, witnessed in the writings of authorities from Isidore of Seville (d. 636) to William Durandus (d. 1296), in which Moses' horns signify the two Testaments,[38] one here visible, the other veiled.

Moses holds the Tables of the Law so that, from the Israelites' point-of-view, both the half-veiled tablets and his veiled hand appear to occlude his face. The Christian viewer of the picture, by contrast, gets a clear view of the prophet's visage.[39] Indeed, one might read Moses' elegant gesture as a simultaneous veiling and unveiling, or revelation: a veiling to the Jews, who are shown as blind to the spiritual truths prefigured in their Law and history, and a revelation to the Christian viewer, who sees and understands the truths beneath the veil of the Old Testament. The details of this picture find a suggestive parallel in the Holkham Bible Picture Book in the depiction of the "three attempts to trap Jesus in argument," a fascinating image whose origins lie in the gospels (especially Matt. 23:1–5) and the *Historia Scholastica* (Fig. 5.14). The Pharisee who "preache[s] a sermon" from the "pulpit of Moses" scrutinizes a small pair of Tables of the Law, while the Jews in his audience wear on their brows phylacteries or *tefillin* – small boxes containing Torah verses worn by Jewish men at morning prayer – here rendered not as boxes but rather as round-topped tablets.[40] In the Holkham Bible image, the Pharisee's tablets and the tablet-shaped "phylacteries," the latter described in the accompanying Anglo-Norman French text as "signs . . . to recall the Law," are veritable blinkers at which the Jews peer intently but uncomprehendingly, and which blind them to the truths of both their own

---

of Seeing and Reading in Anglo-Saxon England (London and Toronto, 2007); Herbert R. Broderick III, "The Veil of Moses as Exegetical Image in the Illustrated Old English Hexateuch (London, B. L. Cotton MS Claudius B. IV)," in *Insular & Anglo-Saxon Art & Thought in the Early Medieval Period*, ed. Colum Hourihane (Princeton, 2011), 271–85; and now Herbert R. Broderick, *Moses the Egyptian in the Illustrated Old English Hexateuch (London, British Library Cotton MS Claudius B. iv)* (South Bend, IN, 2017), 79–109, 155–62. The manuscript is fully digitized on http://www.bl.uk/manuscripts/ (enter "Cotton MS Claudius B IV" in the "Manuscripts" search box).

37 Broderick, *Moses the Egyptian*, 84–86.

38 Mellinkoff, *Horned Moses*, 82–85, 96–99.

39 Brian Britt, *Rewriting Moses: The Narrative Eclipse of the Text* (London and New York, 2004), 103–4.

40 James, "An English Bible Picture Book," 21; Hassall, *Holkham Bible Picture Book*, 124–25; Pickering, *Anglo-Norman Text*, 47, 105.

5.1 *God creating the cosmos; The fall of Lucifer and the rebel angels. Queen Mary Psalter; London, British Library, MS 2 B. VII, fol. 1v.*

Fig. 5.2 God creating the cosmos, OPL Moralized Bible (Oxford, Bodleian Library, MS Bodley 270b, fol. 1v).

5.3 David leads the procession as the Ark of the Covenant is brought back to Jerusalem (top); David propositions
~sheba (bottom), Queen Mary Psalter (London, British Library, MS Royal 2 B. VII, fol. 56v).

Fig. 5.4 Queen Guinevere, the Lady of Malehaut, and other ladies observe the first assembly (left); Knightly combat (right), Lancelot propre; The Pierpont Morgan Library, New York, MS M. 805, fol. 60r.

5.5 Hagar and Sarah ...; Hagar abandons ...nfant Ishmael in the ...erness and is comforted ... angel (bottom), Queen ...y Psalter; London, ...sh Library, MS Royal ... VII, fol. 10r.

5.6 The Lady of the Lake holding the infant Lancelot, ...celot propre; New York, The Morgan Library & ...eum, MS M. 805, fol. 5v.

Fig. 5.7 Michal helps David to escape from Saul's servants (top); Saul orders the slaying of the P[?] of Nob (bottom), Queen Mary Psalter; London, British Librar[y] MS Royal 2 B. VII, fol. 52r.

Fig. 5.8 Michal shows Saul's soldiers the teraph[?] covered by a goatskin as David escapes through th[e] window (left); David tak[es] refuge with Samuel and other prophets (right), Ol[d] Testament Picture Book; Pierpont Morgan Librar[y] New York, MS M. 638, 31r, detail.

5.9 Michal and David (left); Michal helps David to escape through a window (right), Tickhill Psalter; New York Public Library, MS Spencer 26, fol. 23r, detail. Photo: Reproduced from D. D. Egbert, The Tickhill Psalter and Related Manuscripts (New York, 1940), pl. XII, pictures 85 and 86.

5.10 Michal shows Saul's soldiers the teraphim covered by a goatskin (left); Saul's soldiers before the king (right), Tickhill Psalter; New York Public Library, MS Spencer 26, fol. 23v, detail. Photo: Reproduced from D. D. Egbert, The Tickhill Psalter and Related Manuscripts (New York, 1940), pl. XII, pictures 87 and 88.

5.11 Saul's soldiers discover the teraphim – here, a statue of a bishop (left); Michal brought before Saul (right), Tickhill Psalter; New York Public Library, MS Spencer 26, fol. 24r, detail. Photo: Reproduced from D. D. Egbert, The Tickhill Psalter and Related Manuscripts (New York, 1940), pl. XII, pictures 89 and 90.

Fig. 5.12 First kiss of Lancelot and Guinevere, arranged by Galehot (left); the Lady of Malehaut, Laure de Carduel, and the seneschal (right), Lancelot propre; The Pierpont Morgan Library, New York, MS M. 805, fol. 67r.

Fig. 5.14 Three attempts to trap J[esus] in argument, Holkham Bible Picture Book; London, British Library, M[S] Add. 47682, fol. 27v, detail.

Fig. 5.15 (left to right) Miriam's leprosy; God tells Moses that He will show him the Promised Land; Moses passes leadership of the Israelites to Joshua; Moses' burial, Queen Mary Psalter; London, British Library, MS Royal [2B] VII, fol. 27v.

5.16 David cuts off the hem
~aul's garment (top); David
~s the piece of the garment
~ul (bottom), Queen Mary
~ter; London, British Library,
Royal 2 B. VII, fol. 52v.

5.17 David cuts off the
of Saul's garment in
~ve at Ein Gedi, Old
~ment Picture Book; The
~ont Morgan Library,
York, MS M. 638, fol.
~detail

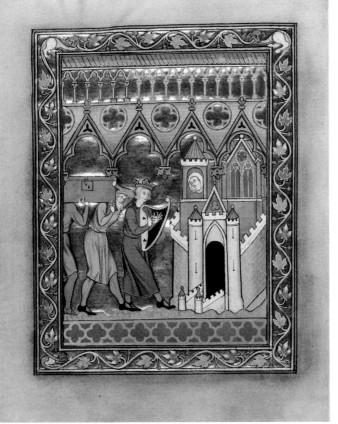

Fig. 5.18 (top) David and his men spy Saul (left); David cuts off the of Saul's garment (right), Tickhill Psalter; New York Public Library, Spencer 26, fol. 36v, detail. Photo Reproduced from D. D. Egbert, T Tickhill Psalter and Related Manuscripts (New York, 1940) XXIII, pictures 143 and 144.

Fig. 5.19 (above) Saul leaves the cave/garderobe (left); David show piece of the garment to Saul (right Tickhill Psalter; New York Public Library, MS Spencer 26, fol. 37r detail. Photo: Reproduced from D. Egbert, The Tickhill Psalter a Related Manuscripts (New Yo 1940), pl. XXIII, pictures 145 146.

Fig. 5.20 (left) David leads the procession as the Ark of the Cover is brought back to Jerusalem, with Michal watching from a window, Psalter and Hours "of Isabelle of France"; Cambridge, Fitzwilliam Museum, MS 300, fol. 1v.

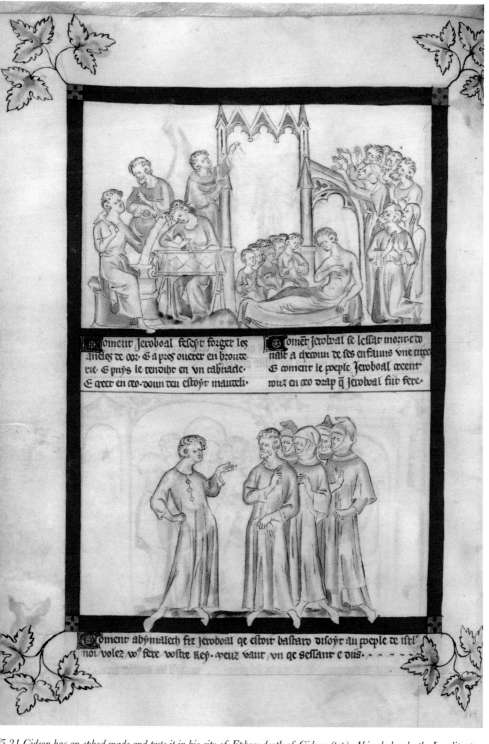

oment Jeroboal fesoyt forger les
andes te cor. E a pres ouerer en broute
rie. E puys le tenoyte en vn tabnacle.
E arer en ceo. doun teu estoyt mauteli.

omet Jerobval se lessar morir. e to
nalt a chenun te ses enfauns vne cipe
E coment le peple Jeroboal accent
wurx en ceo drap q Jeroboal fuit fere.

oment abymalech fiz Jeroboal qe estoit bastard disoyt au peple de isrl
noi volez w? fere vostre Rey. aveuz vaut vn qe sessant e ous.

5.21 *Gideon has an ephod made and puts it in his city of Ephra; death of Gideon (top); Abimelech asks the Israelites to* [make] *him king (bottom), Queen Mary Psalter; London, British Library, MS Royal 2 B. VII, fol. 37v.*

Fig. 5.22 Aaron wearing the ephod, in a manuscript of tables partly based on Nicholas of Lyra's Postillae litterales; *Oxford, Bodleian Library, MS Laud Misc. 156, fol. 6r, detail.*

Postea indutus est Aaron universis ornamentis pontificalibus sicut distinxit et disposuit dominus moysi in monte synai.

Per ornamenta pontificalia aaron in veteri testamento representant ornamenta sacerdotalia in novo.

5.23 *Aaron wearing the ephod (top); a bishop vested in a cope and miter (bottom), OPL Moralized Bible; Oxford, ...eian Library, MS Bodley 270b, fol. 54r, detail.*

Fig. 5.24 Unfinished drawing of Gideon's ephod in the tabernacle, Queen Mary Psalter (London, British Library MS Royal 2 B. VII, fol. 37v, detail). Image captured us the infrared lights set at 1050 nm and taken at The Britt Library as part of a multispectral imaging sequence. Pho Multi-spectral images were captured and processed at Th British Library Centre for Conservation by Dr. Christina Duffy.

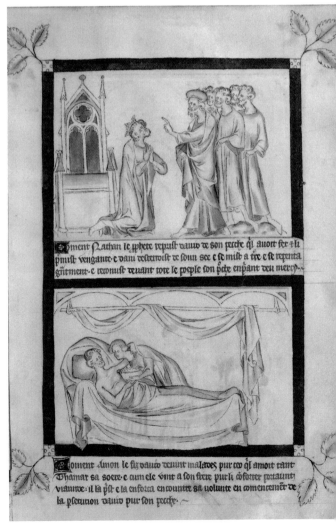

Fig. 5.25 David reproached by Nathan (top); Amnon rapes Tamar (bottom), Queen Mary Psalter; London, British Library, MS Royal 2 B. VII, fol. 58r.

Fig. 5.26(a) St. Edward's Chair: three-quarter view; Westminster Abbey.

Fig 5.26(b) St. Edward's Chair: back, after 2013 restoration; Westminster Abbey.

and Jesus' teachings.[41] In the Queen Mary Master's drawing, both Moses' veil and the tablets he holds up for the Israelites' inspection blind them to the truths contained in their Law.

Yet as striking as the Queen Mary artist's conception of this scene is the explanation for the origin of Moses' horns and use of the veil that is offered in the picture caption. As the Anglo-Norman French text avers, Moses' "countenance is so illumined by the grace of God that no one can look upon him, unless he holds a veil in front of his face, and as a result *they think that Moses has horns*" (emphasis added) (Fig. 5.13, bottom).[42] As Warner observed, an analogous presentation of this idea is found in *Cursor Mundi*:

> Quen Moyses had broght þe lagh (the law)
> And his folk in þe face him sagh,
> Þam thought him hornd apon farr (from afar),
> And duted þam to cum him nerr.[43]
>
> (lines 6653–56)

Thus, rather than a convention of Christian visual representation, the Middle English poem and the captioned prefatory picture present Moses' horns as a figment of the Israelites' fear and ignorance: because Moses hides his face with a veil, the benighted Israelites imagine that he has horns.

A range of negative connotations accrued to horns in medieval Christian thought. Most relevant to the captioned picture in the Psalter preface, it was widely believed in the later Middle Ages (and well beyond) that all Jews had horns that they hid under their hats, a mark of their allegiance to the Devil.[44] It may be, therefore, that the Queen Mary Master's drawing, so unusual in iconography and apparently sophisticated in conception, has a double meaning and function: it is at once a subtle vehicle for Christian exegesis, and the means by which to transform a myth originating in Christian superstition and anti-Judaism into a piquant "proof" of Jewish blindness and witlessness.

Far less complex in visual conception but more enigmatic in inspiration is the final scene in the Moses cycle (Fig. 5.15, top). In the tall, narrow compartment on

41 BL Add. 47682, fol. 27v; Brown, *Holkham Bible Picture Book*, 71.

42 ". . . taunt est son visage alumee de la grace Deu, qe nul ne le poit regarder, si i ne tent un liinge par devant e de ceo quideynt qe il estoit cornu" (BL Royal 2 B. VII, fol. 26r, bottom).

43 *Cursor Mundi*, ed. Morris, Part 2, Early English Text Society o.s. 59 (London, 1875; repr. 1966), 384; Warner, *Queen Mary's Psalter*, 20 n. 1.

44 Joshua Trachtenberg, *The Devil and the Jews: The Medieval Conception of the Jew and its Relation to Modern Anti-Semitism* (New Haven, 1943), 44–52.

the left is the solitary figure of Moses and Aaron's sister Miriam, or "Marie," as the Anglo-Norman French preface calls her, whom God punished with leprosy for speaking against Moses (Num. 12:10–14). In the larger compartment, from left, God tells Moses that he will show him the Promised Land but that Moses will never enter it (Num. 27:12–14, Deut. 32:49–52); next, Moses passes the leadership of the Israelites to Joshua (Num. 27:18–23, Deut. 31:3, 7–8); and, on the right, Moses is buried – neither by God himself in an unknown valley in the land of Moab, as related in scripture (Deut. 34:6), nor on Mount Nebo, as held in Christian tradition, but rather by one of his fellow Jews (possibly Joshua) on "Mt. Thabor." Further, as the caption avers, the Israelites bury Moses "upright, according to Jewish law,"[45] and the picture shows Moses being interred standing up, his face and a hand visible at the mouth of his vertically oriented, vaguely tubular grave.

Medieval depictions of Moses' burial usually show the Lord Himself (following scripture) or one of his angels interring the patriarch's body in a regular, horizontal grave: occasionally, as in an illuminated southwest German manuscript of Rudolf von Ems' *Weltchronik*, the Deity even wields a spade to accomplish this task.[46] Jewish writings, including the Midrash, feature numerous legends surrounding Moses' demise, including the prophet's mourning his impending death and his evasion of the angel that God sent to take his soul, material that apparently informed the program of the copiously illustrated Byzantine Octateuchs.[47]

But the notion that Jews bury their dead standing up is obviously neither a tenet of Judaism nor a motif in Jewish exegesis. What might have been the source of this idea? Perhaps it lies in the artisans' distorted memory, or misinterpretation, of a visual image, such an early Christian, Byzantine, or Italian image of

---

45 "Ici est coment Moyses est enterré en la gyse de lour ley tut en estaunt sur le mount Thabor, dount Josué e les autres feseyent grant doyl. Icii est chevi l'estorie Moyses" (Here Moses is buried upright, according to Jewish law, on Mount Thabor, while Joshua and the others mourned greatly. Here ends the story of Moses) (BL Royal 2 B. VII, fol. 27v, right column).

46 An angel of the Lord buries Moses in the Carolingian San Paolo Bible of c. 870 (Rome, Abbazia di San Paolo fuori le Mura, fol. 50v), for example. God Himself buries the patriarch in the Illustrated Old English Hexateuch (BL Cotton Claudius B. IV, fol. 139v) and in a *Bible Historiale* made c. 1300–25 in Saint-Omer (BnF MS fr. 152, fol. 94v). For the image in the *Weltchronik* manuscript (dated c. 1365) in which God uses a shovel to bury Moses (Karlsruhe, Badische Landesbibliothek, Donaueschingen 79, fol. 85r), see http://digital.blb-karlsruhe.de/blbhs/content/pageview/120513.

47 Kurt Weitzmann, Massimo Bernabò, and Rita Tarasconi, *The Byzantine Octateuchs*, 2 vols. (Princeton, 1999), 1:222–23, and 2:figs. 1117–21.

the Raising of Lazarus, which sometimes show the tightly wrapped Lazarus emerging, standing, from the vertically oriented mouth of his rock-cut tomb.[48] Or perhaps this notion originated in the artisans' memory and misinterpretation of the rituals associated with an actual Jewish burial. At one point in the burial rite, whether the body was interred in a coffin or only a shroud, it was held or tipped upright on a platform in order for water to be poured over it in "a simulacrum of immersion in a *mikveh*," or ritual bath.[49]

Or, most likely, and like the captioned picture showing the Israelites' fear of Moses's "horns," caption and image register a fantasy or myth about Jews widely believed in a Christian culture that, on the one hand, shared with the Jews the God of Abraham, had incorporated the Hebrew scriptures into its own Bible, and regarded the Hebrew prophets, judges, and kings as models of piety, wisdom, and valor or anti-models of their opposite qualities; and on the other hand, perceived contemporary Jews and their customs, whether real or imagined, as inherently alien.[50] The myth of Jewish upright burial may have seemed all the more credible in the England of Edward II, when the Queen Mary Psalter was made, because there were few opportunities to encounter actual Jews, Edward I having expelled them from the realm in 1290.[51] A contemporary Londoner would have been aware of the Domus Conversorum, or House of Converts, established in 1232 by Henry III, and which in Edward II's day provided a home and living for the few former Jews who remained in England after the Expulsion. Located in what is now Chancery Lane, or Chaunceler Lane, as this thoroughfare was called in the early fourteenth century, and therefore not far from Paternoster and Fleet Streets, the loci of the expanding London book trade, the Domus

48 See for example the panel depicting the Raising of Lazarus on the back of Duccio's *Maestà Altarpiece* (c. 1308–11); my thanks to Lucy Freeman Sandler and Kathleen Doyle for this suggestion.

49 Professor Marc Michael Epstein, Vassar College, email correspondence with author, 2/3/14. For Jewish burial and all other customs and traditions, see Ronald L. Eisenberg, *The JPS Guide to Jewish Traditions* (Philadelphia, 2004).

50 For a similarly fantastical explanation for Jewish abstention from pork, devised in connection with the apocryphal Infancy tale known as the Miracle of the Children in the Oven, a theme apparently witnessed solely in English Gothic art, see Kathryn A. Smith, *Art, Identity and Devotion in Fourteenth-Century England: Three Women and their Books of Hours* (London and Toronto, 2003), 275–85, with earlier bibliography.

51 Robin R. Mundill, *England's Jewish Solution: Experiment and Expulsion, 1262–1290* (Cambridge, UK, 1998); idem, *King's Jews: Money, Massacre and Exodus in Medieval England* (London and New York, 2010).

Conversorum housed a mere thirty-four men and women in 1308.[52] Those at court in late 1309 might have known of the visit of Master Elyas, a rabbi or doctor whom Edward II summoned from northern France "to speak with the king concerning his affairs," as London chroniclers noted, or of the delegation of six Jews who came to London the following summer and petitioned Edward in vain to permit the Jews' resettlement in England.[53] The very language of their remembrance in government records illuminates the degree to which the Jews were a "virtual" presence that "haunt[ed]" the consciousness of post-Expulsion England, as Miriamne Ara Krummel has put it, despite the Jews' physical and legal absence from the realm. An entry in the Patent Rolls from 1305 describes a chapel in Colemanestre, London, that was taken over by the Friars of the Sack as "lately the synagogue of the Jews." "Sarra de London, a Jewess" and "Moses son of Jacob de Lond[onia], a Jew" are invoked in Fine Roll entries from 1314 and 1319 – respectively nearly twenty-five and thirty years after the Expulsion – in reference to their former houses in Northampton and Oxford, property that had long since passed to the Crown.[54]

But to return to the image of Moses' burial in the Old Testament preface (Fig. 5.15, top), I know of no extant ancient or medieval textual source for the notion that upright interment is a tenet of Jewish law. Like the idea that Jews have horns, however, the myth that Jews bury their dead standing up is one of exceptional longevity: indeed, it is current to this day, as even a cursory search of the internet reveals.[55] The Queen Mary Psalter thus may preserve the earliest surviving evidence of a long-held belief about Jewish custom and culture born of ignorance and/or curiosity about that custom and culture. That both this idea and the notion that Jews have horns may be called "popular," in the sense of widespread and "normative," is suggested by their currency among a broad audience that encompassed the elite reader-viewers of the Queen Mary Psalter, and, presumably, their associates and advisers, as well as the artisans

---

52 Lauren Fogle, "The *Domus Conversorum*: The Personal Interest of Henry III," *Jewish Historical Studies* 41 (2007): 1–7; Joe Hillaby and Caroline Hillaby, *The Palgrave Dictionary of Medieval Anglo-Jewish History* (Houndmills, Hampshire, 2013), 117–20.

53 *Chronicles of the Reigns of Edward I and Edward II*, ed. William Stubbs, 2 vols. (London, 1882–83), 1 (1882): 269 (June 24, 1310; the petition of the Jews to resettle); Cecil Roth, *A History of the Jews in England* (Oxford, 1941), "The Middle Period, 1290–1609," 132; Miriamne Ara Krummel, *Crafting Jewishness in Medieval England: Legally Absent, Virtually Present* (Houndmills, Hampshire, and New York, 2011), 12.

54 Krummel, *Crafting Jewishness*, 9–11.

55 See for instance Yahoo.com at https://answers.yahoo.com/question/index?qid= 20080110051127AAN8E8M and Ask.com at https://www.reference.com/world-view/ jewish-people-buried-standing-up-51b3a84d336436d1.

who produced the manuscript.[56] Moreover, that these ideas are figured forth in an illuminated manuscript universally held to be among the most elegant, refined productions of early fourteenth-century England is affirmation that popular culture and elite esthetics are in no way mutually exclusive spheres or phenomena.

An ostensible concern of several of the captioned pictures in the preface is the preservation of the monarch's dignity. For example, during his pursuit of David in the desert of Ein Gedi, Saul goes into a cave to relieve himself, not knowing that David and his men are hiding in the cave's recesses. Although David's men urge him to kill Saul, David refuses to do this, and instead cuts off the hem of the unsuspecting king's cloak, later offering it to Saul as evidence of his loyalty (1 Sam. 24:1–7) (Fig. 5.16). Neither the depiction of this episode in the Morgan Old Testament Picture Book (Fig. 5.17) nor the one in the later fourteenth-century English Bohun Psalter-Hours shrinks from portraying Saul's vulnerability: the king squats in the mouth of the cave, drawers lowered or split to reveal bare, white flesh.[57] The makers of the Tickhill Psalter created for Saul an arcaded privy or garderobe in the desert, adding the label "spelunca" to the third and fourth scenes in the *bas-de-page* series in order to clarify the episode's now ambiguous setting (Figs. 5.18–5.19).

The caption for this scene in the Queen Mary Psalter preface preserves both the story's cave locus and the purpose of Saul's visit, yet these elements have been virtually purged from the picture (Fig. 5.16).[58] Saul sits on a draped bench under a row of traceried arches, with neither the setting nor the arrangement of the king's garments suggesting the episode's larger narrative context.

56 For the concept of "popular culture" in relation to premodern societies and in general, see Harriet E. Hudson, "Toward a Theory of Popular Literature: The Case of the Middle English Romances," *Journal of Popular Culture* 23 (1989): 31–50; and Holt N. Parker, "Toward a Definition of Popular Culture," *History and Theory* 50 (2011): 147–70; and also C. M. Kauffmann, "Art and Popular Culture: New Themes in the Holkham Bible Picture Book," in *Studies in Medieval Art and Architecture Presented to Peter Lasko*, ed. David Buckton and T. A. Heslop (Stroud, Gloucestershire, and Dover, NH, 1994), 46–69.

57 BL MS Egerton 3277, fol. 29v; for the manuscript see Sandler, *Gothic Manuscripts*, 2:151–54, no. 135; and idem, *Illuminators and Patrons*; for additional bibliography and the fully digitized manuscript, see the British Library's Digital Catalogue of Illuminated Manuscripts at http://www.bl.uk/catalogues/illuminatedmanuscripts (search for "Egerton 3277").

58 "Coment Saul entra une spelunke pur purger sa ventre, e David estoit dedenz oue ses compaignouns, e ses compaygnouns voleint aver tué Saul e David ne assentast mye e privément trencha une piece de soun mauntel" (BL Royal 2 B. VII, fol. 52v, top).

Similarly, in the depiction in the Morgan Old Testament Picture Book of the triumphant return of the Ark of the Covenant to Jerusalem, the artist portrayed a regally dressed David leaping and dancing vigorously to celebrate the Ark's restoration, conduct that caused Michal, shown wagging a finger at David from a tower window, to despise and criticize her husband for his vulgar, buffoonish behavior (2 Sam. 6:14–20).[59] A sober David enters Jerusalem under the subdued gaze of Michal in the Parisian Psalter-Hours "of Isabelle of France" (Fig. 5.20). The Queen Mary Master's David is a dignified figure who wears a simple gown – the "vestments of a prophet" (vestement de prophete), as the caption explains – a detail apparently derived from scripture (Fig. 5.3, top).[60] The English artist's conception of this scene compares suggestively with that in the Psalter-Hours: perhaps the Queen Mary Master had access to models based on that royal Parisian manuscript or its exemplar (compare Fig. 5.3, top, and Fig. 5.20). Yet in the Queen Mary Psalter preface, as Stanton noted, and in contrast to the miniature in the French Psalter-Hours, Michal and her reproach have been eliminated from the story:[61] in place of the tower and arched window that frame Michal in the Parisian picture, the English artist rendered a void surmounted by a crenellated balcony. In addition to preserving David's dignity, Michal's elimination at this point in the narrative clears the way for Bathsheba, who makes her first appearance in the preface in the bottom register of the same folio (Fig. 5.3, bottom).

David's stately dance before the Ark points to another theme of the Old Testament preface: the role of the Israelites' leaders as models of correct religious observance, and the consequences of their periodic lapses into illicit image-making and -worship. Thus, Abraham rejects his father, Terah or Thare, portrayed in the preface as a maker of calf-shaped idols, and tramples his father's wares before bidding him farewell, renouncing idolatry, and departing his ancestral home, a rare pictorial theme attested in the Midrash, as Michael Camille noted, and in the Jewish *Book of Jubilees* (second century BCE) as well as the Koran.[62] When Solomon lapses into idolatry under the influence of his foreign wives (1 Kings 11:1–8), the idols he adores take the form of devils displayed on an altar.[63]

59   PML M. 638, fol. 39v; http://www.themorgan.org/collection/crusader-bible/78.

60   See 2 Sam. 6:14, ". . . and David was girded with a linen ephod."

61   "Coment l'arke fust amené en Jerusalem, e David en vestement de prophete e autres prophetes e gentz alerent devaunt oue harpes e autres instrumenz de menustracye" (BL Royal 2 B. VII, fol. 56v, top); Stanton, *Queen Mary Psalter*, 174, 178.

62   BL Royal 2 B. VII, fols. 7v–8r; http://jewishencyclopedia.com, s.v. "Jubilees, Book of"; Camille, *Gothic Idol*, 168 and 375 n. 5; Stanton, *Queen Mary Psalter*, 90.

63   BL Royal 2 B. VII, fol. 66r, top.

Also associated with both the crafting of images and their illicit worship are the final scenes in the story of Gideon, or Jerobaal, pictures that offer another window into the crafting of the Psalter preface itself. In the bottom picture on the penultimate page of the Gideon cycle (fol. 37r), after refusing his people's petition to become their king, Gideon caps his victory over the Midianites by asking the Israelites to bring him the defeated enemy's gold earrings (Judg. 8:23–25). The picture at the top of the next page is based on Judg. 8:27, which relates that Gideon had the Midianites' gold made into an ephod, which he placed in the sanctuary of his city of Ephra. The Israelites' worship of the ephod angered God and brought about the tragedy that subsequently befell Gideon's house.

While Gideon's request for the Midianites' gold appears in both Byzantine and Western art, the depiction in Royal 2 B. VII of the *crafting* and *display* of the ephod is an apparently singular medieval survival (Fig. 5.21, top).[64] This may be a function of the tendency in Christian exegesis to interpret Gideon and his story as types of Christ and of the Virgin's purity, as model rather than anti-model. Equally intriguing, the image is unfinished: at the center of the picture, Gideon reaches up to hang the ephod within a gabled Gothic tabernacle. The artist rendered a line or stroke beneath Gideon's hand indicating where the ephod would go, but never drew in that object.

What precisely Gideon's ephod was, is a matter of debate in biblical scholarship. Some writers argue that it was a golden image associated with oracular practices and priestly ritual, while others maintain that it was a splendid garment similar to the ephod crafted at God's command for Aaron to consecrate him as high priest.[65] As described in scripture (Exod. 28:4–40), the high priest's ephod was made of gold, violet, purple, and scarlet linen embroidered with multicolor thread. Outfitted with gold hooks, rings, and bells at the hem and worn with a girdle or sash, shoulder-pieces adorned with precious stones engraved with the names of the children of Israel, and a miter or head covering, these vestments were completed by a breastplate studded with engraved stones commemorating the twelve Israelite tribes. The Gothic visual corpus features numerous evocations of Aaron's ephod, among them a drawing in an early fifteenth-century English manuscript of tables partly based on Nicholas of Lyra's *Postillae litterales* (Fig. 5.22).[66] In the writings of Durandus and in the OPL Moralized Bible, Aaron's

64 Stanton, *Queen Mary Psalter*, 165.

65 http://jewishencyclopedia.com, s.v. "Ephod"; Diane M. Sharon, "Echoes of Gideon's Ephod: An Intertextual Reading," *Journal of the Ancient Near Eastern Society of Columbia University* 30 (2006): 89–102.

66 Bodleian Library, MS Laud misc. 156, fol. 6r; for which see Kathleen L. Scott, "An English Modelbook for Nicholas of Lyra's *Postilla litteralis*," in idem, *Tradition and Innovation in Later Medieval English Manuscripts* (London, 2007), 1–32; and Mary Carruthers, "The

ephod is offered as the forerunner or prototype of Christian ecclesiastical vestments (Fig. 5.23).[67]

This Levitical, typological understanding of the ephod appears to inform the depiction of Gideon's ephod as it was meant to have been portrayed in the Queen Mary Psalter preface (Fig. 5.21, top). In Latin, Anglo-Norman French, and Middle English, the words "ephod," "ephot," and "ephoth" were used to describe both Jewish and Christian vestments: in the Wycliffite Bible (1382), Aaron's ephod is characterized as "a preestis ouermest clothing, that we cleepen a *cope*" (emphasis added).[68] Neither the unillustrated summary of the story of Gideon-Jerobaal in the Psalter preface nor the caption for this drawing employs the term "ephod." But the unillustrated summary describes this object as a "drap" – a "mantle," "cloth," or "drapery" – one "more luxurious than the richest *choir cope* ever created" (emphasis added).[69] An infrared image of the area within the tabernacle taken at the British Library as part of a multispectral imaging sequence reveals what appear to be the curved hem and voluminous folds of a cope, and, perhaps, the triangular panel or vestigial hood included in some examples (Fig. 5.24).[70] Why the artist never finished the drawing is unknown. Perhaps, after sketching in the outlines of the vestment, he consulted the text-compiler or the text itself and simply forgot to finish the job.

That the caption to this image also refers to Gideon's ephod as an "embroidered cloth" or "embroidery" is a reminder of the importance of London and Westminster as centers for the crafting of high-quality embroidery,

'Pictures' of Jerusalem in Oxford, Bodleian Library MS Laud Misc. 156," in *Imagining Jerusalem in the Medieval West*, ed. Lucy Donkin and Hannah Vorholt, *Proceedings of the British Academy* 175 (2012): 97–121. For additional Gothic depictions of the high priest's ephod, see Lesley Smith, "The Imaginary Jerusalem of Nicholas of Lyra," in *Imagining Jerusalem in the Medieval West*, 78–97, figs. 3.1 and 3.2, with additional bibliography.

67 For the origins and symbolism of the cope, see J. Wickham Legg and W. H. St. John Hope, *Inventories of Christchurch Canterbury* (Westminster, 1902), vii–xvii; and Christine Linnell, "Opus Anglicanum with Particular Reference to Copes as Liturgical Show-Pieces, Ecclesiastical Exemplars and Eucharistic Exegetes" (PhD diss., University of St. Andrews, 1995), 22–28, esp. 28.

68 *OED*, s.v. "Ephod"; *Glossarium Mediae et infirmae latinitatis*, s.v. "Ephod," at http://ducange.enc.sorbonne.fr/EPHOT; *The Anglo-Norman Dictionary*, s.v. "Ephot," at http://www.anglo-norman.net/gate/. My great thanks to Alixe Bovey for this reference and for her invaluable help in thinking about the portrayal of the ephod in BL Royal 2 B. VII.

69 "E [Jeroboal] fesoyt fere un drap si com une Chape de quoer la plus riche qe pout estre fet" (BL Royal 2 B. VII, fol. 35r).

70 See for example the Butler-Bowden Cope; London, Victoria & Albert Museum, T.36-1955, c. 1330–50; at http://collections.vam.ac.uk/item/O93441/cope-unknown/.

or *opus anglicanum* (Fig. 5.21).[71] During the thirteenth through fifteenth centuries, the royal court appears to have been the locus of "more or less permanent workshops" for the production of luxury embroidery.[72] Edwards II and III, Isabella of France, and Philippa of Hainault are among the royal patrons recorded as having commissioned copes and other vestments as gifts, as well as items such as counterpanes and other furnishings.[73] In close alliance with the text, the Queen Mary Master depicted some of the steps involved in the ephod's creation. At the extreme left, a man seated at an anvil attends his instructions and prepares to forge the Midianites' earrings into gold thread and ornament (*Coment Jeroboal feseyt forger les aneles de oor*). This vignette reflects the actual setting of much embroidery-making at the royal court, as many (male) embroiderers practiced their craft in the workshops of the royal armorers.[74] To the right of this first craftsman, another artisan sits at a trestle table or a wooden embroidery frame (*E aprés ouerer en brouderie*), perhaps drawing out the design on the fabric or else transferring it by pricking or pouncing.[75] The artisan's left hand is *beneath* the fabric rather than *above* it, however, a detail more readily associated with representations of sewing or embroidering than of drawing or

71   "Coment Jeroboal feseyt forger les aneles de oor. E aprés overer en brouderie, e puis le tendiht en un tabernacle. E creet en ceo, doun Deu estoyt mau de li" (How Jeroboal had the golden earrings melted down, and afterwards had made an embroidered cloth, and hung it in the tabernacle, and worshipped this, which angered God against him) (BL MS Royal 2 B. VII, fol. 37v, top). For *opus anglicanum*, see A. G. I. Christie, *English Medieval Embroidery* (Oxford, 1938); Donald King, *Opus Anglicanum: English Medieval Embroidery* (London, 1963); Kay Staniland, *Medieval Craftsmen: Embroiderers* (London, 1991); Linnell, "Opus Anglicanum;" *English Medieval Embroidery: Opus Anglicanum*, ed. Clare Browne, Glyn Davies, and M. A. Michael, with Michaela Zöschg (New Haven and London, 2016); and *The Age of Opus Anglicanum: A Symposium*, ed. M. A. Michael, Studies in English Medieval Embroidery I (London and Turnhout, 2016).
72   Staniland, *Medieval Craftsmen: Embroiderers*, 49; Glyn Davies, "Embroiderers and the Embroidery Trade," here quoting 42, in Browne et al., eds., *English Medieval Embroidery.*
73   Julian Gardner, "*Opus Anglicanum* and its Medieval Patrons," 52–53; and M. A. Michael, "The Artistic Context of *Opus Anglicanum*," 61–75, both in Browne et al., eds., *English Medieval Embroidery.*
74   Staniland, *Medieval Craftsmen: Embroiderers*, 23, 49; Annemarie Weyl Carr, "Women as Artists in the Middle Ages: 'The Dark is Light Enough,'" in *Dictionary of Women Artists*, ed. Delia Gaze, 2 vols. (London and Chicago, 1997), 2:6; Lisa Monnas, "Embroideries for Edward III," in *The Age of Opus Anglicanum*, ed. Michael, 50–68.
75   Compare the implement in the artisan's hand to the ones shown in Staniland, *Medieval Craftsmen: Embroiderers*, 32, Fig. 29.

pouncing.[76] It appears, then, that the artist sought to evoke here all three steps simultaneously – drawing, pouncing, and embroidering – in order to figure forth for the Psalter's reader-viewers the full "sweep" of the craft process.

Surviving copes and descriptions of them in inventories give a sense of these vestments' material richness and elaborate ornament, which could include gems, pearls, and a range of devices, designs, and imagery, including figural and narrative imagery.[77] Lavishly ornamented copes were among the most visible elements of processions and ceremonials and in the celebration of the liturgy. During the preparatory phases of the mass, the cope marked the celebrant as Christ's representative on earth, "fitting" him to enact "the sacramental mystery on behalf of the assembled congregation."[78] Yet what is most fascinating about this picture and its allied texts is the manner in which they recast the Jews' lapse into idolatry as a lesson in proper Christian worship.[79] The Jews' false god here is neither a calf-shaped idol nor a demonic statue, as in so many Christian representations of idolatry (including several in the Psalter preface itself), but rather a resplendent vestment that was a key element of Christian liturgy and ceremonial. Even in its unfinished state, the prefatory picture would have reminded the Christian reader-viewer that copes in all their glittering magnificence could be admired for their artistry and appreciated for the manner in which they enhanced the solemnity and affirmed the sacrality of the service; yet they were never to be regarded as objects of worship.

A luxurious cope is not the only artifact crafted at Westminster that is evoked on the pages of the Queen Mary Psalter preface. In the picture on fol. 58r, which shows the prophet Nathan's reproof of David for the latter's sexual relations with Bathsheba, his murder of her husband, the soldier Uriah, and subsequent marriage of Bathsheba (2 Sam. 12:1–14), a chastened David kneels on the left, his hands clasped in prayer. The prophet Nathan stands at the head of a phalanx of four men and wags an index finger in stern rebuke of his repentant royal protégé (Fig. 5.25, top). The caption describes the scene thus:

76 Compare the artisan in the drawing in the Psalter to the female embroiderer in the fresco "Allegory of March: The Triumph of Minerva" in the Palazzo Schifanoia in Ferrara (1476–84) by Francesco del Cossa et al., reproduced in Staniland, *Medieval Craftsmen: Embroiderers*, 49, Fig. 54.

77 Wickham Legg and St. John Hope, *Inventories of Christchurch Canterbury*, 53–57; J. Wickham Legg, "On an Inventory of the Vestry of Westminster Abbey, Taken in 1388," *Archaeologia*, s.s. 52 (1890): 205–6, 256ff.

78 Linnell, "Opus Anglicanum," 244; Richard W. Pfaff, *The Liturgy in Medieval England: A History* (Cambridge, UK, 2009), 231–32, and also 108 and 240.

79 Camille, *Gothic Idol*, esp. ch. 4, "Idols of the Jews," 165–95.

How the prophet Nathan reproved David for the sin that he had committed and promised him that [the Lord] would be avenged. And David descended from his seat and submitted himself on the earth and sincerely repented, and acknowledged his sin in front of all the people, praying for God's mercy.[80]

The seat from which David has "descended," shown behind the kneeling monarch at the picture's left edge, features pinnacled corner-posts and a gabled back adorned with tracery and topped by a bulb-like finial. Although it does not match the original in all of its details, I suggest that this image is meant to evoke an artifact crafted at Westminster not long before the Queen Mary Psalter itself: St. Edward's Chair, now commonly known as the Coronation Chair (Figs. 5.26a and b).[81] Originally commissioned in 1296 by Edward I as a form of "trophy case" to enclose the Stone of Scone, the block of red sandstone used in the coronations of the kings of Scotland that Edward captured that year during his successful military campaign against the Scots, St. Edward's Chair was conceived as a gift to Westminster Abbey.[82] Master Walter of Durham, "the king's painter," crafted the chair that survives today c. 1298–99; by 1307, it was installed next to the shrine of Edward the Confessor in St. Edward's Chapel in Westminster Abbey, as an inventory compiled that year confirms. Although the chair is only documented as having been used in the coronation ceremony in 1399, for the coronation of Henry Bolingbroke as Henry IV, many scholars believe that it may have served as the Coronation Chair as early as 1308, for Edward II's crowning.[83]

To the modern eye, the Queen Mary Master's drawing may seem only a distant reflection of the chair's actual appearance. Yet the artist approached the task of rendering the chair in a manner consonant with medieval notions of copying or "portraying," the goal of which was not to reproduce exactly every feature of the original, but rather selectively and meaningfully to "transfer" and

---

80 "Coment Nathan le prophete reprist David de son pecché q'il avoit fet e li promist vengance. E Davi[d] descendist de soun see e se mist a terre e se repenta grantment e reconust devant tote le poeple son pecché en priant Deu mercy" (BL Royal 2 B. VII, fol. 58r, top).

81 Warner, *Queen Mary's Psalter*, did not discuss this scene; Stanton, *Queen Mary Psalter*, 179, identified the object in the picture as an altar. The most recent, detailed study of St. Edward's Chair is Warwick Rodwell, *The Coronation Chair and the Stone of Scone: History, Archaeology and Conservation* (Oxford and Oakville, CT, 2013). This analysis draws on Kathryn A. Smith, "St. Edward's Chair in the Queen Mary Psalter," *Electronic British Library Journal*, art. 10 (2017): 1–18, http://www.bl.uk/eblj/2017articles/article10.html.

82 Paul Binski, *Westminster Abbey and the Plantagenets: Kingship and the Representation of Power 1200–1400* (New Haven and London, 1995), 135–40, at 138.

83 See Rodwell, *Coronation Chair*, 15–21, 37–38, and 42 for a summary of the debates.

reformulate a few of its most important elements.[84] The Queen Mary Master has done just that: the tracery on the throne as rendered on the page conflates and condenses into a single bay the main tracery forms on the various parts of the once richly gilded and polychromed oaken chair, including the open quatrefoils on the bottom grille, the oculus within the gable on the chair's back, the bifora-with-oculus units on the back's upper register, the blind arches on the lower back and arms, and the bulb-like finial that once topped the gabled back.

The importance of the Queen Mary Master's drawing lies in far more than its ostensible status as the earliest known evocation in English art of St. Edward's Chair, however.[85] The narrative context, too, is significant. This image of a repentant Israelite king submitting to reproof by his councilor(s) resonates with the political struggles that dominated the reign of Edward II (Fig. 5.25, top). In large part in consequence of his tendency to promote and rely on unpopular favorites, as well as his poor judgment and perceived abuses, relations between Edward II and his barons and clergy were often contentious – and from even before his coronation.[86] A string of political crises early in the reign resulted in the appointment in March 1310 of the Ordainers, those prelates and nobles of the realm who "were to have full powers to reform the state both of the kingdom and of the king's household."[87] Indeed, as Seymour Phillips notes, citing the account in the London chronicle the *Vita Edwardi Secundi*, during the roughly three weeks preceding the Ordainers' appointment, the conflict between Edward and his barons had become so heated that the barons accused the king of "breaking his coronation oath and threatened him with deposition."[88] The Ordinances, issued in 1311, forced Edward to implement wide-ranging reforms designed to curb royal power and prerogatives in favor of a baronial council, and were confirmed during subsequent crises in 1316 and 1318 as well as 1321, when his barons apparently again threatened Edward with deposition.[89]

---

84   Richard Krautheimer, "Introduction to an 'Iconography of Mediaeval Architecture,'" *Journal of the Warburg and Courtauld Institutes* 5 (1942): 1–33, at 20; Stephen Perkinson, "Portraits and Counterfeits: Villard de Honnecourt and Thirteenth-Century Theories of Representation," in *Excavating the Medieval Image: Manuscripts, Artists, Audiences. Essays in Honor of Sandra Hindman*, ed. David S. Areford and Nina A. Rowe (Aldershot, Hampshire, and Burlington, VT, 2004), 13–35.

85   For other possible medieval representations of the chair, see Rodwell et al., *Coronation Chair*, 18–21.

86   The most recent biography of the king is Seymour Phillips, *Edward II* (New Haven and London, 2010).

87   Ibid., 166.

88   Ibid., 165.

89   Ibid., 387, 522.

The chronology of events presented here overlaps the Psalter's style-generated dating of c. 1310–20. The manuscript might have been produced at any time during the period c. 1310–22, or shortly thereafter:[90] Fresh examination of all of the Queen Mary group manuscripts from the codicological, scribal, stylistic, and iconographical perspectives might produce new insights into their dating as well as that of Royal MS 2 B. VII, among other questions. Moreover, by virtue of the manner in which it romances the Old Testament past, as well as its topical treatment of biblical history, the Psalter preface would have resonated with the experience of any highly placed member of the English court circle. Yet on account of those very qualities, and especially the subtle yet pointed allusion to the contemporary political "moment" in the image of David's rebuke by Nathan (Fig. 5.25, top), it is still congenial to imagine the manuscript as intended for the eyes of a royal reader-viewer. The preface could have functioned as a *speculum principis* for the young Edward III, as Stanton suggested.[91] Equally, however, the messages of this carefully tailored scene of royal submission, and of the illustrated preface as a whole, would have been meaningful to Edward II, whether during his early years as king or later in his tumultuous reign.

This paper has of necessity considered only a fraction of the Queen Mary Psalter's remarkable preface in service of evoking the *imaginaires* of its beholders and makers – the former phantom figures whose royal identity remains unconfirmed but is generally, and plausibly, assumed; the latter a resourceful text-compiler and scribe and an accomplished, *engagé* artist. Michael Prestwich is one of many scholars who have cautioned against the assumption that "particularly splendid" books can only have "originated at the court."[92] Yet if there is no evidence that the Queen Mary Master was a court artist or a member of a court "school," it is nonetheless fitting to imagine the illuminator as based at the royal court at Westminster for the duration of the project, as Deirdre Jackson has most recently suggested.[93] There, the artist would have had the time to dedicate to the assignment, ample support, an insider's perspective, and knowledge of or access to a diverse range of materials available both at court and in the city, from a moralized Bible of Capetian provenance and models based on lavishly

90 Stanton, *Queen Mary Psalter*, 240, plausibly suggested 1322 as an outer date for the production of the Psalter.

91 Ibid., 211–15, 238–39.

92 Michael Prestwich, "The Court of Edward II," in *The Reign of Edward II: New Perspectives*, ed. Gwilym Dodd and Anthony Musson (York, 2006), 68.

93 Jackson, in *Royal Manuscripts*, 272. For royal and noble patronage of both court and city book artisans, and for patrons' employment of book artisans on retainer, see most recently Kathryn A. Smith, *The Taymouth Hours: Stories and the Construction of the Self in Late Medieval England* (London and Toronto, 2012), 27–34.

illuminated French Arthurian romances and devotional manuscripts, to ambitious English works and artifacts of venerable or more recent vintage.

Access to a library or libraries would have served the artisans well. One collection whose riches the manuscript's makers might have mined was the royal library in the Privy Wardrobe in the Tower of London. Books appear in Wardrobe accounts from the reign of Edward I. Nonetheless, some of the most tantalizing evidence for the bibliophilic activities of the royal family and their close associates comes from a roll of issues and receipts submitted by the Keeper of the Wardrobe, John Fleet, that records the loan or return of some 160 "libri diversi," including religious and liturgical manuscripts and romances and other secular works in Latin and French.[94] The roll covers only the period c. 1322–41, yet it is not unreasonable to imagine the court as a book-rich environment in the earlier years of Edward II's reign. Isabella's activities and reputation as a patron and owner of books and other works of art are well established, and Edward owned, acquired, or was gifted manuscripts from his youth.[95] The court was certainly an image-rich environment. Documents record the king's purchase of or payment for religious paintings, tapestries, and murals, and even a tent displaying religious, historical, and political themes, during his adult life.[96]

London book artisans worked in the shadow of religious institutions that housed impressive libraries. The holdings of the library of Old St. Paul's were enriched in 1313 by a bequest by Ralph de Baldock, the energetic dean and later bishop of London, who left some 150 books to that institution in his will, including legal and religious texts, sermon collections, Bible commentaries, scientific works, an

94 Juliet Vale, *Edward III and Chivalry: Chivalric Society and its Context, 1270–1350* (Woodbridge, Suffolk, 1982), 49–50, 169; see also Susan H. Cavanaugh, "Royal Books: King John to Richard II," *The Library* ser. 6, 10, no. 1 (1988): 304–16; Jenny Stratford, "The Royal Library in England before Edward IV," in *England in the Fifteenth Century*, Proceedings of the 1992 Harlaxton Symposium, ed. Nicholas Rogers (Stamford, UK, 1994), 189–90; and Carter Revard, "Courtly Romances in the Privy Wardrobe," in *The Court and Cultural Diversity: Selected Papers from the Eighth Triennial Conference of the International Courtly Literature Society*, ed. Evelyn Mullally and John Thompson (Cambridge, UK, 1997), 297–308.

95 For Isabella's bibliophilic activities, see Susan H. Cavanaugh, "A Study of Books Privately Owned in England 1300–1450," 2 vols. (PhD diss., University of Pennsylvania, 1980), 1:456–60. For Edward's books and education generally, see Cavanaugh, "Study of Books Privately Owned," 1:275–79; and Phillips, *Edward II*, 54–60.

96 Prestwich, "Court of Edward II," 68.

illuminated Apocalypse, and chronicles.[97] The library of the nearby Dominican Priory at Blackfriars also was probably extensive.[98] Moreover, the makers of the Queen Mary Psalter could have tapped the resources of libraries outside of Westminster and London. St. Augustine's, Canterbury, was one of many English monasteries whose holdings included religious, historical, scientific, and literary works not only in Latin but also in French ("in gallico"), including chivalric and courtly romances, among them volumes "de launcelet," "qui vocatur Graal," and "del Rex Htus" (or "Artus").[99] Edward II is known to have borrowed from (and not returned to) the library of Christ Church Cathedral, Canterbury a copy of the *Lives* of saints Thomas Becket and Anselm.[100] Yet if the precise circumstances of the manuscript's production and the identities of its reader-viewers remain uncertain, what *is* certain is that the Queen Mary Psalter Old Testament preface brilliantly synthesizes the diverse intervisual, multilingual strands of early fourteenth-century England's rich artistic and readerly cultures.

97 The manuscripts in Ralph de Baldock's bequest are listed in A. B. Emden, *A Biographical Register of the University of Oxford*, 3 vols. (Oxford, 1957–59), 3 (1959): 2147–49; see also N. R. Ker, *Medieval Libraries of Great Britain: A List of Surviving Books*, 2nd edn. (London, 1964), 120–21; and Nigel Ramsay, "The Library and Archives to 1897," in *St. Paul's: The Cathedral Church of London 604–2004* (New Haven and London, 2004), 414.

98 The libraries of both Old St. Paul's and the Dominican priory at Blackfriars have been discussed by Peter B. Nowell in an unpublished paper titled "Two Lost Libraries in London" (2014), https://www.academia.edu/7883114/Two_Lost_Libraries_in_London.

99 M. R. James, *The Ancient Libraries of Canterbury and Dover* (Cambridge, UK, 1903), 371–74; Madeleine Blaess, "Les Manuscrits français dans les monastères anglais au moyen âge," *Romania* 94 (1973): 351–56.

100 James, *Ancient Libraries*, 148.

Affective Reading
and Walter Hilton's *Scale of Perfection* at Syon

MICHAEL G. SARGENT

When I arrived in New York thirty years ago, one of the first assignments I gave myself was to make sure to meet Mary Erler, an English professor at Fordham who had published an important article elucidating the care for books at Syon Abbey as it was described in the sacristan's account rolls of the early sixteenth century.[1] Mary and I have stayed in touch ever since, sharing our common interest in Henry V's two great religious houses, that of Brigittine nuns and brothers at Syon, northwest across the Thames from Richmond Palace, and the Carthusian monastery of Jesus of Bethlehem at Sheen, on the southeast bank of the Thames, to the west of the palace grounds.[2] Much of Mary's work has been on women's readership, spirituality, and associational networks (particularly through the medium of book production, ownership, gift, and bequest) in the later medieval and early modern period in England – with Syon Abbey as a constant thread in the web of her interests. A major part of my own interest has been in the production, transmission, and ownership of books among the later medieval English Carthusian monks – the *nexus* of textual, material, and social connection that the surviving manuscripts and early prints of these works embody – and the critical edition of some of the texts in these books.[3] One of

1   Mary Carpenter Erler, "Syon Abbey's Care for Books: Its Sacristan's Account Rolls 1506/7–1535/6," *Scriptorium* 39 (1985): 293–307.

2   The king originally envisaged three monasteries of the most austere religious orders at Richmond: the first founded was Jerusalem, a house of Celestine hermit/monks that originally occupied the site where Syon later came to stand, while the Brigittines were originally settled on marshy ground further upriver. A half-dozen Celestine monks were recruited from the house at Paris, but when these recent immigrants refused to pray for the success of the king's military expedition in 1415 (the expedition that was to end in the victory of Agincourt and the Treaty of Troyes, by which Henry would have become king of both England and France), the plan for a Celestine monastery was dropped, and only Sheen and Syon came to be.

3   See, for example, Michael G. Sargent, "The Transmission by the English Carthusians of some Late Medieval Spiritual Writings," *The Journal of Ecclesiastical History* 27 (1976): 225–40 (a revised, expanded version of this article will appear in *The Carthusians in the City: History, Culture and Martyrdom at the London Charterhouse, c. 1370–1545*, ed. Julian Luxford);

the strongest of these *nexus* of connection has been Syon Abbey; and the present paper is a study of the *nexus* of Syon Abbey and *The Scale of Perfection*, for there is a strong link between the two, a link formed in large part by the affective reading of the *Scale* by the nuns of Syon.[4]

Of the twenty-one surviving manuscripts originally containing the complete English text of the *Scale*, three have connections to Syon Abbey. These manuscripts are all affiliated with what I have termed the "Carthusian Group" of manuscripts of *Scale* II,[5] although, to be fair, it could just as well have been given the somewhat more cumbersome title the "Carthusian-Brigittine Group." This group comprises nine manuscripts and the 1494 Wynkyn de Worde *editio princeps* of the *Scale* (*STC* 14042: all later printings in fact derive from this one), plus two manuscripts that represent conflation of the Carthusian group with some other. All manuscripts of the Carthusian group contain both books of the *Scale*.[6] Their texts of *Scale* II originally did not have chapter titles, as other manuscripts do; they end with the phrase "this is the voice of Jesus," approximately half a page before the close of the text in other manuscripts; they share some 384 unique readings throughout the text (readings in which all of these manuscripts agree, and no others); and there is a consistent pattern of comparison and conflation of manuscripts within this group.

Nicholas Love, *The Mirror of the Blessed Life of Jesus Christ: A Full Critical Edition*, based on *Cambridge University Library Additional MSS 6578 and 6686, with Introduction, Notes and Glossary*, ed. Michael G. Sargent (Exeter, UK, 2005); and Walter Hilton, *The Scale of Perfection, Book II*, ed. S. S. Hussey and Michael G. Sargent, Early English Text Society o.s. 348 (Oxford, 2017).

4   The connection of the *Scale* with the brothers of Syon has been explored by Vincent Gillespie, "Dial M for Mystic: Mystical Texts in the Library of Syon Abbey and the Spirituality of the Syon Brethren," in *Looking in Holy Books: Essays on Late Medieval Religious Writing in England*, Brepols Collected Essays in European Cultures 3 (Turnhout, 2011), 175–207; and "Hilton at Syon Abbey," in *"Stand up to Godwards": Essays in Mystical and Monastic Theology in Honour of the Reverend John Clark on his Sixty-Fifth Birthday*, ed. James Hogg, Alain Girard, and Daniel LeBlévec, Analecta Cartusiana 204 (Salzburg, 2002), 9–60.

5   Note that the following observations refer primarily to the text of *Scale* II, to which have been added some observations concerning the text of *Scale* I drawn from Rosemary Birts's (Dorward's) 1951 Oxford M.Litt. thesis, "*The Scale of Perfection* by Walter Hilton, Canon at the Augustinian Priory of Thurgarton, Book I, Chapters 38–52," and from A. J. Bliss's unpublished materials compiled toward the critical edition of *Scale* I, which the Bliss family have given me in order that I might eventually complete the edition.

6   Another seventeen surviving originally complete manuscripts contain *Scale* I alone, two contain *Scale* II alone, and one contains an English *Scale* I followed by a copy of *Scale* II in the Carmelite Thomas Fishlake's contemporary Latin translation.

Of these manuscripts, five are connected with monasteries of the Carthusian order and three with Syon Abbey. As Mary Erler has noted,[7] BL MS Harley 2387 was bequeathed to Syon by Margery Pensax, former anchoress at St. Botolph's, Bishopsgate, who is recorded there in 1399 and 1413 (that is, before the foundation of Syon), and who may have occupied the cell at St. Botolph's as late as 1426. Pensax may have been the anchoress to whom Margery de Nerford left a choice of books in 1417 – making this manuscript, if Margery Pensax received it from Margery Nerford (which is possible) and then passed it along to Syon (which we know she did), a remarkable example of the kind of networks of relationship established through the giving and receiving of books among lay, vowed, and religious women that Mary's work has gone so far in elucidating. Another early fifteenth-century manuscript of the *Scale*, Oxford, All Souls College, MS 25, bears the name of "Rose Pachet, professed in Syon," a nun recorded in 1518 and 1539. A member of the household of survivors of Syon formed around John Green in the 1540s,[8] Rose Paget is recorded as receiving a pension in 1554/5, and was appointed as tenth prioress of the Syon community upon its Marian refoundation in 1557.[9] A third manuscript of the *Scale*, Oxford, Bodleian Library, MS Laud misc. 462, bears, on a fly-leaf within its original covers, a copy of a grant by King Edward IV to Syon, dated October 6, 1462.

Two out of seventeen surviving copies of the 1494 Wynkyn de Worde *editio princeps* of the *Scale* also have Syon connections. The Cambridge University Library copy was given to the former Cluniac monk Anthony Bolney, *quondam* sub-prior of Lewes abbey, by Katherine Palmer, a former Syon nun who led several groups of Syon brothers and sisters into exile in the Low Countries in the 1550s, brought a number of brothers and sisters back for the Marian refoundation of the house in England in 1557, and, as eighth abbess, led them into their Elizabethan exile. The copy of the *Scale* in the Rosenbach Library in Philadelphia was famously annotated by James Grenehalgh of Sheen Charterhouse for Johanna Sewell,

---

7   Mary C. Erler, *Women, Reading, and Piety in Late Medieval England* (Cambridge, UK, 2002), 169–70 n. 51. See also David N. Bell, *What Nuns Read: Books and Libraries in Medieval English Nunneries* (Kalamazoo, 1995), 190 n. 25.

8   Peter Cunich, "The Brothers of Syon, 1420–1695," in *Syon Abbey and its Books: Reading, Writing and Religion, c. 1400–1700*, ed. E. A. Jones and Alexandra Walsham (Woodbridge, Suffolk, 2010), 39–81; see esp. 71. See also Cunich, "Palmer, Katherine, d. 1576, abbess of Syon," in *Oxford Dictionary of National Biography* (Oxford 2004–); Bell, *What Nuns Read*, 196 n. 38; Erler, *Women, Reading, and Piety*, 121.

9   Bell, *What Nuns Read*, 196 n. 38.

probably for presentation to her on the day of her profession in Syon, April 28, 1500.[10]

Finally, there is the equally famous, no longer extant manuscript corresponding to item M.26 in the catalogue of the brothers' library in Syon, a copy that, like the original manuscript of *The Name of the Rose*, is often discussed, but known only by its trace.[11] Unfortunately, unlike the case of Umberto Eco's semiotic detective story, no amount of examination of the signifier seems here to have brought the signified back into existence.

One of the sixteen surviving manuscripts of Thomas Fishlake's contemporary Latin translation of the *Scale* is also connected to the Syon brothers: Uppsala, Universitetsbibliotek, MS C.159, a monastic *vade mecum* containing even a set of notes on the Sarum liturgy (which the Syon brothers used) was donated to the Brigittine mother-house at Vadstena in Sweden by Clement Maidstone, deacon in Syon, who died in 1456.[12]

There are more surviving copies of Walter Hilton's *Scale of Perfection* connected with Syon Abbey than with any other single religious house; and there are more copies of the *Scale* connected with Syon than of any other work written in English in the later Middle Ages. The only books connected with Syon that survive in greater numbers are psalters and other liturgical books. *The Scale of Perfection* was obviously in some sense a good "fit" for Syon, and particularly for the nuns of Syon. In looking at the question why this should be so, I would like to think through Mark Amsler's discussion of the multiple literacies – Latin, vernacular, clerical, lay, multimodal, multilingual – of late medieval Europe.[13]

A singular example of the complexity of the literacy of the Syon nuns may be found in a text more markedly theirs than any other: *The Mirror of Our Lady*.[14]

10 Sargent, *James Grenehalgh as Textual Critic*, Analecta Cartusiana 85 (Salzburg, 1984).

11 Sargent, "Walter Hilton's *Scale of Perfection*: The London Manuscript Group Reconsidered," *Medium Ævum* 53 (1983): 189–216; Vincent Gillespie, "Walter Hilton at Syon Abbey," in *"Stand Up to Godwards,"* 9–60; see esp. 36–44.

12 Monica Hedlund, "*Liber Clementis Maydeston*: Some Remarks on Cod. Ups. C 159," in *English Manuscript Studies 1100–1700*, vol. 3, ed. Peter Beal and Jeremy Griffiths (London, 1992), 73–101.

13 Mark Amsler, *Affective Literacies: Writing and Multilingualism in the Late Middle Ages* (Turnhout, 2011).

14 *The Myroure of oure Ladye*, ed. John Henry Blunt, Early English Text Society e.s. 19 (London, 1873). See Michael G. Sargent, "The Anxiety of Authority, the Fear of Translation: The Prologues to *The Myroure of oure Ladye*," in *"Booldly bot meekly"*: *Essays on the Theory and Practice of Translation in the Middle Ages in Honour of Roger Ellis*, ed. René Tixier and Catherine Batt, The Medieval Translator / Traduire au Moyen Age 14 (Turnhout, 2018), 231–44.

The *Mirror* is a translation and commentary on the *Sermo Angelicus*, the unique liturgy of praise of the Virgin Mary sung over the course of the week by the nuns of the Brigittine order. As a translation and commentary, the *Mirror* is obviously modeled on Richard Rolle's English psalter commentary, which was composed, according to the verse prologue of the text in Bodleian Library MS Laud misc. 286, for Margaret Kirkby (for whom he also wrote *The Form of Living*), a recluse, formerly a nun in the Cistercian convent at Hampole where Rolle died in 1349.

Rolle's commentary comprises the full Latin text of the psalter, verse by verse, with a word-by-word translation provided for each verse, and additional exposition where necessary. In many manuscripts, these three textual elements are disposed on the page in such a way that they are readily distinguishable by eye: the Latin text is written in rubric, often in an engrossed textura hand; the literal translation in black in a cursive (Anglicana or Secretary) hand, often underlined in red; and the further exposition and commentary in black, sometimes in a less formal cursive hand, without underlining. Although Rolle describes these three textual elements (the Latin text, the literal translation and the commentary) in his prologue, he does not himself articulate their differentiation on the page.[15]

The distinction of these three textual elements is made explicit, however, by the author of *The Mirror of Our Lady* in the second part of his introduction, in the description of the intended *mise-en-page* of his text, "how ye shall be gouerned in redyng of this Boke and of all other bokys."[16] The *incipit* of each verse of the Latin text of the Brigittine liturgy is, he says, written in rubric, followed by the word-for-word translation into English written in black with red underlining, and then the exposition in black without underlining. The reader of the *Mirror*, the author points out, can use the *incipit* of each verse to follow the text of the Latin as it is read and can follow along in English, referring the word-for-word text to the commentary both for sentence-by-sentence understanding of the Latin text, and for further exposition of its meaning. The one surviving manuscript of the *Mirror*, written in the early sixteenth century by Robert Tailour, and belonging

---

15 The visual differentiation of the three levels of the text arose in the work of the scribes themselves, presumably under the influence of books in the Latin commentary tradition (which itself had older antecedents), as an aspect of the development of the "hierarchy of scripts" described by Malcolm Parkes in *English Cursive Book Hands, 1250–1500* (Oxford, 1969), xiv; and *Their Hands Before Our Eyes: A Closer Look at Scribes. The Lyell Lectures delivered in the University of Oxford, 1999* (Aldershot, Hampshire, 2008), 106–12.

16 *Myrouere*, ed. Blunt, 65. The following description of the manuscript *mise-en-page* of the *Mirror* is based on the text of Aberdeen University Library, MS 134, fol. 55v; for the description in the Fawkes edition, see *Myroure*, 70.

to Sister Elizabeth Monton,[17] does not distinguish the three textual elements according to the author's directions, either by rubrication (except sporadically) or by any difference in script, although it does preserve the author's description of these distinctions. The 1530 print of the *Mirror*, on the other hand, printed by Richard Fawkes at the instance of Abbess Agnes Jordan, does preserve the textual distinctions, through the use of different type-fonts for the three elements, and it alters the author's description to refer to differences in type rather than hierarchy of script.

Unlike Rolle's psalter commentary, the *Mirror* does not cite the entirety of the Latin text, but only the *incipit* of each verse. And even this, the author notes, may be dispensed with when the text is read aloud (when the frequent interjection of Latin words in a continuous piece of text might be confusing to the hearers), although it should be followed in non-continuous text, like anthems and responses. The author also notes that he does not provide translations or expositions for psalm texts, because the sisters have access to Rolle's commentary for that. Finally, the author of the *Mirror* notes that his sister may wish to follow the service in his book, using the Latin *incipits* of the text to find her place (like the facing-page Latin-English missals used by pre-Vatican II Roman Catholics), but only if she has already said or read the service beforehand; otherwise, she is to attend to the Latin service rather than the English text.

The highly complex experience of reading evoked by *The Mirror of Our Lady*, and by Rolle's English psalter commentary before it, goes far beyond the traditional idea of reading as a conduit for the passage of information. It would be impossible simply to skim one's way down the page of either text: the reader is constantly, intellectually, emotionally, and physically, recruited as a reading subject by the book – a book that, to use the terminology of Bruno Latour, is itself an *actant* in the exchange.[18] Finding and reading the rubricated Latin *incipit* of the particular text she wishes to read, a text that connects her in memory to the hearing and singing of the office in unison with her sisters at a particular hour on a particular day of the week, holding her place on the page with her finger while she reads the word-for-word translation (while remembering the words of the text that follow the *incipit* from her own singing days and weeks before), glancing up, looking ahead, bowing or genuflecting at the recitation of certain

---

17 Written in two volumes, surviving as Aberdeen University Library MS 134, and Bodleian Library MS Rawlinson C.941. Monton is recorded as a sister in Syon in 1518, but does not occur in the 1539 pension list; a Robert Taylor was Clerk of the Works at Syon in the early sixteenth century. See Bell, *What Nuns Read*, 175–76.

18 See Bruno Latour, *Reassembling the Social: An Introduction to Actor-Network-Theory*, Clarendon Lectures in Management Studies (Oxford, 2005), 54–55.

words and phrases, such as the "Gloria Patri," stitching the present moment of reading to the time before or after of actual liturgical performance, to which the present reading is intended to add depth of understanding: the *Mirror* invokes a completely embodied reading – what Amsler describes as an "affective literacy" – a term that he uses to

> describe how we develop physical, somatic, and/or activity-based relationships with texts as part of our reading experiences. We touch, sense, or perceive the text or vocalize it with our eyes, hands, and mouths. Affective literacy also involves the emotive, noncognitive, paralinguistic things we do with texts or to texts during the act of reading.[19]

The affective literacy invoked by Richard Rolle's English commentary on the psalter and *The Mirror of our Lady* is neither clerical nor lay, according to the usual binary: it is neither Latin nor vernacular, it is neither theological nor devotional; it is deeply, materially, both. But it does not, I would propose, or does not just, transgress the binary. I would like to suggest rather that we consider the possibility of another literacy in process of construction between the writers and readers of such texts: a religious women's literacy that occupies not so much a hybrid or liminal space between clerical and lay literacy, but rather a space of its own beside clerical and beside lay literacy.[20] We might profitably look at vernacular translations of Latin theological literature that were made or adapted for religious women in terms of such an affective literacy. Works such as *The Orcherd of Syon*, the translation of the *Dialogo* of Catherine of Siena that disposes its material into seven parts comprising five chapters each, described in some detail in the prologue and epilogue addressed to the abbess and sisters of Syon as a garden in the alleys and paths of which the reader may wander, sampling the sweet fruits and bitter herbs that grow there – linking the sisters' embodied experience of walking in the garden of Syon Abbey with their reading of St. Catherine's book.[21]

19 Amsler, *Affective Literacies*, 102.
20 I am thinking here of Eve Kosofsky Sedgwick's use of the concept of the "beside" as specifically non-dualistic: see Sedgwick, *Touching Feeling: Affect, Pedagogy, Performativity* (Durham, NC, 2003), 8–9. In speaking of a "religious women's literacy," I am describing what I think of as a tendency, not a category; I do not think it appropriate to identify it with a gender or a vocation in a way parallel to the gendering of "feeling like a woman" in Sarah McNamer's *Affective Meditation and the Invention of Medieval Compassion*, The Middle Ages Series (Philadelphia, 2010), esp. 119–49.
21 See C. Annette Grisé, "'In the Blessed Vyneyerd of Oure Holy Saueour': Female Religious Readers and Textual Reception in the 'Myroure of Oure Ladye' and 'The

To speak of affect in the religious and contemplative life in this way is to broaden the terms in which affect is conceptualized. Scholars dealing with late medieval contemplative literature have been used to think of "affective mysticism" in terms of Richard Rolle's characteristic experiences of *calor, canor* and *dulcor*, and the effect of his spirituality on the fourteenth-century religious lyric and its continuation into the fifteenth in *The Book of Margery Kempe,* or the erotic rhetoric of "melting like a candle before the flame" that Nicholas Love invokes to demonstrate the truth of the doctrine of the real presence of the body and blood of Christ in the eucharist in *The Mirror of the Blessed Life of Jesus Christ.*[22] Alternatively, the term is used to describe imaginative meditation on the life and passion of Christ of the type so well described by Sarah McNamer and Michelle Karnes,[23] and detailed in the Queen's University of Belfast-University of St. Andrew's "Geographies of Orthodoxy" project.[24] Both uses of the idea of affect recognize only a limited set of affective relations, responses, or manifestations; and accounts of agency in devotional affect based in medieval theologies of grace foreclose the observation of the foundation of affect in the very embodiedness of human experience. Consideration of physical, spatial, memorial, visual, auditory, haptic, and other agential relations in the arousal of affect tend to be subsumed in debates over the role of operant *versus* co-operant grace and the sensual *versus* the intellectual role of the imagination.[25] What present-day conceptualizations of affect enable is the consideration of not just the furniture of the human mind, but also of a multitude of practices, objects, relations, spaces, and even silences as evocative of affect and performance.[26]

Orcherd of Syon,'" in *The Medieval Mystical Tradition in England, Ireland and Wales: Papers Read at Charney Manor, July 1999,* ed. Marion Glasscoe, Exeter Symposium VI (Cambridge, UK, 1999), 193–211.

22 See Love's *Mirror*, 149–54.

23 McNamer, *Affective Meditation*; Michelle Karnes, *Imagination, Meditation and Cognition in the Middle Ages* (Chicago, 2011).

24 See *The Pseudo-Bonaventuran Lives of Christ: Exploring the Middle English Tradition*, ed. Ian R. Johnson and Allan F. Westphall, Medieval Church Studies 24 (Turnhout, 2013); Ian R. Johnson, *The Middle English Life of Christ: Academic Discourse, Translation, and Vernacular Theology* (Turnhout: 2013); and *Devotional Culture in Late Medieval England and Europe: Diverse Imaginations of Christ's Life*, ed. Stephen Kelly and Ryan Perry, Medieval Church Studies 31 (Turnhout, 2014).

25 See particularly Karnes, who argues that for Bonaventure (although not for the Middle English versions of the pseudo-Bonaventuran *Stimulus amoris* and *Meditationes vitae Christi*, the *Prickynge of Love* and Love's *Mirror*) the imagination is in fact a cognitive faculty.

26 Glenn Burger reminds me that McNamer's use of William Reddy's discussion of "emotive" speech acts in her conceptualization of affective meditation as "intimate

In traditional terms, Walter Hilton would be considered anything but an affective contemplative writer. He places sensory-spiritual gifts such as those that Rolle describes among the lower experiences of the contemplative life, particularly in *Scale* II, Chapter 30:[27]

> Vpon þe same wyse it may be seyd of oþer maner felynges þat are lyke to bodily: as herynge of delytable songe, or felynge of confortable hete in þe body, or seenge of lyȝt, or swetnes of bodily sauour. Þese are not gostly felynges, for gostly felynges are felt in þe myȝtes of þe soule, principally in vnderstondynge and in lufe and lytel in ymaginacion. Bot þese felynges are in ymaginacyon, and þerfor þei are not gostly felynges, bot whan þei arn best and most trewe ȝit are þei bot owtward toknes of þe inly grace þat is felt in þe myȝtes of þe soule.

In his tract *Of Angels' Song*, which summarizes many of the ideas and expressions of *Scale* II,[28] Hilton describes how such experiences may be either physical or spiritual, concluding, "it suffys to me forto lif in trouth principali, and noght in felynge." Yet at the same time, Hilton spends much of the first half of *Scale* II trying to tease out how it is that someone who is reformed to the image of God in faith can still be constantly aware of the feeling of the image of sin within him- or herself, and all of the latter half of *Scale* II describing the reformation of the image of God in the soul in faith and in feeling. As much as Rolle's, Hilton's is a spirituality of affect.

In the remainder of this paper, I would like to take a closer look at the copies of *The Scale of Perfection* read by the nuns in Syon. To begin with, we should note that the writing of the two books of the *Scale* was probably separated by ten or more years. Parallelisms of thought and expression suggest that *Scale* I was written before the composition of Hilton's Latin letter to Adam Horsley *De Utilitate et prerogativis religionis* in the mid-1380s.[29] We first know of Hilton as a canon attached to Ely consistory court in 1371 and 1375, probably at about thirty years of age. By the time he wrote *De Utilitate*, he had given up his promising legal career and unsuccessfully tried his vocation as a hermit, but had not joined a religious order (although he encourages Horsley to do so, he says

scripts" is useful here. See McNamer, *Affective Meditation*, 11–14; William M. Reddy, *The Navigation of Feeling: A Framework for the History of Emotions* (Cambridge, UK, 2001).

27 Hilton, *Scale, Book II*, ed. Hussey and Sargent, 208–11.

28 Hilton, "Of Angels' Song," in *English Mystics of the Middle Ages*, ed. Barry Windeatt (Cambridge, UK, 1994), 131–36, at 136.

29 Hilton, *Scale* II, lxxiv–lxxxvii and explanatory notes; see also Walter Hilton, *The Scale of Perfection*, trans. John P. H. Clark and Rosemary Dorward, Classics of Western Spirituality (Mahwah, NJ, 1991), 13–21.

that he himself does not feel called to that life). The strong similarity between the opening chapters of *Scale* I and the opening section of the letter *On Mixed Life*, too, suggests that Hilton was already being asked to write advice on the contemplative life for people of a variety of social situations by this time. The transmission of the earliest version of *Scale* I in the manuscripts that do not include *Scale* II, and which lack a number of textual interpolations characteristic of later forms of the text, shows that it had reached northwest Yorkshire and the West Country area in which the Vernon and Simeon manuscripts were written before the end of the fourteenth century.[30]

Six manuscripts of this early version of *Scale* I, including the Vernon and Simeon manuscripts, address themselves to a "Ghostly brother or sister," and one of the early version, plus three others of later versions, address themselves to a "Ghostly brother"; the space for the addressee is left blank in one manuscript, and erased in another. Even so, it is probable that Hilton was writing for an enclosed woman. Further, the impression has grown upon me over my years of working with the text of the *Scale* that the disorganized way in which it proceeds from topic to topic – with no original chapter titles and, in *Scale* I, with widely varying systems of chapter division, often shifting topic with chapters opening with the phrases "but now you say," or "but now you ask" – may indicate that *Scale* I at least is the record of a set of conferences between Hilton and an actual advisee. But when read by others, these markers of interlocutory deixis become invocations to the reader to participate in the text as in a conversation.

Following the opening discussion of the stages of the active and contemplative lives in *Scale* I, Hilton discusses the three traditional activities of contemplation: reading, meditation, and prayer. But, he notes, "reading of Holy Writ may thou not well use" – meaning, presumably, that his first reader had limited facility in Latin, and was thus unable to engage in the traditional monastic exercise of meditation and prayer based on the reading of the text of scripture. He therefore proceeds to provide a set of introspective meditative exercises, culminating in a long series of chapters on the eradication of the seven deadly sins from the soul, and the restoration of the image of the triune God in the fallen soul that has become a "foul image of sin."

Scale II, as I have said, may have been written some years after *Scale* I, and I am not certain that it was actually complete when Hilton died on the vigil of the Annunciation, March 24, 1396: the ending is abrupt, and differs in various

---

30   In fact, although I disagree with Jonathan Hughes' contention that Hilton was one of the clerical entourage that the young Thomas Arundel brought with him from Ely to York when he became archbishop there in 1388, it is possible that some members of that entourage brought copies of *Scale* I with them.

manuscripts. He begins by saying that he is writing because his interlocutor "coueytest gretli and askest it per charite" to hear more of the reformation of the soul to the image of God. This reformation, he says, occurs in two ways: in faith, and in faith and feeling. The first half of *Scale* II comprises an Augustinian discussion of justification by faith; the second, starting with the image of the contemplative life as a journey to Jerusalem, deals, ever more rhapsodically, with the reformation of the soul in faith and feeling.

Interestingly, Thomas Fishlake's Latin translation for the word "feeling" throughout *Scale* II is "sensacio," and he inserts numerous references to meditation on the "humble manhood and the glorious passion of our Lord Jesus Christ" – insertions that have no justification in the underlying English text.[31] In fact, I think that Fishlake has totally misunderstood Hilton here: the proper translation for what Hilton describes here as "feeling" is "affectus": Hilton is talking, literally and at length, about the reformation of the soul to the image of God in affect. As someone who has read *Scale* II a number of times (a benefit of collating two dozen manuscripts and then proofreading the text several times afterward), I will have to say that I never fail to notice the shift in the feel of Hilton's text as he proceeds through the discussion of passing through the "lighty mirkness" that is the gate of contemplation into the discussion of the opening of the inner eye and of the sweet murmurings of love in his final chapters – "this is the voice of Jesu." He is in fact modeling the change in affect that his text describes, and calling to his reader to follow him in it.

The two earliest manuscripts of *The Scale of Perfection* to comprise both books are copies of *Scale* I to which *Scale* II has been added in a different hand (BL MS Harley 6579; and Bodleian Library MS Rawlinson C.285). My tabulation of approximately 22,000 variations among the surviving manuscripts of *Scale* II shows six or seven lines of textual transmission, which indicates a relatively large number of first-generation copies of Hilton's original.

The Harley manuscript, the earliest of the Carthusian group of manuscripts, is the most often discussed of the manuscripts of the *Scale*. It was written in the dialect of Ely or extreme southern Lincolnshire around 1400, and was corrected by several hands – with the same Ely/Lincolnshire scribal dialectal profile – that added, among other things, the annotations in *Scale* I that have since come to be called the "Christo-centric additions" (often amounting to little more than the substitution of the name "Jesus" for "God" in other manuscripts), as well as a

---

31   Michael G. Sargent, "Patterns of Circulation and Variation in the English and Latin Texts of Books I and II of Walter Hilton's *Scale of Perfection*," in *Medieval and Early Modern Religious Cultures: Essays Honouring Vincent Gillespie on his Sixty-Fifth Birthday*, ed. Laura Ashe and Ralph Hanna (Woodbridge, Suffolk, 2019).

passage on the devotion to the Holy Name of Jesus at the end of *Scale* I, Chapter 44, and a passage on charity in *Scale* I, Chapter 78. By the middle of the fifteenth century, however, the Harley manuscript belonged to London Charterhouse. Textually affiliated with this manuscript in *Scale* II are the nine others of the "Carthusian" group:[32] of these, the Chatsworth manuscript, written in the first half of the fifteenth century, was probably annotated at Coventry Charterhouse by James Grenehalgh, originally of Sheen Charterhouse, c. 1508; its close congener, San Marino, Huntington Library, MS 266, copied by John Clerk (d. 1472) of Hinton Charterhouse; Cambridge, UK, Trinity College Library, MS 354 was copied by Robert Benet of Sheen (d. 1518) and annotated there by Grenehalgh in 1499. Textually affiliated with these, too, is the Wynkyn de Worde *editio princeps* of 1494, which bears an indulgence block-print on its title page featuring what is obviously a Carthusian monk. An early seventeenth-century manuscript copied from one of the prints of the *Scale* and *Mixed Life* (the *Scale* texts of which all descend directly from the Wynkyn de Worde print of 1494) was made in the early seventeenth century by a Carthusian lay brother at the exiled house of Sheen Anglorum in Belgium. As mentioned before, two other manuscripts of the same affiliational group, BL MS Harley 2387 (the Margery Pensax manuscript), and Bodleian Library MS Laud misc. 602 are both connected to Syon.

Four other manuscripts form what I call the London group. The first is London, Lambeth Palace, MS 472 (the base-text of the Bestul edition of the *Scale*), the famous "Common Profit" manuscript made from the goods of John Killum (d. 1416), grocer of London.[33] The second is London, Inner Temple, MS Petyt 524, which descends directly from the Lambeth manuscript (the scribe of the Petyt manuscript has even copied the marginal annotations of the Lambeth manuscript – even when these are confusing). The Petyt manuscript belonged to Henry Langford, organmaker, dwelling in the Minories (as the street is still known), where the convent of Franciscan nuns – the Poor Clares, or Minoresses – once stood, just northeast of the Tower of London. The third is Bodleian Library MS Bodley 592, a copy that may have been made from the Lambeth manuscript before it was annotated, written in a beautiful quadrata hand in an otherwise unlocalizable Central Midland Standard dialect. The fourth is BL MS Harley 2397, which belonged to Elizabeth Horwood, abbess of the Poor Clares. The

---

32 As noted above, the present discussion deals primarily with the affiliation of the texts of *Scale* II. The second book was added to copies of *Scale* I already in circulation, and the patterns of affiliation need not be the same. The degree of similarity between these patterns will only be clarified by further work on the text of *Scale* I. I am presently working to complete the edition of *Scale* I that was begun by A. J. Bliss.

33 Walter Hilton, *The Scale of Perfection*, ed. Thoms H. Bestul (Kalamazoo, 2000). Available online: http://d.lib.rochester.edu/teams/publication/bestul-hilton-scale-of-perfection.

Lambeth, Petyt, and Harley manuscripts are also the only manuscripts of *Scale* II to contain other works by Hilton.

Another group of three manuscripts centers on the Rawlinson manuscript (the earliest of the northwest Yorkshire manuscripts), and includes BL MS Add. 11748, and New York, Columbia University, MS Plimpton 257, a late fifteenth-century congener of the Vernon and Simeon texts of *Scale* I. The text of *Scale* II in the Rawlinson manuscript and its congeners reads "God" several dozen times where all other manuscripts read "Jesus." This is perhaps the reflex of the "Christo-centric additions" of *Scale* I, in which the original form of the text did not use the name "Jesus." If this is so, then these three manuscripts might represent an early form of *Scale* II, comparable to the early version of *Scale* I.

All Souls College MS 25 (the Rose Pachet manuscript) was written in a scribal dialect of northern Essex. Textually, it is remarkably idiosyncratic, with some 1,800 isolative variants (one variant every other line that is not shared with any other manuscript). It apparently descends from an exemplar conflated with a manuscript of the Rawlinson type over the first half of the text, and with one of the Carthusian-Brigittine type over the latter half of the text. Further, it shows a number of textual displacements that would indicate that a gathering of its exemplar was dropped and picked up in the wrong order. This happens often enough in manuscript transmission, and is usually signaled by the scribe, who has noticed the disorder, with marginal notes to skip forward or back by a folio or two (twice for each folio out of order). There are no remarks on the disorder of the text in the All Souls manuscript; apparently, no one noticed.

Cambridge, Cambridge University Library, MS Ee.iv.30, written in a beautiful textura hand in a Middlesex scribal dialect and belonging to London Charterhouse, also presents a conflated text: in this case, of the Carthusian and the London group versions of the text of *Scale* II.

There are also four other manuscripts of *Scale* II, two of which – Cambridge, Corpus Christi College Library, MS R.5, and Oxford, Magdalen College Library (Old Library), MS F.4.17 (a version in which the *incipit* of *Scale* II is altered so that it can stand alone without reference to *Scale* I) – are remarkably idiosyncratic, but both share the variant chapter division of Fishlake's Latin version of *Scale* II and other readings that may reflect conflation with the Latin text.

Two final manuscripts seldom disagree with the textual consensus of the English manuscripts as a whole. These two – Harley 6573 (an early fifteenth-century manuscript written in the scribal dialect locatable, like that of the Rawlinson manuscript, at the border of Ely and Norfolk, just south of the southwest corner of the Wash),[34] and Philadelphia, University of Pennsylvania Library, Codex 218

---

34 BL MS Harley 6573 is the base-text of Hilton, *Scale, Book II*, ed. Hussey and Sargent.

(the former Stonor manuscript, that also contains a copy of the *Prickynge of Love*, the Middle English version of the *Stimulus amoris* sometimes attributed to Hilton) – not only disagree with the consensus of the English manuscripts less often than any others, but also agree with Fishlake's Latin *Scale* more often than any others. It should also be noted here that the Latin translation is a first-generation witness to the text of the *Scale*, the first manuscript of which predates any of the surviving manuscripts of the English text. The Latin text does not derive from any surviving version of the English text, and must represent a separate line of transmission, through an exemplar that no longer survives.

The affective literacy invoked by *The Scale of Perfection* would probably have made it an ideal guide for a novice at Syon, where the novitiate year was not spent within the community, but in some other residence nearby, with the novice presumably attending services in Syon as a member of the lay congregation and taking instruction. This seems to have been the case for Johanna Sewell, professed in Syon in 1500, who may have taken instruction in the contemplative life from James Grenehalgh, a Carthusian monk at Sheen. Grenehalgh, a former schoolmaster at Wells Cathedral, was something of an expert on the *Scale*, having collated at least three copies against each other (Cambridge, Trinity College Library, MS 354; the Rosenbach copy of the Wynkyn de Worde print of the English text; and BL MS Harley 6576 of the Latin) and corrected each with the reading of the others where they disagreed – even providing English translations of the Latin text in the margins of the de Worde print (his working copy) at several points.[35] He finished his collation of the Trinity and Rosenbach copies of the *Scale* on the Carthusian Feast of the Relics, November 8, 1499, according to a pair of matching notes in the two copies (Trinity 354, fol. 115; Rosenbach *Scale*, fol. 134v).[36] A further note below this in the Rosenbach copy, also in Grenehalgh's hand, indicates that the book was in his possession on the feast of St. Helena and the Finding of the Cross, May 3, 1501. He also seems to have used the fly-leaves of the Rosenbach *Scale* to record theological, literary and devotional commonplaces, dating from as early as 1497, and identifying himself as a northerner like Hilton, "eiusdem partis oriundus, Shene professus".[37] Grenehalgh responded to Hilton at various points, as on fol. 10, where he notes

35 Part of the argument of this section derives from Sargent, *James Grenehalgh as Textual Critic*, esp. 75–109. See also Sargent, "David of Augsburg's *De Exterioris et Interioris Hominis Compositione* in Middle English," in *Satura: Studies in Medieval Literature in Honour of Robert R. Raymo*, ed. Nancy M. Reale and Ruth E. Sternglantz (Donington, Lincolnshire, 2001), 74–102, esp. 99–102.

36 Images are provided in Sargent, *James Grenehalgh as Textual Critic*, 138–39, 199–200.

37 Hilton was probably not a northerner like Grenehalgh (from Grenehalgh in Lancashire, presumably), but – most probably – was from Hilton in Huntingdonshire.

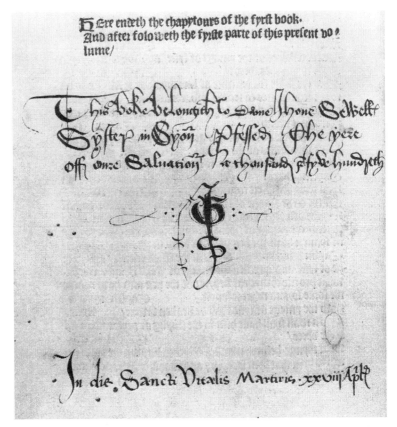

Fig. 6.1 *Walter Hilton,* The Scale of Perfection, *printed 1494 by Wynkyn de Worde (STC 14042): Rosenbach Incun. 494H, fol. 4v. Photo: by permission of The Rosenbach, Philadelphia.*

Hilton's "I wote not," and provides him with a "WH" monogram similar to his own "JG" – a fully embodied, affective reading indeed.

Among Grenehalgh's responsive annotations to the Rosenbach *Scale* are a number that are directed rather to Johanna Sewell.[38] At one point (fol. 3), he playfully puns on her name in telling her to "see well" from the beginning of Hilton's discussion of the eradication of the image of sin in the soul to the end of

Hilton did, however, use such non-standard forms as "mirkness," "ilk," and "ay," which Grenehalgh, reading his text a century later, would recognize as northernisms.

38   Images of Grenehalgh's personal annotations are provided in Sargent, *James Grenehalgh as Textual Critic*, 164–212; for color images of some of these, see Kathryn Kerby-Fulton, Maidie Hilmo, and Linda Olson, *Opening up Middle English Manuscripts: Literary and Visual Approaches* (Ithaca, NY, 2012), 326–35.

Scale I, and provides a matching sign at the appropriate point in the text. At the end of the text of *Scale* II he provides a veritable litany of Trinitarian devotion. Notably, at the bottom of the page he provides himself and Johanna Sewell with a double monogram, "JGS," preceded by the words "Corde sincero / Mente deuota" and followed by a Trinitarian doxology opening with the words "Te Deum laudamus."

Grenehalgh may have intended to give this book to Johanna Sewell (which would have been a violation of strict Carthusian regulations against private disposal of monastic property), since he provides it with a full *ex libris* in her name, furnished with the date of her profession in Syon and a double monogram, in the empty space below the end of the table of chapters of *Scale* I (fol. 4v; Fig. 6.1). The idea that the Rosenbach *Scale* remained in Syon began with Margaret Deanesly's mistranscription of "This boke belongeth to Dame Jhone Sewell" as "This boke belongeth to me, Jhone Sewell," which led to her identification of all of the annotations in this book as Johanna Sewell's.[39] In fact, none of the annotations are in a hand that can be identified as other than Grenehalgh's. He also put the Sewell monogram at the foot of the first page of text of *Scale* I and provided her with a full-page *lorica* of prayers, blessings, and patron saints on the verso of the last folio (fol. 135v; Fig. 6.2).

What happened after James gave Johanna this copy of the *Scale*? If he did manage to give it to her, I suspect that it did not remain in Syon for long: in fact, my private fantasy is of the prior of Sheen knocking on his door that evening, saying, "James, we need to have a talk." What happened between James and Johanna? Lee Paterson has suggested that it was an example of the corruption of spiritual into sensual love (an inversion, he notes, of the Ovidian counsel on how to seduce someone through friendship) that is described in a section of David of Augsburg's *Formula novicorum* cited in the Syon text *Disce mori* with the advice, at the point where it discusses the tendency of corrupted lovers to pour the poison of flattery into each other's ears, that "Of which poison if ye lust more to read, / Seeþ þe tale of Troilus, Creseide and Dyomede." For the Syon sisters also read *Troilus and Criseyde*.[40]

Kathryn Kerby-Fulton agrees with Patterson, enlisting me for support, and citing a difficult note by Grenehalgh that runs off the bottom edge of one page of the *Scale* (fol. 30):

39 *The Incendium Amoris of Richard Rolle of Hampole*, ed. Margaret Deanesly, Publications of the University of Manchester, Historical Series 26 (Manchester, 1959), 82.

40 Lee W. Patterson, "Ambiguity and Interpretation: A Fifteenth-Century Reading of *Troilus and Criseyde*," *Speculum* 54 (1979): 297–330; repr. in Patterson, *Negotiating the Past: The Historical Understanding of Medieval Literature* (Madison, WI, 1987), 115–53.

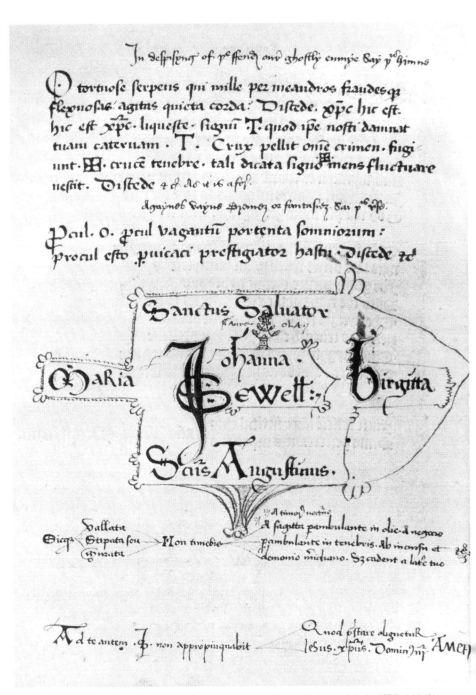

Fig. 6.2 Walter Hilton, The Scale of Perfection, *printed 1494 by Wynkyn de Worde (STC 14042): Rosenbach Incun. 494H, fol. 135v. Photo: by permission of The Rosenbach, Philadelphia.*

hac die, id est vigilia Sancti Valentini, feria 5, sesso ad pred[icandum] venit [JS monogram] ad c[on]tra p[..]o cum qua post difficultatem & processum [uicarii? Kerby-Fulton reads "in carne," which I do not see] colloquabar. 1500[41]

That would appear to be the record of a meeting on the vigil of St. Valentine's day; that is, a month and a half before Johanna Sewell's profession.[42] The remaining strokes, including those that extend up the right-hand edge of the page, do not seem to resolve into letter forms. Grenehalgh certainly seems to be hiding something here, although, *pace* Patterson and Kerby-Fulton, I do not think that it was an affair. And anything that may have happened seems to have been one-sided: there are no Johanna Sewell annotations. Grenehalgh does annotate a number of passages, here and elsewhere, that speak of the evil of false judgment, and of the heavenly reward of those who have resisted temptation.[43]

Heavenly reward or not, a Carthusian monk who resisted the criticism of his superiors was still liable to penance.[44] This, I suspect, is what happened in Grenehalgh's case. Although he seems still to have had the Rosenbach *Scale* in his possession a year later, he may have been subject to penance, perhaps even imprisoned in Sheen; the *carta* of the General Chapter of the order in the spring of 1508 records that he has been sent to Coventry – to Coventry Charterhouse, as a guest (Coventry Charterhouse, we may note, did have a school, and may have had a use for a former schoolmaster) – with the stipulation that no visitation was ever to result in his return to the house of his original profession, but that he might make another profession at Coventry, or in any other house that would have him. His death, as a guest in Hull Charterhouse, is recorded in the *carta* of the General Chapter of 1530.[45]

In all of this, we see a variety of affective strategies by which readers from the end of the fourteenth century through the first half of the sixteenth engaged with Walter Hilton's *Scale of Perfection*. It was read as a guide to a life of personal reflection and moral reform leading eventually to a sense of union with God

41 For Kerby-Fulton's reading "in carne," see Kerby-Fulton, Hilmo, and Olson, *Opening up Middle English Manuscripts*, 333.
42 The vigil of Valentine's Day, February 13, was a Thursday (feria quinta) in 1500. Johanna Sewell's profession would have been on the Tuesday following the first Sunday after Easter.
43 Sargent, *James Grenehalgh as Textual Critic*, 75–212 (esp. 94–109); see esp. 176–77 (fol. 12v) for an annotation in the Rosenbach *Scale* apparently responding to criticism that he thought inappropriate.
44 For the punishment enjoined by the Carthusian *Consuetudines* and *Statuta* upon intractable and obstinate monks, see Sargent, *James Grenehalgh as Textual Critic*, 80–82.
45 Ibid., 115–16.

through grace that is not (or is no longer) based in the imaginative invocation of the senses, but is still somehow affective – a union that may still be called "reformation in faith and in feeling." The initial affective response to the text of the *Scale*, by James Grenehalgh, who identified with Hilton (incorrectly) as a fellow northerner, was the desire to create a "corrected" text, authoritative by reason of its incorporation of variant readings from different manuscript and printed sources. This is a prominent characteristic of the Carthusian group of manuscripts: several bear the marks of conflation and correction, or of descent from a conflated (and thus probably an emended) exemplar.

Grenehalgh also reacted personally to the text of the *Scale* in other annotations in which he responded to the author, explained Hilton's meaning to subsequent readers (Johanna Sewell in particular), and, at least at one point, disagreed with him.

Readers of the Lambeth Palace manuscript, the core of the London manuscript group (a manuscript that actively looked forward to its later readers in its "Common Profit" inscription), also left both textual-critical and content oriented annotations, advice to later readers to pay attention to particular sections of text, and bookmark threads attached to the margins in various places; many of these annotations are copied into the margins of two other of the London group manuscripts by the scribes themselves. In fact, we ought to look at what Kathryn Kerby-Fulton has described as the activity of "the professional reader" in annotating and illustrating manuscripts of texts (like those of *Piers Plowman* with which she and her collaborators have worked) as an aspect of affective literacy.[46]

Finally, as we can see particularly in James Grenehalgh's annotation of the Rosenbach copy of the *Scale* for Johanna Sewell, affective literacy goes where it will. In the mid-1970s, as a graduate student in the University of Toronto, I sat in the Rosenbach Library in Philadelphia, copying out Grenehalgh's hundreds of annotations to the *Scale*, tracing them down the page as I went, and it occurred to me then that my fingers were touching the very words of the text that his fingers had touched as he wrote his annotations: that through the centuries, through the paper wall, I could feel the hand of James Grenehalgh. I have been to where the village of Grenehalgh in Lancashire once stood, somewhere between a garage and a chicken farm, about 10 miles inland from Blackpool. I have seen where Sheen Charterhouse once lay, now beneath the thirteenth, fourteenth and

---

46 Kathryn Kerby-Fulton and Denise Louise Despres, *Iconography and the Professional Reader: The Politics of Book Production in the Douce Piers Plowman*, Medieval Cultures 15 (Minneapolis, 1999); Kerby-Fulton and Maidie Hilmo, eds., *The Medieval Professional Reader at Work: Evidence from Manuscripts of Chaucer, Langland, Kempe, and Gower* (Victoria, BC, 2001).

fifteenth holes, just west of the western wall of the Observatory, on the grounds of the Royal Mid-Surrey Golf Course. Across the river to the north lies Syon House, the residence of the Duke of Northumberland, part of which incorporates the chapel of Syon Abbey, where Johanna Sewell was buried. I always think of that when I fly over it about five minutes before landing at Heathrow. For we, too, are affective readers.

Book Accessories, Gender,
and the Staging of Reading

HEATHER BLATT

In recent decades, reading communities have garnered much interest among medievalists, foremost among whom is Mary Erler, whose focus on women's reading communities drew me to work with her. One of my most vivid memories after my arrival at Fordham as a graduate student involves an occasion on which we met to discuss my academic plans and interests. I was then in the early stages of a project involving the materiality of medieval bookmarks; Mary asked about how they were described, and I offered several of the terms I had found in inventories and wills, one of which was "register." Mary immediately offered me a copy of her essay on the sacristan's rolls from Syon, pointing me to the account records with which she had worked that mentioned register bookmarks. To be able to discuss how my work intersected with that of another scholar was both an exciting and encouraging experience. In this essay, I am delighted to return to this intersection of shared interests to further explore the care for books, reading practices, and gender, beginning in Mary's stomping ground of Syon.

Reinvigorated by interest in the manuscript as a locus of analysis, heightened by awareness of and research into overlooked communities of readers, and facilitated by attention to the diversity of literacy practices in late medieval England, the study of medieval readers and their books has developed into a flourishing subject of study. Women's reading communities, devotional reading practices, the work of manuscript glosses, scribal corrections, and more have drawn attention to the myriad social and cultural influences that shaped reading and interaction with books in the Middle Ages.[1] Absent from this discussion, however, and strikingly

---

1   Pioneering studies of readers, reading practices, and reading communities include Rebecca Krug, *Reading Families: Women's Literate Practice in Late Medieval England* (Ithaca, NY, 2006); Mary C. Erler, *Women, Reading and Piety in Late Medieval England* (Cambridge, UK, 2006); Joyce Coleman, *Public Reading and the Reading Public in Late Medieval England and France* (Cambridge, UK, 1996); Jocelyn Wogan-Browne et al., *The Idea of the Vernacular: An Anthology of Middle English Literary Theory, 1280–1520* (Philadelphia, 1999); and Kathryn Kerby-Fulton and Denise L. Despres, *Iconography and the Professional Reader: The Politics of Book Production in the Douce Piers Plowman* (Minneapolis, 1999). Work on these subjects has been furthered by Jessica Brantley, *Reading in the Wilderness: Private Devotion and Public*

absent given the material turn pursued by medieval studies in recent years, has been assessment of how peripheral objects related to books shaped their use and reading. Book furniture, including desks, lecterns, and prie-dieux, and accessories such as bookmarks, have received little or no attention. The ubiquity of these objects that accompanied and accessorized books perhaps explains some of the ease with which it has been possible to overlook them; the ease with which these objects can be separated and viewed as separable from books surely contributes further. Yet examining such book furniture and accessories reveals differences in representations of medieval readers' interactions with books.

Staging Reading at Syon Abbey

Accordingly, in the first part of this essay I will examine attitudes and habits reflected in the use of book furniture at one of the most significant sites for the study of reading in late medieval England, Syon Abbey, which was established by a charter of Henry V on March 3, 1415. Monks and nuns lived separately and pursued separate routines; their reading practices have been widely studied.[2]

Performance in Late Medieval England (Chicago and London, 2007); Jennifer Bryan, *Looking Inward: Devotional Reading and the Private Self in Late Medieval England* (Philadelphia, 2008); Nicola F. McDonald, "A York Primer and its Alphabet: Reading Women in a Lay Household," in *The Oxford Handbook of Medieval Literature in English*, ed. Elaine Treharne and G. Walker (Oxford, 2010), 181–99; Daniel Wakelin, *Scribal Correction and Literary Craft: English Manuscripts 1375–1510* (Cambridge, UK, 2014); Stephen Partridge and Erik Kwakkel, eds., *Author, Reader, Book: Medieval Authorship in Theory and Practice* (Toronto, 2012); Jane Griffiths, *Diverting Authorities: Experimental Glossing in Manuscript and Print* (Oxford, 2014); Vincent Gillespie, "The Haunted Text: Reflections in *A Mirror to Devout People*," in *The Text in the Community: Essays on Medieval Works, Manuscripts, Authors, and Readers*, ed. Jill Mann and Maura Nolan (South Bend, IN, 2006), 129–72; and Ryan Perry, "'Some sprytuall matter of gostly edyfycacion': Readers and Readings of Nicholas Love's 'Mirror of the Blessed Life of Jesus Christ,'" in *The Pseudo-Bonaventuran Lives of Christ*, ed. Ian Johnson and Allan F. Westphall (Turnhout, 2013), 79–126.

2   The principal account of Syon's foundation and the text of some of its rules are provided in George J. Aungier, *The History and Antiquities of Syon Abbey, the Parish of Isleworth and the Chapelry of Hounslow* (London, 1840). Influential work specifically addressing book use and reading includes Krug's chapter on reading at Syon published in *Reading Families*; the essay collection edited by E. A. Jones and Alexandra Walsham, *Syon Abbey and its Books: Reading, Writing, and Religion, c. 1400–1700* (Woodbridge, Suffolk, 2010); Erler, *Women, Reading and Piety in Late Medieval England*; Ann Hutchison, "What the Nuns Read: Literary Evidence from the English Bridgettine House, Syon Abbey," *Mediaeval Studies* 57 (1995): 205–22; Elizabeth Schirmer, "Reading Lessons at Syon Abbey: *The Myroure of Oure Ladye* and the Mandates of Vernacular Theology," in *Voices in Dialogue: Reading Women in the Middle Ages*, ed. Linda Olson and Katherine Kerby-Fulton (Notre Dame, IN, 2006),

Nevertheless, how surviving rules for Syon address the practices of both nuns and monks in ways that cast light on their different interactions with books, book furniture, and book accessories, has passed unnoticed. In the second part of this essay, I assess one particular type of accessory mentioned at Syon, the register bookmarker, and trace its uses in late medieval England and Europe more generally, before and after the Reformation. I argue that treatment of book accessories and book furniture demonstrates that gender emerges as an influence affecting treatment and representations of book furniture and accessories. These, in turn, helped shape habits of book use in the late Middle Ages, even as they also reflect the cultural pressures that influenced such use. In consequence, studying book furniture and accessories reveals their significant role in contributing to attitudes shaping book use and reading among individuals and communities.

Syon, though young in its foundation, was esteemed not only for the rigor of its religious observance, but also for its learning. Its oldest version of the rule governing the monastery establishes it as intended for the nuns, with priests nearby to provide mass and daily offices for them.[3] The rule also explicitly recommended and supported reading and access to books: "bookes they shall haue as many as they wyll in whiche ys to lerne or to studye."[4] Nuns and monks enjoyed access to separate libraries, presided over by individual librarians.[5] The important role of books at Syon has thus left scholars with a rich documentary archive. This archive, though sadly far from being intact, includes the catalog

345–76. On nuns' literacy more generally, see David N. Bell, *What Nuns Read: Books and Libraries in Medieval English Nunneries* (Kalamazoo, 1995); its update, "What Nuns Read: The State of the Question," in *The Culture of Medieval English Monasticism*, ed. James G. Clark (Woodbridge, Suffolk, 2007), 113–33; and the survey by Jocelyn Wogan-Browne, "Analytical Survey 5: 'Reading is Good Prayer': Recent Research on Female Reading Communities," *New Medieval Literatures* 5 (2002): 229–97. The reading and book practices of Syon recusants following the dissolution of Syon have been studied by Mary C. Erler, *Reading and Writing during the Dissolution: Monks, Friars, and Nuns 1530–1558* (Cambridge, UK, 2013).

3   Elin Andersson, *Responsiones Vadstenenses: Perspectives on the Birgittine Rule in Two Texts from Vadstena and Syon Abbey: A Critical Edition with Translation and Introduction*, Studia Latina Stockholmiensia 60 (Stockholm, 2011), 3, 32. Editions of the Rules are provided in the facsimile edition edited by James Hogg, and by George Aungier in *The History and Antiquities of Syon*. See James Hogg, ed. *The Rewyll of Seynt Sauioure*, 3 vols , Salzburger Studien zur Anglistik und Amerikanistik 6, (Salzburg, 1978–80). While Aungier refers to as the *Additions to the Rule of Syon*, Hogg follows instead the nomenclature applied to the manuscript text developed by the British Library, calling them *The Orders and Constitutions of the Nuns at Syon* (4:v). The additions provided localized practices specific to Syon.

4   From the facsimile printed by James Hogg, *The Rewyll of Seynt Sauioure*, 2:50.

5   Hutchison, "What the Nuns Read," 205.

to the men's half of Syon's unique double library, letters, manuscripts, and other records. Such written resources demonstrate the community's intellectual vibrancy on the eve of the Reformation until its suppression and dissolution in 1539. Less attention has been given, however, to the accessories and artifacts that surrounded Syon's book culture and are noted in references in these written records.[6] For example, the rules of the house specify that the sacristan was to supply the house with "penners, pennes, ynke, ynkhornes, [and] tables,"[7] and the additional rules also make references to desks and lecterns to be used with books at various times and places. These details demonstrate how richly material the textual lives of the monks and nuns at Syon could be.

Furthermore, these details suggest that gender affected not just patterns of reading, but also the manipulation of books as physical objects. Addressing reading practices in Syon, Rebecca Krug has noted that the abbey promoted "an intense experience of identification with books as both material and spiritual objects."[8] Krug relates this to the nuns' expression of individuality, but her point also serves to specify the importance of book materiality to Syon's book culture. In studying the rules regulating life at Syon, it becomes clear that such identification was further facilitated through instructions regulating how the monks and nuns were to manipulate and accessorize their books. Specifically, examining references to the use of book furniture that supported the reading and use of books, such as desks and lecterns described in the Syon records, shows that differences emerge in the rules of Syon that point to divergences in how the monks and nuns used, or were expected to relate to, such accessories.

In particular, the rules and their addenda primarily associate book furniture with the monks of Syon, whereas the nuns' relation to books emphasizes body and gesture. For example, the rules for the monks specifies when to hold or place books, such as a gospel book, on a chair or desk or lectern during mass and other occasions, in and outside of liturgy. The keeper of the high mass exemplifies this behavior when enjoined during mass to "be redy at hand to holde the boke to the bisshop, and after he haue seid iii verses, than toward the professed lay the boke ayeyn on the chaer." That is, he should hand the book to the bishop

6 The most extensive study of the objects contributing to book use at Syon, which focuses on the maintenance of books, is the essay by Mary C. Erler, "Syon Abbey's Care for Books: Its Sacristan's Account Rolls 1506/7–1535/6," *Scriptorium* 39 (1985): 293–307.
7 Aungier, *The History and Antiquities of Syon*, 367. Here, "tables" most likely refers to wax tablets, often used for note-taking purposes, soon to be supplanted by erasable tables incorporated into printed books like almanacs. On both types of tables, see Peter Stallybrass et al., "Hamlet's Tables and the Technologies of Writing in Renaissance England," *Shakespeare Quarterly* 55:4 (2004): 379–419.
8 Krug, *Reading Families*, 157.

during the liturgy, and then, upon taking it back, place it upon a ready chair.[9] In comparison, young nuns – not allowed to celebrate mass, a task left up to the monks – should hold their elders "in dewe reuerence," demonstrating such by "puttyng to their handes to helpe them in beryng of heuy bokes." By lending their hands to the carrying of books, the nuns show respect to their seniors in the abbey. Monks have chairs for book support; nuns have their own bodies, and the use of their bodies to support books demonstrates appropriate etiquette toward other nuns. Furthermore, during any "conuentual acte," the nuns should be "lokynge upon ther bokes . . . ffor God loueth more to be worchypped and seyn with the eyen of the soule," and the abbess, at her installation, should "hau[e] the boke of the rewles and constitucions in her lappe."[10] In these moments, the additional rules for the monks at Syon often describe when and under what circumstances they should manipulate books, and what furniture they should use in doing so (practices found in liturgical instructions to this day). In contrast, the additional rules specify that the nuns should help carry books for each other, look at their books rather than try to peek at the altar, and recognize the authority of the abbess while she holds Syon's rules in her lap. In this moment the book of the rule becomes a cultic object as well as a text, with a function equivalent to a relic or a crozier; even as the function of the book shifts from text to sacral object, it remains contextualized with reference to the body of the woman using it.

These examples not only demonstrate how the monks' and nuns' reading was differently articulated in liturgical and non-liturgical contexts, but also reflect how the monks' relation to books at Syon was mediated through furniture and treated procedurally as part of their professional duties and ritual activity, whereas the nuns' bodies mediated their relation to books, depicted primarily as reading for non-liturgical devotional purposes. The additional rules situate the

---

9   Aungier, *History and Antiquities of Syon*, 309, 345, 363; in these Aungier draws on the additions to the Syon rules in BL MS Arundel 146; see also James Hogg, *The Rewyll of Seynt Sauioure* for similar passages drawn from the St. Paul's Cathedral Library manuscript of the Syon additions for the brothers. For example, in discussing the observance of matins, the St. Paul's manuscript asserts that the duty of the hebdomadary is to "ley the legende on the lectron" (3:55); when hallowing holy water, "the holder of the boke schal . . . se that the desk be remouyd and sette aȝen / whan tyme is" (3:66). In other places, the additions for the monks described in the St. Paul's manuscript omit reference to the furniture in a way that, especially given the noted presence of the furniture in the Arundel 146 additions for the brothers, treats the monk holding the book as furniture himself: "He also must hold the bok to the buschop knelyng or stondyng as the case requireth" (3:49). Even in the absence of furniture, the monks are still associated with it by filling its role.

10   Hogg 4:154, 4:117, 4:52.

nuns' use of books in the context of devotional observance, and, furthermore, reflect guidance about community etiquette. The relationship between monks and their books focuses on their professional life and activities, whereas the nuns' relationship to books, in ways consistent with affective devotional practice, focuses on their behavior and emotional responses.[11] These moments thus contribute to our understanding of readers and reading at Syon: liturgical and non-liturgical reading become gendered activities, and also similarly gender relationships between bodies and furniture, which become markers of these gendered reading practices. As C. Annette Grisé has observed more generally, the woman engaged in devotional reading "came to understand her gendered subjectivity through her reading."[12] This subjectivity both enforced cultural norms of gender and empowered readers through them. How the Syon rules model and instruct behavior toward books demonstrates that such cultural norms even extended to the manipulation of books as physical objects.[13] Furthermore, the way these practices shaped different modes of book manipulation suggests that dual models for gendered readers persisted from a variety of angles. It is not simply that nuns were constituted as gendered readers through book manipulation; so, too, were monks.

Such attitudes toward the gendered manipulation of books find reflection outside the walls of Syon in the broader culture of late medieval Europe. In panel paintings of the fifteenth century, for example, women reading seldom use book furniture, which predominates in paintings of men reading. This distinction between gender and the presence or absence of book furniture also reflects the gendered nature of writing, since many of the men pictured reading were also known for their writing, as in the case of St. Jerome. Consequently, the use of book furniture in paintings of a period contemporary to Syon's documentary archive

---

11 This focus on affective response intersects more generally with affectively emphatic devotional practices that also emphasized women as their specific audience. On such practices see, for example, David Green's chapter on "Figurative Reading" in *Women Readers in the Middle Ages* (Cambridge, UK, 2007); Mark Amsler on "Affective Literacy" in *Affective Literacies: Writing and Multilingualism in the Late Middle Ages* (Turnhout, 2011); and Sarah McNamer's discussion of why women engaged so fervently in affective devotion in *Affective Meditation and the Invention of Medieval Compassion* (Philadelphia, 2011), 25–57.

12 C. Annette Grisé, "Women's Devotional Reading in Late-Medieval England and the Gendered Reader," *Medium Ævum* 71 (2002): 209–25, at 210.

13 Grisé makes a related point in her essay "The Textual Community of Syon Abbey," *Florilegium* 19 (2002): 149–62. Discussing how the Syon rules sought to create community, Grisé quotes Elizabeth Grosz's argument that "cultural and personal values, norms, and commitments" can be used to inscribe a body with cultural ideas of gender and sexuality (155).

supports the visual iconography that encodes gender-differentiated practices predicated upon the increased access of men to scholarly work, university education, and writing. The archive's descriptions of how book furniture should be used also emphasize gender differentiated practices, particularly in the context of liturgical and non-liturgical reading. Together, the Syon rules and contemporary visual imagery suggest that book furniture contributed to and even regulated gender differentiated habits of book use and manipulation in the late Middle Ages.

Accordingly, the different ways the monks and nuns of Syon acted and were guided to interact with books can be traced through examining their use of and relationship to the accessories that surround and shape experiences with books. Book furniture contributed to the engendering of masculine reading practice, whereas the intimate proximity of the book to the reader's body reflects a more feminized practice of reading and book manipulation. The references at Syon also suggest that reading was a highly mobile practice, particularly as applied to women devotional readers. That is, the presence of book furniture in the context of men reading represents a locationally fixed activity: book use occurs in studies, closets, and other spaces dedicated to the work of reading and writing. These contexts also relate to the size of books; men, more routinely using books for study, and male clergy, routinely making use of large books for mass, would have found these uses better served by taking advantage of furniture that allowed books to remain fixed in place. Thus at Syon the keeper of the mass uses a chair – possibly a lectern – upon which he can "lay the boke ayeyn." In contrast, the emphasis on the relation between the bodies of Syon's women readers and their books, and the visual record that similarly emphasizes that devotional reading involved holding the book close and intimately proximate to the body, suggest that this non-liturgical, primarily devotional reading was less fixed locationally. Scenes of devotional readers in late medieval art, particularly when including women readers, routinely depict women reading outdoors, or seated on floors indoors, in public rooms of the household and in private spaces. Rarely do any of these spaces indicate a purpose dedicated to reading or writing.

Examining the absence of book furniture, as a result, reveals women's reading practice and book use not only as intimately bound up with the body, but in consequence of that reliance on the body, as more mobile, dynamic, and often domestically centered. The nuns of Syon move their books from space to space and room to room, bringing the books to where they wish to read or study, whereas the monks of Syon take themselves to their books. While the records of Syon indicate that the women enjoyed their own library space, what nevertheless emerges in the rules is a rhetoric of gendered difference that depicts men's relation to books as static and fixed, and women's relation to books as dynamic and mobile. Similar mobility is depicted in Rogier van der Weyden's iconic painting "The Magdalen Reading," in which Mary Magdalen sits in a domestic interior room upon a pillow placed upon the floor. Her back is turned to a convenient cabinet so that she can hold the book close, cradling it in her hands and lap as she reads.[14] While she reads in one place, her reading is not bound to that place. Such locationally dynamic reading is not exclusive to women in this period; men can be identified in similar poses. However, the predominant associations represent masculine reading as characterized by the presence and use of furniture, with consequent spatial fixity; and devotional reading, particularly identified with women, as characterized by the absence of furniture and the resulting intimate proximity of book and body. The material context of books, from the architecture of libraries and desks to the details of bindings, can thus facilitate an understanding the physical practices surrounding their use, at the level of both the individual and the community, and the values and attitudes that shaped interaction with them.

Bookmarkers at Syon

In the light of how one category of book accessory, book furniture, reflects gendered habits of book use, a particular detail in the sacristans' accounts at Syon deserves further consideration. The sacristan (or sexton) shared with the chantress of Syon responsibility for physical maintenance of the library.[15] Between 1519 and 1531, the sacristans' accounts rolls record the purchase, a dozen at a time, of "pynnes for to Register bookes."[16] This phrase identifies a type of bookmarker popular before and after the provision of these accounts, one characterized by multiple textile strands, often braided, that were knotted around or otherwise fixed to an anchor – here a "pynne." The anchor rests above the pages of the book, parallel to the spine, allowing the individual strands of the bookmarker to be placed at and moved between various pages. A number of types of end finishes, most employing tasseled knots, completed the strands. Such objects are referenced in a variety of other contemporary documents, from wills to inventories, where they may be referred to using a number of terms: "signaculum" and "registrum" in Latin (usually in the ablative form following the preposition "cum"), "pip(p)e" and "signe(t)" in French, "register," "register pynne," and "marker" in Middle

---

14 London, National Gallery, ca. 1435–38. The image is reproduced on the cover of this volume.

15 E. A. Jones and Alexandra Walsham, "Introduction: Syon Abbey and its Books: Origins, Influences and Transitions," in *Syon Abbey and its Books*, 1–38, at 24.

16 Erler, "Syon Abbey's Care for Books," 303.

and Early Modern English.[17] These bookmarkers could be both practical and decorative, supporting readers' nonlinear access to the contents of a book and sometimes individuating one book by distinguishing it from others. In consequence of their use and individuating role, this sort of bookmarker exemplifies another type of accessory that could affect how individuals read, handled, and otherwise perceived the books they encountered. Given that Syon bought such markers by the dozen on a near-annual basis over the course of several years, they clearly held significance for the community of readers at the abbey, as they did beyond the abbey's walls. In effect, the multiple-strand bookmarker provides a vehicle to explore the implications book accessories have for how we understand the use and perception of books, and shows that women's devotional reading practices could extend not only to the books they read, but also to the accessories that accompanied the manuscripts and printed books that they used.

In considering women's use of bookmarkers, it is worth noting women's roles in producing them as well. While goldsmiths or other metalworkers – almost always men – might be responsible for producing the anchor of a bookmarker, particularly when fashioned from gold, silver, or enamel, or when the less expensive and more pedestrian brass-like alloy latten was used, other bookmarkers could be made from cheap turned wood or even sewn using button-making or embroidery techniques, practices more accessible to women. Women's participation in bookmarker making has generally gone unacknowledged, with one exception: in the production of the laces often used for the strands of bookmarkers. One such example is documented in the inventories of Henry VIII: the inventory references, within the Jewel-House at the Tower of London, enclosed inside a "coofer Marked with the Lettre V [. . .] a litle purse of lether with iiij Registre pynnes whereof twoo Silke womens worke."[18] Silkwomen commonly produced both purses and the braided laces used to tie them closed; in fact, the craft of silk-working in the late Middle Ages was one practiced almost exclusively by women,

---

17 For more details on the terminology used here and the construction of such bookmarkers, see Heather Blatt and Lois Swales, "Multi-Page Bookmarkers: Tiny Textiles and Diverse Passementerie Hidden in Books," in *Medieval Clothing and Textiles* 3, ed. Robin Netherton and Gale R. Owen-Crocker (Woodbridge, Suffolk, 2007), 145–79. For subsequent work on bookmarkers and other means for marking places, see Daniel Sawyer, "Navigation by Tab and Thread: Place-Markers and Readers' Movements in Books," in *Spaces for Reading in Later Medieval England*, ed. Mary Flannery and Carrie Griffin (New York, 2016), 99–114. Sawyer surveys the different methods readers used to negotiate the density of texts, from formal place-markers such as tabs and bookmarkers to slitting or folding pages.

18 David Starkey, ed., *The Inventory of King Henry VIII: Society of Antiquaries MS 129 and British Library MS Harley 1419: The Transcript* (London, 1998), 76.

particularly in England, where it was situated around London's Soper Lane.[19] For Henry VIII's register pins, they clearly produced the braided silk laces fixed to the anchors, and perhaps embroidered the anchors themselves.

Silk frequently appears in inventories that describe bookmarkers, and also in accounts recording the funds disbursed in payment for the binding and dressing of books. There, bookmarkers receive separate itemization, as in the accounts of the Mercers of London, which mention in the accounts of 1400–1401 four pence paid for "seignes de soie a cest livre" – that is, "bookmarkers of silk" – for a late fourteenth-century account book belonging to the company.[20] The preponderance of silk laces for bookmarkers, and the role of silkwomen as the primary source of these laces,[21] consequently suggest that women's work and women's labor often contributed to the production of bookmarkers.

Interestingly, while the Syon sacristans' accounts reference the purchase of register pins, they do not mention the material of the strands themselves. Silk was discouraged at Syon, according to the additional rules, which note when discussing the Chambress' responsibilities and the work and items she oversees, such as "sewynge, making, reparyng . . . gyrdelles, purses, knyues, laces, poyntes, nedelles, threde," that one should "in nowise . . . be ouer curious, but playne and homly, witheoute weuynge of any straunge colours of sylke."[22] Silk conveyed vanity and luxury. Instead, the rules directed Syon's nuns to plainer material, such as linen. This preference for less luxurious goods might have, in turn, had an impact on the materials used in Syon's bookmarkers. Perhaps the sacristans' accounts mention only the pins because the price included the finished object

---

19 Anne F. Sutton, *The Mercery of London: Trade, Goods and People, 1130–1578* (Farnham, Surrey, and Burlington, VT, 2005), esp. 202–3, 207. Marjorie Keniston McIntosh, *Working Women in English Society, 1300–1620* (Cambridge, UK, 2005), 223. Women's participation in the silk-working industry declined, however, over the course of the sixteenth century as merchants imported more work from abroad (224). See also Anne F. Sutton, "Two Dozen and More Silkwomen of Fifteenth-Century London," *The Ricardian* 16 (2006): 46–58. For a more extended discussion of the economic and social context of silkwomen, see Sutton, *The Mercery of London*, esp. 202–3, 207, 445, 454, which charts their centrality to mercers' businesses in the fifteenth century and earlier, and their decline and supplanting by silkmen in the sixteenth.

20 Lisa Jefferson, ed., *The Medieval Account Books of the Mercers of London* (Farnham, Surrey, and Burlington, VT, 2009), 156–57.

21 Sutton, *Mercery of London*, describes silkwomen as lynchpins of mercery businesses, either *sole* or working in partnership with their husbands. Alice Claver, a silkwoman who supplied the great wardrobe of Henry VIII, sold to the great wardrobe tassels, buttons, laces, and silk thread, all of which she could have made, spun, and dyed herself (207).

22 Aungier, *History and Antiquities of Syon*, 392.

as made with inexpensive linen. Another possibility could be that the nuns themselves – well-resourced by the Chambress – produced the strands on their own. Certainly, women of both low and high social estates learned how to make the kinds of laces typically used for bookmarkers, and were likely to have been the intended audience of instructional texts about lacemaking that circulated at this time in manuscript.[23] Even if Syon purchased the bookmarkers in their final form, ready to use, the frequency with which people associated "loveley ladies with youre longe fyngres"[24] as sources of laces like those used for bookmarker strands points to a gendered material history for bookmarkers from the fourteenth to the seventeenth century. Addressing the linkage between women's bodies and lacemaking, Edmund Waller wrote in his poem "On a Brede of Divers Colours" about how "Twice twenty slender Virgins' Fingers twine / This curious Web, where all their Fancies shine."[25] This focus on the role of women's bodies in the creation of bookmarkers demonstrates how the familiar methods of production affected perception of the items produced. In this way, bookmarkers become associated with feminized qualities of beauty, slimness, virginity, and fancy. Above all, bookmarkers, in and out of Syon, used materials whose past positioned them to convey meaning in the present, meaning associated with women's productive labor and gendered work.

Gendered connotations and practice were not exclusive to the material culture of bookmarkers; gender also influenced their use in reading practice. Bookmarkers specifically facilitated a nonlinear mode of reading, in which the reader could use the bookmarker to approach passages out of sequence. This mode of reading connects explicitly to devotional reading practices, as in those recommended by the translator of the *Orcherd of Syon* – a text itself translated and designed for the nuns of the abbey. In its prologue, the translator compares reading the text to traversing the many alleys of an orchard ("ȝe mowe chese if ȝe wole of xxxv aleyes where ȝe wolen walke, þat is to seye of xxxv chapitres, o tyme in oon, anoþir tyme in anoþir").[26] This passage has become well enough

---

23 Ruth Carroll, "Recipes for Laces: A Discourse Colony," in *Discourse Perspectives on English: Medieval to Modern*, ed. Risto Hiltunen and Janne Skaffari (Amsterdam and Philadelphia, 2003), 137–66, at 142.

24 *Piers Plowman: The B Version*, ed. George E. Kane and E. Talbot Donaldson (London, 1975), line VI.10, also cited by Stephanie Trigg in "'Ye louely ladyes with youre longe fyngres': The Silkwomen of Medieval London," *Studia Anglica Posnaniensia* 38 (2002): 469–84.

25 "On a Brede," from *Witts recreations*, 3rd edn. (London, 1645), quoted in Mrs. Bury Palliser, *A History of Lace* (London, 1865), 292.

26 *Orcherd of Syon*, ed. Phyllis Hodgson and Gabriel M. Liegey, Early English Text Society o.s. 258 (Oxford, 1966), 1.

known that it will suffice to touch upon it only briefly. This mode of devotional reading, promoted explicitly by the *Orcherd* to a female audience and facilitated further still by bookmarkers, could be performative, even as it sought to regulate behavior and cognitive processes.[27]

Here, the difference in the monks' and the nuns' relationships to books as evidenced by their accessories appears once more. While the *Orcherd* links this nonlinear mode of reading to the nuns' ability to dwell over passages and "savoren" their "fruyt" and "herbis," whether sweet or "scharpe, hard, or bitter,"[28] the monks are encouraged in their rules to ensure that books are "markyd that whan he leyth any boke up on any lectron or deske, he schal open it in the myddes, and so schett it aȝene whan he taketh it away."[29] In other words, the monks' books should be managed so that they can be immediately opened to a predetermined place, and that place maintained after the book was taken away, presumably as they make their way through the liturgical year. There were several methods available to the monks for marking their books, such as the use of historiated initials or illuminations, though these would require thumbing through the pages to locate. More direct methods might involve adding tabs to the edge of pages, which would allow books to be opened to predetermined, fixed locations.[30] More apropos yet would be the dial bookmarker, which used a dial to identify a specific column and passage on a page. The dial would be affixed to a string that could extrude from the book and mark the specific opening where the passage of interest was located.[31] Most flexible for developing needs, however, would be the multiple-strand bookmarker, which would allow multiple passages to be flagged for attention. The strands would make those passages identifiable when the book was closed, and the different colors used for the textile strands would assist in distinguishing one opening from another (a system still in use today).[32]

---

27 See Jessica Brantley, *Reading in the Wilderness*, 16; and C. Annette Grisé, "Prayer, Meditation, and Women Readers in Late Medieval England: Teaching and Sharing Through Books," in *Texts and Traditions of Medieval Pastoral Care: Essays in Honour of Bella Millett*, ed. Cate Gunn and Catherine Innes-Parker (York, 2009), 178–92. See also Sarah Noonan, "'Bycause the redyng shold not turne hem to enoye': Reading, Selectivity, and *Pietatis Affectum* in Late Medieval England," *New Medieval Literatures* 15 (2013): 225–54.

28 Ibid., 1 and 421.

29 Hogg, 3:55.

30 On such tabs, see Sawyer, "Navigation by Tab and Thread."

31 For the use of dial bookmarkers in medieval England, see Richard Emms, "Medieval Rotating Column-Indicators," *Transactions of the Cambridge Bibliographical Society* 12 (2001): 179–84.

32 Indeed, one extant bookmarker, likely contemporary to the thirteenth-century gradual in which it is located, used multiple colors (green, pink, yellow, and perhaps

As a reader's needs changed – for example, as when utilizing different parts of a missal according to the liturgical calendar – the bookmarker strands might be relocated to identify the most immediately relevant passages within a text.

To return in conclusion to Syon and its bookmarkers: did the nuns use the bookmarkers obtained by the sacristan? Almost certainly. We know they were recommended to read nonlinearly, as advised and described by the translator of the *Orcherd of Syon*. Moreover, among the extant surviving manuscripts from Syon Abbey is the martyrology used initially by the monks and later by the nuns to record the nuns' obits and provide the daily lessons of the "Martirloge." It includes its original bookmarker.[33] Of a notable style, the two woven strands of the bookmarker, one originally blue and the other red, have sewn to them large vellum rectangles that provide prompts to the reader about, for example, Latin: "Soror" and "Sorores" appear next to each other as reminders of the words' grammatical number. The bookmarker thus evidences another way the inhabitants of Syon could employ such accessories: not only to mark places, but also to provide Latin education and reference. Even the image of a bookmarker alone could signal nonlinear, selective reading, as demonstrated in BL MS Harley 612, which marked in the margin passages to be inserted in its text of the *Revelations of St. Bridget*. Around several of these insertions are drawings, in particular on fols. 82v and 218v, the images of chemise-bound manuscripts spread open. Upon their pages are written the passages to be inserted, and from between their pages dangle strands of bookmarkers.[34] Readers would thus negotiate the text nonlinearly, pausing in their reading of the central passage to look to the margin, take note of the insertion, and then return to the central passage. These examples also demonstrate a final point about the reading practices of Syon. Despite the rules' attempt to construct and impose the gendered performance of relationships to books, which parallels similar attitudes evident in the broader culture of secular readers outside the abbey, the monks and nuns of Syon shared reading practices reliant upon a communal book accessory. While their relationships to books may have been constructed differently, as articulated in the gender-specific advice for books' handling and apprehension, there are yet

cream) for its bookmarker strands. This is the New York, Morgan Library & Museum, MS 711, the bookmarker of which is analyzed in greater detail in Blatt and Swales, "Multi-Page Bookmarkers," 176.

33   BL MS Add. 22285, pictured and further discussed in Christopher Wordsworth and Henry Littlehales, *The Old Service-Books of the English Church* (London, 1904), 278–79; and Claes Gejrot, "The Syon Martiloge," in *Syon Abbey and its Books*, 203–27.

34   Christopher De Hamel, *Syon Abbey: The Library of the Bridgettine Nuns and their Peregrinations after the Reformation* (Otley, West Yorkshire, 1991), 58–59.

certain similarities in how the monks and nuns read those books and used the accessories they shared.

This similarity between the use of bookmarkers by nuns and monks at Syon is particularly interesting because it contrasts with the other evidence regarding the status of bookmarkers, where gendered distinctions emerge in their treatment, use, and presentation. When writers and translators associated with Syon, like that of the *Orcherd*, recommend nonlinear reading, they typically do so to audiences explicitly or implicitly made up of nuns; when nonlinearity becomes similarly explicit in texts addressed to male audiences, as it does in the additions to the rule above, the valence of the relationship between reader and book changes.[35] The nuns' nonlinear reading evokes affective responses – savoring, sweetness, bitterness – whereas the nonlinear engagement of the monks demonstrates their mastery in handling and teaching from books, and in using accessories to support their use. Absent from male encounters with book accessories is reference to devotional reading. Instead, the monks are encouraged to become adept users of books and book-related tools. These distinctions between the gendering of reading practice and reading responses align generally with the rhetoric of affective devotion, and more broadly still with cultural emphasis on women's predisposition to experiences of flesh, physicality, and corporeality.[36] Only recently have critics begun to argue that affective devotion was not predominately the practice of women – an opinion that has hitherto persisted in part because the discourse and texts advocating such devotion survive primarily in works associated with female audiences.[37] In this context, tracing the role of the bookmarkers at Syon suggests

35 I discuss the gendering of nonlinear reading instructions in the second chapter of *Participatory Reading in Late-Medieval England* (Manchester, 2018). An example of nonlinear reading advocated to men is given in a biblical concordance to the Wycliffite Bible, which explains that, "If a man haue mynde oonly of oo word or two of sum long text of þe newe lawe . . . þis concordaunce wole lede him bi þe fewe wordis þat ben confrid in his mynde vnto þe ful text, and shewe him in what book and in what chapitre he shal fynde þo textis which him list to haue," quoted in Anne Hudson, *The Premature Reformation: Wycliffite Texts and Lollard History* (Oxford and New York, 1988), 234.

36 For example, Caroline Walker Bynum, in *Holy Feast, Holy Fast: The Religious Significance of Food to Medieval Women* (Berkeley, 1987), discusses at length how, by the thirteenth century, the flesh and physicality of Christ were considered symbolically feminine because of these very associations between embodiment and women. This affinity between women's corporeality and the book extends to reading and metaphors of authorship, as addressed by Amy Hollywood in *The Soul as Virgin Wife: Mechthild of Magdeburg, Marguerite Porete, and Meister Eckhart* (Notre Dame, IN, 1995), 114.

37 For assessment of the gendered audience of affective devotion, see Sarah McNamer, *Affective Devotion*. McNamer argues that "compassionate meditation" produced by affective reading "originated as a practice among female religious," and that "gender

the perception that even the same accessory, depending on whether it supported the monks' or the nuns' divergent textual, material, and interpretive practices, might convey different meaning to contemporary audiences.

Bookmarkers outside Syon

Even as the past of the production of bookmarkers as objects and their use as accessories of reading could convey significance, so too could the moment of their completion, as when presented for gifts or fashioned in memory of a place. Instances in which the commissioning and transmission of bookmarkers express meaning can be seen in the royal accounts of Isabeau of Bavaria, queen consort of France and wife of Charles VI.[38] Isabeau played an influential role as patron in the Valois court; for example, while presiding over the regency council on behalf of the mentally ill Charles VI in 1396, she became the patron of Johan Maelwel, uncle to the Limbourg monks who later produced the *Tres Riches Heures*, and commissioned his work as a painter.[39] Books figure prominently in accounts detailing purchases supporting her patronage and gift-giving practices. Her accounts also reveal that bookmarkers played a role in her use of books as gifts. These accounts record several payments made to the queen's goldsmith, Jean Clerboure, between 1395 and 1403, for work associated with the dressing of books. One of these payments describes "une pipe d'or, esmaillliez des armes de la royne" – a gold bookmarker enameled with the arms of the queen – for

performance became an enduring, core mechanism for the production" of compassion (7). Sarah Noonan has argued that affective reading emerges from nonlinear reading practices. See Noonan, "'Bycause the redyng shold not turne hem to enoye.'"

38   These accounts have been transcribed by Bernard Prost in "Documents sur l'histoire de la reliure: Extraits de comptes royaux des XIVe et XVe siècles," *Bulletin du Bibliophile* 64 (1897): 607–18, 645–60. Isabeau of Bavaria has long been viewed dismissively by a variety of audiences, assessed primarily through the lens of gossip and propaganda. The latter years of the twentieth century ushered in a re-evaluation of her role in the court of France and its political and cultural affairs during the late fourteenth and early fifteenth centuries. Such revisionist work finds its most extended study of Isabeau to date in Tracy Adams, *The Life and Afterlife of Isabeau of Bavaria* (Baltimore, 2012). For specific context on Isabeau's use of books as gifts, see "Female Book Collectors in the Valois Courts," in Joni M. Hand, *Women, Manuscripts, and Identity in Northern Europe, 1350–1550* (Farnham, Surrey, and Burlington, VT, 2013), 11–56. For the practice of gift-giving specific to New Year in the Valois Courts, see Brigitte Buettner, "Past Presents: New Year's Gifts at the Valois Courts, ca. 1400," *The Art Bulletin* 83/4 (December 2001): 598–625.

39   Timothy B. Husband, *The Art of Illumination: The Limbourg Brothers and the Belles Heures of Jean de France, Duc de Berry* (New Haven and London, 2008), 279.

the book of hours of her daughter, Michelle of Valois.[40] Another describes "une pipe d'or pour un breviaire . . . esmailliez aux armes de lad. dame," a gold bookmarker for the breviary of the queen of England, Joan of Navarre, enameled with her arms.[41] The latter, given the account's dating to the year of Joan's marriage to Henry IV of England, may well have been a wedding gift, or a commission via Isabeau for Joan before the latter's departure to England. (Jean Clerboure was additionally paid in this account to repair the clasps of a book of hours that also belonged to Joan, suggesting an ongoing relationship between Joan and the goldsmith, rather than a one-off interaction associated with a single gift.)[42] In contrast, when the queen paid the goldsmith for a bookmarker for a book of hours for her son Louis the Dauphin, the bookmarker is described only as a "pippe d'or," gold, but apparently not decorated with arms or other individuating details.[43] More attention seems to be paid by Isabeau – or her accountant – to the decorative elements of the bookmarker when the recipient is a woman. Furthermore, women predominate both as givers and as recipients of bookmarkers. In these accounts, the ratio of occasions when the king and his artisans provide a bookmark, to when the queen and hers do, is 1:1.7. Similarly, women receive bookmarkers almost twice as frequently as men, the ratio here being 1:2.3.[44]

Around Isabeau thus coalesces a network of women, their books, and their book accessories. Bookmarkers play key roles among these accessories as accompaniments to the luxuriously finished manuscript, as transmitters of identity, and as vehicles of memory that denote relationships between women through their creation and decoration. Michelle of France, taking the book with her into her subsequent marriage, would carry a visual reminder, in the bookmarker's existence and even more specifically in its decoration, of her mother; Joan of Navarre, using the breviary while resident in England, would have occasion to think of France and its queen, who provided her with such a gift

---

40   Ibid., 651. Michelle herself married Philip III (Philip the Good), duke of Burgundy, in July 1409. This was not Isabeau's only gift of a book to her daughter, for she also provided Michelle with an "ABC of psalms" on a birthday, testifying to Isabeau's interest in her daughter's education (Adams, 232).

41   Ibid., 653.

42   Ibid.

43   Ibid.

44   Prost quotes every account related to the king's and queen's expenses of the fourteenth and fifteenth centuries that mentions items related to books, from coverings to clasps to illumination. Between 1378 and 1405, these accounts refer to bookmarker purchases a total of nineteen times; seven of these purchases are associated with the king, and twelve with the queen. Fourteen recipients of bookmarkers are women; six are men.

(or with contact to a master of French gold work).[45] In addition, the creation and use of these bookmarkers manifest a narrative of relationships between women – narratives mediated through the form of a book accessory. Isabeau arranges for bookmarkers to be provided along with books given to women including her daughters Jehanne, Michelle, and Katherine, and her daughter-in-law Margaret of Burgundy, as well as the queen of England. In contrast, she only once arranges for a similar bookmarker to be given to one of her sons. As Joni Hand argues, books served as "vehicles for the expression" of ideologies important to the aristocratic women who owned them.[46] The evidence of Isabeau's accounts suggests that bookmarkers contributed to the ideological expressiveness and memorial function of books by emphasizing political and familial connections. It was not only through the manuscripts themselves that "dynastic, familial, and private intent" could be conveyed.[47] Bookmarkers also, as accessories that could be decorated with heraldic arms as well as other imagery, contributed to the aim of such gifts.

Such a narrative furthers our understanding of women's participation in late medieval literary culture. Commissioning a bookmarker as a gift that accompanies the commission of a book suggests that bookmarkers played several roles. First, in crafting the finished look of a well-dressed book, bookmarkers contributed to how the book's material form might signal wealth and beauty, adding to the role that clasps and binding already played.[48] Second, a bookmarker's function was not merely fashionably decorative or practical, but also enabled readers to shape their reading experience in a way that bypassed the text's navigational layout. That is, while the *mis-en-page* and organizational elements – historiated initials, illuminations, and chapter divisions – functioned to denote place, a bookmarker facilitated readers' determination of their own navigational strategies. Consequently, the presence of a bookmarker as part of a book commissioned by a woman suggests that women readers like Isabeau of Bavaria paid attention to how the recipient might want or need to navigate the text above and beyond those

45   In this way, bookmarkers, through their creation and decoration, provide a material testimony to the user's or giver's identity.

46   Hand, *Women, Manuscripts, and Identity*, 2.

47   Diane E. Booton, in chapter 4, "Ducal Patronage and Ownership," of *Manuscripts, Market and the Transition to Print in Late Medieval Brittany* (Farnham, Surrey, and Burlington, VT, 2010), 135.

48   On the way that embellishments to a book's binding, particularly through its "furniture" – that is, clasps and other external elements, like bosses – contributed to its beauty and signified conspicuous consumption, see Virginia Reinburg, *French Books of Hours: Making an Archive of Prayer, c. 1400–1600* (Cambridge, UK, 2012), in the section on "Treasured Possession and Devotional Object," 76–83.

ways supported by the text's layout. Bookmarkers commissioned by Isabeau most frequently accompanied missals and books of hours and breviaries, works whose contents were not designed to be read in a linear sequence; bookmarkers served a practical navigational role in facilitating apprehension of such volumes.[49] In addition, that these bookmarkers, in Isabeau's accounts, consistently accompany devotional texts given to women again signals their use for particular reading purposes: in the hands of a woman reader, the bookmarker does not represent an accessory to nonsequential reading applied to texts in any genre. Instead, it is an accessory specific to nonsequential reading in the service of devotional practice.

This role of bookmarkers as devotional reading aids used especially by women finds plentiful representation in North European art of the fifteenth and early sixteenth centuries. Works of art that depict bookmarkers show them predominantly used by, or in books held or identifiable with, female figures – particularly saints, Mary, and angels presented as women.[50] That the numbers favor female figures so markedly must be credited to the late medieval popularity of Marian devotion and, in particular, to the iconography of the Virgin as an exemplary reader. In contrast, few women of the fifteenth and sixteenth centuries, the contemporary subjects of the paintings, are shown with bookmarker-bearing books in hand. In addition to Mary, painters most frequently depict Anne, Mary Magdalene, and a few angels gendered female; these women use, hold, or are otherwise associated visually with books accompanied by bookmarkers. Here, too, differences surface in the handling of books with bookmarkers: female figures usually hold books with bookmarkers in their hands or laps (by a factor of four to one when compared to men), while the use of lecterns, desks, or tables is roughly equal between the genders. As we saw with the Syon monks and nuns, visual art of the same period employs a gendered vocabulary in which women's

49 Isabeau arranges for bookmarkers accompanying a missal for her daughter Jehanne (Prost, 617); a missal of her own (Prost, 646); in unspecified books for Michelle de France and Margaret of Burgundy (Prost, 649, 650); in books of hours for herself (Prost, 649–50); in a book of hours for Margaret of Burgundy (Prost, 650); a missal for Catherine de France (Prost, 651); a book of hours for the dauphin (Prost, 653); in the breviary of the queen of England (Prost, 653) and the missal of Margaret of Burgundy (Prost, 654).
50 A survey of sixty-seven images depicting bookmarkers in art of the fourteenth to mid-sixteenth centuries (listed in Blatt and Swales, "Multi-Page Bookmarkers," 171–73) provides interesting data. Often several people in a single image are shown with bookmarkers, providing a total of ninety-four users of bookmarkers. Men – whether saints or figures contemporary to the painting – are depicted as bookmarker users a total of forty times. Women – whether legendary or contemporary – appear as bookmarker users a total of fifty-four times. That indicates a ratio of 1:1.35. In other words, for every one man using a bookmarker, 1.35 women use them, an increase of 35%.

167

reading and book-handling predominately relates to the body, and men's reading and book-handling is accessorized with furniture.

A representative example of the visual encoding that surrounds the depiction of books with bookmarkers can be seen in Jan van Eyck's Ghent Altarpiece, which depicts both Mary and John the Baptist holding books accessorized with bookmarkers.[51] Their bookmarkers are largely identical, anchors formed in the shape of a domed cluster of pearls, and possibly meant to evoke the iconography of cleanness and virginity that applies to both figures, or memories formed from reading as pearls of wisdom. Mary holds a smaller, chemise-bound book at mid-chest height, while John the Baptist carries a larger, leather-bound volume open upon his lap. Her reading experience is intimate, private, as she looks down at the manuscript, which she holds at an angle that prevents viewers from seeing much more than a slice of its text. Furthermore, the size of the book and its textile chemise binding also characterize her reading experience as one of smallness and softness. In its closeness to her body, her reading also betokens urgency and focus; she reads for learning and devotion. In contrast, John's bookmarker-facilitated experience depicts the book tipped visually toward the viewer so that both folios of the open manuscript are in evidence, making it clear that he reads a text with a denser, two-column layout. His reading seems more leisurely, even though his posture is upright and outward-looking, his book harder and less decorative. Together with the greater size of his book, John as reader conveys more authority. He knows what his book contains and needs to consult it only to refresh his memory. The text he reads likely gestures to the Bible, with a familiar two-column *ordinatio*, whereas Mary's text probably represents a small devotional work, such as a book of hours. In sum, then, the portrait of Mary as reader indicates an experience that is intimate, private, and devotional, while John engages in a more open, public mode of reading that appears to involve consultation of a learned text rather than intense devotional practice.

The practice of carrying or using books flourished in medieval art. It was familiar in the iconography of saints, and was especially connected in the

---

51   The altarpiece is the work of Hubert and Jan van Eyck (at Ghent, Belgium, in the St. Bavo Cathedral), begun c. 1425 and finished in 1432. The initial design is thought to have been the work of Hubert, who died in 1426, leaving the execution and finalization of the paintings to his brother. A foundational and still authoritative work on the van Eycks and the altarpiece is that by Elisabeth Dhanens, *Van Eyck: The Ghent Altarpiece* (New York, 1973); more recent and influential studies include the substantive conversation about the altarpiece staged in *Investigating Jan van Eyck*, ed. Susan Foister, Sue Jones, and Delphine Cool, Museums at the Crossroads 6 (Turnhout, 2000). The altarpiece can be studied through high-resolution images online in the digital humanities project "Closer to Van Eyck: Rediscovering the Ghent Altarpiece," http://closertovaneyck.kikirpa.be/#intro.

late Middle Ages to the popularity of books of hours, objects of conspicuous consumption.[52] This practice, in its intersection with bookmarkers, reveals further details regarding habits of use and relation. For example, closer analysis of the bookmarkers depicted in the altarpiece further illuminates how the use of the bookmarkers and books reflects gendered practices. In the portrait of John as reader, multiple strands of bookmarkers in a Bible would facilitate comparative analysis of similar or seemingly contradictory passages and themes, and would also enable accessing and consulting the text out of its linear sequence in order to follow liturgical navigation of the Bible or – since the reader here is John the Baptist, and thus belongs temporally to a period that pre-dates the formation of the Catholic liturgy – to anticipate the order of liturgical reading. In the portrait of Mary as reader, multiple strands of bookmarkers in a work like a book of hours promote easy access to the various included texts, making it easier for readers to navigate between sections of the book and thus extend their devotions; the bookmarker's presence thus signifies attentiveness to the many texts or passages marked by the strands.

These differing portraits of John and Mary as readers using books that include bookmarkers gesture to differing book-body relationships that parallel the differences found in the Syon discourse surrounding books. Mary holds the book close to her body, cradling it with her hands and holding it close to her heart and head, while John keeps his book at a distance and looks elsewhere. This intimacy between women's bodies and books could even eroticize portraits of women readers, particularly Mary as a reader.[53] For John, the book supplements activity, whereas for Mary the book provides a focal point for her efforts. In this way, tracking the visual imagery of bookmarkers in late medieval art provides further evidence demonstrating, on the eve of the Reformation, a gender-differentiated intellectual and material relationship to books. Such differentiation depicts women's relationships to books as private, personal, closed, devotional,

---

52 Eamon Duffy refers to books of hours as "this most chic of devotional fashion accessories" in *Marking the Hours: English People and their Prayers 1240–1570* (New Haven, 2006), 22. Gertrude Schiller identifies books as common objects in Annunciation scenes from the eleventh century onward in *Iconography of Christian Art*, vol. 1, trans. Janet Seligman (Greenwich, CT, 1971), 33–52, at 42. For assessment of how book owners would gaze at themselves in portraits of reading, see Alexa Sand, *Vision, Devotion, and Self-Representation in Late Medieval Art* (Cambridge, UK, and New York, 2014).

53 See David Linton, "Reading the Virgin Reader," in *The Book and the Magic of Reading in the Middle Ages*, ed. Albrecht Classen (New York and London, 1998), 253–76. Linton observes that painters and illuminators were ambivalent regarding the representation of women readers; as Linton notes, "the book and the act of reading are highly eroticized in Annunciation scenes" (254).

and physically intimate, and depicts men's relationships to books as more public, learned, authoritative, and physically distant. Furthermore, these different representations of how the books and their accessories are represented in the Ghent Altarpiece confirm how devotional reading was becoming perceived as a gendered activity associated with women, whereas other, more academic forms of reading – consulting or referencing passages, for example – connoted men's work, and how these attitudes find reflection even in the treatment of book accessories.[54]

In England, bookmarkers largely disappear from sight in the years following the Reformation.[55] This absence may correspond to how nonlinear, selective reading becomes associated in the early years of the English Reformation with Catholicism, creating the possibility that bookmarkers, as visible tools of this reading practice, became tainted by association.[56] Evidencing this perception of nonlinear reading, Edward VI's *Book of Common Prayer*, printed in 1549, prejudicially contended that the common treatment of the Bible itself – with legends, responses, and other passages or texts collected with it – left the work fragmented in ways that

---

54 See, in particular, Grisé, "Women's Devotional Reading," and the other resources identified in n. 37 above.

55 The finding list of extant bookmarkers in Blatt and Swales, "Multi-Page Bookmarkers," 148–54, with the catalog of depictions of bookmarkers in art in the same, 171–73, demonstrates a similar absence of examples in the mid-sixteenth century.

56 On nonlinear reading, its association with Catholic religious practice, and the resulting tension surrounding it as Protestants continued to critique its use while practicing it nevertheless, see Matthew P. Brown, "The Thick Style: Steady Sellers, Textual Aesthetics, and Devotional Reading," *PMLA* 121 (2006): 67–86; Matthew P. Brown, *The Pilgrim and the Bee: Reading Rituals and Book Culture in Early New England* (Philadelphia, 2007); and John N. King, *Foxe's "Book of Martyrs" and Early Modern Print Culture* (Cambridge, UK, 2006), 266–67. Scant references to bookmarkers and a gap in extant survivals makes certainty difficult, and the correlation between the dearth of bookmarkers and the tension between Protestant and Catholic reading practices is not the only possible explanation. Other possibilities include changing textile trends rendering textile bookmarkers unfashionable, or changing interest in books as popular accessories and symbols of personal identity. Another possibility may be suggested by developing pressure in the sixteenth century on mercer husbands to maintain wives who did not engage in trade (Sutton, *Mercery of London*, 445), which may have impacted silkwomen's production of bookmarks or their laces, as silkwomen were encouraged to set aside their trade; by the mid-sixteenth century, precisely when documentation of bookmarkers in England disappears for a few decades, silkwomen were increasingly supplanted by silkmen (ibid., 454).

"breake the continual course of the reading of the scripture."[57] Proper Protestant reading, the *Book* thus suggests, should be unbroken, linear, and continuous. Almost certainly in consequence, the arrangement of the liturgies in the *Book of Common Prayer* (Morning and Evening Prayer and Holy Communion) are similarly straightforward and sequentially ordered, which requires a minimum of nonlinear negotiation. In contrast to Catholic liturgical books, the *Book of Common Prayer* is (perhaps unsurprisingly in this context) not bound with multiple-strand bookmarkers to mark the places. Indeed, in the years preceding the landmark publication of the *Book of Common Prayer*, the bookmarkers mentioned in the inventories of Henry VIII's property made after his death in 1547 (which we encountered above) are described as being maintained quietly out of the way in coffers kept in the Tower of London.[58] The argument against nonlinear, selective reading and textual collation represented in the *Book of Common Prayer* thus intersects with, and perhaps even motivated, diminished use of the primary tool to facilitate that mode of reading, the multiple-strand bookmarker.

In secular portraiture, the use of books and bookmarks could similarly be charged with meaning. For women, holding a book might "connote reading as an aspect of female virtue and piety," in which closed pages are "implicitly religious or didactic in content."[59] During this period, the association between male users of books and book-related furniture nevertheless continues.[60] The furniture in question is usually a table or desk of some sort, as seen in the 1546 portrait by Gerlach Flicke of Archbishop Cranmer, which depicts him holding one book

---

57 *The boke of the common praier and administratio[n] of the sacramentes and other rytes and ceremonies of the Churche, after the vse of the churche of Englande* (Worcester, 1549, *STC* 16271), Aii^r–iii^r.

58 See *The Inventory of King Henry VIII* (n. 18 above), 71–72.

59 Stephanie Dickey, "'Meet een wenendze ziel . . . dock droge ogen': Women Holding Handkerchiefs in Seventeenth-Century Dutch Portraits," *Nederlands Kunsthistorisch Jaarboek* 46 (1995): 332–67, at 342.

60 This period also witnesses increasing numbers of books held in personal libraries in England, in part due to the transference of books from ecclesiastical libraries to private hands in the 1530s, and in part due to how less expensive printed books made book-collecting a more economically accessible activity. For more discussion of such, see Sears Jayne, *Library Catalogues of the English Renaissance* (Godalming, Surrey, 1983), 39–43. On the correspondence between private libraries and book ownership of this period, see Kristian Jensen, "Printing at Oxford in its European Context 1478–1584," in *History of Oxford University Press*, vol. 1: *Beginnings to 1780*, ed. Ian Gadd (Oxford, 2013), 31–50, at 37–40. The seminal study edited by R. J. Fehrenbach, *Private Libraries in Renaissance England*, vol. 1 (New York, 1992), which initiated a multivolume series and online database hosted by the Folger Shakespeare Library, continues to be influential.

in his hand, with two other books and a letter upon the table before him.[61] In contrast, women continue to be consistently shown holding books exclusively in their hands or laps – or, as was briefly fashionable in the 1550s and 1560s, in small format at the end of a girdle chain draping along the front of a skirt.[62] One of the few examples of a bookmarker in portraiture from this period comes, perhaps unsurprisingly, from Italy, a region less beset by the rising tides of anti-Catholicism. In 1551, the Italian artist Sophonisba Anguissola painted a woman, usually identified as her sister Elena, in the habit of a nun; Elena had entered the monastery of San Vincenzo in Mantua, adopting the name Sister Minerva.[63] In this portrait, Elena holds a volume in her hands, her thumb inserted in the opening. The red strands of a bookmarker dangle toward her waist. She thus represents the tradition of female religious use of bookmarkers and depicts the gendered mode of book interaction also witnessed at Syon, even though this portrait dates to a period that, in England, is more dominated by images of secular readers. These trends in depicting how men and women were associated with books show that some of the gendered behavior evident in the Syon records also applies outside Syon, to secular readers, even as bookmarkers, for a time, fade from sight.

61   London, National Portrait Gallery, NPG 535, originally painted 1545–46.

62   See, for example, the "Portrait of an Unknown Lady" by Hans Eworth (Cambridge, UK, Fitzwilliam Museum, PD.1–1963, c. 1557), and the portrait of Elizabeth I when a princess, c. 1546, usually attributed to William Scrots (London, Windsor Castle, RCIN 404444). These books reached their peak of popularity between 1530 and 1560, on which see Hugh Tait, "The Girdle-Prayerbook or 'Tablett': An Important Class of Renaissance Jewelry at the Court of Henry VIII," *Jewelry Studies* 2 (1985): 29–57. Mary Ellen Lamb argues that the placement of the girdle book lent it a sexual charge when worn by women, in her essay "Inventing the Early Modern Woman Reader through the World of Goods: Lyly's Gentlewoman Reader and Katherine Stubbes," in Heidi B. Hackel and Catherine E. Kelley, eds., *Reading Women: Literacy, Authorship, and Culture in the Atlantic World, 1500–1800* (Philadelphia, 2009), 15–35, at 24. This trend of representing women holding books close to their bodies in hands or laps continues into the seventeenth century, as represented in the image series known as "The Painted Life of Mary Ward," in several of which Mary holds a book in her hands (artist unknown; Mary Ward Hall, Augsburg, Germany, and available online at http://www.congregatiojesu.org/en/maryward_painted_life.asp).

63   Anguissola, "The Artist's Sister in the Garb of a Nun," Southampton, Southampton City Art Gallery, SCAG 3. For details about the artist, see Marco Tanzi, "Sofonisba Anguissola," in *The Dictionary of Art*, vol. 2, ed. J. Turner (London, 1996), 92; Christopher Wright, *Renaissance to Impressionism: Masterpieces from Southampton City Art Gallery* (London, 1998), 17, 27, 81.

By the late sixteenth and early seventeenth centuries, however, as the initial Protestant condemnation of nonlinear reading fades and the fashion for small, highly decorative embroidered book-bindings rises, bookmarkers again come back into view.[64] Their rise and fall highlights how closely they had become linked not to all kinds of nonlinear reading, but particularly to devotional, religious reading. By the time George Webb and his associates write and publish *A Garden of Spirituall Flowers* (1609), nonlinear, selective reading was once more recommended. These authors write that a conscientious reader should, "marke the Text, observe the division . . . fold down a leafe in your Bible from which the place is recited, that so at your leasure after your returne from the Church, you may examine it." In his 1647 conduct manual, John White too recommends "comparing Scripture to Scripture."[65] Such place-marking as described by Webb and White both facilitates selective reading and could be made easier through the use of a bookmarker. In addition, the bookmarker could enhance the decorative accessorization of a volume granted the luxury of an embroidered binding, and it is in this particular context – the embroidered bindings most often used to decorate printed psalms and testaments – that bookmarkers return to a limited popularity.[66]

Personalized Bookmarkers

Bookmarkers of the late sixteenth and seventeenth centuries personalize books that were printed en masse, but which also functioned as personal accessories of devotion. Continuing the association of bookmarkers with religious reading practices, the psalters and Bibles they accessorized are primarily associated with women readers and makers.[67] Perhaps because of their highly personalized role,

64 On the early seventeenth-century fashion for embroidered bookbindings, the classic work remains Cyril Davenport's *English Embroidered Bookbindings* (London, 1899), although it bears updating from less comprehensive, but more recent, scholarship such as that in Mirjam M. Foot, *Pictorial Bookbindings* (London, 1986).

65 Webb and White are quoted in Michael Brown, *The Pilgrim and the Bee*, 116, 80. For more on such nonsequential reading, see Patrick Collinson, "The Coherence of the Text: How it Hangeth Together: the Bible in Reformation England," *Journal for the Study of the New Testament*, supplement series, 105 (Sheffield, 1995), 84–108; and Peter Stallybrass, "Books and Scrolls: Navigating the Bible," in Jennifer Andersen and Elizabeth Sauer, eds., *Books and Readers in Early Modern England* (Philadelphia, 2002), 42–79.

66 On the changing popularity of bookmarkers, see n. 56 above.

67 For the practice of embroidered bookbindings and their users and creators, see Femke Molekamp, *Women and the Bible in Early Modern England: Religious Reading and Writing* (Oxford, 2013), 44ff. For the cultural context surrounding women's textile use and production, see Susan Frye, *Pens and Needles: Women's Textualities in Early Modern England*

two extant bookmarkers from this period also demonstrate characteristics evocative of personal religious and political identity. The first example, a bookmarker in a copy of a 1633 edition of the Bible and Thomas Sternhold's verse psalms, bears two portraits of Charles I and adds this couplet: "From prison bring / Youre captive king." It has been suggested that the book and bookmarker were owned by one of the ladies-in-waiting of Queen Henrietta Maria, wife of King Charles I, and a person certainly sympathetic to Charles I during the English Civil War.[68] This use of a rhymed couplet on a bookmark associates it with the traditions of short, rhymed texts and sentences called "posies," which were popular on rings and other personal items. By the early seventeenth century, posies could be used to decorate and personalize handkerchiefs, gloves, and bracelets, often as a testament of a man's sentiment toward his beloved.[69] They could also be used to express royalist sentiment, as this couplet and others do.[70] This example of a bookmarker suggests a connection between their use and female ownership in the early seventeenth century, and specifically gestures to the use of a bookmarker as a book accessory expressing a woman reader's political sentiment.

The second example of a bookmarker – this one in a copy, with an embroidered binding, of a 1632 printing of Robert Barker's Bible and Sternhold's psalms –

(Philadelphia, 2010); and Ann Rosalind Jones and Peter Stallybrass, *Renaissance Clothing and the Materials of Memory* (Cambridge, UK, 2000).

68   Quoted in *The British Museum Library* by Gertrude Burford Rawlings (Edinburgh, 1916), 195.

69   For example, in the work *Cupids posies. For bracelets, hand kerchers and rings, with scarfes, gloves, and other things; written by Cupid on a day, when Venus gave him leave to play. Verbum sat amanti. The lover sheweth his intent, by guises that are with posies sent* (London, 1642, Wing C7608A), one posy is described as "A Posie sent to a Maid, being cunningly enterwoven in a silke Bracelet." It reads: "Kindly take this guift of mine, / For guift and giver both are thine" (*A7*). All the items described in *Cupids posies* that identify the gender of giver or recipient represent women as recipients, not as givers; that may simply correspond to the focus of this particular collection on love and courtship, though it does suggest that items with posies upon them may have been strongly connected to women's ownership.

70   Several politically oriented posies for fingerloop braids are given in two braiding pattern-books: BL MS Add. 6293, fol. 38r; and Nottingham, Nottinghamshire Archives DD/E/222/3, fol. 1r. For more on these and other forms of textile textuality see Claire Canavan, "Textual and Textile Literacies in Early Modern Braids," *Renaissance Studies* 30.5 (2015): 684–707, with thanks to the author for sharing a copy of the essay with me, along with information on the Nottingham Archives braid book. These political, royalist posies include, "The ffall of Kings / Confusion brings," and "The time is cominge that you shall see / The Kinge to Raigne in Royaltie" in the Nottingham Archives manuscript; the former is also included in BL MS Add. 6293 (with thanks to Carissa Harris for assistance with this manuscript).

bears lines in Latin from the Magnificat, a few psalms, a verse from the Song of Solomon, and the complete text of the "Anima Christi," a prayer associated with St. Ignatius Loyola (see the Appendix, below).[71] Each quotation has been braided into a single strand, thirteen strands in total, each less than two millimeters wide. The bookmarker provides a brilliantly executed integration of private political and religious identity within a volume popularly associated with Protestantism, publicly representing the reader in a diametrically different fashion.[72] The bookmarker would have been too small to be read by a neighbor in the congregation; indeed, at less than two millimeters in width, the strands are difficult to read without magnification. In this way, the user of this bookmarker was able to privately and personally acknowledge religious identity while conforming to the outward fashions of a Protestant. Even as the owner read through the Bible, movement of the bookmarker strands would once again lace the text with the material representation of self-identity. This bookmarker, along with the bookmarker mentioned above, demonstrates how book accessories, made readable through provision of their own texts, could intersect with the religious and political concerns that shaped the identities of their owners.

Taken together, what the book furniture and bookmarkers alike indicate is that the material culture of book history extends beyond the materiality of books themselves. Books were profoundly socialized material objects. Yet the objects that surrounded them and supported their use – what might be called the paracodexical materialities of books – similarly influenced both perceptions and use of books. Objects such as bookmarkers, desks, lecterns, in their absence and in their presence, contributed to how use of the book could be regulated and how it could participate in gendered social practice. Consequently, assessment of the material history of books must also take into account their wider material context.

71 Cambridge University Library, BSS.201.C32.15.
72 Sternhold's psalms participated in the explosive popularity of metrical psalters in the sixteenth and early seventeenth centuries; on their popularity and influence, see Hannibal Hamlin, *Psalm Culture and Early Modern English Literature* (Cambridge, UK, 2004), particularly the first chapter, "'Vere mete to be used of all sortes of people': the 'Sternhold and Hopkins' Psalter." Hamlin notes that sung metrical psalms were, for Protestants, "a means of spreading doctrine" (22).

Appendix

Transcription of verses from the bookmarker in Cambridge University Library, BSS.201.C32.15.

The bookmarker consists of thirteen strands. Each strand is transcribed separately below, identified first by color of strand and second by color of text.[73]

1 Red/white: ANIMA CHRISTI SANCTIFICA ME CORPVS CHRISTI SALVA ME

   Translation and source: "Soul of Christ, sanctify me, / Body of Christ, save me." ("Anima Christi," 1–2).[74]

2 Blue/yellow: SANGVIS CHRISTI INEBRIA ME · AQVA LATERIS CHRISTI LAVA ME

   Translation and source: "Blood of Christ, inebriate me, / Water from the side of Christ, wash me" ("Anima Christi," 3–4).

3 Brown/white: PASSIO CHRISTI CONFORTA ME · O BONE IESV EXAVDI ME

   Translation and source: "Passion of Christ, strengthen me, / O good Jesus, hear me." ("Anima Christi," 5–6).

4 Blue/white: INTRA VVLNERA TVA ABSCONDE ME · NE PERMITTAS ME SEPARARI A TE

   Translation and source: "Within your wounds hide me. / Let me never be separated from you." ("Anima Christi," 7–8).

5 Orange/yellow: AB HOSTE MALIGNO DEFENDE ME

   Translation and source: "From the evil enemy defend me." ("Anima Christi," 9).

---

73 The technique by which the strands of this bookmarker were produced is known as fingerloop braiding, a technique in which silkwomen and (later) silkmen were skilled (see Blatt and Swales, n. 17 above, 162–63). On the subject of fingerloop braids with text (also known as letter braids), see Noémi Speiser and Joy Boutrup, *European Loop Braiding: Investigations and Results, Part II: Instructions for Letter Braids in 17th Century Manuscripts* (Leicester, 2009).

Thanks are due to Liam Sims, who arranged for me to view the bookmark and provided some details about the Bible with which it is associated, and to Jim Bloxam of Cambridge University Library and his colleagues, who provided the initial details about the texts on the strands via email in 2005.

74 Anonymous translation here and below from *The Westminster Collection of Christian Prayers*, ed. Dorothy M. Stewart (Louisville and London, 2002), 182.

6 Green/yellow: IN HORA MORTIS MEAE VOCA ME · ET IVBE ME VENIRE AD TE

Translation and source: "In the hour of my death call me, / And bid me come to you." ("Anima Christi," 10–11).

7 Red/white: VT CVM SANCTIS TVIS LAVDEM TE IN SAECVLA SECVLORVM AMEN

Translation and source: "That with your saints I may praise you / Forever and ever. Amen." ("Anima Christi," 12–13).

8 Blue/yellow: SIT NOMEN DOMINI BENEDICTVM · ET HOC NVNC ET VSQVE IN SAECVLVM

Translation and source: "Blessed be the name of the Lord: from this time forth and for euermore" (Psalm 112/13:2).[75]

9 White/red: EXSVRGAT DEVS ET DISSIPENTVR INIMICI EIVS · [ET FVGIANT] QVI ODERVNT EVM A FACIE EIVS ·

Translation and source: "Let God arise, let his enemies be scattered: let them also that hate him, flee before him" (Psalm 67/8:1).

10 Yellow/green: DILECTVS MEVS MIHI · ET EGO ILLI

Translation and source: "My beloued is mine, and I am his" (Song of Solomon 2:16).

11 White/yellow: too faded to read.

12 Red/white: QVID ENIM MIHI ET IN CAELO · ET A TE QVID VOLVI SVPER TERRAM

Translation and source: "Whom haue I in heauen but thee? and there is none vpon earth that I desire besides thee" (Psalm 72/3:25).

13 Green/yellow strand: MAGNIFICAT ANIMA MEA DOMINVM · EXVLTAVIT SPIRITVS MEVS IN DEO SALVTARI MEO

Translation and source: "My soule doth magnifie the Lord. And my spirit hath reioyced in God my Sauiour" (Luke 1:46–7). This is the beginning of the canticle Magnificat, based on the first words of Mary's greeting to her cousin Elizabeth.

75 Translation here and below from Robert Barker's Authorized Version of the Bible, the book with which the bookmark is associated.

Enska Vísan:
Sir Orfeo in Iceland?

MARTIN CHASE

Enska Vísan, literally "The English Verse," is a little-known and never-published Icelandic poem from the end of the Middle Ages. Because of its affinity to the Middle English *Sir Orfeo*, it seems a good subject for this volume in honor of Mary Erler: *Sir Orfeo* is one of the many texts Mary and I have enjoyed teaching together over the years at Fordham, and I hope she will take pleasure in this analogue. The text of *Enska Vísan* has been transmitted through scribal networks and reading communities in Iceland, not unlike those in England that Mary's work has done so much to elucidate. Because *Enska Vísan* defies classification in the usual sub-genres of late medieval Icelandic poetry – *rímur* (long narrative poems), *fornkvæði* (ballads), and *trúarkvæði* (devotional poems) – and because this body of literature traditionally has been published in genre-specific collections, the poem has never appeared in print.[1] The *rímur* have long been subject to scholarly study, and the *fornkvæði* have come into their own with the critical edition by Jón Helgason[2] and the masterful survey by Vésteinn Ólason,[3] but the *truarkvæði* have received less attention.[4] *Enska Vísan* shares characteristics with Icelandic (and English) metrical romances, ballads, and devotional poems, but there are also differences enough to prevent its being placed squarely in any one traditional genre. What follows is a presentation of the text of the poem along with a discussion of its context. I have found *Enska Vísan* transmitted in eleven manuscripts – there may well be more – from the seventeenth through the nineteenth centuries, and it is known to have existed in two others, now lost. The dating of the poem itself is uncertain.

1   Marius Kristensen printed the ten fragmentary stanzas that appear in Reykjavík, Árni Magnússon Institute, MS AM 622, 4to as an appendix to *En Klosterbog fra Middelalderens Slutning*, Samfund til Udgivelse af Gammel Nordisk Litteratur 54 (Copenhagen, 1928), 236–37.
2   Jón Helgason, ed., *Íslenzk Fornkvæði / Islandske Folkeviser*, 8 vols., Editiones Arnamagnæanæ B10–B17 (Copenhagen, 1962–81).
3   Vésteinn Ólason, *The Traditional Ballads of Iceland*, Stofnun Árna Magnússonar á Íslandi Rit 22 (Reykjavík, 1982).
4   Jón Helgason began a critical edition of the *trúarkvæði* and published vol. 1, part 2 and vol. 2 of a projected 3 vols.: Jón Helgason, ed., *Íslenzk Miðaldakvæði / Islandske Digte fra Senmiddelalderen* (Copenhagen, 1936–38).

Enska Vísan presents a narrative that shares elements with the Middle English *Sir Orfeo*. The story can be summarized as follows: an unnamed knight and his beloved have promised one another to join their lives in all ways and to share fully in all things. The knight wants to go to court, while his beloved must remain behind. The knight goes on his way, and Death comes quickly on the scene to seize his beloved and escort the unwilling lady to the otherworld. As they proceed, they come to where the knight lies sleeping, and he sees (as he dreams?) a dragon fly through the air with his wife in its claws. He draws his bow and shoots down the "demon" as it flies by, rescuing his beloved, who commands him to take her "to the land where joy never fails." He obediently carries the lady for seven months over many paths, across a broad bridge, over cold ice and hot ground bubbling with molten liquid. He carries her through a thick forest and across a burning desert, where wild beasts threaten to harm her. They finally come to a fair plain, where they are greeted by "angels and apostles," who say, "Give us the one you carry. It is good to be here, and here she will regain her health." The knight indignantly refuses ("I wouldn't give you a bean"), saying that they have ignored him in his trials and refused to hear his cries for help. Then a "peaceful man" who calls himself "Sunday" appears. "Give me the sinful soul," he says, "I can see that it is time for her to rest. I am mighty and I will never fail her." The knight replies "I gladly give her to you. You have always come to help me." "Sunday" replies, "I am the God you believe in. I give you leave for three days: you must go back into the world and tell of your journey, then *seculorum secula* will be sung." The knight returns to the world and parts with his wealth and worldly glory. He tells of his journey, and all sing *seculorum secula*.

Manuscript Tradition

The earliest surviving manuscript that contains *Enska Vísan* is BL MS Add. 11177 (**B**),[5] a verse collection entitled in the scribal hand "Fornkuæde Nockur til gamans af Jmsumm ort" ("ancient songs for amusement, by various poets"). The manuscript is the product of two scribes working together: the first scribe copied pp. 1–8 and 36–128, while pp. 9–36 are in a second hand.[6] Comparison with signed manuscripts identifies Oddur *digri* (the Fat) Jónsson (1648–1711)[7] as the main scribe of **B**,[8] and shows that while the manuscript cannot date from

5   H. L. D. Ward, *Catalogue of Romances of the Department of Manuscripts in the British Museum*, vol. 1 (London, 1883), 81–108.

6   Jón Helgason, *Íslenzk Fornkvæði*, 1:XIV.

7   *Íslenzkar æviskrár frá landnámstímum til ársloka 1940*, ed. Páll Eggert Ólason, 6 vols. (Reykjavík, 1948–76), 4:15.

8   Jón Helgason, *Íslenzk Fornkvæði*, 1:XVI, XXVIII.

earlier than c. 1670, when Oddur's hand reached its adult form, it may have been produced as late as 1711, the year of his death.[9] Oddur was the son of Jón Arason (1606–73),[10] priest (and poet) at Vatnsfjörður in the West Fjords of Iceland, though Oddur himself lived for many years at Reynistaðir, 350 kilometers to the east. Oddur was a well-known poet, antiquarian, and collector of manuscripts who was an associate of the Danish antiquarian Ole Worm.[11] All that is known of the history and provenance of **B** is that by 1837 it was in Copenhagen in the possession of the Icelandic emigré Finn Magnusen (Finnur Magnússon, 1781–1847),[12] founder of Det Kongelige nordiske Oldskriftselskab (The Royal Society for Northern Antiquities), who sold it to the British Museum that year.[13]

Sometime before 1837, perhaps in conjunction with the sale, Finn Magnusen made a list of the manuscript's contents and transcribed a number of poems, including *Enska Vísan*. His transcript was among the materials the folklorist Svend Grundtvig (1824–83) acquired in preparation for the edition of *Íslenzk Fornkvæði* (Icelandic ballads)[14] he edited with Jón Sigurðsson (1811–79), the leader of the Icelandic independence movement,[15] and which after his death became the Svend Grundtvig Collection at the Dansk Folkemindesamling (Danish Folklore Collection) in Copenhagen. Finn's transcript now has the shelfmark DFS 66, pp. 311–46, in the Royal Danish Library.

There is another nineteenth-century transcript of **B**, this one of the entire manuscript. In 1866 the young Icelandic scholar Jón Andrésson Hjaltalín (1840–1908)[16] moved to London, where he supported himself by writing and teaching until he was hired by the Advocates' Library in Edinburgh in 1870 as Assistant Librarian and editor of the library's *Catalogue of Printed Books* (1873–78).[17] During the winter of 1868–69, he made a trip to Copenhagen and delivered a transcript of **B** to Jón Sigurðsson,[18] presumably commissioned for the *Íslenzk Fornkvæði*

9   Ibid., 1:XVI, XXVIII.

10 *Íslenzkar æviskrár*, 3:41–42.

11 *Menn og Menntir Siðskiptaaldarinnar á Íslandi*, ed. Páll Eggert Ólason, 4 vols. (Reykjavík, 1919–26), 1:433, 4:672–73, and *passim*; *Íslenzkar æviskrár*, 3:41–42.

12 Ibid., 2:13–14.

13 Jón Helgason, *Íslenzk Fornkvæði*, 1:XVI–XVII.

14 Svend Grundtvig and Jón Sigurðsson, eds., *Íslenzk Fornkvæði*, 2 vols. (Copenhagen, 1854–85). This edition is not to be confused with the later eight-volume *Íslenzk Fornkvæði / Islandske Folkeviser* edited by Jón Helgason as part of the Editiones Arnamagnæanæ series.

15 *Íslenzkar æviskrár*, 3:266–68.

16 Ibid., 3:40.

17 "Jón A. Hjaltalín" [obituary], *Norðri*, October 20, 1908.

18 Copenhagen, DFS 65, p. 148, cited by Jón Helgason, *Íslenzk Fornkvæði*, 1:XVIII.

edition. After Jón Sigurðsson's death his library became part of the National and University Library of Iceland in Reykjavík, where the transcript of **B** has the shelfmark JS 126, fol.[19] The manuscript contains seventy-four numbered poems, of which *Enska Vísan* is number 29. It is the only poem in the manuscript with devotional content.

B is closely related to two contemporary manuscripts from the West Fjords region: Árni Magnússon Institute MS AM 147, 8vo (**G**),[20] the *Kvæðabók* (verse collection) of Gissur Sveinsson; and a now-lost manuscript (**V**), known through two copies, Copenhagen, Royal Danish Library, MS NKS 1141, fol. (**V¹**),[21] and Reykjavík, National and University Library of Iceland, MS JS 405, 4to (**V²**).[22] Gissur Sveinsson (1604–83) was priest at Álftamýri on the Arnarfjörður in the West Fjords.[23] AM 147, 8vo has a colophon identifying Gissur as the scribe,[24] and a dedication on fol. 1r tells that the book was a gift to Gissur's friend and neighbor Jón Arason, the above-named priest at Vatnsfjord, on June 12, 1665. There is no title page, but a heading above the first poem in the anthology on fol. 1v reads "Nøckur fornnkvæde til gamans" ("some *fornkvæði* for amusement"). The seventy-one poems in the collection represent a variety of genres: Icelandic ballads, many of much earlier origin; translations from Anders Sørensen Vedel's book of Danish ballads, *Hundredvisebogen* (1591); traditional Icelandic *sagnakvæði* or alliterative narrative poems; and a variety of poems by sixteenth- and seventeenth-century Icelandic poets. Comparison with **B** shows that forty-eight pages, including those that would have contained *Enska Vísan*, are missing.[25] Apart from *Enska Vísan*, all the poems have clearly secular themes.

The title-page dedication of the lost manuscript **V** is reproduced in **V¹**: we read here that it was copied for another son of Jón Arason, Magnús *digri* (like his brother, "the Fat") Jónsson (1637–1702)[26] of the island of Vigur in

---

19 *Skrá um handritasöfn Landsbókasafnsins*, ed. Páll Eggert Ólason, 7 vols. (Reykjavík, 1918–96), 2:478–79.

20 Available online through https://handrit.is/en (search by shelfmark for "AM 147 8vo"); Kristian Kålund, *Katalog over Den Arnamagnæanske Håndskriftsamling*, 2 vols. (Copenhagen, 1889–94), 2:413.

21 Kristian Kålund, *Katalog over de oldnorsk-islandske håndskrifter i Det store kongelige bibliotek og i Universitetsbiblioteket* (Copenhagen, 1900), 119.

22 Available online through https://handrit.is/en (search by shelfmark for "JS 405 4to"); *Skrá*, 1:567.

23 There is a facsimile edition edited by Jón Helgason, *Kvæðabók séra Gissurar Sveinssonar, AM 147, 8vo*, 2 vols., Íslenzk rit síðari alda 2 (Copenhagen, 1960).

24 Jón Helgason, *Íslenzk Fornkvæði*, 1:X, 247. See also *Kvæðabók séra Gissurar Sveinssonar*.

25 Jón Helgason, *Íslenzk Fornkvæði*, 1:XII.

26 *Íslenzkar æviskrár*, 3:433–34.

the Ísafjarðardjúp, by his scribes Magnús Ketilsson (c. 1675–1709),[27] who copied his portion in 1699, and Jón *dettir* (the Faller) Þórðarson (c. 1676–1755), who worked on the manuscript 1699–1700.[28] This unfortunate priest (and accomplished scribe) acquired his nickname by being so drunk while celebrating mass one day that he collapsed on the church floor in front of the altar.[29] Magnús Jónsson bequeathed the manuscript to his daughter Kristín, who lived nearby in Mýrar on the Dýrafjörður, and while it was in her possession Árni Magnússen examined it: his description, including ascription of ownership to Kristín and a list of its contents, catalogued as AM 153, 8vo, has since been lost, but the catalogue his assistant Jón Ólafsson of Grunnavík made in 1730 (Árni Magnússon Institute MS AM 383 and Árni Magnússon Institute MS AM 456, fol.) attests to the "Fornqvædabók Kristinar Magnüsdöttur ä Mÿrum."[30] Kristín died in 1712, leaving the manuscript to her husband, Snæbjörn Pálsson, himself a noted collector of manuscripts, who lived on until 1767.[31] When he died the manuscript was sent to the Danish scholar and collector P. F. Suhm (1728–98)[32] in Copenhagen, presumably in hopes of selling it to him. Suhm did not buy it, perhaps because mixed in with the poems of historical interest were many translations from printed Danish collections. Suhm had a copy (**V¹**) made of what interested him (including *Enska Vísan*), and sent the original back to the West Fjords.[33]

Exchanges like this between rural Icelanders and Danish philologists became increasingly common. A turning point came on July 17, 1845, when the English philologist George Stephens made a passionate appeal at the annual meeting of Det Kongelige Nordiske Oldskriftselskab in Copenhagen. Alarmed that interest in folktales and folksongs was waning in Iceland, as everywhere, and fearing that a vast amount of unpublished folk literature was in danger of being lost, he urged that a circular be sent to "priests, students [i.e. secondary-school graduates], and other educated men in Iceland" who were in a position to gather and transcribe relevant materials from among the general populace for preservation in the Society's archives. His exhortation was published in *Antiquarisk Tidsskrift* for

---

27 Ibid., 3:440.
28 Jón Helgason, *Íslenzk Fornkvæði*, 1:XIX.
29 *Íslenzkar æviskrár*, 3:307.
30 Jón Helgason, *Íslenzk Fornkvæði*, 1:XIX; *Kvæðabók séra Gissurar Sveinssonar*, 2:39; Kålund, *Katalog over den Arnamagnæanske Håndskriftsamling*, 2:419.
31 *Íslenzkar æviskrár*, 4:310.
32 Leo Tandrup, "P. F. Suhm," *Dansk Biografisk Leksikon*, 3rd edn. (Copenhagen, 1979–84), http://denstoredanske.dk/Dansk_Biografisk_Leksikon/Historie/Historiker/P.F._Suhm.
33 *Kvæðabók séra Gissurar Sveinssonar*, 2:39–40; Jón Helgason, *Íslenzk Fornkvæði*, 1:XX–XXI

1845,[34] and the following year the journal printed a formal *Boðsbréf til Íslendínga* (Invitation to Icelanders), dated April 28, 1846, urging Icelanders to submit information about ancient documents such as manuscripts and letters, historical sites and ancient place names, and popular folk traditions.[35] The response was immediate. Among the first to write was Jón Ingjaldsson (1800–76),[36] priest at Húsavík in Steingrímsfjörður (West Fjords), who wrote of spending the decade 1810–20 under the tutelage of his uncle Arnór Jónsson, priest at Vatnsfjörður in Ísafjarðardjúp. He recalled borrowing Kristín Magnúsdóttir's manuscript from the local doctor, Jón Einarsson[37] ("or his children Hjálmar and Þórunn"), who owned it at the time, perhaps as her descendants. Arnór may well have borrowed the book to use in the instruction of his nephew. Jón Ingjaldsson writes as one who has studied the book and knows it well: he assures the Oldskriftselskab that the manuscript is of interest, and that "there is much desirable, old and new, to be had, valuable gold to be plucked *ex stercore Ennii*" (from the dung of Ennius).[38] Jón Einarsson was the doctor at Ármúli in Langadalsströnd (just across the Ísafjarðardjúp from Vatnsfjörður) from 1788 until he died in 1816, so Jón Ingjaldsson's memory of the manuscript and its contents must date from the period 1810–16.

JS 405, 4to (**V²**), the second copy of **V**, was made in the West Fjords by Þórður Þorsteinsson (1760–1846),[39] who was priest at Ögur, the parish in which the island of Vigur is located, from 1809 to 1837 and was a renowned scribe known to have copied "mikinn fjölda allskonar íslenzkra bóka" (a great multitude of all kinds of Icelandic books).[40] Unlike **V¹**, **V²** is a copy of the entire exemplar. On the title page and in the colophon of the manuscript, Þórður names himself as the scribe and gives 1819 as the date of completion, so he must have had access to the manuscript just a few years after Jón Ingjaldsson and Arnór Jónsson – they may well have known one another. The manuscript had lost a leaf since Suhm's copy was made, and Þórður notes that he made the transcription lest the text of the original, which was "miög rotinn og sumstadar nærri ólæs" (very rotten and in places nearly illegible) should be lost altogether.[41] Unfortunately, that is what in

---

34 *Antiquarisk Tidsskrift* (1843–45): 91–92.
35 Printed in ibid., "Det kongliga nordiska Fornskrift-Sällskapet," i–viii.
36 *Íslenzkar æviskrár*, 3:160–61.
37 Ibid., 3:98–99.
38 His letter is preserved as Copenhagen, DFS 67, pp. 457–63, printed in Jón Helgason, *Íslenzk Fornkvæði*, 1:XXIII.
39 Ibid., 1:XXIII–XXIV.
40 *Antiquarisk Tidsskrift* (1849–51): 219.
41 National and University Library of Iceland, MS JS 405, 4to, p. 2.

fact most likely happened – nothing has since been seen of **V**. Þorður's copy, **V²**, remained in the West Fjords for a time.

Another early respondent to George Stephens's appeal was a merchant and scholar in the West Fjords market town of Ísafjörður, Gísli Ívarsson (1807–60),[42] who by the middle of the nineteenth century had become the owner of **V²**. He sent the manuscript on loan to Jón Sigurðsson, who published a detailed description of it in the 1849–51 issue of *Antiquarisk Tidsskrift*,[43] clearly pleased to have a complete copy of the lost manuscript. Jón Sigurðsson and Svend Grundtvig used it for their edition of *Íslenzk Fornkvæði*, and at some point Jón acquired it for his own collection, whence it has come to the National and University Library of Iceland as MS JS 405, 4to.[44] It is characteristic of the culture of reading and writing in Iceland at the time that a provincial merchant would be collecting manuscripts (transmitted through a local scribal network and circulated among local readers), reading scholarly journals from Denmark, and corresponding with the great scholar and statesman Jón Sigurðsson.

Jón Helgason studied this neighborly sharing of manuscripts in the West Fjords and determined from the contents and common errors that **G**, **B**, **V¹**, and **V²** are related according to the stemma shown in Fig. 8.1, to which I have added the transcripts of the related manuscripts DFS 66 and JS 126, fol.[45] **G** was copied from a hypothetical exemplar ***X**, as was a hypothetical manuscript ***Y**, from which **B** and **V** were copied. DFS 66 and JS 126, fol., were subsequently copied from **B**, while **V¹** and **V²** were copied from **V**.

A version of *Enska Vísan* representing a different tradition occurs in AM 622, 4to, the *Kvæðabók* of bishop Gísli Jónsson, also known as *Hólmsbók*.[46] The manuscript itself, as Gísli's colophon dedicating it to his daughter Helga states, was completed by 1549, but *Enska Vísan* was not added until the seventeenth century.[47] The manuscript must have been produced while Gísli was priest at Selárdal in Arnarfjörður (West Fjords), where he served from 1546 until 1550, when the turbulent year of Reformation in Iceland made a move to Denmark expedient. On return to Iceland he became bishop of Skálholt in 1556, a position he held until his death in 1587. AM 622, 4to is a large and important collection

---

42 *Íslenzkar æviskrár*, 2:58–59.

43 *Antiquarisk Tidsskrift* (1849–51): 219–55.

44 Jón Helgason, *Íslenzk Fornkvæði*, 1:XXVI.

45 Ibid., 1:XXXI.

46 Available online through https://handrit.is/en (search by shelfmark for "AM 622 4to"); Kålund, *Katalog over Den Arnamagnæanske Håndskriftsamling*, 2:34–37.

47 There is a transcription of the text of "Suenska Vísan" from AM 622, 4to by the nineteenth-century scholar Jón Þorkelsson in Reykjavík, National and University Library of Iceland, MS Lbs 2033, 4to. I have not yet had an opportunity to examine this manuscript.

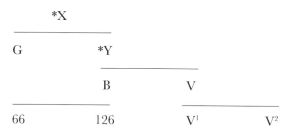

Fig. 8.1 Manuscript stemma showing the relationship of MSS G, B, V¹, and V² of Enska Vísan.

of devotional poems that reflect pre-Reformation sensibilities. Born in 1513 and educated by the monks of Viðey, Gísli Jónsson is a bridge figure, who saw his country before, during, and after the Reformation.[48] His *Kvæðabók*, a primary manuscript witness for the texts of many of the great late medieval Icelandic devotional poems, attests to his devotion to the Virgin Mary and the saints, but his long and vigorous career as a post-Reformation leader of the Church of Iceland leaves no doubt as to his Lutheran sensibilities. Bishop Gísli is iconic in that he produced both an important manuscript collection of Catholic poetry and one of the earliest translations of Reformation hymns printed in Icelandic.[49] This was typical of the time: printing was reserved for officially approved Lutheran texts, while pre-Reformation materials were copied by hand, but it is remarkable that the pattern is reflected even in the works of a bishop.

AM 622, 4to is made up of three booklets in Gísli's hand, which were already bound together when the manuscript was acquired by Árni Magnússon at the beginning of the eighteenth century. The first booklet, fols. 1–11 of the present manuscript, contains an assortment of Latin, Icelandic, and German hymns and secular songs, most with musical notation, as well as a table of Sunday gospels, a calendar of church holidays, and a list of the books of the Bible. In the blank space at the end of the booklet (fol. 11r–v), immediately following a Latin Marian hymn ("Sol nascitur de virgine"), stanzas 1–7 and 9–12 of *Enska Vísan* – here called *Svenska Vísan* ("The Swedish Verse") are written in a seventeenth-

48 Guðrún Nordal, "Á mörkum tveggja tíma: Kaþólskt kvæðahandrit með handi siðbótarmanns, Gísla biskups Jónssonar," *Gripla* 16 (2005): 209–28, at 209.
49 *At Gudz lof meigi ætiid auckazt aa medal Kristinna manna, Þa eru hier nockrer Psalmar, vtsetter alss mier Gilbert Jonssyne aa Islensku med Litaniu og scriptar gangi* (Copenhagen, 1558). Gísli also translated numerous German theological works, including Johannes Bugenhagen's *Historia Des lydendes unde upstandige/ unses Heren IesuChristi:/ uth den veer Euangelisten* (Icelandic titel, *Historía pínunnar og upprisu drottins vors Jesú Kristi*) and Johann Spangenberg's *Margarita theologica*.

185

century hand. Rather than an alternate geographical association for the poem, "Svenska" is probably a mistaken reading for "Sú enska" ("the English"), *sú* being the nominative singular feminine form of the definite article reduplicating the alternate form -*an* suffixed to *vísa*. The inscription on fol. 1r names Gísli's daughter Helga, at the time just a child, as the owner, but somehow it became the property of her younger sister Vilborg, from whom it eventually passed to her great-great-great granddaughter, Kristín Ísleifsdóttir, and Árni Mágnússon acquired the manuscript from Kristín's husband Þórður Pétursson (1655–1730).[50] Vilborg and her husband, Þorvarður Þórólfsson, lived at Syðri-Reykir, not far from Skálholt; generations later, Kristín and Þórður lived at Innri-Hólmur.

In Jón Ólafsson's catalogue of Árni Magnússon's collection, there is a section titled "Feminae post Reformationem doctiores" ("Highly Learned Post-Reformation Women") in which he provides brief accounts of a number of learned women of the seventeenth century. One of them is Vilborg Gísladóttir, who "taught singing to boys and thereby kept a kind of school."[51] Guðrún Nordal hypothesizes that the booklet with musical notation was produced for the instruction of Vilborg's singing students (the prose lists would also be suited to classroom use), and notes that manuscripts (along with other moveable property) were customarily handed down through the female line of a family, while the land went to the sons (as we have seen was the case with Kristín Magnúsdóttir).[52] Whether it was Vilborg or one of her descendants who added *Enska/Svenska Vísan* to the book, it was there by about 1700 when the book came to Árni Magnússon. The scribes of these early versions of *Enska Vísan* seem to be as uncertain of the poem's genre as modern scholars: while bishop Gissur copied *Enska Vísan* into a miscellany of secular *fornkvæði* or ballads, someone who was his contemporary saw fit to add it to bishop Gísli's manuscript of Catholic devotional poetry. The Danish scholar Marius Kristensen, who printed a text of "Suenska Vísan," comments:

---

50 Jón Helgason, *Íslenzk Fornkvæði*, 4:XIII. The line of descent: Gísli Jónsson m. Kristín Eyjólfsdóttir → Vilborg Gísladóttir m. Þorvarður Þórólfsson → Erlendur Þórvarðarson m. ? → Þórður Erlendsson m. ? → Ísleifur Þórðarson m. ? → Kristín Ísleifsdóttir m. Þórður Pétursson.

51 "kenndi piltum söng og hélt svo sem skóla þar með," Copenhagen, University Library, Add. MS 3, fol., quoted in Margrét Eggertsdóttir, "'Í blíðum faðmi brúðgumans': Hlutur kvenna í trúarlegum kveðskap á sautjándu og átjándu öld," in *Konur og kristmenn: Þættir úr kristnisögu Íslands*, ed. Inga Huld Hákonardóttir (Reykjavík, 1996), 167–89, at 181. See also *Menn og Menntir*, 4:10; and Jón Helgason, *Jón Ólafsson of Grunnavík*, Safn Fræðafjelagsins um Ísland og Íslendinga 5 (Copenhagen, 1926), 194–95.

52 Guðrún Nordal, "Á mörkum tveggja tíma," 211.

"Svenska vísan" stands alone: it is added by a later owner, and it bears witness to continued contact with other cultures, since its form alone shows that it cannot originally have been Icelandic. Whoever reworked it clearly had much better poetic abilities than Gísli Jónsson.[53]

AM 622, 4to is the earliest of a group of manuscripts that represent a version of *Enska Vísan* different from the one we see in the West Fjords tradition. Another response to the appeal from the Oldskriftselskab came from the elderly priest Brynjólfr Árnason (1777–1852).[54] Brynjólfr was parish priest at Langholt in Meðalland, and apart from school days in Reykjavík, had lived on the south coast of Iceland his entire life, so was not associated with one of the northern scribal networks. He contributed the texts of nine poems, including *Enska Vísan*, in his own hand. His transcripts are preserved as MS DFS 67 C in the Royal Danish Library. He says nothing about their origin, but he was clearly copying from an exemplar: after stanza 9 (his stanza 6) he notes in parentheses, "the next stanza and the beginning or opening lines of the following are missing."[55] Brynjólfr must have known another version of the text to have been aware of this. The first stanza of each appears in *Antiquarisk Tidsskrift* for 1846–48, where Jón Sigurðsson comments:

It appears – as it most likely is in fact the case – that people in the Skaptafell district know by memory most of the folksongs and folktales that until now have not been collected.[56]

With respect to *Enska Vísan* in particular, he observes:

The poem here has fifteen stanzas, but something is missing . . . there are transcripts where the poem has eighteen stanzas. There are strange word forms here and there in this transcript, and the last stanza is different from other versions.[57]

---

53 "'Svenska vísan' står for sig selv; den er . . . indföjet af en senere ejer, og den vidner om vedvarende forbindelse med udlandet, da den efter hele sin form ikke kan være oprindelig islandsk. Bearbejderen har dog haft betydelig större digterævner end Gísli Jónsson" (Kristensen, *En Klosterbog*, XX).
54 *Íslenzkar æviskrár*, 1:271.
55 ". . . vantar næsta erindid og upphaf id eda næstu hendinguna af ödru," DFS 67, fol. 237r.
56 *Antiquarisk Tidsskrift* (1846–48): 162–63, 170.
57 Ibid., 162–63. (In fact there are sixteen stanzas in Brynjólfr's version.)

The order of the stanzas in Brynjólfr's version is likewise different from what we find in the **B** tradition: DFS 67 C stanza 1 = **B** stanza 1, but then 2=4, 3=5, 4=6, 5=7, 6=9, 7=12, 8=10, 9=11, 10=13, 11=14, 12=15, 13=16, 14=17, and 15 has no corresponding stanza in **B**. DFS 67 is clearly, if not closely, related to AM 622, 4to: as in **622**, **B**'s stanza 8 is missing in **67**, likewise the first two lines of stanza 12. There are a number of distinctive readings where **67** agrees with **622** against **B**: "reid" for "bið" in stanza 4/1, "breid" for "greid" in 4/2, "vnnustu" for "kærustu" (4/3), "matt" for "skallt" (9/1), "vaxa" for "er" (9/3). All of these readings are reflected in a group of four related manuscripts from the Skagafjörður region now in the National and University Library of Iceland in Reykjavík: Lbs 1587, 4to; JS 255, 4to; JS 591, 4to; and Lbs 202, 8vo. But there are also readings where the Skagafjörður manuscripts agree with **622** against **B** and **67** ("deyd" for "neijd" [2/5], "strang" for "streing" [6/1]); where they agree with **B** and **67** against **622** ("heitann" for "breidann" [12/3]); where they agree with **67** against **B** and **622** ("heil og sæl" for "velkominn" [7/1]); and, after **622** breaks off, with **67** against **B** ("gef" for "sel" [14/1], "fiærri" for "mikelle" [14/2], "vinum og frendum" for "ferdum j" [17/4]). Thus **67** is related to both **B** and **622**, but more closely to **622**, and the Skagafjörður manuscripts are related to all three traditions, but correspond most closely to **67**. Slight variations in the closely-linked Skagafjörður manuscripts show that scribes were quite willing to emend their exemplars, and the influence of various oral traditions must also have played a role.

The Skagafjörður manuscripts distinguish themselves by naming the poem "Spanska Vísan" ("The Spanish Verse"). If there is a reasonable explanation for the shift from "Enska" to "Svenska," it is not as easy to see how the development to "Spanska" came about. There may have been confusion with the poem known as "Spönskuvísur," by the popular seventeenth-century Skagafjörður poet Ólafur Jónsson (1560–1627),[58] or perhaps "Spanska" was just a step away from "Svenska" in the oral transmission of this exotic poem. Despite the shift in the title, this tradition continues to associate the poem with England: in stanza 11/1 the "broad bridge" ("breijdu brv̋") the knight carries his lady across has become "Einglands bru" ("England's bridge"), and in 13/1 the "fair plain" ("þann fagra vǫll") they reach is now "Einglans hil" ("England's hill").

---

58 Ólafur Jónsson, "Ein lítil drápa um þá spönsku ránsmenn eða Bischaios, er hér voru fyrir nokkrum árum (1615)" (A little poem on the Spanish pirates or bischaios, who were here a few years ago), Reykjavík, National and University Library of Iceland, ÍB 70, 4to, fols. 100r–103v, digital version accessible through https://handrit.is/en (search by shelfmark for "ÍB 70 4to" and move through to fol. 102r).

The earliest of the Skagafjörður group of manuscripts is Lbs 1587, 4to.[59] It is a "Lioodasafn" ("poetry collection") copied by the farmer, fisherman, and distinguished scribe Þorsteinn Þorsteinsson á Heiði (1791–1863) in 1829. The Skagafjörður district, like the West Fjords, was a center of manuscript culture from the Middle Ages up to the end of the nineteenth century. On the north coast of Iceland, just to the east of the West Fjords, it is not so far away that occasional contact would be unthinkable. In her study of the scribal network surrounding Þorsteinn Þorsteinsson, Tereza Lansing suggests that the unusual flourishing of local scribal and reading networks was in part due to the continuing influence of the diocese of Hólar, an important center of manuscript production in the Middle Ages and the site of the first (and for many years only) printing press in Iceland.[60] Between 1741 and 1745 the Danish theologian Ludvig Harboe (later bishop of Nidaros in Norway) was sent to Iceland to assess the state of the church there. As a part of his survey, in the summer of 1743 he tested the literacy of all the children of the Skagafjörður district between the ages of twelve and seventeen, and found that nearly all could read.[61] There was less emphasis on instruction in writing, and many who had managed to learn to write were self-taught.[62] Nevertheless, the response from the local clergy to a questionnaire sent by Hið íslenzka Bókmenntafélag (The Icelandic Literary Society) in 1838–40 estimated that a third of the population of Skagafjörður could write.[63]

Þorsteinn Þorsteinsson may have been one of the self-taught boys of this literate community – there is no indication that he received schooling beyond what he would have received from the local priest as a child. He was born at Hamar, on the northeast side of the Skagafjörður, and lived most of his life on the farm at Heiði, a few kilometers to the west. He supported himself by farming and fishing, but his passion was manuscripts. The manuscript collection at the National and University Library of Iceland contains seventy-six manuscripts (500 texts, 15,000

---

59 *Skrá*, 1:557.

60 Tereza Lansing, "Manuscript Culture in Nineteenth Century Northern Iceland: The Case of Þorsteinn Þorsteinsson á Heiði," in *Vernacular Literacies – Past, Present and Future*, ed. Ann-Catrine Edlund, Lars-Erik Edlund, and Susanne Haugen, Vardagligt skriftbruk 3 (Umeå, Sweden, 2014), 193–211.

61 Kristmundur Bjarnason, "Alþýðufræðsla í Skagafirði fram um síðustu aldamót: Nokkrar athuganir," in *Gefið og þegið: Afmælisrit til heiðurs Brodda Jóhannessyni sjötugum*, ed. Þuríður J. Kristjánsdóttir (Reykjavík, 1987), 221–46, at 221–24; Silvia Hufnagel, "The Farmer, Scribe and Lay Historian Gunnlaugur Jónsson from Skuggabjörg and his Scribal Network," *Gripla* 24 (2013): 235–68, at 236–39.

62 Hufnagel, "The Farmer, Scribe and Lay Historian," 236.

63 Kristmundur Bjarnason, "Alþýðufræðsla í Skagafirði," 224; Hufnagel, "The Farmer, Scribe and Lay Historian," 238.

pages) produced by Þorsteinn. He copied the first in 1809, when he was just eighteen, and the last in 1862, the year before he died at seventy-two.[64] Tereza Lansing has surveyed the various genres included in his books and determined that about 20% of the texts are medieval (pre-1550) works, and the rest includes *rímur* and other poetry, local history, folktales, and travel stories, as well as translations of chapbooks, novels, and historical texts.[65] Jóhannes Guðmundsson of Hólabær in Langadal,[66] the local district administrator ("hreppstjóri"), making rounds as a collector for the folklorist Jón Árnason,[67] visited Þorsteinn in 1859 and reported, "He had no other place for his library than an old shed so bad that I could not look at any book and put things aside elsewhere than on the clay floor. His collection is so large that it would take several days to make a clear catalogue of it."[68] Notes in the manuscripts indicate that manuscripts circulated through a dense local network of scribes, who borrowed one another's books to make their own copies. Lansing has identified thirty-four members of Þorsteinn's network, including three priests, two government officials (which means that 11.5% of the network's members were university educated), a merchant, a bookseller, and two clerks (another 11.5%), and twenty-six farmers (77%).[69] This community may have been one of the most productive, but it is typical of the reading and scribal communities that flourished in rural Iceland from the late Middle Ages right up to the early twentieth century. The *Ljóðasafn* that became Lbs 1587, 4to particularly caught Jóhannes Guðmundsson's eye when he first saw it in Þorsteinn's shed, and he convinced Þorsteinn to loan it to him. But he wrote to Jón Árnason on February 9, 1863, that "the old guy" (karlinn), now a widower boarding with female relatives on the island of Málmey offshore from his former home at Heiði, had asked for it back and that it was clearly not for sale.[70] Þorsteinn died the following June,[71] and Jóhannes wrote on February 10, 1864, that Þorsteinn had died "and I was so unlucky as to just have sent back the poetry books I had

---

64 Lansing, "Manuscript Culture," 195.

65 Ibid.

66 *Íslenzkar æviskrár*, 3:32–33.

67 Ibid., 3:48–49.

68 "Ekki hafði hann annað pláss fyrir bókasafn sitt en svo lélegan kofa, að ég gat enga bók skoðað til að geta lagt meitt frá mér annars staðar en ofan í forargólf, og svo er safn hans svo mikið, að ekki hefði veitt af nokkrum dögum til að fá greinilegt registur yfir það alt." Finnur Sigmundsson, ed., *Úr fórum Jóns Árnasonar*, 2 vols. (Reykjavík, 1950–51), 1:360, see Lansing, "Manuscript Culture," 195.

69 Lansing, "Manuscript Culture," 203, 206–9.

70 *Úr fórum Jóns Árnasonar*, 1:360, see Jón Helgason, *Íslenzk Fornkvæði*, 7:207.

71 Obituary, *Norðanfari*, vol. 2, nr. 25–28 (July 1863), p. 60, accessible online at http://timarit.is/view_page_init.jsp?pageId=2039403&issId=138708&lang=4.

borrowed; otherwise I probably could have got them."[72] Finally, on February 11, 1866, he writes that after a long struggle he has managed to get the one book (Lbs 1587, 4to), but not the other.[73] At some point thereafter the manuscript became the property of the publisher Valdimar Ásmundsson (1852–1902), and it was sold to the National and University Library of Iceland in 1911.[74]

Gunnlaugur Jónsson (1786–1866), like Þorsteinn Þorsteinsson a farmer, lived at Skuggabjörg, 15 kilometers down the coast of the Skagafjörður from Þorsteinn's home at Heiði, and he was a member of Þorsteinn's scribal network. The National and University Library of Iceland has thirty manuscripts produced by Gunnlaugur in its collections, and two of them are poetry anthologies that contain *Spanska Vísan*: JS 255, 4to,[75] written in 1841, and JS 591, 4to,[76] written in 1854, not long before Gunnlaugur gave up his scribal work as blindness set in.[77] The contents of the manuscripts are unrelated – presumably each is a copy of a different borrowed collection. JS 255, 4to is one of five booklets (JS 254–258, 4to) that originally made up a single "Kvæda Book".[78] When Páll Erlendsson, parish priest at Brúarland (the parish for Skuggabjörg), read the appeal of the Oldskriftselskab in *Antiquarisk Tidsskrift*, he wrote to the journal with the information that the farmer Gunnlaugur Jónsson had himself written a large poetry collection of about 300 poems in three [a misunderstanding?] volumes.[79] Jón Sigurðsson wrote to Gunnlaugur, who sent him the first volume of his collection, now JS 258, 4to, on June 20, 1851.[80] In 1859 Gunnlaugur sold another volume, now JS 254, 4to, to his younger neighbor Þorsteinn Þorsteinsson á Upsum (1825–1912)[81] – not to be confused with Þorsteinn Þorsteinsson á Heiði, the scribe of Lbs 1587, 4to. Upsir, Heiði, and Skuggabjörg lie within a 10-kilometer radius in the Skagafjörður district, and the local network included two scribes and collectors with the same name.[82] Þorsteinn Þorsteinsson á Upsum

---

72 *Úr fórum Jóns Árnasonar*, 2:44, see Jón Helgason, *Íslenzk Fornkvæði*, 7:207.

73 *Úr fórum Jóns Árnasonar*, 2:94, see Jón Helgason, *Íslenzk Fornkvæði*, 7:208.

74 *Skrá*, 1:555, 557.

75 Accessible online through https://handrit.is/en (search by shelfmark for "JS 225 4to"); *Skrá*, 2:537–38.

76 See the online description available through https://handrit.is/en (search by shelfmark for "JS 591 4to"); *Skrá*, 2:602–5.

77 Hufnagel, "The Farmer, Scribe and Lay Historian," 243.

78 *Skrá*, 2:537–38; Jón Helgason, *Íslenzk Fornkvæði*, 6:XI–XIII.

79 *Antiquarisk Tidsskrift* (1846–48): 41.

80 Jón Helgason, *Íslenzk Fornkvæði*, 6:XII.

81 *Íslenzkar æviskrár*, 5:236.

82 Þorsteinn Þorsteinsson á Upsum emigrated to Canada in his old age and died at the home of his son Þorsteinn Þ. Þorsteinsson, a noted Icelandic-language poet and author

wrote on the title page, "The poetry collection of Gunnlaugur was four volumes in all, but I have not seen the other three. I have heard that Gísli Brynjólfsson got two of them, and I know nothing of the other one."[83] JS 258, 4to had already been separated from the originally five-volume collection, hence Þorsteinn's reference to four.

Gísli Brynjólfsson (1827–88)[84] spent his adult life in Copenhagen, where he was stipendiarius of the Arnamagnæan Commission, docent in Icelandic at the University, and Jón Sigurðsson's assistant.[85] It is telling of the reading and scribal networks of the time that a farmer-scribe in rural northern Iceland could casually drop the name of an academic in Copenhagen along with that of his farmer-scribe neighbor in the same note. Þorsteinn had sold JS 254, 4to to Hið íslenzka Bókmentafélag (The Icelandic Literary Society) by 1885, when it was described in the society's manuscript catalogue,[86] and the entire collection was acquired by the National and University Library of Iceland in 1902. How the three remaining booklets, JS 255–257, 4to, found their way into the library's collection is less certain. The catalogue entry for JS 254–258, 4to says vaguely of all five that "J[ón] S[igurðsson] got the manuscripts from Þorsteinn Þorsteinsson á Upsum and pastor Sveinn Skúlason."[87] In his 1880 edition of the poems of pastor Stefán Ólafsson (1619–1688), some of which are preserved in Gunnlaugur's kvæðabók, Jón Þorkelsson comments:

> The collection was written about 1840 and thereafter, and it is extremely remarkable. I do not now know of more than five volumes. Jón Sigurðsson owned four, and he got most of them about 1860 from pastor Sveinn Skúlason (now of Kirkjubær in Tunga), but one volume is in the collection of the Icelandic Literary Society in Copenhagen, nr. 272, 4to [i.e. JS 254]. When Jón Sigurðsson's collection was moved to Iceland in 1880, these volumes belonging to the Society were supposed to go along, but one volume [JS 258] that had been lent to Professor Svend Grundtvig remained behind, and when he died in the summer of 1883 it came into the hands of the Arnamagnæan Commission,

in Winnepeg.

83 "Kvæða sirpur Gunnlaugs voru alls 4 enn eg hefi ekki seð hinar 3r. 2 hefi eg heyrt að Gísli Brynjólfson hafi feingið enn eg veit ikki um eina," quoted in Jón Helgason, Íslenzk Fornkvæði, 6:XII.

84 Íslenzkar æviskrár, 2:45–46.

85 Jón Helgason, Íslendingar í Danmörku (Reykjavík, 1931), 75–76.

86 Sigurð L. Jónasson and Finn Jónsson, Skýrsla um Handritasafn hins íslenzka Bókmentafélags, vol. 2 (Copenhagen, 1885), 15–16.

87 Skrá, 2:538.

and it is now in their keeping. The volumes that were moved to Iceland with Jón Sigurðsson's books are numbers 254–257, 4to in his collection.[88]

JS 255, 4to has a notation on the flyleaf, "Sv. Skúlason 16/965," so it is definitely one of the volumes acquired by Sveinn Skúlason. After university studies in Copenhagen, Sveinn was editor of the newspaper *Norðri* in Akureyri from 1856 to 1862 before moving to Reykjavík and eventually to Kirkjubær.[89] He probably acquired the manuscript during this period: he was living in the area, and Gunnlaugur's sale of JS 258, 4to to Jón Sigurðsson in 1851 suggests that he was beginning to part with his books as his eyesight failed.

JS 591, 4to, written by Gunnlaugur in 1854, is the second volume of a five-part "Kvæðasirpa," now catalogued as JS 588–592, 4to. Gunnlaugur was the scribe of the first four volumes, and JS 592, 4to is a compilation by various hands. This second poetry anthology is not a copy of JS 255, 4to – it is a completely different collection. Both manuscripts are collections of learned poetry, hymns, and folk poetry by named and unnamed poets from the sixteenth through the nineteenth centuries, but there is very little overlap. Apart from "Spanska Vísan," JS 591, 4to has just two poems that are also found in JS 255, 4to: the ballad "Frísa kvæði"[90] and "Það var einn Riddari Kóngs." There are three more poems in JS 591, 4to that appear in JS 258, 4to (the first volume of Gunnlaugur's other collection),[91] but the manuscripts are clearly conceived and produced independently of one another. It is possible that each is a copy of a separate exemplar, or Gunnlaugur may have simply assembled a second collection after producing the first. "Spanska Vísan" may well have been copied from two exemplars. It is not surprising that there are many orthographical variants between the two versions, but there are also five lexical variants: **591** has "getin" for **255**'s "gefin" (1/2), "finn" for "fryn" (6/2), "þaug þa" for "þaug" (8/2), "brunnan" for "brunnanum" (10/4), and "i vil" for "ej vil" (11/3). I have not been able to trace the manuscript's progress from Gunnlaugur Jónsson in 1854 to the Jón Sigurðsson collection, where it appears in the printed catalogue of 1927: sometime between 1850 and 1870 Páll Pálsson (1806–77),[92] who was instrumental in the establishment and organization

---

88 [Jón Þorkelsson, ed.,] *Kvæði eptir Stefán Ólafsson, Gefin út af hinu Íslenzka Bókmentafélagi* 2 (Copenhagen, 1886), VIII–IX. By 1927 JS 258, 4to had also been transferred to the National and University Library of Iceland.

89 *Íslenzkar æviskrár*, 4:375.

90 Edited in Jón Helgason, *Íslenzk Fornkvæði*, 8: 62–72; see also Jón Samsonarson, ed., *Kvæði og Dansleikir*, Íslenzk Þjóðfræði, 2 vols. (Reykjavík, 1964), 1: CCXV.

91 "Klerks kvæði," "Kvæði um tvær systur," and "Draumkvæði," edited in Jón Helgason, *Íslenzk Fornkvæði*, 6:5–11.

92 *Íslenzkar æviskrár*, 4:136–37.

of the manuscript collection at the National and University Library of Iceland, made a copy of the entire manuscript, now catalogued as National and University Library of Iceland MS Lbs 202, 8vo.[93] On the first page he notes, "Fornkvædi nokkur (eftir hnd. í s. JA)" (Some ballads from a manuscript in the collection of JA). Jón Helgason identified "JA" as Jón Árnason (1819–88),[94] who was Librarian of the National and University Library of Iceland and a noted scholar and collector of folklore. Jón Þorkelsson, writing in 1888, likewise identified poems in Lbs 202, 8vo as having been copied from a manuscript in Jón Árnason's collection, which suggests that the manuscript became part of the Jón Sigurðsson collection after Jón Árnason's death the same year.[95]

These manuscripts show the transmission of a text through local reading and scribal communities in rural Iceland over a period of three centuries or more. Its origin is unknown: perhaps it was composed by a poet who had heard, or heard of, or read, a similar text in English. *Enska Vísan* shows clear signs of being transmitted orally: there are repeated lines and phrases, and the many variants in the manuscripts bear witness to an evolution that is more than scribal. On the other hand, the many manuscript copies are themselves witnesses of a written tradition, and the opening stanza refers to reading and writing: "The English poem, it is so long, / It was *written* in organ's song, / it was *set* by the master's art, / it was *read* on the lily-branch." The opening line of *Sir Orfeo* likewise has a reference to literacy: "We redeth oft and findeth y-write" (We often read and find in writing).

Poetic Form

The poetic form of *Enska Vísan*, like its subject matter, is strangely ambiguous. Jón Helgason edited the poems of the **B** manuscript tradition in *Íslenzk Fornkvæði* – with the exception of this one, remarking that it "associates itself with the ballad tradition by its lack of alliteration, but diverges from it by its meter: five lines rhyming *aabbb*, with the last line longer than the others."[96] Jón Helgason planned to include the poem in the third volume of *Íslenzk Miðaldakvæði*, his edition of late medieval devotional poetry. To say that *Enska Vísan* lacks alliteration is something of an overstatement (more striking is the complete absence of kennings): the stanza of *Enska Vísan* is considerably more complex than the *fornkvæði* or ballad stanza or the *ferskeytt* stanza of the Icelandic *rímur*. In his authoritative study of

93 *Skrá*, 2:49.
94 *Íslenzkar æviskrár*, 3:48–49.
95 Jón Þorkelsson, *Om Digtningen på Island i det 15. og 16. Århundrede* (Copenhagen, 1888), 45, 47, 48, 55, 56, 161.
96 Jón Helgason, *Íslenzk Fornkvæði*, 1:XL.

the Icelandic ballads, Vésteinn Ólason describes the standard form of the ballad stanza:

> The Icelandic ballad meters are the same as those used in Scandinavia, viz., either couplets with four-stress lines rhymed *aa* accompanied by a refrain, usually split (the first half of which is inserted between the lines of the couplet), or quatrains rhymed *xaya*, in most cases with a refrain following upon each strophe, the usual number of stresses in each half-strophe being 4 + 3, but in some cases 4 + 2, or occasionally 3 + 3.[97]

He notes that, "Apart from a few late imitations, these meters are not used in other kinds of Icelandic poetry; and they are distinguished from almost all Icelandic verse before the twentieth century by using no regular alliteration."[98] The Icelandic *rímur*, or long metrical romances, are typically in *ferskeytt* stanzas: four lines of alternating four and three stresses, rhymed *abab*. The meter of *Enska Vísan*, on the other hand, is more like the highly wrought meters we see in late medieval Icelandic devotional poetry. These meters, clearly an evolution of the skaldic meters of the High Middle Ages, use a great variety of stanza forms that pay careful attention to rhyme, alliteration, and regular patterns of stress.

In the *Enska Vísan* stanza lines 1–4, rhymed *aabb*, have four stresses, and line 5, chiming with a third *b* rhyme, has six. And *Enska Vísan* does make an attempt at alliteration, though it is not very consistent. A more regular version of this stanza, where lines 1–2 and lines 3–4 are linked by alliteration, with internal triple alliteration in line 5, is otherwise associated with devotional poetry: it is used in three late medieval Marian poems and a poem on St. Christopher published in *Íslenzk Miðaldakvæði*,[99] two seventeenth-century imitations by Einar Sigurðsson í Eydölum printed in Bishop Guðbrandur Þorláksson's *Vísnabók*,[100] a *lausavísa* by Hallgrímur Pétursson,[101] and an exquisite little poem in a manuscript

---

97 Vésteinn Ólason, *The Traditional Ballads of Iceland*, 15.

98 Ibid., 15.

99 Jón Helgason, *Íslenzk Miðaldakvæði*, 2:53–59 ("Bioda vil eg þier bragsins smid"), 2:148–55 ("Fliodit eicki finnazt mä"), 2:200–3 ("Mariu nafn med gledi ok pris"), 2:349–59 ("Christeforusvísur").

100 *Vísnabók Guðbrands*, ed. Jón Torfason and Kristján Eiríksson (Reykjavík, 2000), 125–26 ("Huggunarvísur fyrir þá sem syrgja eftir ástmenn sína"), 126–27 ("Önnur huggunarvísa í móti barnamissir").

101 Hallgrímur Pétursson, *Sálmar og Kvæði*, ed. Grímur Thomsen, 2 vols. (Reykjavík, 1887–90), 2:448 (Lausavísa XXVIII, "Þarfa ráðin minstu mín").

Kvæðabók composed by Bjarni Gissurarson for his daughter.[102] The use of this meter suggests that the poet considered *Enska Vísan* a devotional poem.

The meter is not as strictly regular as in the poems of *Íslenzk Miðaldakvæði* or the baroque poems, and this irregularity is certainly the result of oral circulation. The most regular stanza in *Enska Vísan* is stanza 6:

> Rid*d*ar*e*n*n* spente sin*n* boga*nn* å streing,
> Han*n* skaut vnder falkans væng,
> gio*r*di h*a*n*n* kross þ*ar* kolfuren*n* flő,
> krǎkan*n* þeg*ar* j gegnum [smó]
> felmtradi årin*n* og felldi þ*ad* nid*ur* s*em* falsklega drő.

To see an alliterative pattern in lines 1 and 2, we need to grant that *sp-*, *st-*, and *sk-* can alliterate with one another, which would admittedly be unusual, but it does seem to be what the poet (or at least the scribe) is asking of us. While *Enska Vísan* does not consistently maintain the line-linking alliteration of traditional Icelandic meters, it does have abundant, if irregular, alliteration within the line, as we find in English alliterative verse. Consider stanza 15:

> Þ*ar* kom fram*m* eir*n*n fri*j*d*ur* ma*d*ur,
> sagdest heijta su*nn*udag*ur*
> "selldu mier þå hina syndugu sǎl,
> "eg sie he*nn*e er huijld*ar* mal,
> "e*g* er so rijkur eg skal henni alldrei veijta tǎl."

We see "*f*ramm" and "*f*ridur" alliterating in line 1, "*s*agdest" and "*s*unnudagur" in line 2, "*s*elldu"/"*s*yndugu"/"*s*ǎl" in line 3, "*h*enne" and "*h*uijldar" in line 4, and the vowel alliteration of "eg"/"eg"/"alldrei" in line 5.

Theme

There are a number of motific parallels between *Enska Vísan* and *Sir Orfeo*: I have listed some of them in Appendix B below. They are by no means close enough to suggest that the author knew *Sir Orfeo*, but the poems may well have roots in a common body of material. There is a fragmentary ballad from Shetland, first recorded in 1880, that narrates a similar story. Child printed it as the "Ballad of

---

102 "Heilsa eg dottir hyr og god," *Kvæðasafn síra Bjarna Gissurarsonar á Þingmúla*, Copenhagen, Royal Danish Library, MS Thott 473, 4to.

King Orfeo," although, as in *Enska Vísan*, the king is not named.[103] His beloved is called "Lady Isabel." Child reprinted a version of the ballad collected by Jessie M. Saxby and published in *The Leisure Hour*;[104] Saxby does not state whether the ballad was traditionally associated with "King Orfeo," but the affinity was clear to Child, who printed a summary of *Sir Orfeo* and a discussion of the manuscript versions along with the ballad. Its language is an attempt to sound Scandinavian: the two refrain lines are "Scowan ürla grün," perhaps for Danish *skoven årle grøn* ("Early green's the wood"), and "Whar giorten han grün oarlac," which Svend Grundtvig thought was an attempt at *Hvor hjorten han går årlig* ("Where the hart goes yearly").[105] The first line of the recorded version is "Der lived a king inta da aste," locating the king "in the east," i.e. in Scandinavia – as it made its way around the North Atlantic, the strangely foreign poem seemed to be from elsewhere no matter where it landed. It should be noted that there is yet another fragmentary version of the story, the Old Scots *King Orphius* (c. 1400–c. 1550).[106] This is a fuller treatment of the narrative, and the most recent editor, Rhiannon Purdie, suggests that it is derived from *Sir Orfeo*, though significantly modified through oral transmission.[107]

Allegory

The evocative mythical character of the poem shifts to Christian allegory in stanza 15 with the appearance of a figure named "Sunday." This interpretation of the Orpheus myth reflects a tradition associated with the fourteenth-century *Metamorphosis Ovidiana* of the Benedictine Pierre Bersuire. He records a variety of allegorical interpretations of Ovid's Orpheus narrative, and in one of them, Orpheus is understood as an allegorical representation of Christ, as we see here in the final stanzas of *Enska Vísan*.[108] Pierre says that Orpheus represents Christ, the eternal Son, and Eurydice, the human soul. They are joined from the beginning, but the devil/serpent pursues the bride, also associated with Eve, and kills her with sin. Orpheus/Christ descends to the depths to reclaim his wife, that is, *natura humana*, human nature, and leads her to the blessed world above. In

---

103 Francis James Child, ed., *The English and Scottish Popular Ballads*, 5 vols. (1883–98; repr. New York, 1957), 1:215–17.

104 [Jessie Margaret Edmonston] Saxby, "Folk-Lore from Unst, Shetland," *The Leisure Hour* 1880, 108–10.

105 Child, *The English and Scottish Popular Ballads*, 1:217.

106 Rhiannon Purdie, ed., *Shorter Scottish Medieval Romances*, Scottish Text Society ser. 5, no. 11 (Edinburgh, 2013), 23–123, 218–27.

107 Ibid., 23–27.

108 See John Block Friedman, *Orpheus in the Middle Ages* (Cambridge, MA, 1970), 126.

stanza 15 of *Enska Vísan*, the lady is referred to as *synduga sál*, the sinful human soul, and the mighty heavenly figure *Sunnudagur* identifies himself as *sá Guð þú trúir upp á*, "the God you believe in," God the Father. The three-days' leave, or *orðlof*, granted the knight/Christ seems to be a reference to the descent into hell, which suggests pre-Reformation piety, but the knight's contemptuous refusal to hand the lady over to the angels and apostles in stanza 14 may be a Lutheran rejection of any mediators between God and humans – it seems to say that prayers to angels and saints are wasted effort and that one should appeal directly to God. The seven months of the journey may be a reference to the Ptolemaic seven ages of man, an image familiar from both classical and patristic authors that appears in fifteenth- and sixteenth-century literature.[109] *Enska Vísan* is an appealing poem that transcends genres (myth, allegory, ballad, *rímur*, devotional poetry, folktale, learned allegory), religious sensibilities (pre- and post-Reformation), and locality. Its transmission is both scribal and oral – the scribal facilitating oral performance in evening reading sessions or *kvöldvökur*, and memories of the *kvöldvökur* leading to further oral revisions. All these things make it both remarkable and characteristic of literary culture in Iceland at the end of the Middle Ages.

109 See, for example, J. A. Burrow, *The Ages of Man: A Study in Medieval Writing and Thought* (Oxford, 1986), 38–54.

Appendix A: *Enska Vísan*

1. Enska vijsan*n* h*v*n er sig so lòng,
h*v*n *var* skrifud *ã* organs sòng,
h*v*n *var* sett *ã* meijsta*ra* list,
h*v*n *var* lesin*n* *ã* liliukuist,
huòrsú hin*n* vng[e] hofma*n* hef*ur*
sin*n*[ar] vnnustu mist.

The English verse, it is so long,
it was written in organ's song,
it was set in masterly art,
it was read on the lily stalk,
how the young courtier had lost his
beloved.

Mss: B, 66, 126, V¹, V², 622, 67, 1587 [orthographical variants in the group 1587, 255, 591, and 202 are not noted in the variant readings], 255, 591, 202.
— *Readings*: **1/1** Enska] Suen*n*ska 622; Spanska 1587, 255, 591, 202. sig] ≏ 67, 1587, 255, 591, 202. **1/2** *var* skrifud *ã*] var skrifud af 622, er te[k]in af 67; var getinn vid 1587, 591, 202; var gefinn við 255. **1/3** *var* sett *ã*] var sett með V¹; *var* sett in V², *var* sleiginn af 622; er kvedin af 67; var getinn af 1587, 255, 591, 202. meijsta*ra*] meistaran*n*s 622, 1587, 255. **1/4** h*v*n var] og 67. lesin*n*] sleigin*n* 622; skrifud 67, 1587, 255, 591, 202. *ã*] af 622; uppá 67; med 1587, 255, 591, 202. liliukuist] eirn Liliu kvist 67. **1/5** huòrsú] hvornin 67. hin*n*] sá 67. vngi] vnga B; ungv 255; unga 591. sinnar] sin*n*ur B; sína V², 622, 67, 1587, 255, 591, 202. vnnustu] ki*æ*ru vn*n*ustu 1587, 255, 591; k*æ*rustu 202.

Notes: **1/1** *h*v*n er sig so lóng*. The unusual use of the reflexive pronoun with the verb *vera* ("to be") and a predicate adjective is a Danism: it occurs in Early Modern Danish as well as German, typically in ballads. The pronoun adds nothing to the meaning of the sentence and should not be translated. See *Ordbog over det danske Sprog* s.v. "være, *v.*, 25" (http://ordnet.dk/ods/ordbog?select=være,2&query=være). For examples of "er sig + adj." in Early Modern Icelandic see *ÍF* 1:19 ("Kvæði af herra Jóni og Ásbirni"), *ÍF* 1:36 ("Kvæði af Sigmundi"), *KD* 2:329 ("Kvæði móður og dóttur"), *ÍGSVÞ* 3:126 ("Kellingarleikur"). **1/2** *organs sóng*. Organs were rare in medieval and early modern Iceland, and *organssöng* is a rare word associated with exotic contexts. Apart from this text it occurs in a fourteenth-century translation of the biblical Book of Judith translating Latin *organis* (Svanhildur Óskarsdóttir, "The Book of Judith: A Medieval Icelandic Translation," *Gripla* 11 [2000]: 79–124, at 120), and in *Skikkjurímur*'s account of the Pentecost celebrations at the court of King Arthur (*Skikkjurímur*, ed. and trans. Matthew James Driscoll, in *Norse Romance II: Knights of the Round Table*, ed. Marianne E. Kalinke, Arthurian Archives 4 [Woodbridge, Suffolk, 1999], 2:267–325, at 281). **1/4** *liliukuist*. Another rare word, associated with Catholic piety. It occurs in the pre-Reformation "Kvæði af Imnar og Elínu," where the repentant lovers' sins fall from them like leaves from the lily's stalk (*ÍF* 6:195). The concluding stanza of the fifteenth-century

199

Marian poem *Gjörði í einu* exhorts the reader "to read Maria's verse . . . praise of the *liliu kuist*," i.e. praise-poem written with the lily's stalk – note the shift from the traditional skaldic mention of declaming and listening to reading and writing (*ÍM* 1:169). The word is also known in Swedish ballads. **1/5** sin*n*[ar]: *missa* normally takes a genitive object.

2. Þau gafu sam*an* sijna æ*ru* og digd,	They gave each other their honor and worth,
þau skilldu vn*n*ast j frelse og frigd,	they would love one another in freedom and joy,
þau gắfu sam*an* sijn gull so reijd,	they gave each other their gold so red,
þ*au* skilldu vn*n*ast j lijfe og j deijd,	they would love one another in life and in death
þ*au* skilldi e*c*ki skilia vtan*n* s*v* hin krắnka neijd.	they would not be parted save by crippling constraint.

Mss: B, 66, 126, V¹, V², 622, 1587, 255, 591, 202. — *Readings*: **2/1** gáfu] bun*n*du 622, 1587, 255, 591, 202. sijna æ*ru* og digd] sin*n* gull ofinn reir 1587, 255, 591, 202. **2/2** frelsi] lyst 622; lijfi 1587, 591, 202. og] og j 622. frigd] deid 1587, 591, 202. **2/3** ÷ 1587, 255, 591, 202. sín] sitt 622. so] og V¹, V². **2/4** ÷ 1587, 255, 591, 202. lijfe og j] lífi og 66, 126, V²; lijf og j 622. deyð] neyd 622. **2/5** skilldi] skilldu 1587, 255, 591, 202. ekki] alldrei (corrected to ecki) 1587; ein*n*gin 622. skilia] skiliast 1587, 255, 591, 202. vtan*n*] fijren*n* 1587, 255, 591, 202. s*v* hin] sú 66, V¹, V²; þan*n* 622; j 1587, 255, 591, 202. krắnka] krankan*n* 1587; kraunkum 255, 591, 202. neijd] deyd 622, 1587, 255, 591, 202.
Notes: **2/3** *reijd*. The Old Norse/Icelandic word is *rauðr*. The form here shows influence from elsewhere in the North Atlantic: cf. Faroese *reyður* and Middle English/Middle Scots *rēd*, *reid*, etc. See *Føroysk Orðabók*, s.v. "reyður" (http://www.obg.fo/fob/fob.php?leitord=reyður&button_leita=&action=1&pageno=0), *MED*, s.v. "rēd (adj.)" (http://quod.lib.umich.edu/cgi/m/mec/med-idx?type=id&id=MED36283), and *Dictionary of the Older Scottish Tongue*, s.v. "Red(e, Reid, adj.*" (http://www.dsl.ac.uk/entry/dost/rede_adj). In *Sir Orfeo* cf. lines 150, "It nas of silver, no of gold red," and 362, "Of rede gold y-arched riche."

3. Ridd*are*nn villdi sig til hőfan*n*a gã,
h*a*nz ki*æ*ra vn*n*ustan eft*t*er skilldi þrã,
h*v̆*n klappar vnder h*a*nz huijtu kin*n*,
"fardu vel ki*æ*rí vn*n*usten*n* min*n*,
og er e*g* vm*m* þad hrædd, e*g* siãj þ*i*g
nu j sijdasta sin*n*."

The knight desired to go to the court,
his dear beloved had to pine at home,
she stroked him under his white cheek,
"Farewell my dear beloved,
and I am afraid that I see you now for
the last time."

Mss: B, 66, 126, V¹, V², 622. — *Readings*: **3/1** villdi] vill 622. hőfan*n*a] Höfan*n* 126. **3/2** ki*æ*ra] ÷ 622. vn*n*ustan] vn*n*ustu*a*n 126. eft*er* skilldi] skylldi ept*er* 622. þrã] stá 622. **3/3** h*v̆*n] h*a*nn 622. hanz] h*e*nnar 622. **3/4** fardu] lif 622. ki*æ*rí] ki*æ*ra 622. vn*n*usten*n*] vn*n*ustan*n* 622. **3/5** og] Eg 66 ÷ 622. er e*g*] óttaz ad 66; er er V². e*g*] ÷ 622. vm*m* þad hrædd] ÷ 66; um þad hræddur 622. nu] ÷ V¹, V².

4. Ridd*are*nn biő sijna ferdina ã
leijd,
daudin*n* kom j h*a*nz gard so greijd,
fangadi h*a*nz kærustu og taladi so,
"þu skallt þ*i*g burt vr verőlldin*n*e gã,
þin*n* vn*n*ustan sijd*a*n alldrej m*ed*
augu*m* siã."

The knight made ready and set on his
way,
Death came so quickly into his yard,
seized his beloved and spoke thus,
"You must depart from the world,
never again to set eyes on your
beloved."

Mss: B, 66, 126, V¹, V², 622, 67, 1587, 255, 591, 202. — *Readings*: **4/1** biő sijna ferdina ã] reid fr*a*m*m* sina 622; reid á burt sina 67; reid j burtu sijna 1587, 255, 591, 202. **4/2** h*a*nz gard so] gard hans 1587, 255, 591, 202. greijd] B, V¹, V²; breid 622, 67, 1587, 255, 591, 202. **4/3** fangadi] greip 622; tók 67, 1587, 255, 591, 202. kærustu] vn*n*ustu 622, 67, 1587, 255, 591, 202. taladi] sagdi 622; svaradi 1587, 255, 591, 202. so] þá 67. **4/4** þ*i*g burt vr] þig j burt vr 622; med mér i burtu 67; hiedan ur verőlldin*n*i 1587, 255, 591, 202. verőlldin*n*e] ÷ 67. **4/5** þin*n* vn*n*ustan sijd*a*n alldrej] þinn unnustan síðan aldrei aptr V¹, V²; *og* alld*r*i sidan*n* þin*n* vn*n*ustan 622; þinn unnusta skaltu nú alldrei framar 67; hier med þin*n* ún*n*ustan*n* alldrei 1587, 255, 591, 202. augu*m*] augm 126; augunum V¹, V², 67, 1587, 255, 591, 202.

5. Daudin*n* filgdi hen*ne* ã veg,
hv̆n vard ad gắnga þő hv̆n vær*i*
  treg,
kom þar ad s*e*m ridd*a*rin*n* lắ,
han*n* sắ drekan*n* j lofttinu flő;
han*n* þekte þ*ad* vijfed h*a*n*n* hiellt ã j
  sin*ne* haturlegre klő.

Death escorted her on the path,
she was made to go, though she was
  loath,
came there where the knight lay,
he saw the dragon fly in the air;
he knew that woman he held in his
  hateful claws.

Mss: B, 66, 126, V¹, V², 622, 67, 1587, 255, 591, 202. — *Readings*: **5/1** filgdi]
gieck m*ed* 622; fór med 67. hen*ne*] hana 67. **5/2** vard] hlaut 622, 67, 1587, 255,
591, 202. gắnga] fara 67, 1587, 255, 591, 202. **5/3** kom þar ad s*e*m ridd*a*rin*n*]
Kom þar ad sin*n* ridd*a*rin*n* 126; vacknadi riddarin*n* 622, 67. lắ] þar ed han la
622, 67, 1587, 591, 202; þar ad han*n* lá 255. **5/4** han*n*] og 67. drckan*n* j lofttinu]
loftinni V¹; hatt þar narin*n* 622; hvar han*n* álki álfta 67; organ*n* so hạtt hún 1587,
255, 591, 202. **5/5** han*n*] ÷ 67. þekte] kenndi 622. þad vijfed] þad vijf 622; sitt
vijf 1587, 255, 591, 202. han*n*] sem 67, 591, 202; so 1587, 255. hiellt ã j sin*ne*
haturlegre] hellt á i sinni haturlegu 66, V¹, V²; haturliga hiellt vti sine 622, 67;
haturlega hiellt nú j sin*n*i kló, 1587, 255, 591; hardlega helt nú í sinni kló 202.

6. Ridd*a*ren*n* spente sin*n* bogan*n* ã
  streing,
Han*n* skaut vnder falkans væng,
gi*o*rdi h*a*n*n* kross þar kolfuren*n* flő,
krắkan*n* þeg*a*r j gegnum [smó]
felmtradi ắrin*n* og felldi þ*ad* nid*ur* s*e*m
  falsklega drő.

The knight braced his bow on the
  string,
he shot under the falcon's wing,
he aimed across the demon's flight,
the devil intersected the arrow's path,
the fiend shuddered, and he felled it
  as it deceitfully fled.

Mss: B, 66, 126, V¹, V², 622, 67, 1587, 255, 591, 202. — *Readings*: **6/1** Ridd*a*ren*n*]
Han*n* 1587, 255, 591, 202. spente] spennar 622; setti 67; tók þá 255, 591, 202; ÷
1587. sin*n*] sína 67; sin*n* hin*n* 1587, 255, 591. bogann] B, V¹, V², 622; örina 67. ã
streing] suo strann*g* 622; stranga 1587, 255, 591, 202. **6/2** han*n*] ÷ 67; og 1587,
255, 591, 202. skaut] skaut svo 67; skaut hónum 1587, 255, 591, 202. falkans]
pukans (correction in a later hand) B; drekans 66; pukans V¹, V², 622, 1587, 255,
591, 202; vargsins 67. **6/3** ÷ 1587, 255, 591, 202. han*n*] ÷ 67. þar] þar ed 622.
flő] smó 66; stód 67. **6/4** ÷ 1587, 255, 591, 202. krắkan*n*] krátinz V¹, V²; k . . . nis
(the MS is damaged) 622; grátid 67. þeg*a*r] vielid V¹, V², 622; hel 67. smó] flő B
(corrected to "smó" in a later hand), 66, 126, 1587, 255, 591, 202. **6/5** felmtradi]
felmtradurin 67. ắrin*n*] áranum V¹, V², 622; arminum 1587, 255, 591, 202. og]

÷ 67; han*n* 1587, 255, 591, 202. þa*d*] ÷ 67; hana 1587, 255, 591, 202. s*e*m] hann 622; þad 67; so 1587, 255, 591, 202. falsklega] fastlega V^1, V^2, 1587, 202. *Notes:* **6/3** *kolfurenn.* A *kólfur* is an arrow with a blunt head used with a bow or crossbow. Lines 3–4 read, literally, "He made a cross where the arrow flew, the devil sped right through it." **6/5** *árinn.* In Old Norse, *árr* means simply "messenger," and "fjandans árr" ("devil's messenger") is used to denote an evil spirit. But by the fifteenth century, *árr* had assumed an exclusively negative meaning. See Ásgeir Blöndal Magnússon, *Íslensk Orðsifjabók* (Reykjavík, 1989), s.v. "1 ár."

7. "Velkomin*n* ki*æra* vn*n*ustan*n* mijn,
hu*ar* er yd*ar* litur so fijnn?
bliknad er holld en*n* fölnad er hår,
mi*er* lijst þu orden*n* folnud sem
     når,
og var eg vm*m* þad hrædd*ur* eg mundi
     þ*i*g alldrei aftt*ur* siå."

"Welcome, my dear beloved,
where is your hue so fine?
Your flesh is wan, and dun your hair,
I think you have grown pale as a
     corpse!
And that made me fear that I would
     never see you again."

Mss: B, 66, 126, V^1, V^2, 622, 67, 1587, 255, 591, 202. — *Readings:* **7/1** Velkomin*n*] Komdu nú heil og sæl 67; Heil og sæl 1587, 255, 591, 202. ki*æra*] ki*æ*ri 622; ÷ 67, 1587, 255, 591, 202. vn*n*ustan*n*] unnusta 67, 1587, 255, 591, 202. **7/2** hu*ar*] hví 66. er] er nú V^1, V^2. ydar] þinn nu 622; þinn 67; nú þinn 1587, 255, 591, 202. litur so] liturin klár og 67; so liturin*n* 1587, 255, 591; liturinn só 202. fijn] frijn 1587, 255. **7/3** ÷ 1587, 255, 591, 202. bliknad] fölnud 67. holld] kinn 622; þin kinnin 67. en*n*] ÷ 67. fölnad] klár 67. er hår] ÷ 67. **7/4** orden*n*] vera 622; ÷ 67. bleik V^1, V^2; fól 1587, 255, 591, 202. folnud] bliknud (correction made in a later hand) B, 66; ÷ 622, 67, 1587, 255, 591, 202. når] annar nar 622, 67. **7/5** Eg óttadiz ad eg mundi aldre mundi þig aptur mundi sjá 66. og] ec 622; því 1587, 255, 591, 202. var] er 622, 1587, 255, 591, 202; er svo 67. eg] ÷ V^1, V^2, 622, 67. vm*m* þad] ÷ 622, 67, 1587, 255, 591, 202. eg mundi þ*i*g] þu muner hann 622, 67; þu múnir heilsun*n*i 1587, 255, 591; um þu múnir heilsun*n*i 202. sjå] faa 622, 67; ná 1587, 255, 591, 202.

8. "Þu skallt bera m*ig* ã *þad* l*a*nd,
   þar er hu*or*ki ad ottast meijn nie
      grand,
   þar er jlm*ur* og *þar* er r*ő*s,
   þar skijn s*ő*l bædi fő*gur* og
      [ljós],
   þar er sã jlmur s*em* alldrei þrotn*ar*
      en*n* ãvallt ő́x."

"You must carry me to that land,
   where there is no fear of harm or
      hurt,
   There is fragrance and there are roses,
   The sun shines there both fair and
      fine,
   There is the sweet scent that always
      waxes and never wanes."

Mss: B, 66, 126, V¹, V². — *Readings*: **8/2** er hu*or*ki] hvorki er V¹, V². **8/4** ljós]
fijn (corrected to ljós in a later hand) B, 126. **8/5** sã jlmur] þad yndi B (corrected
from sã jlmur in a later hand), 66.

9. "Þu skallt be*ra* m*ig* j *þan* stad,
   þar skijn s*ő*l bæde nott og dag,
   þar er jlm*ur* og *þar* er ber,
   og er sã sæll s*em* *þang*a*d* fer,
   skiæ*rasta* blő́mstred skijn so fagurt
      sem skijra gler."

"You shall carry me into that place
   where sun shines both night and day,
   there is fragrance and there are berries,
   and blessed are those who travel there,
   brightest flowers shine as fair as sheer
      glass."

Mss: B, 66, 126, V¹, V², 622, 67, 1587, 255, 591, 202. — *Readings*: **9/1** Þu] Eg
67. skallt] matt 622, 1587, 255, 591, 202; skal 67. m*ig*] þíg 67. j] á 67. **9/2** þar
skijn sől] er sólin skín V¹, V²; þar skin 202. bæde] ÷ 67. **9/3** er jlm*ur*] vex plomur
622; vaxa blómstur 67; vaxa laukar 1587, 255, 591, 202. og] ÷ 67. er] eru V¹,
V²; vaxa 622, 67, 1587, 255, 591, 202. **9/4** o*c*] Æ (corrected from o*c* in a later
hand) B, 66; og því V¹, V²; ÷ 67; 1587, 255, 591, 202. er sã sæll] sæll er sá 67; sa
er sæll 1587, 255, 591; sú er sæll 202. **9/5** skiæ*rasta*] skiæra 126, V¹, V²; skyra
622; skín 622, 67; skiærasti 1587, 255, 591, 202. blő́mstred] blomit 622; lióminn
1587, 255, 591, 202. so fagurt sem] þar fegra enn 1587, 255, 591, 202. skijra] þat
skærasta 622; skiæra 67; skijrasta 1587, 255, 591, 202.

10. Hann bar hana fulla manudi siő̀,
   m*ar*gan*n* stijgin*n* kő́n*n*udu þau,
   þau þoldu kallt og *þau* þoldu
      heijtt,
   þeim v*ar*d ei til hialp*ar* neijtt,
   þar kom en*n* ad *þeim* v*ar*d hialp og
      huggun veijtt.

He carried her for a full seven months,
   many a path they came to know,
   they suffered cold and they suffered
      heat,
   for them there was no help at all,
   though as it happened, help and
      solace came to them at last.

Mss: B, 66, 126, V¹, V², 622, 67, 1587, 255, 591, 202. — *Readings*: **10/1** fulla]
heila 67, 1587, 255, 591, 202. manudi] mánud 67. sið] þriá 1587, 255, 591, 202.
10/2 þau] þaug þá 591, 202. **10/3** kallt] heitt 1587, 255, 591, 202. og] ÷ 67.
heijtt] kallt 1587, 255, 591, 202. **10/4** þeim] þau 67. vard] var 622; sáu sér 67.
ei] ecki B, V¹, 67; eigi 622. hialpar] lijknar 622. neijtt] margt 1587, 255, 591, 202.
10/5 þar kom enn ad] þar næst mun 622; þar næst var 67; hier næst vár 1587,
255, 591; hér var 202. vard hialp] varð stoð V¹, V²; hialpinn von 622; huggun
send 67; hiálpinn synd 1587, 255, 591, 202. huggun] hjálpin 67.

11. Hann [bar] hana yfer þã breijdu brṽ,	He carried her over the broad bridge,
hṽn var ecki stittre enn ståljarn þriu;	it was not shorter than three steelyards;
hann bar hana yfer þann kalldann ijs,	he carried her over the cold ice,
vellandi biked fra grunnunum rijs,	molten liquid rose from the ground,
þar var so jllt og þotte honum sier daudenn vijs.	it was so evil there, and he thought he was sure to die.

Mss: B, 66, 126, V¹, V², 622, 67, 1587, 255, 591, 202. — *Readings*: **11/1** bar]
bara B. þã breijdu] þá brottu V¹, V²; eina breida 622, 67; Einglands 1587, 255,
591, 202. **11/2** ecki] ei 126, V¹, V², 67; eigi 622. stittre] stærri 1587, 255, 591,
202. ståljarn] staddiann 622; stafiel 67; stafroinn 1587; stafrofinn 255, 591, 202.
11/3 hann bar hana yfer þann kalldann ijs] hann bar hana yfir þann kallda ís
V¹, V²; han bar hana yfir eirnn breidann sannd 622; þar brann undir, þar fraus
ís 67; þar vall elldur og þar vall j 1587, 255, 591, 202 . **11/4** vellandi biked fra
grunnunum rijs] Vellandi bikid frá grunninur rís 66; vellandi biked fra grundunum
rijs 126; er vellanda bikið frá grunnenum rís V¹, V²; brenndandi badi hans fot og
hannd 622; vellandi bik frá grunni er i 67; brennandi bickid brúnanúm j 1587,
255; brennandi bikid brunan i 591, 202 (scribal note "anum?"). **11/5** þar var so
jllt og þotte honum sier daudenn vijs] þar var svo illt að þótti honum ser dauða vís
V¹; þar var so illt, at þótti honum sér daudinn vís V²; armer arar villdu hans vnnustu
veita grannd 622; þar var svo illt, þeim þókti sér þar daudin vís 67; þar var so
heitt ad þeim þotti sier daudinn vijs 1587, 255, 591, 202.
Notes: **11/2** *ståljarn.* The meaning of the word is unclear. Literally "steel-iron,"
the word exits in Modern Icelandic as a term for iron used to make steel, or for
an instrument made of steel: a *stáljárn-karl* is a crowbar; a waffle iron (*vaffeljárn*)
can be referred to as a *stáljárn* if it is made of steel. Here, it may be related to the
English word "steelyard" ("stalliard, stellere," etc.), the name of an iron balance
consisting of a lever with unequal arms, which moves on a fulcrum to weigh
objects. The size can vary from a portable instrument just a foot or so in length

to very large implements used to weigh freight in shipyards. The name seems to come from "steelyard" as the name for the headquarters of the Hanseatic merchants in London or for similar establishments in provincial towns (*OED*, s.v. "steelyard" [http://www.oed.com/view/Entry/189568]). The normal Icelandic term for a steelyard is *reisla*. The variant readings reflect scribal confusion about the unfamiliar term: **622**'s "staddiann" is probably a version of English (Latin) *stadium* as a measure of length. **67**'s "stafiel" is obscure — is may be confused with *stadial*, an early alternate English form of *stadium*. Stafróf ("alphabet") in **1587**, **255**, **591**, and **202** is perplexing. Perhaps there is some association with the basic meaning of *stafur* ("staff"). **11/4–5** The imagery of these lines reflects the landscape of Iceland.

12. Hann bar hana á einn þickuann skőg,
þyrnir vöktu hanns jliumm blőd,
hann bar hana yfer þann heijta sand,
þar brendi hann sinn főt og hannd,
þeir olmu vargar villdu hanz vnnustu veijta grand.

He carried her through a thick forest,
thorns drew blood from his footsoles,
he carried her over the hot sand,
where he burned his feet and hands,
the violent beasts wanted to harm his beloved.

Mss: B, 66, 126, V¹, V², 622, 67, 1587, 255, 591, 202. — *Readings*: **12/1** ÷ 622, 67, 1587, 255, 591, 202. **12/2** ÷ 622, 67, 1587, 255, 591, 202. **12/3** þann heijta] eirnn breidann 622; eirn heitan 67; þann hvíta V¹; heitann 1587, 255, 591, 202. **12/4** þar brendi hann sinn] brenndandi badi hans 622. **12/5** þeir olmu vargar] amer arar 622; þeir vondu andar 67; hier med Judar 1587, 255, 591, 202. hanz] ÷ V¹, 622, 67.

Notes: **12/5** *vargar*. The variants reflect scribal confusion here: *vargar* ("beasts, wolves, wild men"), *árar* ("demons," cf. **6/5**), *þeir vöndu andar* ("the evil spirits"). The most disturbing is *júðar* ("Jews") in the nineteenth-century Skagafjörður manuscripts. Jews may have been on the minds of these scribes due to recent events: in 1815 the Dane Ruben Henriques was the first Jew to register in Iceland and began trading in Akureyri, though he never actually settled in Iceland. In 1850 the Danish parliament enacted a law permitting non-Danish Jews to enter the country, but the Icelandic Alþingi debated the law and voted not to ratify it for Iceland. It was eventually approved after a second vote in 1855, when the Danish government lifted the last restrictions on trade. Jews have always been rare in Iceland: *The Encyclopedia of the Jewish Diaspora* listed the Jewish population of Iceland as ten in 2009 (Snorri G. Bergsson, "Jews in Iceland," *The Encyclopedia of the Jewish Diaspora*, ed. M. Avrum Ehrlich, 3 vols. [Santa Barbara, 2009], 1:1077).

13. Hann bar hana a þann fagra völl,
einglar og postular geingu honum ã
  gen,
"selldu mier þad þu helldur vppa,"
einglar og postular toludu þã,
"hier er so gott og hier mã hvn sijna
  heijlsuna fã."

He carried her to that fair plain,
angels and apostles came to meet
  him,
"Give me what you are holding onto,"
angels and apostles said then,
"Here it is so good and here she can
  regain her health."

Mss: B, 66, 126, V¹, V², 67, 1587, 255, 591, 202. — *Readings*: **13/1** a] of
(corrected to a) B; fram á 67; yfir 1587, 255, 591, 202. þann fagra völl] völl fagran
er feckst þar sien V¹, V²; völl svo græn 67; Einglans hil 1587, 255, 591, 202. **13/2**
einglar og postular geingu honum ã gen] englar og postular stódu honum igen
67; postúlar og Einglar stodú hónum ey vil 1587, 255; postúlar og Einglar stodú
hönum i vil 591, 202. **13/3** selldu mier þad] gefdu mér þad sem 67; liädú mier
þá sem 1587, 255, 591, 202. vppa] á 67. **13/4** ÷ 1587, 255, 591, 202. toludu]
svörudu 67. **13/5** gott] ÷ V¹. og] að V¹, 1587, 255, 591, 202, ÷ 67. hier mã hvn
sijna heijlsuna fã] her má hún sína heilsu fá V¹; her er so blídt má hún sina heilsu
fá V²; hér máttu alla þína heilsu fá 67; hier meiga allir sælúna fa 1587, 255, 591,
202.

14. "Jeg sel ydur ecki eina baun!
þier stõdud mier so lijtt j minne
  mikelle raun!
hrõpadi eg hatt og kalladi þã;
þier villdud mig huõrke heijra nie siã
hier er so gott og hier er so blijdt, og
  hier skal eg stã."

"I will not give you a bean!
You helped me so little in my great
  need!
I cried aloud and called on you then,
You would not hear or see me.
Here it is so good and here so mild,
  and here will I stand."

Mss: B, 66, 126, V¹, V², 67, 1587, 255, 591, 202. — *Readings*: **14/1** Jeg sel ydur
ecki] eg gef yckur 67; Ecki gief eg ydúr 1587, 255, 591, 202. eina] enga 67; neina
1587. **14/2** þier stõdud] þer stóðuðuð V¹, V²; ætid stódud 67; ävallt vorú þid]
1587, 255, 591, 202. mier] mig V¹, V². so] ÷ V¹, V², 67. lijtt j minne mikelle] lítt
í mikilli V¹, V²; fiærri i 67, 1587, 255, 591, 202. **14/3** hrõpadi eg] eg hrópaðe
V¹; hrópadi V²; kalladi eg 1587, 255, 591, 202. og kalladi þã] og kalladi eg þá
67; enn hrópadi þrátt 1587, 255, 591, 202. **14/4** þier villdud mig] þid vildud mig
67; þú skilldud 1587, 255, 591, 202. huõrke] hvörgin V². hiejra] heira mig 1587,
255, 591, 202. **14/5** er so gott og hier er so blijdt, og hier skal eg stã] hér er svo
gott, hedan skal eg alldrei i burtu fara 67; skal eg vera og hier skal eg stä 1587,
255, 591, 202.

15. Þar kom framm eirnn frijdur madur,
sagdest heijta sunnudagur
"selldu mier þá hina syndugu sál,
eg sie henne er huijldar mal,
eg er so rijkur eg skal henni alldrei
veijta tál."

There came forth a peaceful man,
he said his name was Sunday.
"Give to me the sinful soul,
I see it is time for her to rest.
I am so mighty, I will never lead her
astray."

Mss: B, 66, 126, V¹, V², 67. — *Readings*: **15/1** frijdur] velborin 67. **15/2** sagdest]
og sagdist 67. **15/3** selldu] gefdu 67. **15/4** eg sis] se eg að V¹; sir ec at V². **15/5**
skal] vil V¹, V², 67. alldrei] eckert 67.
Notes: **15/4** *huijldar mal.* The phrase "þótti flestum mál hvíldar" ("most thought it
was time for rest") also occurs in *Göngu-Hrólfs saga* (ed. Guðni Jónsson, Fornaldar
Sögur Norðurlanda [Reykjavík, 1954], 3:264) and *Gunnars saga Keldugnúpsfífls* (ed.
Jóhannes Halldórsson, *Kjalnesinga Saga*, Íf 14 [Reykjavík, 1959], 14:357).

16. "Giarnann eg þier hana sel
ætijd komstu ad hialpa mier.
[huórt] þad sinn eg heijrdi þitt nafn,
þá varstu mier til hialpar giarn,
blijdaste byrinn bar mig alldrei á betre
hafn."

"I will gladly give her to you,
you always came to help me,
and every time I heard your name,
you were there eager to help,
the softest breeze never bore me to a
better harbor."

Mss: B, 66, 126, V¹, V², 67, 1587, 255, 591, 202. **16/1** Giarnann eg þier hana
sel] gjarnan eg hana gef og sel þér V¹, V²; giarna gef eg hana þér 67; Giarnann
eg hana þier giefa vil 1587, 255, 591; Gjaran þér hana eg gefa vil 202. **16/2**
hialpa] biarga 1587, 255, 591, 202. **16/3** huórt þad sinn] eg huórt (eg crossed out
by a later hand) B; hvort það sinn er V¹, V²; hvonær þá 67; alltijd ä 1587, 255,
591, 202. heijrdi] ad heidra alltijd ä 1587, 255, 591, 202. **16/4** þá] ÷ 66, V¹, V²;
ætijd 1587, 255, 591, 202. til hjálpar gjarn] jafnan til hjálpar gjarn V¹, V²; ætid
ástargiarn 67; lijknargiarn 1587, 255, 591, 202. **16/5** blijdaste byrinn bar mig
alldrei á betre hafn] þin blidi birin bar mig ætid i betri hafn 67; blijdi herra eg
ber mitt alldrei á betra nafn 1587; blijdi herra eg ber mitt alldrei betra nafn 255,
591, 202.

17. "Eg er sa Gud þu trver vppa,
gef eg þier ordlof vmm dagana þriá,
þu skallt þig afttur j verólldina gá,
og seigia so þijnum ferdum j frá,
þá mun sunged seculorum secula."

"I am the God you believe in,
I give you leave for three days,
you shall go back to the world,
and tell of your journey,
then will be sung *seculorum secula.*"

Mss: B, 66, 126, V¹, V², 67, 1587, 255, 591, 202. — *Readings*: **17/1** Gud] gúd sem 1587, 255, 591, 202. trv̆er] treystir 1587, 255, 591, 202. vppa] á 67. **17/2** gef *eg* þier ordlof vm*m*] eg vil ljá þér 67; ordlof gief eg þier 1587, 255, 591, 202. vm*m*] ÷ 1587, 255, 591, 202. dagana] daga V¹. **17/3** ÷ 67. þu skallt þig] ÷ 1587, 255, 591, 202. j] á 255. gå] ad gä 1587, 255, 591, 202. **17/4** og] ad 67, 1587, 255, 591, 202. so] ÷ 67, 1587, 255, 591, 202. ferd*um* j] ferðunum V¹, V²; vinum og frendum 67, 1587, 255, 591, 202. **14/5** þå mun] þá er mín 67; sie þa 1587, 255, 591, 202. sunged] súngin 67. seculor*um*] seculo og 67.

18. Aftt*ur* kom så j þen*n*an*n* heijm,
s*e*m skildi vid aud og verall*dar* seijm,
gi*o*rdi ha*n*n allt ad greijna þå,
glögt so sijnum*m* ferdun*um* frå,
þå sungu aller Seculor*um* Secula.

Then he went back to this world
and parted with wealth and worldly glory,
he then did all to give a clear account,
of the travels he had made.
Then all sang *seculorum secula*.

Mss: B, 66, 126, V¹, V². **18/1** þen*n*an*n*] þenna V¹, V². **18/2** s*e*m] er V¹, V². **18/4** glögt so] eð gl*o*ggvasta V¹, V². ferdun*um*] ferðum V¹, V². **18/5** sungu aller] var sungid (corrected to sungu allir) 66. **18/1–5** Hofmann aptur i veröldu bió, / Itum ad byrta jardteikn stór, / drengurin lifdi dagana þriá, / dír og sagdi óttu frá, hann var fús ad fara ad deya og þagnadi þá – ("Back in the world, the courtier had the joy / Of making the great miracle known to men, / The man lived for three days, / Holy, and told of the terror, / He was eager to meet death, and then was silent – ") 67.

Appendix B: *Enska Vísan/Sir Orfeo* Parallels

Enska vísan	*Sir Orfeo* [Auchinleck version][110]
[title] *Enska Vísan*	**40** In Jnglond an heiʒe lording
1/2 hv̆n var skrifud ã organs sõng	**1** We redeþ oft & findeþ y-write
1/4 hv̆n var lesinn ã liliukuist	
2/1 Þau gafu saman sijna æru og digd,	**121** "Seþþen we first to-gider were
þau skilldu vnnast j frelse og frigd,	Ones wroþ neuer we nere,
þau gãfu saman sijn gull so reijd,	Bot euer ich haue y-loued þe
þau skilldu vnnast j lijfe og j deijd,	As mi liif, & so þou me;
þau skilldi ecki skilia vtann sv̆ hin	Ac now we mot delen ato"
krãnka neijd.	**129** "Whider þou gost ichil wiþ þe,
	& whider y go þou schalt wiþ me."
3/5 "og er eg vmm þad hrædd, eg siãj	**125** "Ac now we mot delen ato
þig nu j sijdasta sinn."	– Do þi best, for y mot go."
4/2 daudinn kom j hanz gard so	**191** Ac ʒete amiddes hem ful riʒt
greijd,	Þe quen was oway y-tviʒt,
fangadi hanz kærustu og taladi so	Wiþ fairi forþ y-nome
4/4 "þu skallt þig burt vr verõlldinne	**167** "& þan þou schalt wiþ ous go,
gã,	& liue wiþ ous euer-mo;"
þinn vnnustan sijdan alldrej med augum	
siã."	
7/2 "huar er ydar litur so fijnn?	**107** "Allas! þi rode, þat was so red,
bliknad er holld enn fõlnad er hãr,	Is al wan, as þou were ded;"
mier lijst þu ordenn folnud sem nãr,	
11/3 hann bar hana yfer þann	**247** Now, þei it comenci to snewe &
kalldann ijs,	frese,
12/1 Hann bar hana ã einn þickuann	**237** Þurth wode & ouer heþ
skõg,	In-to þe wildernes he geþ.
12/5 þeir olmu vargar villdu hanz	**252** Bot wilde wormes bi him strikeþ
vnnustu veijta grand.	
13/1 Hann bar hana a þann fagra	**351** He com in-to a fair cuntray,
võll,	As briʒt so sonne on somers day
einglar og postular geingu honum ã	Smoþe & plain & al grene
gen,	**375** Bi al þing him þink þat it is
	Þe proude court of Paradis.

---

110 *Sir Orfeo*, ed. A. J. Bliss, 2nd ed. (Oxford, 1966).

Reading the Real Housewives
of John Foxe's *Book of Martyrs*

ALLISON ADAIR ALBERTS

In her diary entry for September 28, 1599, Lady Margaret Hoby writes:

> In the morninge, after priuat praier, I tooke order for things about the house, and at 9 : I did eate my breakfast : then I hard Mr Rhodes [her chaplain] read tell allmost dinner time : after dinner I talked with Tho: Adesone about the purchassinge his owne farme : then I wrought [did needlepoint] tell allmost supper time, and after I had priuatly praied, I went to supper : after that I walked tell Lector time, and after that I hard one of the men read of the book of Marters, and so went to bed.[1]

Lady Hoby's diary records the events of her life in Hackness from 1599 to 1605, where she managed her large manor house and estates. Typical of other entries, September 28 demonstrates how her day is divided between domestic duty and devotional practice. Her entry moves seamlessly between the two types of activity, painting a picture of a life in which these two spheres – domestic and spiritual – abut and overlap. The same intersection of domesticity and spirituality is echoed throughout the text Lady Hoby names – the "book of Marters." In John Foxe's *Book of Martyrs*, women are often characterized by their distinctly domestic spirituality: their devotion intermingles with their everyday responsibilities as wives, mothers, and daughters. This similarity between readers like Lady Hoby and Foxe's female martyrs has inspired over thirty years of scholarship. In an early and influential article, Carole Levin argues that Foxe's female martyrs constituted role models for Tudor women, though she concludes by noting the difficulty of fitting all of Foxe's women into this model.[2] Since then, critics have

---

1 Margaret Hoby, *The Private Life of an Elizabethan Lady: The Diary of Lady Margaret Hoby, 1599–1605*, ed. Joanna Moody (Stroud, Gloucestershire, 1998), 22.
2 Carole Levin, "Women in The *Book of Martyrs* as Models of Behavior in Tudor England," *International Journal of Women's Studies* 4 (1981): 196–207.

often sought to understand how these martyrs align with patriarchal expectations for wives, such as those outlined in conduct manuals and other such texts.[3]

Yet Foxe's women are not intended to be mirrors for their readers' behavior. Instead, Foxe's female martyrs are part of a much longer trajectory of women in hagiography, whose examples are intended to teach and inspire, rather than provide models for emulation. While the *Book of Martyrs* has been described as an innovative, forward-thinking collection, indicative of its author's break from medieval, Catholic England, the text is deeply indebted to the great store of medieval writing about martyrs, an immensely popular genre, which would have been familiar to Foxe's contemporary readers through texts, sermons, drama, art, or personal devotion to saints.[4] Acknowledging Foxe's medieval inheritance renders his project legible, revealing where he borrows and where he innovates. Recognizing both reveals what Alice Dailey has called the "genius" of the text, which "is not the invention of Protestant martyrdom but the text's successful positioning of the martyr figure within the double framework of local specificity and transcendent typology."[5] This double positioning is particularly visible in Foxe's treatment of women: Foxe's "new" Protestant female martyrs reflect the generic range of classical and medieval female martyrs as well as sixteenth-century perceptions of women's domestic roles and family dynamics.

Unless we take account of the "generic residue" of medieval martyrologies, Foxe's women can appear to be perplexing and contradictory.[6] This essay recovers the influence of the medieval on the *Book of Martyrs* in its examination of mother martyrs, whose accounts reflect the traditional mother saint or martyr who abandons her family in order to pursue a life (or death) inspired by her faith.

---

3   See, for example, Megan L. Hickerson, *Making Women Martyrs in Tudor England* (Houndmills, Hampshire, 2005); Susannah Brietz Monta, "Foxe's Female Martyrs and the Sanctity of Transgression," *Renaissance and Reformation / Renaissance et Reforme* 25 (2001): 3–22; and Edith Wilks Dolnikowski, "Feminine Exemplars for Reform: Women's Voices in John Foxe's Acts and Monuments," in *Women Preachers and Prophets through Two Millennia of Christianity*, ed. Anne Brenon, Karen L. King, Beverly Mayne Kienzle, and Pamela J. Walker (Berkeley, 1998), 199–211.

4   Janel M. Mueller describes Foxe's treatment of martyrdom as a "new species of sacramentalism." Similarly, John Knott writes that Foxe illustrates a "new kind of heroism." Mueller, "Pain, Persecution, and the Construction of Selfhood in Foxe's Acts and Monuments," in *Religion and Culture in Renaissance England*, ed. Claire McEachern and Debora Shuger (Cambridge, UK, 1997), 172; Knott, *Discourses of Martyrdom in English Literature, 1563–1694* (Cambridge, UK, 1993), 38.

5   Alice Dailey, *The English Martyr from Reformation to Revolution* (South Bend, IN, 2012), 59. See also Dailey's discussion of Foxe's medieval inheritance, *English Martyr*, 53–97.

6   The term is Dailey's, *English Martyr*, 53.

While abandonment is a standard element of hagiography, conduct literature of Foxe's period emphasizes intense, immersive devotion to the education and care of family.[7] Critics have often settled this conflict by subordinating the women's expression of faith (perceived as "misbehavior") to their domestic relationships, privileging roles such as mother, daughter, or wife over the role of martyr.[8] In doing so, though, these arguments ignore the larger context of the *Book*'s genre, judging Foxe's mothers as sixteenth-century women, not as the generic type of mother martyrs. Foxe's mothers are indebted to the typology of mother martyrs from classical and medieval hagiography; likewise, they are connected with late medieval female spirituality through their emphasis on domesticity.

One cause of this critical oversight is a contemporary overemphasis of Foxe's own proposal that his *Book* breaks with the tradition of the *Golden Legend*, a well-known medieval hagiography. The first edition of the *Book of Martyrs* includes a Latin preface entitled "Ad Doctum Lectorum" in which Foxe describes the *Golden Legend* as a "book abounding with unnatural monstrosities of lies and most empty inventions."[9] He differentiates the *Golden Legend* from his own project by claiming:

> I would like it to be made manifest to all that I have taken pains to ensure that there should not be anything legendary in the work, or of such a kind as either could have been invented by me, or could not be everywhere very unlike that *Golden* (I should rather say *Leaden*) *Legend*.[10]

7 For an overview of the genre of practical guidebooks for women in marriage, see Suzanne W. Hull, *Chaste, Silent and Obedient: English Books for Women, 1475–1640* (San Marino, CA, 1982), 31–70.

8 For instance, Megan L. Hickerson has argued that for Foxe's women, "disorderliness itself, while exemplifying godly defiance of unjust political authority, at the same time proved their virtuous adherence to patriarchal principles." Hickerson, "Gospelling Sisters 'goinge up and downe': John Foxe and Disorderly Women," *Sixteenth Century Journal* 35 (2004), 1036, 1051. Edith Wilks Dolnikowski suggests that Foxe's women testify to their faith, but "do so, according to Foxe, within the conventional institutions of marriage and family." Dolnikowski, "Feminine Exemplars," 201. Susannah Brietz Monta has located a "tension between martyrdom as an expression of a God-given self and as a gendered role . . . suggesting inconsistent explanations for female martyrs' boldness and steadfastness" (Monta, "Foxe's Female Martyrs," 10).

9 John Foxe, *The Unabridged Acts and Monuments Online* or TAMO (London, 1563), "Ad Doctum Lectorem," trans. John Wade (HRI Online, 2011, *STC* 11222), 6. All citations from the *Book of Martyrs* come from TAMO, which presents unabridged the four editions published during Foxe's lifetime (1563, 1570, 1576, 1583) at www.johnfoxe.org. Hereafter cited as TAMO, followed by the edition in parentheses.

10 Ibid.

This claim is often construed to mean that Foxe completely disregards the medieval tradition of hagiography. Yet Foxe does not necessarily object to medieval saints themselves, but rather to the way hagiographers have added "fabulous inuentions of men" to saints' stories, rendering them superstitious and corrupt.[11] Foxe rejects medieval hagiographers' methodologies, rather than the saints themselves or the devotion that they inspire.[12]

Rather than reading "Ad Doctum Lectorum" [To the learned reader] as a wall erected between medieval and early modern hagiographies, the prologue should instead be read within the collection of prefaces first published in the 1563 *Book of Martyrs*. These five prefaces, three of which are composed in Latin, comprise a collection of reading guides and introductory material that precede the stories of martyrs.[13] As the title of "Ad Doctum Lectorum" [To the learned reader] indicates, this particular preface is intended for the *literati*, erudite readers of the text. Largely concerned with justifying the text's composition in English, rather than Latin, the 1563 prefaces reflect Foxe's anxiety that his text be taken seriously.[14] All but one of these early prefaces – including "Ad Doctum Lectorum" – are removed in the 1570 edition, revealing a change in the way Foxe understands his readership: this second edition is designed with the common reader in mind, a revision that reflects the tremendous popularity of the 1563 edition among readers of all classes.[15]

As the prefaces change from edition to edition, their content reflects Foxe's concerns for his anticipated audience. The 1570 edition reveals that his attention has shifted to readers who have misunderstood the first text, those "waspes & buszyng drones" who gave him such "sufficient triall."[16] The revised prefaces are

---

11 Foxe, TAMO (London, 1583, *STC* 11225) Book 1, 118.

12 On the similarities between Foxe's Book and the *Golden Legend*, see Fiona Kao, "John Foxe's Golden Saints? Ways of Reading Foxe's Female Martyrs in Light of Voragine's *Golden Legend*," in *Contextualizing Miracles in the Christian West, 1100–1500: New Historical Approaches* (Oxford, 2014), 197–228; and Alice Dailey, *English Martyr*, 53–97.

13 On the prefaces and their revisions, see Susanna Felch, "Shaping the Reader in the Acts and Monuments," in *John Foxe and the English Reformation*, ed. David Loades (Aldershot, Hampshire, 1997), 52–65; and John N. King, "Guides to Reading Foxe's 'Book of Martyrs,'" *The Huntington Library Quarterly* 68 (2005): 133–50.

14 King, "Guides to Reading," 134–35; Felch, "Shaping the Reader," 57–58.

15 The order that the *Book of Martyrs* should be placed in every cathedral church did not come until 1571; thus, as Felch points out, the 1570 edition is still intended for the individual reader and as such functions as a "manual on how to read." Felch, "Shaping the Reader," 60. See also John N. King, *Foxe's Book of Martyrs and Early Modern Print Culture* (Cambridge, UK, 2006), 246.

16 Foxe, TAMO (London, 1570, *STC* 11223) Preface.

intended to facilitate the reader's comprehension and navigation of the text.[17] As such, a dominating theme of the 1570 prefaces is the distinction between "true" and "false" believers made through their respective reading practices. On one hand, false readers are the ones who

> neither readyng the whole, nor rightly vnderstandyng that they read, inueigh and maligne so peruersly the setting out therof, as though neither any word in all that story were true, nor any other story false in all the word [*sic*] besides.[18]

On the other hand, "studious" readers recognize the continuity between the primitive church and the reformed church and thus are able to distinguish "better betwene antiquitie and noueltie" of the Catholic church.[19] For Foxe, reading practices characterize the reader's doctrinal beliefs more broadly.

In response to the anxiety over false readers, the "fundamental" revision of 1570 abandons the Latin prefaces in favor of a series of extensive vernacular guides intended for the common reader.[20] While either Foxe or his publisher John Day reintroduced "Ad Doctum Lectorum" to the final edition published in Foxe's lifetime, in 1583, its absence from the 1570 and 1576 editions demonstrates that Foxe's attack on the *Golden Legend* was not of primary importance to him, or to the massive body of readers for whom he revised. Instead, the project remains invested in teaching readers about the differences between Protestant and Catholic doctrine in its juxtaposition of martyrs and their antagonists.

One effect of the text's didactic focus is to make visible women's devotional practices. In Foxe's description of the trial of Richard Belward of Ersham, who was suspected "greatly of lollardy" in 1424, he explains that Belward is charged with preaching that "no saintes which are in heauen, ought in no case to be prayed vnto, but onlye God," and that "he councelled diuers wemen, that they shuld not offer in the Church for þe dead, neither with wemen that were purified."[21] Nearly 100 years later, Robert Cosin and Thomas Man, executed in 1518, instruct Joan Norman of Amersham "not to go on pilgrimage, nor to worship any Images of saints. Also when she had vowed a peece of siluer to a saint for the health of her child they disswaded her from the same."[22] According

---

17 Additions to the preface include an index of martyrs' first names, authors cited, a chart to convert Arabic to Roman numerals, a section on ecclesiastical history intended to convert hostile readers, and other "cautions" from the author to his readers.
18 Foxe, TAMO (1570), Preface, 9.
19 Foxe, TAMO (1570), Preface, 2.
20 The adjective is King's in "Guides to Reading," 133.
21 Foxe, TAMO (1583), Book 6, 684.
22 Foxe, TAMO (1583), Book 7, 842.

to the Protestant martyrs, the Catholic women's transgressions are vested in the domestic, corporeal elements of spirituality that had been long associated with women throughout the Middle Ages.[23] The women are motivated by care for the dead, the postpartum body, or the sick child. These examples remind the reader that female devotional practices were often shaped by the everyday domestic experiences of caretaking.

Continuous with these late medieval traditions, the *Book of Martyrs* responds to and even incorporates the domestic experiences of Protestant women as they relate to faith and spirituality. Like the Catholic women, the Protestant wives and mothers in Foxe's accounts are often deeply invested in domestic responsibilities of caring for family members. Across the *Book*, martyrdom constitutes grief at the loss of a husband, the challenges of caring for a child, or the protection of the vulnerable, postpartum body – not just the suffering at the moment of the martyr's death. For the most part, these are not the spectacular accounts of public torture and execution. Rather, in their focus on "domestic" suffering, Foxe's accounts of contemporary mother martyrs are punctuated by moments of private devotion. Similar to Lady Hoby's interludes of "priuat praier," these moments would certainly be recognizable to the everyday female reader.

A later edition of the text suggests that female readers would be particularly interested in women martyrs. Nathaniel Homes, an editor of the 1632 edition, assigns types of readers particular stories based on their presumed interests. Homes's "A table of tables" generally lists readers by their profession (lawyers, kings, historians, or farmers, for instance), except for female readers, who are divided between two categories: virgins and women. For "virgins," Homes recommends a maiden warrior who defends her town against the invading Turks; Rose Allin, a young Protestant girl who withstands physical torture; and Blandina, a second-century mother martyr of Lyon.[24] At the conclusion of his list, Homes writes, "Virgins may behold here for their instruction mirrors."[25] Under "Women," Homes includes a Roman wife; the early Christian mother martyrs Symphorissa and Sophia; and a note that the reader will find "many more women, sometimes mother and daughter embracing flamse [*sic*] for Christ, in the third volume."[26] Homes's "A table of tables" suggests that he perceives

23 Diana M. Webb, "Women and the Home: The Domestic Setting of Late Medieval Spirituality," in *Women in the Church: Papers Read at 1989 Summer Meeting and 1990 Winter Meeting of Ecclesiastical Historical Society*, ed. W. J. Sheils and Diana Wood (Oxford, 1990), 159–73.

24 John Foxe, *Acts and monuments of matters most speciall and memorable happening in the Church* (London, 1632), 25. Early English Books Online, *STC* 11228, accessed 3 January 2018.

25 Ibid.

26 Ibid., 26. The third volume includes martyrs from Edward III to Henry V.

women to be interested in stories of women like them in some particular way: in the "Women" section, the common element between readers and subject is defined as motherhood. Thus, from the vast number of entries in Foxe's *Book*, a female reader might seek out stories of other women whose domestic setting or matrimonial status may have reflected her own.

While readers' interpretations of Foxe's *Book* were shaped by a number of influences, it is possible to identify some common practices among female readers of the text.[27] Records of some female readers indicate that the *Book of Martyrs* was read both communally and privately, for daily meditation or public gatherings, and as part of a larger religious education carried out though reading and listening. Katherine Brettergh, a young woman noted for her piety, read the *Book of Martyrs* alongside scripture and other religious texts. After her death at the age of twenty-two, in 1601, Brettergh's devout life and spectacular crisis of faith on her deathbed inspired two sermons, later published seven times between 1602 and 1641. The second sermon describes her daily commitment to "[t]o reade, to pray, to sing, to meditate."[28] Katherine, who engaged in prayer and instruction with her family and in private, was also praised for her rigorous reading schedule: she challenged herself to read at least eight chapters of Scripture per day, an assignment she would pair with "some godly writer, or expositer of Scripture, or in the book of Martyrs."[29] Reading the *Book of Martyrs*, in particular, would cause her to

> weepe most bitterly, when either shee had read of that which touched her afflictions neere, or of the cruell martyrdome, which the deere children of God were put vnto, by the cruell and wicked tyrants of former dais.[30]

Katherine's intense emotional reaction to the *Book of Martyrs* is described as evidence not only of her extreme piety but also of the sermon's proposal that she is a good reader: in her reading, she was "not like the simple Popish women

---

27　On the variety of responses to the text, see King, "Reading Foxe's *Book of Martyrs*," in *Acts of Reading: Interpretation, Reading Practices, and the Idea of the Book in John Foxe's Acts and Monuments*, ed. Thomas Page Anderson and Ryan Netzley (Newark, DE, 2010), 133; and King, *Foxe's Book of Martyrs*, 243.

28　William Harrison and William Leygh, *Deaths advantage little rewarded, and the soules solace against sorrow* (London, 1602), 3. Early English Books Online, *STC* 12866, accessed 3 January 2018.

29　Ibid., 9.

30　Ibid.

of our daies, which are euer learning and neuer able to come to the knowledge of the truth."[31]

Lady Margaret Hoby's diary describes the different settings in which a reader might experience reading or listening to Foxe's *Book*. Lady Hoby was first introduced to the *Book* as a child under the tutelage of Katherine, Countess of Huntingdon.[32] As her diary indicates, she continued to read and listen to the text as an adult. On four occasions between September 28 and October 4, 1599, Lady Hoby notes that she listens to the *Book of Martyrs* read aloud after supper in the company of others. Shortly after, on October 24, 1599, she records that she reads the *Book of Martyrs* on her own before she retires to bed. Three years later, on June 11, 1601, she describes how "After privat prairs I went about the house and wrought [did needlepoint] amonge my Maides, and hard one read of the Booke of Marters."[33] Lady Hoby's communal and private reading is coupled with other devotional activities: her daily records include accounts of reading and writing notes in her Testament, attending church, privately praying and meditating, writing in her sermon book, and discussing various religious topics and questions with friends and members of her household.

Lady Grace Mildmay's autobiography depicts her lifelong study of the *Book of Martyrs* as central to her spiritual education. Like Lady Hoby, Lady Mildmay first encounters the *Book of Martyrs* as a child. She writes that "The Bible, [Wolfgang] Musculus's *Common Places*, *The Imitation of Christ*, Mr Foxe's *Book of Martyrs* were the only books [my mother] laid before me, which gave me the first taste of Christ Jesus."[34] As Lady Mildmay continues to study these texts into adulthood, she elevates Foxe's *Book* to the second most important book on her list (a post previously held by Musculus's *Common Book*) in a late revision of the autobiography in 1617.[35] Similar to the affective devotion inspired by *The Imitation of Christ*, she describes how, in reading Foxe's *Book*, "our faith may be increased and strengthened and our hearts encouraged manfully to suffer death and to give our lives for the testimony of the truth of God."[36] Teaching her family to read the *Book of Martyrs* is part of Lady Mildmay's legacy, which she

---

31 Ibid., 4.

32 Moody, *Private Life*, 22 n. 59.

33 Ibid., 151.

34 Transcribed by Linda A. Pollock in *With Faith and Physic: The Life of a Tudor Gentlewoman, Lady Grace Mildmay, 1552–1620* (London, 1993), 28. As a young girl, Lady Mildmay must have read the first edition of the *Book of Martyrs* (1563), as she left home to marry at the age of fifteen, in 1567, before the publication of the second 1570 edition.

35 Retha M. Warnicke, "Lady Mildmay's Journal: A Study in Autobiography and Meditation in Reformation England," *Sixteenth Century Journal* 20 (1989): 61.

36 Pollock, *With Faith and Physic*, 23.

imagines as both spiritual and material. She tells her daughter that though she might give her "jewels and pearl and costly apparel," she must first be "furnished with virtue in [her] mind."[37]

For each of these women, their interaction with the *Book of Martyrs* reveals that their spiritual devotion is rooted in experiences in and around their homes. Katherine Brettergh's daily prayer and meditation are performed "both in her chamber, as also abroad secretly and solitarily in the orchard, garden, or fields."[38] Lady Hoby's diary shifts easily between domestic responsibility and devotion. Her prayers, readings, and devotions are interspersed between gardening, needlepoint, meals, and conversation. Finally, as Lady Mildmay wills her *Book of Martyrs* to her daughter and grandchildren, she understands her gift of spiritual education as part of her duty as mother and grandmother to pass the "holy seed from generation to generation."[39] These women demonstrate that their domestic space is also a spiritual space, and their domestic duties are laid against the background of a larger devotional program.

The *Book of Martyrs*, likewise, does not separate the domestic and spiritual trials and responsibilities of women, whose worth as martyrs is proved through their roles as mothers or wives. In his accounts of mothers, Foxe often draws on a basic narrative of the mother martyr or mother saint that revises Genesis 22: God commands Abraham to sacrifice Isaac, and in agreeing to do so, Abraham demonstrates the extent of his love and obedience. The test is shocking because it asks Abraham to act against his natural love for, and his desire to protect, his own child; it pits loyalty to God against loyalty to family. This conflict is particularly startling in stories of mothers, whose service to family is often imagined in conduct literature as service to God. Yet in Genesis 22 and elsewhere in religious writing, child sacrifice functions as "a supreme test of religious devotion or honor[;] the primitive command to slay a child presupposes intense parental love – no sacrifice could be more painful, and therefore more precious," as Barbara Newman has argued in her analysis of mother martyrs.[40] Thus, despite the variety of historical circumstances that mother saints and martyrs faced, hagiography assumes that giving up a child is the most extreme of all sacrifices for the mother.[41] When reading a religious genre like hagiography, contemporary readers would be

---

37 Ibid., 28.

38 Harrison and William Leygh, *Deaths advantage*, 8.

39 Pollock, *With Faith and Physic*, 30.

40 Barbara Newman, *From Virile Woman to Womanchrist: Studies in Medieval Religion and Literature* (Philadelphia, 1995), 77.

41 Mary Dunn, *The Cruelest of All Mothers: Marie de l'Incarnation, Motherhood, and Christian Tradition* (New York, 2016), 111, and Newman, *Virile Woman*, 94–95.

struck by the extent of the woman's sacrifice, rather than shocked by its seeming unnatural or cruel.

In classical and medieval typology, a mother martyr or mother saint is not holy and powerful because of her motherhood, but rather in the way that she loses or relinquishes her status as a mother. From the early Roman martyrs onward, mother martyrs renounce their families — including their children — as they choose a life solely devoted to Christ. While God saves Isaac, satisfied with his father's devotion, many holy mothers carry this sacrifice through as they abandon or give up their families in order to pursue lives of poverty, pilgrimage, religious service, or even martyrdom. The early Roman martyrs Perpetua and Felicitas cast aside their maternal love and responsibility as they approach martyrdom. After Perpetua is imprisoned, the *Golden Legend* describes how her father brings her infant son with him to the jail as a means of convincing her to reject Christianity.[42] Perpetua "threw the infant from her and repulsed her parents, saying: 'Get away from me, you enemies of God, because I do not know you!'"[43] Felicitas, a slave of Perpetua's family, is imprisoned alongside her former mistress. At eight months pregnant, she gives birth after her fellow prisoners pray that she might be delivered of the child so that she could be offered to the wild beasts along with her compatriots (pregnant women were not permitted to enter the arena).[44] In these stories, motherhood is depicted as incompatible with the mother's path toward martyrdom: the woman must first separate herself from her child and her extended family in order to be united with God.[45]

Perpetua's attitude toward children and family reflects Matthew 10:37, in which Christ states, "Whoever loves father or mother more than me is not worthy of me, and whoever loves son or daughter more than me is not worthy of me." This idea is also echoed in the writings of influential church fathers, who felt that a woman's love for her children prevented her from wholly loving Christ.[46] St. Jerome praises his follower Paula for leaving her five children to go on pilgrimage after her husband died. He explains that, despite her grief and sadness, "[h]er full faith made her able to bear this suffering."[47] Like Perpetua, Paula must release

---

42 While Perpetua's written account of her imprisonment and martyrdom, composed in 203 AD, reveals a far more complex maternal identity, Jacobus de Voragine's version abbreviates the story significantly. Joyce E. Salisbury, *Perpetua's Passion: The Death and Memory of a Young Roman Woman* (New York, 1997), 85–90.

43 Voragine, *Golden Legend*, 729. Foxe names Perpetua only when he lists saints who are praised during the mass. Foxe, TAMO (1583), Book 10, 1423.

44 Salisbury, *Perpetua's Passion*, 16.

45 Newman, *Virile Woman*, 93.

46 Ibid., 81.

47 Voragine, *Golden Legend*, 122.

herself from motherhood before she can fully devote herself to Christ: her vita describes how "[s]he knew not herself as mother in order to prove herself Christ's handmaid."[48] Elizabeth of Hungary, a princess and thirteenth-century saint, and Margaret of Cortona, a thirteenth-century Italian saint, also abandon their children to prove that they are principally dedicated to Christ. After Elizabeth's husband dies, she sends her children to other caretakers as she pursues a life of chaste, pious poverty. In response to criticism, she declares:

> The Lord has heard my voice graciously, because I regard all temporal things as dung, I care for my children no more than for others around me, I make light of all contempt and disrespect, and it seems to me that I no longer love any but God.[49]

Elizabeth characterizes her maternal duties as a distraction from her love of God; only without this distraction can she reach the degree of spiritual devotion she desires. Margaret's renunciation takes the form of neglect of her own son. Her *Life and Revelations* describes how she "preferred the divine Love to the child of her womb, to such an extent as not even to prepare for him his meals, in order not to interrupt her prayers."[50] Margaret's care for the poor replaces care for her child: her confessor describes how Margaret's "son was the only person she took no care of, as if she had forgotten a mother's love."[51] When her son's master relays a rumor that the child has drowned himself because of "sorrow and want of maternal aid," Margaret's refusal to respond proves that she has "disengaged from all worldly matters that could impede her progress in spiritual life."[52] In hagiography, these women's decisions are justified through the idea that love of children and love of Christ are incompatible because of the assumption that mothers naturally love their children above God. Renunciation, then, is the only option for mothers who wholly pursue a spiritual life.

In classical and medieval hagiography, while Abraham's test demonstrates the woman's extreme devotion to Christ, it also associates her with other models of holiness. In abandoning her family, the woman also abandons wealth and material comforts, dedicating herself to a life of poverty and religious service. Thus, the woman is aligned with the apostles and religious men and women

---

48 Ibid.
49 Ibid., 695.
50 Giunta Revegnati, *Life and Revelations of Saint Margaret of Cortona*, trans. F. McDonogh Mahony (London, 1883), 13.
51 Ibid., 14.
52 Ibid., 21.

who had done the same.[53] Freed of her domestic and marital duties, the woman also returns to a life of chastity, a state associated with purity by hagiographers. Furthermore, in renouncing her children, the mother likewise renounces her own identity as a mother. This sacrifice is important because it removes the part of the woman's identity that is associated with weakness in devotion, as early interpretations of Matthew 10:37 suggest. In this way, the woman becomes more masculine, and thus, more laudable in her faith.[54] Finally, as the woman breaks from her maternal identity, she is brought closer to Christ. The woman's self-sacrifice "operates as a proxy for the painful renunciation of self in the image of the crucified Christ," casting her renunciation as the ultimate act of heroic virtue.[55]

The arc of classical and medieval mother martyrs provides a context for Foxe's contemporary mothers. Foxe intends for these narratives to be read against each other, since part of his agenda is to legitimize the reformist church by drawing a connection between early Roman martyrs and Protestant martyrs. Because the martyr was a divinely sanctioned figure, the correlation between the two ages proved that the Protestant church was a continuation of the Apostolic church, whereas the Catholic church represented discontinuity, and therefore, heresy.[56] For this reason, Foxe gives considerable space to the passions of early martyrs. He stresses the resonance between the martyrs of the "primitiue church" and the "Martyrs of our time," arguing that they are both worthy of commendation. He writes:

> for those [early martyrs] did but water the truth with their bloud, that was nowe springinge vppe. And these [contemporary martyrs] by their deaths did restore it againe, when it was sore decayed and fallen downe.[57]

Because he wishes to cast the medieval Catholic church as "sore decayed and fallen downe," Foxe cannot acknowledge the continuity between his project and medieval hagiography. Returning to Abraham's test in his depiction of contemporary mother martyrs links them to the Apostolic martyrs, but it also allows Foxe to enter into an ongoing conversation – carried on throughout the Middle Ages – about how mothers are perceived to be holy.

53 Clarissa W. Atkinson, *The Oldest Vocation: Christian Motherhood in the Middle Ages* (Ithaca, NY, 1991), 165, 192.

54 Dunn, *The Cruelest of Mothers*, 100.

55 Ibid.

56 Brad S. Gregory, *Salvation at Stake: Christian Martyrdom in Early Modern Europe* (Cambridge, MA, 1999), 177.

57 Foxe, TAMO (1563), Preface, 16.

While earlier hagiography often depicts motherhood as an "obstacle that stood in the way" of sanctity, Foxe's accounts of contemporary mother martyrs are far more sensitive to the relationship between mother and child, reflecting a deep interest in the intersection between spirituality and domesticity.[58] Foxe's innovations mirror developments in reformist thinking: in particular, his extension of the category "holy woman" to include the family woman reflects a sense that women's duties as wives, mothers, and daughters contributed to the spiritual well-being of the family.[59] Conduct literature of the period imagined the wife and mother as the manager of the household, a role which included caring for and educating children. This education was multifaceted, shaping children's knowledge and character alike. In "The New Mother, or Puerpera," Erasmus explains that, "Thou has not fully performed the duty of the mother, unless thou shalt first fashion the tender little body of thy son and afterward his no less tender mind with good education."[60] Similarly, Juan Vives' *Instruction of a Christen Woman* advises that the

> babe fyrste hereth her mother and fyrste begynneth to enforme her speche after hers. For that age can do nothyng itself but counterfet and folowe other: and is counnyng in this thing only she taketh her fyrst conditions and information of mynde by suche as she hereth or seeth by her mother.[61]

Vives' emphasis on "counterfet" or modeling is echoed in *The Monument of Matrones* by Thomas Bentley, a compendium of women's writing that includes several prayers for women as they enter motherhood. One prayer intended for "childrens good education" asks that Christ might give the mother "thy gifts both spirituall and bodily, that I may have competent wherewith to educate and bring

---

58 The phrase is Dunn's, *The Cruelest of All Mothers*, 98–99.

59 Patricia Crawford, "The Construction and Experience of Maternity in Seventeenth Century England," in *Women as Mothers in Pre-industrial England: Essays in Memory of Dorothy McLaren*, ed. Valerie A. Fildes (London, 1990), 12.

60 Desiderius Erasmus, *Collected Works of Erasmus: Colloquies*, 2 vols., trans. Craig R. Thompson (Toronto, 1997), 606 (lines 14–17).

61 Juan Luis Vives, *A Very Frutefull and Pleasant Boke Called the Instructio[n] of a Christen Woma[n], Made Fyrst in Laten, and Dedicated Vnto the Quenes Good Grace, by the Right Famous Clerke Mayster Lewes Vives, and Turned Out of Laten into Englysshe by Rycharde Hyrd. Whiche Boke Who so Redeth Diligently Shal Haue Knowlege of Many Thynges, Wherin He Shal Take Great Pleasure, and Specially Women Shall Take Great Co[m]modyte and Frute Towarde The[n]creace of Vertue [and] Good Maners*, trans. Richard Hyrde (London, 1529), 14. Early English Books Online, *STC* 24856, accessed 4 January 2018. Vives' advice was so popular that his text was published eight times in English between 1529 and 1592.

them vp."[62] Emphasized throughout the genre, these ideals reveal that sixteenth-century readers understood a mother's responsibilities to encompass two equally important roles as physical caretaker and spiritual educator.

Foxe's book takes seriously the idea that mothers fulfilled these dual roles, as his accounts of mothers show how they care for their families' spiritual and physical wellbeing. His focus on family expands the scope of the stories from the narrow trajectory of birth-to-martyrdom of many early martyrologies to a greater focus on the everyday details of his martyrs' lives. This broader interest underscores the quotidian, rather than the spectacular. As a result, the text often incorporates the domestic experiences of women as evidence of their faith, and thus, justification of their martyrdom. The example of Helen Stirke, a Scottish martyr, demonstrates how Foxe revises Abraham's test to be more sympathetic to the woman's role as a wife and mother. Helen is accused of heresy when she calls out the name of Jesus, rather than the Virgin Mary, during childbirth.[63] In her trial, Helen explains that

> if she her selfe had beene in the time of the virgin Mary, God might haue looked to her humilitie and base estate, as hee did to the virgines, in making her the mother of Christe, thereby meaninge, that there was no merites in the virgine, whyche procured her that honour, to be made the mother of Christe, and to bee preferred before other women, but Gods only free mercy exalted her to that estate.[64]

Typical of Foxe's martyrs, Helen's response aims to teach readers about the distinction between Catholic and Protestant beliefs. Helen shocks her Catholic interrogators in claiming that Mary was not exceptional except through God's mercy – and especially not because of her virginity. Because of this, Helen concludes that she could have been chosen as Christ's mother herself. Thus, Helen sees no reason why she should call upon Mary, rather than Christ, during childbirth, an often-perilous experience for mother and child. When she is condemned to death, Helen "desired earnestly to dye with her husband."[65] However, upon receiving her sentence that she would be executed separately, she comforts her husband and bids him:

62 Thomas Bentley, *Monument of Matrones, the fifth lamp of virginity* (London, 1582), 156. Early English Books Online, *STC* 1893, accessed 3 January 2018. 156. See also "Another praier to be vsed of the mother, for the good education of hir youth and children," ibid., 158.

63 Foxe, TAMO (1583), Book 8, 1291.

64 Ibid.

65 Ibid.

Husband, reioyce, for we haue liued together many ioyful dayes: but this day, in which we must die, ought to be most ioyfull to vs both, because we must haue ioy for euer. Therefore I will not bid you good night, for we shall sodainely meete with ioy in the kingdome of heauen.[66]

With this joyful farewell, Helen is led to the place where she will be drowned, at which point she must also give up her newborn. The account concludes by observing that although

she had a child sucking on her brest, yet this moued nothing the vnmercifull hearts of the enemies. So after she had commended her children to the neighbors of the towne for Gods sake, and the sucking barne was geuen to the nurse, she sealed vp the truth by her death.[67]

In many ways, Helen's narrative recalls the story of Perpetua or Felicitas, mother martyrs who give up their newborns in order to seek martyrdom, in the way that she is fiercely faithful to her beliefs and unafraid in the face of danger. Yet unlike the early martyrs' stories, Helen seals her fate as a martyr through the act of giving birth – the act of becoming a mother, rather than the act of refusing this role. Helen describes this moment as one that brings her closer to Jesus. Her story also marks a significant departure from the classical and medieval mother saints, for whom marriage is often interpreted as a barrier to be overcome through widowhood. When Elizabeth of Hungary marries at the insistence of her father, her hagiographer is quick to note that she immediately promises her confessor that should she reach widowhood, she will keep "perpetual continence."[68] Helen, though, is described not only as a mother but as a faithful, loving wife as well. As she kisses her husband goodbye, she reminds him of their joyful life together and looks forward to their reunion in heaven. Moreover, instead of emphasizing her independence from her family, Helen's separation from her child is a detail clearly intended to invoke the reader's pity, since it has failed to do so in the "unmerciful hearts of the enemies."[69] Rather than perceiving motherhood and wifehood as burdensome, as the earlier stories do, Helen's example does not separate the role of martyr, wife, and mother. Though her trials and her unwavering resolve recall the early Roman martyrs, Helen's story is distinguished in the way that the narrator's claim to her martyrdom is folded into her domestic roles.

66 Ibid.
67 Ibid.
68 Voragine, *Golden Legend*, 695.
69 Foxe, TAMO (1583), Book 8, 1291.

As in Helen's story, the emphasis on verbal proclamations of faith, rather than physical endurance of torture, is common among Foxe's accounts of mothers and wives. While physical trials are still present, Foxe often describes mother martyrs' trials in terms of domestic conflict. The perseverance required to resolve these domestic conflicts is portrayed to be equal to that of martyrs who endure physical torture. Crossman's Wife, for example, is said to be "preserued" by the Lord because her infant stops crying when persecutors search her house, allowing her to remain safely in hiding.[70] Marbeck's Wife, a "poore woman, which had her owne mother lying bedred vpon her hands, beside 5 or 6 children," leaves her nursing infant behind to seek out her husband in London, who has been imprisoned. She stays there eighteen days and endures much heckling from the porter before she is permitted to see him.[71] In the case of Joan Seaman, family responsibilities cause her to return from hiding after she has been accused of heresy. When her eighty-year-old husband falls ill, Mother Seaman takes care of him until his death. Though she dies of sickness, Foxe praises her for "not regarding her life but considering her duetie, and shewed her dilligence to her husband most faythfully," as is the "duety of a good wife."[72] In these accounts, Foxe's focus on the domestic roles of women replaces earlier martyrologists' inclusion of miraculous or supernatural elements. I. Ross Bartlett rightly observes that "[i]n contrast to the legendary *acta* of the early and medieval church, Foxe's characters have a more tangible reality."[73] In his focus on the quotidian details of the contemporary martyrs' lives, Foxe provides points of contact with his readers as he celebrates all types of Protestant women, inclusive of a wide range of class and sexual status.

While the martyr's endurance of trials and welcoming of death remain the central signifiers that her death is meaningful, Foxe's martyrs are more accessible because of his interest in the details of their everyday lives. His interest in the "tangible" elements can shift the portrayal of the martyr's suffering, which is always cast as exemplary and heroic in medieval and classical hagiography. Throughout the *Book of Martyrs*, the endurance of physical pain signifies the martyr's worthiness, as it does across all periods of the genre. Yet Foxe's treatment of pain is inconsistent, as Fiona Kao argues: it both ties and distances his martyrs from classical and medieval hagiography. One constant and important element of early martyrs is their divine analgesia, or inability to feel pain. Foxe retains the

---

70 Foxe, TAMO (1583), Book 12, 2073.
71 Foxe, TAMO (1583), Book 8, 1240.
72 Foxe, TAMO (1583), Book 12, 2060.
73 I. Ross Bartlett, "John Foxe as Hagiographer: The Question Revisited," *Sixteenth Century Journal* 26 (1995): 774.

portrayal of divine analgesia as it appears in his sources; otherwise, a primary difference between his portrayal of classical and contemporary martyrs is the way that the latter feel (and at times, are undone by) the pain that they suffer.[74] This suffering encompasses both physical and emotional pain, casting shadows of human frailty: guilt, fear, anger, and even doubt trouble these women in their passage to martyrdom. Like the stories of medieval martyrs, Foxe's narratives often linger over the suffering the martyr undergoes on the way to her execution. But these scenes also reveal that Foxe's martyrs are not the invincible icons of medieval hagiography. Foxe's contemporary martyrs are differentiated from the stories of medieval martyrs, which generally admit no imperfection of the heroine.[75] In offering imperfect heroines, one of the effects of Foxe's accounts is to focus on the way the women navigate their challenges. The sole emphasis on the martyr's life distinguishes her from the medieval saint, whose role as an intercessor ensures that her afterlife is tantamount to her actions while alive. Freed of the role of intercessor, Foxe's female martyrs confront their own suffering rather than mediate the suffering of others. They tell personal stories, and it is these diverse experiences that the narrator values, rather than their afterlives.

The story of Agnes Bongeor, a young mother, explicitly rewrites Abraham's sacrifice in terms of the maternal experience in its description of a woman who becomes a martyr by overcoming self-doubt. The story begins as Agnes descends into "dispayre" when she is separated from her fellow prisoners, and kept alive while her companions are sent to their death because the bailiff has mistakenly recorded her name as Agnes Bowyer.[76] Upon learning that she would not be taken with the others, "what piteous mone that good woman made, how bitterly shee wepte, what strange thoughts came into her mynde, how naked and desolate she esteemed her selfe."[77] This disappointment is especially acute since Agnes has already made preparations for her martyrdom. Foxe describes how,

> hauyng a child, a little yong Infant suckyng on her, whom she kept with her tenderly all the tyme she was in prison, agaynst þat day likewyse did she send it away to another Nurse, and prepared her selfe presently to geue her selfe for the testimonie of the glorious Gospell of Iesus Christ.[78]

---

74 Kao, "John Foxe's Golden Saints?" 200.
75 Bartlett, "John Foxe as Hagiographer," 773.
76 Foxe, TAMO (1583), Book 12, 2044.
77 Ibid.
78 Ibid.

Without her child or companions, Agnes is left to contemplate her fate. A friend comes to visit her, and, finding the young woman in a "greate perplexity of mynde," he reminds her of the way God tested Abraham.[79] Agnes anticipates the friend's comparison between Abraham and herself and argues against the similarities. She points out that she has not been chosen for martyrdom, and thus, "the Lord thinketh me not worthye of this dignitie, and therfore Abrahams case & mine is not alyke."[80] Furthermore, she states, their cases are dissimilar because Abraham was tried with offering his own child, whereas she gave her child away of her own accord. Yet her friend presses the comparison:

> Good sister . . . way [weigh] the matter but indifferently. Abraham I graunt . . . would haue offered his sonne: and haue not you done the lyke in your little suckyng babe? But consider further then this, my good sister . . . where Abraham was commanded but to offer his sonne, you are heuy and grieued because you offer not your selfe, which goeth somewhat more neere you then Abrahams obedience did, & therefore before God assuredly, is no lesse accepted & allowed in his holy presence: which further the preparing of your shroud also doth argue full well, &c.[81]

Agnes finds solace in her friend's words and returns to reading and prayer, "wherein she found no litle comfort."[82] Soon after, a writ arrives from London, and she is martyred on September 17, 1557.

By offering Abraham's test as a parable for Agnes's situation, the friend underscores several parallel circumstances between them. First, Agnes's obedience to God inspires her to seek martyrdom, just as Abraham's obedience inspires him to willingly offer Isaac for sacrifice. Likewise, though Agnes does not offer her child to be killed, giving the baby to the nurse is characterized as a sacrifice similar to Abraham's because of the emotional anguish it causes. The way in which the narrator describes her tender relationship with her child underscores Agnes's affection for the infant, and her sadness at losing it. Finally, her friend argues that she has actually made double the sacrifice of Abraham – offering her little suckling babe and as well as herself – and this assuredly finds God's grace. While Agnes's death is described in the briefest way, the reader understands her to be worthy because she suffers as a result of her sacrifice. In this way, she resembles a mother like Paula, whose grief is described as if "her

79   Ibid.
80   Ibid.
81   Ibid.
82   Ibid.

entrails were twisted in pain as if being torn from her body."[83] However, while Paula overcomes this pain when "[f]or love of God she put aside love of sons and daughters," Foxe's mother martyr is not required to give up her maternal love or forget the suffering she endures as a mother.[84] Agnes's account rewrites the narrative of Paula's transcendence: her narrative describes Abraham's test in a way that understands her release of her child as a compassionate sacrifice. In this way, Agnes's story intertwines the roles of mother and martyr, recognizing her suffering in each role as valuable evidence of her faith.

As in Agnes Bongeor's story, Foxe's accounts of contemporary martyrs often depict the martyr's suffering as fluid, varying between heroic and pathetic. This portrayal of suffering separates Foxe's polemic from that of the early martyrologists. Martyrdom is celebrated by classical and medieval martyrs in a way that precludes pity. For instance, the *Book of Martyrs* includes the story of a second-century martyr of Lyon, Blandina, who "like a worthy mother" sends her children to the conquerors before she hastens to her own death with such joy as if "she had bene bydden to a bridall, and not in case to be throwne to the wilde beast."[85] This comparison of martyrdom to marriage is common among early martyrs, who often describe their deaths as a joyful celebration. Yet suffering for the contemporary martyrs is not always described with the same language of celebration and heroism. By borrowing the shape of his stories from medieval iterations of the genre, Foxe helps his readers to recognize the accounts of "true" martyrs. Yet from time to time, Foxe's devotion to a realistic portrayal of pain breaks down the paradigm of exemplary suffering found throughout stories of medieval and classical martyrs. When pain is portrayed with realism, rather than the spectacular analgesia of early martyrs, the stories open themselves to pathos, rather than awe.

Joan Dangerfield's story, for instance, is framed to evoke pity in its introduction as "an other story of such vnmercifulnes shewed agaynst a woman in childbed, as farre from all charitie and humanitie, as hath ben anye other storye yet hetherto rehearsed."[86] Joan, a mother of ten, and her husband, William, are reported by their neighbors on charges of heresy. The pair are imprisoned separately, and Joan, pulled from childbed, "was caryed into the common Iayle, and there placed amongst theues and murderers" with her youngest child, just fourteen

---

83 Voragine, *Golden Legend*, 122.
84 Ibid.
85 Foxe, TAMO (1583), Book 1, 71.
86 Foxe, TAMO (1583), Book 11, 1977. Here Foxe says this is "an other story," implying that there are multiple stories of cruelty to women in childbed. The only other story I have found about a woman specifically accused while in childbed is that of Helen Stirke, recounted above.

days old.[87] After they are incarcerated, the "Bishop beginneth to practise not with the woman first, as the serpent did with Eue, but with the man, craftily deceiuing his simplicitie, with fayre glosing wordes, falsely perswading him that his wife had recanted." William recants as a result of the bishop's words, but soon discovers the truth: his wife has remained stedfast. He regrets his decision immediately. Soon after, he dies while Joan is still imprisoned with her infant. After the bishop examines Joan, Foxe describes how the "poor woman" remained imprisoned

> together with her tender babe, which also remayned with her in þe Iayle, partaker of her Martyrdome, so long as her milke would serue to geue it sucke, till at length the childe being starued for colde and famine, was sent away when it was past al remedie, and so shortly after dyed.[88]

The death of the child is not the end of the Dangerfields' sad story, though. Foxe relays how, not long afterward, William's elderly mother perished at the couple's home "for lacke of comfort." Lamenting the death of the four Dangerfields – husband, wife, infant and grandmother – Foxe concludes by speculating that the other nine children "were all vndone by the same."[89]

When Foxe casts the bishop as the serpent and William as Eve, he positions Joan as the new head of the Protestant household, stoic and unfailing in her faith. This rhetorical move challenges the medieval Catholic church, in which the Virgin Mary is imagined to replace Eve. Foxe's Protestant history imagines this triumph quite differently: Mary, whose role as a mother was so central in the Middle Ages, is replaced by an ordinary mother, Joan. As the new Protestant mother, however, Joan presents a difficult example, not in the least because her story is suffused with her extreme physical suffering and the suffering of her family. Foxe's speculation of the demise of the old mother and the other children may in fact be a logical one, especially since the neighbors who reported the parents in the first place may not have been likely to take on nine additional mouths to feed. Moreover, the prison conditions for both parents are clearly horrendous. William's experience seems particularly cruel, as he was imprisoned "so longe till hys legges almost were freated off with yrons."[90] Why does Foxe include these other stories, peripheral to Joan's imprisonment? Perhaps it is because part of Joan's suffering includes the knowledge that her loved ones also suffer, and for

87 Ibid.
88 Ibid.
89 Ibid.
90 Ibid.

Foxe, the emotional pain she endures as a mother and wife contributes to the physical pain she endures in prison.

Joan Dangerfield demonstrates that suffering for Foxe is not always as transcendent as it is in classical or medieval hagiography. In contrast to Blandina's celebratory language of matrimony, the language of Joan's suffering is stark in its description of cold, hunger, and betrayal. Left to die in prison, her story lacks elements of spiritual comfort that are present in the other stories. As Foxe suggests in his conclusion, she cannot turn to others to secure the wellbeing of her children, as Helen Stirke and Agnes Bongeor do. She is not anchored by her husband's love, as Helen seems to be. She finds no comfort in reading or writing of her faith, as Agnes does. As with the other mothers, Joan gives up her infant – and sacrifices the rest of her children to hunger – yet Foxe cannot bring himself to celebrate her sacrifice. Instead, he laments her story as one "farre from all charitie and humanitie," disappointed in his wish to "haue found no moe such stories of vnmerciful cruelty shewed vppon seely women with theyr children and young infants."[91] Abraham's test links Joan to the other women, but it does not have the same effect: while Helen's and Agnes's children are delivered into safety, Joan's child dies – not because of its mother's willing sacrifice, but because of the pathetic conditions of imprisonment. Foxe's focus on Joan's suffering brings about a shift in the martyr's heroism. No longer a joyful occasion, the tone of Joan's martyrdom contrasts with that of Agnes and Helen because of the isolated nature of her suffering. The unbridled charge toward martyrdom by the early Roman martyrs does not transfer perfectly to the Reformation-era martyrs, and Foxe struggles to negotiate the sadness of the story within the framework of the genre.

In Foxe's stories about mothers, the martyrs' experiences are so intertwined with their domestic roles that these elements must have seemed very familiar to readers. Throughout the *Book*, the depiction of the martyr's relationship with her family, ranging from dependence to partnership to antagonism, reflects a spectrum recognizable to the sixteenth-century reader. Foxe's narratives demonstrate that family responsibilities continued to have major influence over these women's lives, and his inclusion of these stories demonstrates his interest in the way women must navigate familial barriers to their faith. For instance, Agnes Prest, aged fifty-four, claims that she is persecuted by her husband and children and leaves them to pursue her faith, earning her own living through spinning. She tells her interrogators, "I must either forsake Christ, or my husband, [and] I am contented to sticke only to Christ my heauenly spouse, and renounce the other."[92] Joyce Lewes rebels against her husband's orders: she refuses to go to church, but when she is forced to do so, she turns her back on the crucifix. Eventually, Joyce is delivered to persecutors by her own husband.[93] While these women do not face situations identical to Abraham's test, like Abraham, their faith is tested through their relationships with their families. Their roles as wives and mothers are integral parts of their stories, and the conflicts they must negotiate are presented as evidence of their fortitude and status as true martyrs and true believers. The equal presentation of female experiences as martyrs and as wives and mothers presents a new view of the female martyr, one that understands her domestic struggles as part of her journey to martyrdom.

In classical and medieval hagiography, Abraham's test is used to praise the way women are able to move beyond the temporal responsibilities of family in order to unite with Christ. After separating from their children, these women pursue a holy life or martyrdom, without regard for sorrow or grief felt as a result of the lost family. In contrast, Foxe's revision of Abraham's test argues that women need not forsake their roles as mothers, and thus, they also need not be portrayed in terms of chastity or masculinity.[94] This emphasis on "domestic" suffering – pain that results from a woman's role as a mother or wife – constitutes a great contribution to hagiography, which had heretofore separated the roles of saint and mother. For Foxe, motherhood and martyrdom are not mutually exclusive: his stories are invested in women as family members, and the suffering they endure in these roles indicates that their domestic trials are valued as part of their martyrdom. Foxe's interest in women's trials as wives and mothers was surely a compelling element of his *Book* for female readers, whose spiritual lives were so often influenced by their domestic roles, as well.

---

92 Foxe, TAMO (1583), Book 12, 2074.

93 Foxe, TAMO (1583), Book 12, 2036–2037.

94 On the tradition of masculinizing female martyrs, see Christine Peters, *Patterns of Piety: Women, Gender and Religion in Late Medieval and Reformation England*, Cambridge Studies in Early Modern British History (Cambridge, UK, 2003), 272.

The Writings of Mary Carpenter Erler

Books

Reading and Writing during the Dissolution: Monks, Nuns, and Friars 1530–1558 (Cambridge, UK, 2013).

Records of Early English Drama (REED): Ecclesiastical London (Toronto, 2008).

Women, Reading, and Piety in Late Medieval England (Cambridge, UK, 2002).

Robert Copland: Poems (Toronto, 1993).

Poems of Cupid, God of Love, ed. Thelma S. Fenster and Mary C. Erler (Leiden, 1991). [An edition of Christine de Pizan's "Epistre de Dieu d'Amour" and "Dit de la Rose" (Fenster) and Thomas Hoccleve's "Letter of Cupid" (Erler)].

Edited Collections

Gendering the Master Narrative: Women and Power in the Middle Ages, ed. Mary Erler and Maryanne Kowaleski (Ithaca, NY, 2003).

Women and Power in the Middle Ages, ed. Mary Erler and Maryanne Kowaleski (Athens, GA, 1988).

Articles

"The Transmission of Images between Flemish and English Birgittine Houses." In *Nuns' Literacies in Medieval Europe: The Antwerp Dialogue*, ed. V. Blanton, V. O'Mara, and P. Stoop, 367–82. Turnhout, 2017.

"The Guildhall Library, Robert Bale and the Writing of London History." *Historical Research* 89 (2016): 176–86.

"The Laity." In *A Companion to the Early Printed Book in Britain 1476–1558*, ed. Vincent Gillespie and Susan Powell, 134–49. Cambridge,UK, 2014.

"London Commercial Theatre 1500–1576." In *Editing, Performance, Texts: New Practices in Medieval and Early Modern English Drama*, ed. Jacqueline Jenkins and Julie Sanders, 93–106. New York, 2014.

"Thomas Cromwell's Abbess, Margaret Vernon." *History Today* 64 (2014): 23–29.

"The Book of Hours as *Album Amicorum*: Jane Guildford's Book." In *The Social Life of Illumination: Manuscripts, Images, and Communities in the Late Middle Ages*, ed. Joyce Coleman, Mark Cruse, and Kathryn A. Smith, 505–35. Turnhout, 2013.

"The Effects of Exile on English Monastic Spirituality." *Journal of Medieval and Early Modern Studies* 42 (2012): 519–38.

"A Revelation of Purgatory." In *History of British Women's Writing*, vol. 1: *700–1500*, ed. Liz Herbert McAvoy, 241–50. New York, 2011.

"Home Visits: Mary, Elizabeth, Margery Kempe and the Feast of the Visitation." In *Medieval Domesticity*, ed. Maryanne Kowaleski and P. J. P. Goldberg, 259–76. Cambridge, UK, 2009.

"Religious Women after the Dissolution: Continuing Community?" In *London and the Kingdom: Essays in Honour of Caroline M. Barron*, ed. Matthew Davies and Andrew Prescott, 135–46. Harlaxton Medieval Studies 6. Donington, Lincolnshire, 2008.

"Private Reading in the Fifteenth- and Sixteenth-Century English Nunnery." In *The Culture of Medieval English Monasticism*, ed. James Clark, 134–46. Studies in the History of Medieval Religion 30. Woodbridge, Suffolk, 2007.

"'A Revelation of Purgatory'(1422): Reform and the Politics of Female Visions." *Viator* 38 (2007): 321–48.

"Widows in Retirement: Locale, Patronage, Spirituality, Reading at the Gaunts, Bristol." *Religion and Literature* 37 (2005): 51–75.

"Fifteenth-Century Owners of Chaucer's Work: Cambridge, Magdalene College, MS Pepys 2006." *Chaucer Review* 38 (2004): 402–14.

"'Hoccleve's Portrait'? in London, British Library, MS Arundel 38." In *Tant d'Emprises: So Many Undertakings: Essays in Honour of Anne F. Sutton*, ed. Livia Visser-Fuchs [*The Ricardian* 13], 221–29. Bury St. Edmunds, 2003.

"The Abbess of Malling's Gift Manuscript (1520)." In *Prestige, Authority, and Power in Late Medieval Manuscripts and Texts*, ed. Felicity Riddy, 147–57. York Manuscripts Conferences 4. York, 2000.

"The Making of Syon's Altar Table of Our Lady c. 1490–96" (with Caroline M. Barron). In *England and the Continent in the Middle Ages: Studies in Memory of Andrew Martindale*, ed. John Mitchell and Matthew Moran, 318–35. Harlaxton Medieval Studies 8. Stamford, Lincolnshire, 2000.

"Devotional Literature." In *Cambridge History of the Book in Britain*, vol. 3: *1400–1557*, ed. Lotte Hellinga and J. B. Trapp, 495–525. Cambridge, UK, 1999.

"A London Anchorite, Simon Appulby His Fruyte of Redempcyon and Its Milieu." *Viator* 29 (1998): 227–39.

"Printers' Copy: MS Bodley 638 and the Parliament of Fowls." *Chaucer Review* 33 (1998): 221–19.

"'Chaste Sports, Juste Prayses & All Softe Delight': Harefield 1602 and Ashby 1607, Two Female Entertainments." In *The Elizabethan Theatre XIV: Papers Given at the International Conference on Elizabethan Theatre held at the University of Waterloo, Ontario, in July 1991*, ed. J. Leeds Barroll, C. E. McGee, and Augusta Lynne Magnusson, 1–25. Toronto, 1996.

"Syon's 'Special Benefactors and Friends': Some Vowed Women." *Birgittiana* 2 (1996): 209–22.

"English Vowed Women at the End of the Middle Ages." *Mediaeval Studies* 57 (1995): 155–203.

"Exchange of Books between Nuns and Laywomen: Three Surviving Examples." In *New Science Out of Old Books: Studies in Manuscripts and Early Printed Books in Honour of A. I. Doyle*, ed. Richard Beadle and A. J. Piper, 360–73. London, 1995.

"Palm Sunday Prophets and Processions and Eucharistic Controversy." *Renaissance Quarterly* 48 (1995): 58–81.

"Three Fifteenth-Century Vowesses." In *Medieval London Widows*, ed. Caroline M. Barron and Anne F. Sutton, 163–84. London, 1994.

"The Books and Lives of Three Tudor Women." In *Privileging Gender in Early Modern England*, ed. Jean R. Brink, 5–17. Sixteenth Century Essays and Studies 23. Kirksville, MO, 1993.

"Pasted-In Embellishments in English Manuscripts and Printed Books c. 1480–1533." *The Library* 6th ser. 14 (1992): 185–206.

"Davies's Astraea and other Contexts of the Countess of Pembroke's 'A Dialogue.'" *Studies in English Literature* 30 (1990): 41–61.

"Wynkyn de Worde's Will: Legatees and Bequests." *The Library* 6th ser. 10 (1988): 107–21.

"Sir John Davies and the Rainbow Portrait of Queen Elizabeth." *Modern Philology* 84 (1987): 359–71.

"Suleyman's 1532 Vienna Campaign: An English News Dispatch." *Slavonic and East European Review* 65 (1987): 101–12.

"Early Woodcuts of John Skelton: The Uses of Convention." *Bulletin of Research in the Humanities* (formerly *Bulletin of The New York Public Library*) 87 (1986/7): 7–28.

"Print into Manuscripts: A Flodden Field News Pamphlet (BL Additional MS 29506)" (with Nancy Gutierrez). *Studies in Medieval and Renaissance History* n.s. 8 (1986): 187–230.

"The First English Printing of Galen: The Formation of the Company of Barber-Surgeons." *Huntington Library Quarterly* 48 (1985): 159–71.

"Syon Abbey's Care of Books." *Scriptorium* 39 (1985): 61–91.

"'The Maner to Lyue Well' and the Coming of English in Francois Regnault's Primers of the 1530s." *The Library* 6th ser. 6 (1984): 229–43.

Notes

"Vernon, Margaret (d. in or after 1546), abbess of Malling and friend of Thomas Cromwell, *Oxford Dictionary of National Biography*. Oxford, 2004–.

"A Possible Syon Book Owner after the Dissolution: William Mownselowe, 1543." *Notes & Queries* 58 (2011): 202–4.

"Robert Copland, d. 1547" and "William Copland," *Oxford Dictionary of National Biography*. Oxford, 2004–.

"Bishop Richard Fox's Manuscript Gifts to his Winchester Nuns: A Second Surviving Example." *Journal of Ecclesiastical History* 52 (2001): 1–4.

"Spectacle and Sacrament: A London Parish Play in the 1530s." *Modern Philology* 91 (1994): 449–54.

"Margery Kempe's White Clothes." *Medium Ævum* 62 (1993): 78–83.

Reviews

Cambridge Companion to Medieval English Mysticism, ed. Samuel Fanous and Vincent Gillespie. *Religion & Literature* 44 (2012): 205–7.

The Queen's Library: Image-Making at the Court of Anne of Brittany 1477–1514, C. J. Brown. *Publication of the Bibliographical Society of America (PBSA)* 106 (2012): 119–21.

Affective Meditation and the Invention of Medieval Compassion, Sarah McNamer. *American Historical Review* 116 (2011): 505–6.

Lay Piety and Religious Discipline in Middle English Literature, Nicole Rice. *Studies in the Age of Chaucer* 32 (2011): 462–65.

Allegories of Love in Marguerite Porete's "Mirror of Simple Souls", Suzanne Kocher. *Speculum* 85 (2010): 416–18.

Women and Writing c. 1340–c. 1650: The Domestication of Print Culture, ed. Anne Lawrence-Mathers and P. Hardman. *Review of English Studies* 61 (2010): 632–34.

Reading in the Wilderness: Private Devotion and Public Performance in Late Medieval England, Jessica Brantley. *Manuscripta* 53 (2009): 131–34.

John Capgrave's Fifteenth Century, Karen Winstead. *English Historical Review* 123 (2008): 1532–33.

Medieval Wall Paintings in English and Welsh Churches, Roger Rosewall. *TMR (The Medieval Review)*, October 3, 2008.

Marking the Hours: English People and their Prayers, Eamon Duffy. *Catholic Historical Review* 93 (2007): 929–30.

Women's Books of Hours in Medieval England: Selected Texts, Charity Scott-Stokes. *The Ricardian* 17 (2007): 146–48.

Lives of the Anchoresses: The Rise of the Urban Recluse in Medieval Europe, Anneke Mulder-Bakker. *TMR (The Medieval Review)*, October 2, 2006.

Cambridge Companion to Medieval Womens' Writing, ed. Carolyn Dinshaw and David Wallace. *Journal of English and Germanic Philology (JEGP)* 104 (2005): 291–94.

The Uses of Script and Print 1300–1700, ed. Julia Crick and Alexandra Walsham. *TMR (The Medieval Review)*, January 25, 2005.

Women and Religion in Medieval England, ed. Diana Wood. *The Ricardian* 14 (2004): 174–77.

Shaping Community: The Art and Archaeology of Monasticism, ed. Sheila McNally. *Journal of Ecclesiastical History* 54 (2003): 732–33.

Reading Families: Women's Literate Practice in Late Medieval England, Rebecca Krug. *Arthuriana* 14 (2002): 207–09.

Richard III's Books: Ideals and Reality in the Life and Library of a Medieval Prince, Anne F. Sutton and Livia Visser-Fuchs. *The Ricardian* 11 (1998): 302–4.

Northern English Books, Owners, and Makers in the Late Middle Ages, John Block Friedman. *History of Education Quarterly* 36 (1996): 552–54.

A Study and Edition of Selected Middle English Sermons, ed. V. M. O'Mara. *Medieval Sermon Studies* 38 (1996): 56–57.

England in the Fifteenth Century, ed. Nicholas Rogers. *The Ricardian* 10 (1995): 201–4.

Syon Abbey: The Library of the Bridgittine Nuns and Their Peregrinations after the Reformation, Christopher de Hamel. *Scriptorium* 48 (1994): 349–52.

The Medieval Translator, ed. Roger Ellis. *Translation and Literature* 2 (1993): 143–47.

Upon My Husband's Death: Widows in the Literature and Histories of Medieval Europe, ed. Louise Mirrer. *Medieval Feminist Newsletter* 14 (1992): 30–32.

Margaret of York, Duchess of Burgundy, 1446–1503, Christine Weightman. *American Historical Review* 96 (1991): 150.

Seeking the Woman in Late Medieval and Renaissance Writings, ed. Sheila Fisher and Janet E. Halley. *Modern Language Review* 86 (1991): 161–63.

"Crimes and Misdemeanors," Woody Allen. *New York Times*, October 15, 1989, 16.

Editing Early Drama, ed. Alexandra Johnston. *The Library* 6th ser. 11 (1989): 158–60.

World's Fair, E. L. Doctorow. *America* 154, March 8, 1986, 193.

Index

239

Tabula Gratulatoria

Allison Alberts
Andrew Albin
Caroline M. Barron
Catherine Batt
Felisa Baynes-Ross
Maija Birenbaum
Heather Blatt
Julia Boffey
Frank Boyle
Clive Burgess
David R. Carlson
Christopher S. Celenza
Martin Chase
Joyce Coleman
Rita Copeland
Heather Dubrow
Lara Farina
Jessica Freeman
Susan Celia Greenfield
Richard Gyug
Susanne Hafner
Franklin T. Harkins
Constance W. Hassett
Glenn Hendler
J. Patrick Hornbeck II
Ann M. Hutchison
Henry Ansgar Kelly
Maryanne Kowaleski

Joseph T. Lienhard, S. J.
Sheila Lindenbaum
Katherine C. Little
Cathryn McCarthy Donahue
Nicola McDonald
Thomas O'Donnell
Veronica O'Mara
Nick Paul
Sara S. Poor
Sue Powell
Denis Renevey
Joel T. Rosenthal
Nina Rowe
Michael G. Sargent
Kathryn A. Smith
Christian Steer
Kara Stone
William P. Stoneman
Anne F. Sutton
Norman Tanner
Livia Visser-Fuchs
David Wallace
Jocelyn Wogan-Browne
Robert A. Wood
Suzanne M. Yeager

Fordham College Rose Hill Honors
Program